ODYSSEY SERIES IN LITERATURE

ROBERT SHAFER, *General Editor*

JAMES RUSSELL LOWELL

ESSAYS, POEMS, AND LETTERS

J. R. Lowell.

LOWELL

ESSAYS, POEMS
AND
LETTERS

Selected and Edited by

WILLIAM SMITH CLARK II

Professor of English, University of Cincinnati

THE ODYSSEY PRESS

New York

Till America has learned to love art, not as an amusement, not as the mere ornament of her cities, not as a superstition of what is *comme il faut* for a great nation, but for its humanising and ennobling energy, for its power of making men better by arousing in them a perception of their own instincts for what is beautiful, and therefore sacred and religious, and an eternal rebuke of the base and worldly, she will not have succeeded in that high sense which alone makes a nation out of a people, and raises it from a dead name to a living power.

—JAMES RUSSELL LOWELL, *The Function of the Poet.*

PREFACE

James Russell Lowell has been, and will remain, a considerable figure in American literature—not merely a figure of historical significance, but an author of perennial interest to the lovers of *belles-lettres*. No satisfactory anthology of his writings has been available, however, to those readers who possess neither leisure nor inclination to find their way through the large mass of Lowell's literary effort. This volume aims to supply that lack by presenting a selection of his more enduring work in both poetry and prose. The editor has tried to assemble representative specimens of Lowell's varied art at its best, but he harbors no illusions as to the impeccability of his judgment. He would wish, above all else, that the collection should reveal a delightful personality, the epitome of that highly articulate refinement to be found in nineteenth-century New England.

The entire contents of this volume have been thoroughly annotated—the first extensive annotation of Lowell's writings. Even those which have enjoyed frequent editing and reprinting have not, in most cases, been fully supplied with explanatory comment. Because Lowell had a lifelong fondness for erudite and topical allusion, the annotating of his works in any detail becomes an arduous undertaking. It is not, however, the rather herculean labors of scholarly detection which give importance to this undertaking. Annotation makes vivid and complete the evidence that Lowell possessed a mind with a remarkable breadth of interests.

A large section of this volume is purposely allotted to Lowell's letters. Almost never reprinted in literary collections of any kind, they have continued too little known and appreciated. Happily there is now a growing realization that Lowell's cor-

respondence constitutes as interesting and distinguished a body
of epistolary art as has yet come from the pen of any American.
The fifty-nine examples included herein have been chosen for
their style as well as substance; none has been inserted simply
for its biographical value. With the gracious permission of
Lowell's granddaughter, Mrs. Lois Burnett Rantoul, three letters (Nos. 40, 41, 47), in the possession of the University of
Cincinnati Library, are published for the first time, and a fourth
(No. 4), also in the possession of the same library, appears in
its entirety after the previous publication of a fragment only.
Letter No. 10 has never before been printed in full. The kindness of the authorities of the Harvard College Library, where
the original of this letter reposes, has made available the complete text. The remaining letters in the present collection are
reproduced without textual change from the chief printed
sources: *Letters of James Russell Lowell,* edited in two volumes by Charles Eliot Norton; *New Letters of James Russell
Lowell,* edited by M. A. DeWolfe Howe; and *James Russell
Lowell: a Biography* by Horace E. Scudder. The selections
from the Norton and Howe volumes are published by permission of, and arrangement with, Harper and Brothers; and the
selections from Scudder's biography by permission of, and arrangement with, Houghton Mifflin Company.

The essays and the poems in this volume are reprinted from
the definitive Riverside edition to Lowell's prose and poetry,
with the single exception of "The Function of the Poet." The
text of this essay is drawn from *The Function of the Poet, and
Other Essays,* edited by Albert Mordell. All the essay and
poetry selections are published by permission of, and arrangement with, Houghton Mifflin Company.

The editor wishes to thank the aforementioned publishers
for their courteous cooperation. He is deeply grateful to the
Charles P. Taft Memorial Fund of the University of Cincinnati for aid toward publication of this volume, and to Dr. Robert Shafer for his cordial interest and invaluable editorial
advice.

W. S. C.

CONTENTS

ix

CHRONOLOGY

1819. February 22. Lowell born at Elmwood, Cambridge, Massachusetts.

1834–38. Attended Harvard College.

1840. August. Took the degree of LL.B. at Dane College Law School, Cambridge.

1841. January. Published his first volume, *A Year's Life*.

1841–43. Contributed to the *Boston Miscellany, Dial,* and *The Pioneer*.

1844. December 26. Married Maria White of Watertown, Massachusetts.

1845. January–May. Resided in Philadelphia and wrote for the *Pennsylvania Freeman*.

June. Returned to Cambridge and made his home at Elmwood.

1846–50. Contributed to the *National Anti-Slavery Standard*.

1847. September 9. His daughter Mabel born.

1851. July 12. Sailed for Europe with his family.

1851–52. Visited Italy, Germany, France, and England.

1852. November. Returned to Elmwood.

1853. October 27. Maria White Lowell died.

1855. January–February. Lectured upon the English poets at the Lowell Institute in Boston.

February. Appointed to succeed Longfellow as Smith Professor of the French and Spanish Languages and Literatures, and as Professor of Belles Lettres, in Harvard College.

June 4. Sailed for Europe to study.

1855–56. Resided at Dresden except for a spring sojourn in Italy.

1856. August. Returned to Cambridge and went to live with his brother-in-law, Dr. Estes Howe.

September. Began his professorial duties at Harvard.

1857. June. Appointed the first editor of the *Atlantic Monthly*.

September. Married Frances Dunlap.

1861. January. His father died. Moved to Elmwood with his family.

May. Resigned as editor of the *Atlantic Monthly*.

1864. Became, along with C. E. Norton, co-editor of the *North American Review*.

1872. June. Resigned his professorship at Harvard.

July 9. Sailed with Mrs. Lowell for Europe.

1872–74. Traveled in England and on the Continent.

1873. June. Received the honorary degree of Doctor of Civil Law at Oxford University.

1874. June. Received the same honorary degree at Cambridge University.

July. Returned to Elmwood.

September. Resumed teaching at Harvard.

1876. July. Delegate to the Republican convention at Cincinnati. Presidential elector from Massachusetts.

1877. June. Appointed American Minister to Spain.

1877–80. Resided at Madrid.

1880. January. Appointed Minister to England.

1880–85. Resided at London.

1885. February 19. Frances Dunlap Lowell died.

June. Left England and his ministerial post. Retired to his daughter's estate at Southboro, Massachusetts.

1886–89. Spent the summers in England.

1887. March. Lectured at the Lowell Institute on the old English dramatists.

1889. November. Took up residence at Elmwood upon his return from England.

1891. August 12. Died at Elmwood.

INTRODUCTION

1. THE ELMWOOD SQUIRE

Seldom does a man play his role on the world's stage in a scene so attuned to the temper of his personality as did James Russell Lowell amid his family acres in Cambridge, Massachusetts. Even now, a half-century after his death, the setting stands with its lines and tone little disturbed—a large, square, three-storied frame mansion of yellow and white, still surrounded by broad lawns and lofty trees within a Cambridge urbanized beyond Lowell's dourest dreams. The mansion's proportions and dignity attest to its construction for a colonial Tory of the mid-eighteenth century. To the spell of Elmwood's aristocratic atmosphere Lowell gradually succumbed. In 1873 he addressed a whimsical warning to Thomas Bailey Aldrich, who was temporarily occupying the estate: "It will make a frightful conservative of you before you know it. It was born a Tory and will die so. Don't get too used to it. I often wish I had not grown into it so." [1]

On Elmwood's top floor Lowell began the lifelong process of "growing in." There, while a student at Harvard College and then at law school, he dwelt happily with his books, and on winter evenings he sat by the fire to write romantically: "Our old mansion is a complete Temple of the Winds to which Eolus's cave was as calm as a maiden's dream. . . . Through every chink the blasts are talking to each other as lovingly as did Pyramus and Thisbe through the 'crannied' one in the walls of which I believe the respectable Snout was the counterfeit presentment. Every one of them telling a different story of his prowess among the rotten boughs and loose shingles without." [2] To the

[1] *Letters*, II, 100.
[2] *New Letters*, 4–5.

garret apartment he brought his bride, Maria White, in June, 1845; and there during the succeeding years all his four children were born. But the untimely death of his wife in October, 1853, caused Elmwood to lose all its attraction as "home." Within two years Lowell left the place, not to return until his father's death in January, 1861, made him master of the property. Then, as a distinguished professor at Harvard College, he came back with the second Mrs. Lowell to the scene of his deepest affections, and took a new lease on life: "I am sitting in my old garret, at my old desk, smoking my old pipe, and loving my old friends. I begin already to feel more like my old self than I have these ten years. . . . I hope I shall find my old inspiration on tap here. It would not bear bottling and transportation." [3]

During the 1860's Lowell derived increasing satisfaction from the oversight of his rural domain. He participated in the tending of gardens and fields, in the cutting of hay, in the harvesting of crops; and, to a considerable degree, he followed the life of a country squire. He became so wedded to Elmwood's isolation and repose that he grew less and less content away from his manor. One July day in 1867, James T. Fields, Lowell's publisher, called and discovered his author, after only a week's stay in the fashionable resort of Newport, back "alone in his library, looking into an empty fireplace and smoking a pipe," and "delighted to return to find his 'own sponge hanging on its nail' and to his books." [4] Indeed his best friends were forced to lure him to the convivial gatherings which formerly had been his constant joy. Sarah Fields, then the most famous hostess in Boston, noted in her journal of December, 1871, that at a Sunday dinner to honor the actress Charlotte Cushman, Lowell proved a sparkling guest, "as he always does *when he can once work himself up to the pitch of going out at all.*" [5] Even after diplomatic appointments to Spain and to England had opened to him the wider courses of public life abroad, he often yearned for his "squiredom" and its meadows by the Charles. Finally, at the

---

[3] *Letters*, I, 310.
[4] *Memories of a Hostess* (Mrs. James T. Fields), 109.
[5] *Ibid.*, 124.

age of seventy, he returned to the cherished seclusion of Elm-wood. Two years later, on August 12, 1891, he died in the house where he had been born and where he had always wanted to die.

The Elmwood home early inculcated in Lowell an admiration for social grace. From his student days onward he preserved an immaculate appearance in public. Of his careful grooming F. H. Underwood, a Cambridge neighbor, remarked, "One might as soon expect to find a smirch on the petals of a new Easter lily as upon his linen or hands." [6] This meticulousness in dress was but a minor evidence of the high valuation which Lowell placed upon dignity and polish of manner as civilizing forces in human society. At twenty-seven he expressed to his intimate friend, Charles F. Briggs, this self-revealing comment upon American culture: "There is as striking a want of external as of internal culture among our men. We ought to have pro-duced the purest race of gentlemen in the world. . . . I have often remarked that educated Americans have the least dignified bearing of any cultivated people. They all stoop in the shoul-der, intellectually as well as physically. . . . The great power of the English aristocracy lies in their polish that impresses the great middle class who have a sort of dim conception of its value. A man gains in *power* as he gains in ease. It is a great advan-tage to him to be cultivated in all parts of his nature. . . . I go so far as to believe that all great men have felt the importance of the outward and visible impression they should produce. Soc-rates was as wise as Plato, indeed he was Plato's master, but Plato dressed better, and dressed his speech better and has the greater name. Pericles was the first gentleman of Greece." [7] Such convictions helped to determine Lowell's preference for the brilliant Charles Street salon of Sarah Fields, and for the ex-clusive Saturday Club. When, as American minister first to Spain and then to England, he had to engage in a continual round of international sociability, he was perfectly suited by

---

[6] *The Poet and the Man, Recollections and Appreciations of James Russell Lowell*, 43.

[7] *New Letters*, 18.

inclination and discipline to that vital responsibility of his office. By the charm of his intercourse he served the American nation far more significantly than most of his countrymen realized.

Though Elmwood led Lowell to value highly social as well as intellectual cultivation, it balanced that training by providing homely activity and contact. With neighborhood youths he gathered pond-lilies, angled for hornpouts, went nutting, walked over the creaking snow-crust, and watched the warm breath of the house chimneys curl silently up in the keen blue air. In summer he chatted under the willows with the highway workers and the travelers on the "New Road" to Old Cambridge, or haunted the "Old-Road" blacksmith shop near the Common to exchange quips with the cartmen. In winter he mingled with the ice-cutters at Fresh Pond or skated sociably with the hired help on the frozen Charles. The homespun quality of this boyhood environment prevented him from ever displaying snobbishness in respect to either labor or persons.

Thus, despite his bent for refinement, Lowell rarely failed to appraise individuals strictly on their merits as *men*. His wise judgments are well illustrated by his remarks to a fellow-townswoman concerning his experience as a delegate to the Republican convention of 1876 at Cincinnati: "It was very interesting, also, to meet men from Kansas and Nevada and California, to see how manly and intelligent they were, and especially what large heads they had. They had not the manners of Vere de Vere perhaps, but they had an independence and self-respect which are the prime elements of a fine bearing. I think I never . . . sat at meat with so many men who used their knives as shovels, nor so many who were so quiet and self-restrained in their demeanor. The Westerners . . . have the unmistakable makings of *men* in them." [8] Lowell's loyalty to American democracy was founded on this enthusiasm for what he conceived to be the manliness of the genuine American. His definition of the essence of Americanism remains unsurpassed: "That 'dignity of human nature' which the philosophers of the last century were

---

[8] *Letters,* II, 169–70.

always seeking and never finding, and which, after all, consists, perhaps, in not thinking yourself either better or worse than your neighbors by reason of any artificial distinction." [9]

The pleasant stability of Elmwood's physical and spiritual order fostered in him a devotion to tradition. He developed an inveterate desire to feel old ground under his feet; he came to hate all changes in familiar earth. "I need a good screen of the past behind me, or I feel an uncomfortable draft on my shoulders and begin to feel a twinge of rheumatism, even if it be only in fancy," he once confessed in a letter to a friend.[10] This strong dependence upon the past grew out of no unreasoning sentiment, no childish dreaming about the glamor of antiquity, but out of early observation that "we carry the Past on our crupper, as immovably seated there as the black Care of the Roman poet. The generations of men are braided inextricably together and the very trick of our gait may be countless generations older than we." [11] Lowell, however, more and more found in tradition not merely a necessitous factor of all human existence, but an element of paramount importance in the cultural ongoing of the race. At fifty-five he had reached this conviction: "For myself, I look upon belief as none the worse but rather the better for being hereditary, prizing as I do whatever helps to give continuity to the being and doing of man, and an accumulated force to his character." [12] Thus Elmwood's venerable associations so quickened in Lowell a conserving instinct that the dominant characteristic of his mind became its acute consciousness of "the forces that are gathered by duration and continuity."

Elmwood, therefore, became the natural center of Lowell's cosmos, the one spot on the planet's surface for which he felt an almost cat-like attachment. It gave him something definite to begin with, it gave him something in particular to love permanently, and hence it gave him what all thoughtful men have need of—a touchstone by which to direct and measure the spiritual

---

[9] *Ibid.*, II, 196.
[10] *New Letters*, 126.
[11] *Works*, VI, 137–38.
[12] *Letters*, II, 152.

progress of their own lives.   At Elmwood he was able to strike
his roots deeply into world-wide knowledge and native earth.
He emerged cosmopolitan in culture, but in mental attitude
redolent of the Yankee soil.

2. THE ROMANTIC AND THE MYSTIC

> But faith and wonder and the primal earth
> Are born into the world with every child.[1]

Wonder and faith Lowell looked upon as the most precious
endowments of man's nature.   He early appreciated that without these elements living would be possessed of neither flavor nor
meaning.   Life, as he often pointed out, is poetic in essence, and
faith holds the only key to heaven.   He preserved to the end
much of childhood's passion for enchantment and mystery.   His
deepest fear was that life might be turned to prose and man be
trapped by actuality: "I have my own suspicions sometimes that
the true age of flint is before, and not behind us, an age harden-
ing itself more and more to those subtle influences which ransom
our lives from the captivity of the actual, from that dungeon
whose warder is the Giant Despair." [2]

Hence Lowell viewed with some foreboding the exploration
of the "huge wonder-horn of the World" by modern scientists.
On one occasion he even went so far as to say of science: "I hate
it as a savage does writing, because he fears it will hurt him
somehow." [3]   He, the poet and artist, was worried lest science
with its rationalizing should dissipate entirely the mythology
which man through the ages has discovered in the universe under one guise or another, and out of which the raw stuff of the
arts has grown.   "Earth is no longer the fine work of art it was,
for nothing is left to the imagination. . . .   The Mysterious
bounds nothing now on the North, South, East, or West," he
lamented in *At Sea*.   Poetry needs the presence of mystery and

[1] *The Cathedral*, ll. 602–3.
[2] Epilogue to *Lectures on the Old English Dramatists*.
[3] *Letters*, II, 230.

conjecture, but the "large, vague world of our fathers" seems almost to have disappeared. "With us poetry is science," [4] a perilous state indeed for humanity, because the very springs of the imagination, man's "common sense of the invisible world," stand threatened. Now since "wonder is crude imagination," [5] the avenue to wonder, damaged by science's incursions, should be repaired at once. To Lowell the situation appeared sufficiently critical to demand a prophet's appeal. "Renew the Age of Wonder," he pleaded in the sonnet, *Science and Poetry.*

Lowell's real quarrel lay not with science *per se,* the disinterested pursuit of truth, but with the deleterious spirit of much contemporary scientific investigation. Yet it will have to be admitted that he never possessed warm sympathy for the basic methods of scientific research. "Faith was never found in the bottom of a crucible, nor peace arrived at by analysis or synthesis," [6] he once remarked disparagingly. He never had the scientist's curiosity for exact knowledge of the physical world, nor did he rejoice over the current rapid accumulation of phenomenal data. For him the world was not primarily a museum of natural history; he much preferred to consider it a museum of supernatural history. While many of his fellow-men were hastening to examine the contents of the universe, he experienced ironic amusement at the sight of "scientific explorers skipping like so many incarnate notes of interrogation." [7] The descriptions by such explorers as Thomas Huxley of geological and zoological evolution Lowell somewhat sarcastically denominated in 1887 as "the new nursery-tales of science." [8]

But, after all, his true hostility was directed against the materialistic attitude which more or less dominated scientists of the period. "Give us science . . . that ennobles life and makes it generous," [9] he urged at the Harvard anniversary of 1886, prompted by his long-held conviction that "science has become

---

[4] *At Sea.*
[5] *The Function of the Poet.*
[6] *Ibid.*
[7] *Ibid.*
[8] *Credidimus Jovem Regnare.*
[9] *Works,* VI, 160–61.

too grimly intellectual, has divorced itself from the moral and imaginative part of man." [10] He felt not a little anxious lest a development of disastrous human consequence might be preparing; namely, a triumphant science which is of the intellect alone, treading "with indifferent foot upon the dead body of Belief." [11] Already, in Lowell's opinion, scientific knowledge had had destructive effects upon the temper of his age:

> This age that blots out life with question marks,
> This nineteenth century with its knife and glass
> That make thought physical, and thrust far off
> The Heaven, so neighborly with man of old,
> To voids sparse-sown with alienated stars.[12]

It had engendered prosaic questioning and substituted demonstration for intuition. The "strange sense of sense escaping things," [13] which in earlier ages had supplied the dynamic force behind cathedral building, symbol of the noblest human aspiration, had now grown faint. "This is no age to get cathedrals built." [14] In that telling observation lies Lowell's final indictment of the prevalent scientific materialism.

There he let the argument rest, and tried to arm himself with the weapons of his time. "Science was faith once; Faith were Science now, would she but lay her bow and arrows by." [15] But to accept wholeheartedly this point of view proved impossible for him in the face of Science's apparent spiritual callousness. Forgetting his own admonition, "Nothing that keeps thought out is safe from thought," [16] he frankly avowed to the well-known English man of letters Leslie Stephen: "But I continue to shut my eyes resolutely in certain speculative directions, and am willing to find solace in certain intimations that seem to me from a region higher than reason." [17] The mechanistic

---

[10] *The Function of the Poet.*
[11] *Ibid.*
[12] *The Cathedral*, ll. 375–79.
[13] *How I Consulted the Oracle of the Goldfishes.*
[14] *The Cathedral*, l. 524.
[15] *Ibid.*, ll. 387–88.
[16] *Ibid.*, l. 390.
[17] *Letters*, II, 168.

philosophy then in the air irritated his religious convictions: "I think the evolutionists will have to make a fetish of their proto-plasm before long. Such a mush seems to me a poor substitute for the Rock of Ages." [18] He refused to be misled as to the sig-nificance of the evolutionary theory. Unlike Leslie Stephen, he did not allow it to upset the foundations of his spiritual beliefs. "However we may explain it, whether as implanted by God or the result of long and laborious evolution, there is something in the flesh that is superior to the flesh . . . and it is to this we must cleave." [19]

Though Lowell took "great comfort in God," [20] he had no interest in church doctrine or denominationalism. Despite the fact that his father was a prominent Unitarian minister, he did not become a regular attendant at any church and in later years did not consider himself a subscriber to any sectarian forms. In 1875 he answered a query about his religious persuasions in these words: "I am not much of a churchgoer, because I so seldom find any preaching that does not make me impatient and do more harm than good. I confess to a strong lurch toward Calvinism (in some of its doctrines) that strengthens as I grow older." [21] But whatever tentative Calvinistic leanings he may have cher-ished never grew to a point of serious philosophic import. He more truly described his state of mind to Leslie Stephen in 1876: "I don't think a view of the universe from the stocks of any creed a very satisfactory one." [22]

Disinclined to be a metaphysical logician, he rarely expressed any explicit concept of the Deity. The "Rock of Ages" he once defined as "a certain set of higher instincts which mankind have found solid under their feet in all weathers." [23] God is pictured from a quite different point of view in *The Cathedral:*

> A Grace of being, finer than himself,
> That beckons and is gone,—a larger life

---

[18] *Ibid.,* II, 245.
[19] *Ibid.,* II, 244.
[20] *Ibid.,* II, 51.
[21] *Ibid.,* II, 148.
[22] *Ibid.,* II, 168.
[23] *Ibid.,* II, 245.

> Upon his own impinging, with swift glimpse
> Of spacious circles luminous with mind,
> To which the ethereal substance of his own
> Seems but a gross cloud to make that visible . . .[24]

The first somewhat nebulous definition suggests an immanent deity, while this second portrays a transcendent one. It was the latter concept which Lowell had usually in mind, nowhere more picturesquely phrased than in his observation to his Cambridge friend and colleague, Charles Eliot Norton: "I think He [*i.e.,* God] is considerably amused with us sometimes, but that He likes us, on the whole, and would not let us get at the match-box so carelessly as He does, unless He knew that the frame of His Universe was fireproof." [25]   In truth, Lowell's theistic speculation took the form of fragmentary and often contradictory ideas. He put far more store by religious sensibility than by systematic theology.

From youth to old age Lowell's faith subsisted chiefly on shadowy, evanescent intimations of a supernal existence. He often lost himself in mystical reverie, where his mind was visited by ghostly presences and phantom dreams. In 1847, at the age of twenty-eight, he called himself a "mystic" with this testimony: "Indeed, during that part of my life in which I lived most alone, I was never a single night unvisited by visions, and once I thought I had a personal revelation from God himself." [26] A half-century later these revelations of what he believed another realm were still haunting him. In *How I Consulted the Oracle of the Goldfishes* (1889) he speaks of

> Wraiths some transfigured nerve divines;
> Approaches, premonitions, signs;
> Voices of Ariel that die out
> In the dim No Man's Land of Doubt.

Except for occasional moments of uncertainty over the ultimate significance of life, such as that expressed in the last line of the

[24] Ll. 444–49.
[25] *Letters,* II, 51.
[26] *Ibid.,* I, 117.

foregoing quotation, Lowell enjoyed an unbroken experience with the "phantasmas of the silences," [27] deeply moving evidence to him of a world invisible and immortal.

3. HYPOCHONDRIAC AND WIT

A psychoanalyst would have found in Lowell a "case" of the greatest interest. He possessed from youth a sensitive and volatile temperament, wherein reserve and expansiveness alternated. His whole being, therefore, was habitually turning in one of two contrary directions: either toward pensiveness, introspection, and morbidity, or toward exuberance, sportiveness, and wit. Of this inner antithesis Lowell was early aware. In a letter of 1847 to Briggs he says, "I find myself very curiously compounded of two utterly distinct characters." [1]

The moments of gloomy discontent, moments not unusual to his private life, grew out of brooding apart. He then found it easy to magnify the slight checks which occurred in his daily round. During 1845, amid marital bliss and professional success, he complained to Briggs: "My sorrows are not literary ones, but those of daily life. I pass through the world and meet with scarcely a response to the affectionateness of my nature." [2] In 1867, when the *Atlantic Monthly,* in the absence of Mr. Fields, the editor, had sent Lowell a smaller sum than usual for a submitted poem, the poet at once took this action as a hint that his contributions were no longer considered so desirable, and sank into a fit of despondency, which only a visit from Mr. Fields himself could dispel. After this episode Mrs. Fields commented significantly in her journal: "Lowell is a man deeply pervaded with fine discontents. I do not believe the most favorable circumstances would improve him." [3] A few years later, while enjoying a long vacation in Europe, he confided to Norton: "I

---

[27] *How I Consulted the Oracle of the Goldfishes.*

[1] *Letters,* I, 117.

[2] *Ibid.,* I, 101.

[3] *Op. cit.,* 109.

have not been overwell since I have been in England. 'Flying
gout' I am fain to call it . . . But it is partly *dumps,* I fancy,
for traveling bores me terribly. I am wretched at not finding a
letter from Mabel here, and J. H. and Rowse have vanished,
leaving no sign. . . . You will find me dull, but honestly willing to brighten." [4]

The strain of mental depression persisted throughout Lowell's
life. It came to the surface when he had been dwelling too
much with his own restive ego. The temperamental dangers
for him in solitary living he well understood: "As for happiness,
a man with a sense of humor (as I in some measure have) has
always a clot of black blood in his veins, always circulating,
always lodging in the most unforeseen and discomfiting places,
and if it once gets into the heart or brain, always fatal to all that
illusion which is the substance of content. And then I have inherited a Puritan conscience that will not let me alone. Every
now and then my good spirits carry me away and people find
me amusing, but reaction always sets in the moment I am left to
myself." [5] The Puritan conscience Lowell would, in a more
objective mood, have admitted to be but another name for that
common complaint of artistic genius, hypochondria.

The dark vein of melancholy, however, was by far the less
important side of his personality and of his creative power.
Some of his briefer lyrics, such as *A Mood,* and certain passages
in longer poems like *The Cathedral,* are pervaded with a morbid
sadness, but for the most part the hypochondriac element does
not assume significance in Lowell's writing. It is the expression
of his other self—"the humorist," as he aptly designated it [6]—
which made him beloved by all acquaintances, won him wide
public esteem, and produced his finest literature, both poetry
and prose. And the humorist in him was almost invariably
aroused by the presence of a friendly audience, even the self-
imagined one to which a letter is addressed. Then his spirits
rose high, wit flowed, and an ineradicable boyishness cropped

[4] Scudder, *James Russell Lowell: a Biography,* II, 157.
[5] *Letters,* II, 289.
[6] *Ibid.,* I, 117.

out. Especially in a crowd of intimates was Lowell prompted to boyish antics. One night, en route home from a Saturday Club meeting in Boston, Louis Agassiz, Dr. Estes Howe, Oliver Wendell Holmes, W. J. Stillman, and Lowell were passing through the Harvard College grounds, with Agassiz and Lowell in weighty discussion of Biblical inspiration. As they reached one of the yard gates with its row of low stone picket columns, Lowell abruptly ceased arguing, vaulted upon a nearby pillar, clapped his hands to his sides, and gave a lusty cockcrow. Then he jumped down and took up the thread of his discourse.[7] After the same manner, his writing now and again betrays youthful exhibitionism in a startling figure or phrase.

This playfulness contributed much to Lowell's popularity, for he could be counted on to add greatly to the conviviality of a gathering. When in 1857 the exploring party of the so-called Adirondack Club, to which Emerson, Agassiz, and Lowell belonged, went into the wilds for a summer sojourn, Stillman, the leader of the group, reported that Lowell was "the soul of the merriment of the company, fullest of witticisms, keenest in appreciation of the liberty of the occasion, and the *genius loci.*"[8] On occasion his sportiveness would take the form of mimicry or impersonation. During the 1850's he belonged to a whist club in Cambridge, an informal group of six or eight congenial spirits, which met on Friday evenings. At these meetings he frequently regaled the members with "his audacious inventions, his deft touches in dressing a story, his assumption of rural shrewdness or clownishness, or his mimicry of antique pedants. Sometimes he would *assume* an imaginary character, and sustain it during an evening."[9] Perhaps he occasionally provided rare entertainment by bringing to life those famous Yankee characters of his, Hosea Biglow and Parson Homer Wilbur.

In spite of his playful and mimetic proclivities, Lowell most enjoyed good talk. Apparently he began quite early to cultivate conversational talents within the family circle, and soon felt sat-

---

[7] W. J. Stillman, *The Old Rome and the New,* 159–60.
[8] *Ibid.,* 160.
[9] F. H. Underwood, *op. cit.,* 42.

isfied with his ability, for in 1847 he wrote to Briggs: "The better qualities of my humor I have never shown except at home, and you would probably be astonished to find what an opinion of my wit obtains among my own family." [10]   Two years later he quickly impressed a distinguished guest at Elmwood with his capacity as a wit.   For three weeks of December, 1849, Fredrika Bremer, the famous Swedish authoress, stayed with the Lowell family, and described the young poet as "predominantly brilliant, witty, gay, especially in the evening when he has what he calls his 'evening fever,' and his talk is then an incessant play of fireworks." [11]   This pyrotechnical brilliance became characteristic of his language, both oral and written.   "Wit was as natural to him as breathing, and when the mood was on he could not help seeing and signalling puns." [12]   Punning constituted in those days a fashionable mode of amusement for the intelligentsia—at least in local circles.   Arthur Clough, the English poet, who had settled in Cambridge in 1852, wrote of a supper at Elmwood in January, 1853: "Thackeray came at ten; Longfellow, Dana, Quincy, Estes Howe, Felton, Fields, and another. Puns chiefly." [13]   Stillman has painted an amusing picture of Lowell and himself engaged in punning contests during the summer of 1858 on the Estes Howe porch, much to the delight of Mrs. Lowell, who gloried in her husband's prowess. [14]   In course of time Lowell's inclination for making puns became a deeply rooted habit, manifesting itself even in his last letters.

Punning, however, was but a minor feature of the wit which brought Lowell fame as a conversationalist, and which made him popular at home and in England as a dinner guest and as an after-dinner speaker.   Sarah Fields again and again awarded to Lowell the palm for scintillating talk at her dinner parties. For example, on November 18, 1868, she gave a dinner at which Bayard Taylor, Thomas Bailey Aldrich, Mr. and Mrs. Scott Sid-

[10] *Letters*, I, 118.
[11] *America of the Fifties: Letters of Fredrika Bremer* (edited by A. B. Benson), 52.
[12] Underwood, *op. cit.*, 41.
[13] *Prose Remains*, 197.
[14] *Op. cit.*, 159.

dons, and Lowell were guests. Afterwards she noted in her diary: "Lowell talked most interestingly, head and shoulders beyond everybody else."[15] Lowell loved to exchange jests, and nowhere more than at the Saturday Club. At a club dinner in honor of G. W. Curtis and several others on February 23, 1867, Oliver Wendell Holmes started playing the wag. Lowell, however, could not contentedly see the Doctor hold the floor alone and harried him with humorous interruptions so constantly that Holmes at last said in mild vexation, "Now, James, let *me* talk and don't interrupt me."[16] This must have been an unwelcome request to a man who, according to Henry James, "was more fond of talking than any one else I ever knew."[17] A great part of Lowell's pleasure in verbal activity resulted from its tonic effect. "His conversation stimulated him in the same way that it stimulated other people."[18] It offered a ready vent for his richer self and, in so doing, brought about a feeling of inward exhilaration.

Playful caper, mimic gleam, and sparkling wit—these qualities found their way into most of Lowell's literary effort. Their charm dominates his writings now, just as it once dominated his conversation. Contact with him was so delightful that friends overlooked the occasional traces of hypochondria. But they never forgot the sweetly provocative presence of Lowell the humorist, whose lively fancy and speech endeared him to all kinds of company, from children in the nursery to guests at diplomatic banquets.

4. THE YANKEE POET

For Lowell no friends were "so constant as the poets."[1] The realm of poetry early became the land of his heart's desire; to be one of its rulers, the dream of his youth and the ambition of a

---

[15] *Op. cit.*, 110.
[16] *Memories of a Hostess*, 33.
[17] "Conversations with Mr. Lowell," *Atlantic Monthly*, LXXIX, 129.
[18] *Ibid.*

[1] *Works*, VI, 69.

lifetime. At twenty-six he wrote to his friend Briggs: "My calling is clear to me. . . . I feel how great is the office of the Poet, could I but even dare to hope to fill it." [2] As a matter of fact, however, he had no real doubt of his capacity. During 1845 he had remarked in a letter to Longfellow concerning his first volume of poems, *A Year's Life:* "My volume, I knew, was crude and immature, and did not do me justice." [3] Lowell's determination to be a poet grew into the supreme passion of his life. Over and over his correspondence repeats the sentiment of this statement made at the age of fifty: "I long to give myself to poetry again before I am so old that I have only thought and no music left." [4] Even in his last years the role of poet lost none of its glamor.

Lowell's lifelong devotion to the profession of poetry was the enthusiasm of a man fundamentally poetic in outlook. To the whole gamut of life his mind instinctively reacted in terms of figurative concept. His correspondence, with its effervescence of metaphors and similes, testifies to the habitual presence of the poet's imaginative power, the immediate and vivid association of feelings and symbols. The richness of Lowell's fancy even in the unpremeditated expression of his letters can only be suggested here. To one correspondent he epitomized the tranquillity of a perfect May day by saying, "Time leans on his scythe and rests." [5] On another occasion he viewed time as a unique kind of property: "One's time is an estate which one can have the pleasure of running through all his life." [6] A visit to the Louvre made him feel the fascination of Titian's cherubs—"little Cupids who have been baptized into the Church without losing a bit of their animal spirits, and who would contrive to get bows and arrows to make mischief with if ever they got into a nunnery." [7] A friend called for Lowell's opinion on the ideal structure of a lyric poem and learned that "the meaning should float

[2] *Letters,* I, 104.
[3] *Ibid.,* I, 99.
[4] *Ibid.,* II, 64.
[5] *Ibid.,* II, 405.
[6] *New Letters,* 43.
[7] *Letters,* I, 265.

steadfast in the center of every stanza, while the vapory emotions (protean in form as you will) float up to it, and wreathe it with an opal halo which seems their own, but is truly its own work." [8] When autumn color came to Elmwood in 1861, he wrote Miss Norton that "the Virginia creeper . . . planted against the old horse-chestnut stump trickles down in blood as if its support were one of Dante's living wood." [9] A walk during his last sojourn at Whitby, England, moved him to whimsical reminiscence: "Thunderstorms loitered about over the valley, like 'Arries on a bank holiday, at a loss what to do with their leisure, but ducking us now and then by way of showing their good-humor. However, there were parentheses of sunshine." [10] Thus at any turn of experience Lowell's faculty for image-making might suddenly illuminate one of life's myriad subjects with a fresh significance.

At the opening of his poetic career his creative energy was directed toward an unfortunate goal. Sensitive to the mood of his youthful intimates and to the general ferment in the New England social attitude, he believed that his "heart would break in pouring out one glorious song that should be the gospel of Reform." [11] Thus, for nearly a decade, preaching became for him inseparably associated with singing. His wide reading at this same period in the great poets, especially in the highly romantic and lyrical masters, Coleridge, Shelley, and Keats, did not affect his essentially moralistic view of poetry. Even after his poetic intentions had changed, it proved hard for him to escape the moralizing habit. Once in the course of a letter to Norton he inadvertently offered an amusing illustration of his unhappy tendency: "We do not care to see our own footprints on the edge [of the water] again, still less to tread in them. Somehow the geese always follow where the songbirds have been, and leave their slumpy stars in the mud themselves have made. There, by ginger! I meant to give the merest hint of

---

[8] *Ibid.*, I, 281–82.
[9] *Ibid.*, I, 315.
[10] *Ibid.*, II, 358.
[11] *Ibid.*, I, 104.

a sentiment, and I have gone splash into a moral. I shall never be a poet till I get out of the pulpit, and New England was all meetinghouse when I was growing up." [12]

Around 1850 he consciously set about trying to break the pulpit's domination of his poetic utterance, which was, he began to realize, growing thin and monotonous: "I am going to try more *wholly* after Beauty herself. . . . I have preached sermons enow, and now I am going to come down out of the pulpit and *go about among my parish.* . . . I find that Reform cannot take up the whole of me, and I am quite sure that eyes were given us to look about us with sometimes, and not to be always looking forward." [13] Thus stirred, he undertook to capture a purer lyric aestheticism. In particular he sought to cultivate more largely a delicate sensuousness arising from his deep-rooted passion for Nature's beauty. Whenever that particular vein of sensation was touched, then he mounted most easily to lyric ecstasy. A gorgeous September day roused his whole being to exaltation: "What glorious fall weather we are having, clear and champagney, the northwest wind crisping Fresh Pond to steel-blue and curling the wet lily-pads over till they bloom in a sudden flash of golden sunshine. How I do love the earth! I feel it thrill under my feet. I feel somehow as if it were conscious of my love, as if something passed into my dancing blood from it, and I get rid of that dreadful duty-feeling— What right have I to be? . . . I wish I could reach you a cup of this wine over those briny leagues." [14] This intense inward excitement over outdoor beauty occasionally brought forth from Lowell moments of moving song. For example, the sun-brush's peculiar magic on Appledore's cliff at the close of day he thus transmuted into verse:

> Now pink it blooms, now glimmers gray,
> Now shadows to a filmy blue,
> Tries one, tries all, and will not stay,
> But flits from opal hue to hue, . . .

[12] *Ibid.*, I, 348.
[13] *Ibid.*, I, 173.
[14] *Ibid.*, I, 273.

So soft that sun-brush in the west,
That asks no costlier pigments' aids,
But mingling knobs, flaws, angles, dints,
Indifferent of worst or best,
Enchants the cliffs with wraiths and hints
And gracious preludings of tints,
Where all seems fixed, yet all evades,
And indefinably pervades
Perpetual movement with perpetual rest.[15]

Such passages of limpid lyricism are, however, rare and never long sustained. Lowell's serious poetry in general contains too many echoes of patterns and styles from classic English poesy to permit the authentic note of originality. More often than not his lyrics lack, as Emerson once privately remarked, "the uncontrollable interior impulse . . . which is felt in the pervading tone, rather than in brilliant parts or lines; as if the sound of a bell, or a certain cadence expressed in a low whistle or booming, or humming, to which the poet first timed his step, as he looked at the sunset, or thought, was the incipient form of the piece, and was regnant through the whole." [16] Yet he chose to labor most in the field of the formal lyric, because it was surrounded with a lofty tradition.

Lowell, nevertheless, eventually came to question the merit of his lyric accomplishment, and hence, since that had always been his chief concern, to doubt his stature as a poet. A sense of unfulfilled promise now and again visited him from about his fiftieth year. In *The Cathedral* (1869) he likened himself to its Gothic architects, "builders of aspiration incomplete." Fifteen years later his dissatisfaction expressed itself more forcibly: "I feel that my life has been mainly wasted—that I have thrown away more than most men ever had." [17] By then he had commenced to excuse the unsatisfying results to his friends. In a letter to the English novelist Thomas Hughes he asserted: "I suppose I should have been a more poetical poet if I had not been

---

[15] *Pictures from Appledore*, II.
[16] *Journals*, December 9, 1869.
[17] *Letters*, II, 280.

a professor. A poet should feed on nothing but poetry, as they used to say a drone could be turned into a queen-bee by a diet of bee-bread." [18] To conceal his trepidation over the decreasing popularity of his poetry he tried to cast aspersion on a changing literary taste: "People want sensation rather than sense nowadays." [19] Three years before his death he wrote to Norton: "I am wondering more and more if my poems are good for anything at all. They are old-fashioned in their simplicity and straightforwardness of style—and everybody writes so plaguily well nowadays." [20]

Lowell in his later years complained that certain obstacles of temperament and circumstance had prevented the complete success of his poetic career. As a particularly important deficiency in his make-up he stressed a lack of perseverance: "I have never been able to shake off the indolence (I know not whether to call it intellectual or physical) that I inherited from my father." [21] This vein of laziness seems to have exerted more than a little influence upon his imaginative processes. It evidently caused him to tire of detailed elaboration when he was dealing with large themes. Even at thirty he acknowledged: "It fags me to deal with particulars. The tendency of my mind is too reflective. I can interest myself in general ideas . . . but weary of their application to the present." [22] Hence, in his lyric endeavors, architectonic power is frequently absent. He himself recognized his weakness in this fundamental quality of true lyric verse and attempted an excuse: "One of my great defects (I have always been conscious of it) is an impatience of mind. . . . The germ of a poem (the idée mère) is always delightful to me, but I have no pleasure in working it up. I carry them [*i.e.*, verses] in my head sometimes for years before they insist on being written. . . . But what can a poor devil do who must gather a stick here and another there to keep the domestic pot a-boiling? My eggs take long in hatching, because I need to

---

[18] *Ibid.*, II, 332.
[19] Scudder, *op. cit.*, II, 358.
[20] *Letters*, II, 345–46.
[21] *Ibid.*, II, 280.
[22] *Ibid.*, I, 134.

brood a good while—and if one is called away from the nest long
enough to let it grow cold? . . . The Muse asks *all* of a man,
and for many years I have been unable to give myself up as I
would." [23]   Thus Lowell repeatedly claimed to the end of his
life that his enforced career as college professor on the one hand
absorbed too much of his energy, and, on the other, cultivated to
an excess his critical sense, so that it "rose like a forbidden apparition in his poetic production." [24]

If Lowell, however, had been less obstinate in the direction of
his poetic ambitions, he would have had little cause for disappointment or apology regarding his poetic accomplishments.
He made the mistake of persisting in over-lofty Parnassian
dreams which distracted him from the essential originality of his
own muse. His forte in verse had been clearly revealed before
his thirtieth year in *A Fable for Critics* and *The Biglow Papers,
First Series*. These works display nothing of the stilted teaching and bookish language so prevalent in his serious poems of
that period. The lighter, more informal tone which their character permitted freed Lowell's tongue from all imitative inhibi-
tions. Here he spoke with a wit and a satiric deftness of greater
potency than that achieved by any other American poet of the
nineteenth century. In *A Fable* there are delightful critical
thrusts, such as this characterization of the English attitude
toward the United States:

> Like most fathers, Bull hates to see Number One
> Displacing himself in the mind of his son,
> And detests the same faults in himself he's neglected
> When he sees them again in his child's glass reflected; . . .

The Biglow Papers with their vigorous Yankee dialect contain
many an incisive passage like the following, the irony of which
remains unimpaired by time or politics:

> I du believe hard coin the stuff
> For 'lectioneers to spout on;
> The people's ollers soft enough

---

[23] *Ibid.*, II, 10–11.
[24] *Works*, VI, 73.

To make hard money out on;
Dear Uncle Sam pervides for this,
An' gives a good-sized junk to all,—
I don't care *how* hard money is,
Ez long ez mine's paid punctooal.

In these humorous pieces, then, there is exhibited a rich and individual vein of poetic inspiration. Lowell should have regarded that vein with more professional earnestness than he apparently ever did, and should have cultivated it more extensively. Thackeray in 1857 well put the matter to Lowell's neighbor and friend, F. H. Underwood:

With such a genius for comedy, greater, I believe, than any English poet ever had,—with such wit, drollery, Yankee sense and spirit. I wonder he does not see his "best hold" and stick to it. Why a man who can delight the world with such creations as *Hosea Biglow* should insist upon writing second-rate serious verse I cannot see.[25]

After the opening of the Civil War Lowell in a second series of *Biglow Papers* did exploit the vein of homely Yankee humor somewhat further. To the political material he added descriptive lyrical touches, the choicest of which appear in *Sunthin' in the Pastoral Line*. The graphic picture of early spring is typical of the imaginative virility shown throughout this comic idyll:

Fust come the blackbirds clatt'rin' in tall trees,
An' settlin' things in windy Congresses,—
Queer politicians, though, for I'll be skinned
Ef all on 'em don't head aginst the wind.
'Fore long the trees begin to show belief,—
The maple crimsons to a coral-reef,
Then saffern swarms swing off from all the willers
So plump they look like yaller caterpillars . . .

Sunthin' in the Pastoral Line is Lowell's masterpiece in his unique genre of poetry. It is an achievement of considerable artistry, for, despite the provincialism of its style, it portrays with superb vitality those elements in a local speech, environment, and morality which provoke universal appreciation.

---

[25] Underwood, *op. cit.,* 121.

A few years later Lowell followed out the dramatic bent visible in *Sunthin' in the Pastoral Line* and others of *The Biglow Papers* by composing in formal English verse a full-fledged narrative of Yankee life and character, *Fitz Adam's Story*. Though much of the Biglow quality lurks in its lines, the piece is a decidedly more ambitious effort in poetic art. The tale of Deacon Bitters, while it is copiously decorated with pungent observations of the New England locale, moves forward with tension sustained, and reaches a perfect dramatic climax. Sly whimsy colors the depiction of both characters and setting, as, for example, that of the parlor in the Eagle Inn:

> The furniture stood round with such an air,
> There seemed an old maid's ghost in every chair,
> Which looked as it had scuttled to its place
> And pulled extempore a Sunday face,
> Too smugly proper for a world of sin,
> Like boys on whom the minister comes in . . .
> Each piece appeared to do its chilly best
> To seem an utter stranger to the rest,
> As if acquaintanceship were deadly sin,
> Like Britons meeting in a foreign inn.

Fitz Adam's description of October weather and of its effect on himself finds Lowell startlingly close to that quiet tone of elfish irony so characteristic of a later member of the New England poetic fraternity, Robert Frost:

> Well, there I lingered all October through,
> In that sweet atmosphere of hazy blue,
> So leisurely, so soothing, so forgiving,
> That sometimes makes New England fit for living.
> I watched the landscape, erst so granite glum,
> Bloom like the south side of a ripening plum,
> And each rock-maple on the hillside make
> His ten days' sunset doubled in the lake;
> The very stone walls draggling up the hills
> Seemed touched, and wavered in their roundhead wills.
> Ah! there's a deal of sugar in the sun!
> Tap me in Indian summer, I should run

> A juice to make rock-candy of,—but then
> We get such weather scarce one year in ten.

From beginning to end the narrative is thus lighted up by flashes of shrewd indigenous fancy. It arouses something of that special flavor of emotion which comes with walking along a New England country road in early autumn—"stone walls on either hand, a somewhat thrifty landscape, and yet fringed all along with hardhack and golden-rod." [26] The piquancy of this New England flavor and the excellence of the structural design combine to place *Fitz Adam's Story* among the best of Lowell's poetic creations.

Its superior merit offers decisive evidence that Lowell's muse was most happily inspired when under the spell of Yankee background. The homespun beauty and humor of rural New England provided the proper outlet for that raciness of imagination and language which constituted his choicest gift. Then, as at no other time, his singing took on a notable individuality and revealed the honorable position which is his in the great choir of the poets. The rightful place of Lowell the poet will always be as a seer of perhaps the purest Yankee spirit produced by New England.

5. THE HUMANE CRITIC

Throughout the prose writings of Lowell a conservatism, at once vigorous and humane, expresses itself. Lowell cultivated, more than any other of the critic's faculties, the capacity to saturate one's self with age-ripened feeling and thought. In a letter of 1868 to James T. Fields, he remarked concerning his possible future activities for the *Atlantic Monthly* audience: "I suppose they'll stand another essay or two yet, if I can divine, or rather if I have absorbed enough of the general feeling about something to put a point on it." [1] This statement describes his habit-

---

[26] *Letters*, II, 292.

[1] *Memories of a Hostess*, 112.

ual approach. As a literary and political essayist he aimed to give polished articulation to ideas already mellowed by men's reflections. To conserve, in the best sense of the word, he conceived as the most important function of the critic.

Lowell grew up with an enthusiasm for the cultural heritage of the Old World, but he early perceived that his countrymen in general lacked a feeling of allegiance to any such common body of cultural ideals as the nations of the Old World possessed. This need in American society for the stabilizing force of traditions caused him, both as a man of letters and as a public speaker, to urge upon his fellow citizens the value of closer acquaintance with their English and European inheritance. It was his unceasing belief that any solid culture in the New World must rest upon the groundwork of Old World civilization, and that only out of contacts with the experience and the achievement of its forebears could the still young American nation gain the proper perspective by which to form its own moral and aesthetic standards. Thus he labored earnestly to spread abroad in the country the gospel of "sweetness and light," though, unlike Matthew Arnold, he engaged in little public tilting with Philistinism. The quiet, persistent influence of his writings and addresses made him one of the outstanding forces for cultural advancement in the United States of the late nineteenth century.

Lowell reiterated again and again the indispensability of traditions to the creation of a strong native literature. "Literature thrives in an air laden with tradition, in a soil ripe with immemorial culture," he declared in one of his last public utterances.[2] He more than once lamented the literary birthright of New England because the Puritans "disinherited us of the past."[3] Whenever he pictured the future American poet of great genius, he prophesied that this poet would "owe his inspiration quite as much to the accumulations of the Old World as to the promises of the New."[4] Such emphatic traditionalism

---

[2] An address in New York City on November 28, 1887, as quoted in Scudder, *op. cit.*, II, 362–63.

[3] *The Function of the Poet and Other Essays*, 134.

[4] *Ibid.*, 144.

sprang from Lowell's perception that the American past was "wellnigh desolate of aesthetic stimulus. We have none or next to none . . . of these coigns of vantage for the tendrils of memory or affection." [5]

In consequence of that realization Lowell sought by his lectures and essays to place before the American public a sound basis for artistic understanding. To him the point of primary importance was the significant continuities in life and art, which the masterpieces of every age and race exemplify: "The masters of prose and the masters of verse in all tongues teach the same lesson and exact the same fee." [6] He came to that basic conclusion after a thorough study of the accepted literary masters from the ancient Greeks to Goethe and Keats. He found certain fundamental conventions of thought, emotion, and form persisting through the centuries. These he set up as the fixed criteria to which he subjected both the works of the "lesser lights" of the past and the writings of his own contemporaries. The strictness of his critical procedure Lowell once described to Sarah Fields in an after-dinner avowal, the gist of which she preserved in her private journal: "He always looked for certain qualities in writers, which if he could not discover, they no longer interested him and he did not care to read them. He discovered, for instance, in the writers who had survived the centuries the same kindred points; those points he studied until he discovered what the adamant was and where it was founded; then he would look into the writers of our own age to see if he could find the same stuff; there was little enough of it unfortunately." [7] His awareness of the immutable spiritual and aesthetic principles which underlie great literature would seem, by the subsequent uncertain progress of American letters, to be still lacking in our national artistic consciousness.

Lowell's conviction was so intense that he took pains to warn against an American overestimate of the creative values to be derived from "the flavor of the climate," and the "gift of the sun

[5] Works, VI, 140.
[6] Ibid., VII, 157.
[7] Memories of a Hostess, 124.

peculiar to the region." [8]   Because he foresaw the artistic dangers, he gave rather guarded approval to the idea that, in the development of American writing, "the novel aspects of life under our novel conditions may give some freshness of color to our literature." [9]   Such deliberately untraditional endeavor as Walt Whitman's *Leaves of Grass* at once aroused his hostility. When Norton wrote Lowell at Dresden soon after the first publication of *Leaves of Grass* in 1855 and described its poetic nature, the latter replied: "No, no, the kind of thing you describe won't do.   When a man aims at originality he acknowledges himself consciously unoriginal." [10]   In 1868 Lowell delivered a final and more vitriolic judgment on the author of *Leaves of Grass:* "Of the shamshaggy, who have tried the trick of Jacob upon us, we have had quite enough, and may safely doubt whether this satyr of masquerade is to be our representative singer." [11]   His antipathy for "the poet of democracy" had increased as he had observed Whitman's effort to achieve a complete divorce from "the inspiration of the past."   In the end he became profoundly irritated by the youthful ignorance of artistic fundamentals which Whitman's poetry seemed to him to display in its superficial novelty, loose technique, and untutored flamboyance.

Yet Lowell felt altogether sympathetic toward the larger poetic movement of which *Leaves of Grass* was an early manifestation. Whitman intended to voice the emotions and aspirations of the common man as he faced swiftly changing social, political, and industrial conditions.   Thus he thought to construct "the epos of the New World."   Lowell had envisioned such an epos and had perceived that its substance, by the very nature of the case, must break sharply with the material and figure of preceding poetry.   In *The Function of the Poet* he welcomed its challenge to the poetic imagination with words of keen critical prophecy. He declared that the poet must "find out what there is imagina-

---

[8] *The Function of the Poet and Other Essays*, 141–42.
[9] *Ibid.*, 142.
[10] *Letters*, I, 242.
[11] *The Function of the Poet and Other Essays*, 143.

tive in steam and iron and telegraph-wires. After all, there is as much poetry in the iron horses that eat fire as in those of Diomed that fed on men." When Walt Whitman, however, attempted to lead the way toward a poetry drawn from the fresh currents of men's interests in the nineteenth century, he went about the undertaking with a heterodoxy so blatant that it shocked Lowell's concept of artistic decency.

The latter's dislike of Whitman did not proceed purely from aesthetic considerations. The tradition of great literature, he believed, established certain bounds of moral propriety. The critic, therefore, should be concerned as much with ethical tone as with aesthetic quality. In that concern Lowell was strongly affected by his sense of contemporary moral convention. It caused him considerable disquiet at times in his critical valuations. A striking example occurs in the eulogy on Fielding which he delivered at Taunton, England, in 1883. Just as years before, at a dinner party in the James T. Fields' home, he had said "he could not tell his boys at Cambridge to read *Tom Jones,* for it might do them harm," [12] so, early in this Taunton address, he pointed out that Fielding's books "cannot be recommended *virginibus puerisque* . . . not because they would corrupt but because they would shock." [13] Nevertheless, on this commemorative occasion, he finally assured his audience that the novelist had an underlying and "earnest moral purpose," [14] even if "the woof of his nature was coarse and animal." [15] But as for Whitman, Lowell did not hesitate to condemn his poetry as "downright animality." [16] He also castigated the young English poet Algernon Swinburne for immorality. In a letter of 1866 to a fellow critic, E. C. Stedman, he wrote: "I have not seen Swinburne's new volume—but a poem or two from it which I have seen shocked me, and I am not squeamish. . . . I am too old to have a painted *hetaira* palmed off on me for a Muse and I hold unchastity of mind to be worse than of body. . . . *Virginibus*

---

[12] *Memories of a Hostess,* 110.
[13] *Works,* VI, 57.
[14] *Ibid.,* 61.
[15] *Ibid.,* 59.
[16] *New Letters,* 115.

puerisque? To be sure! Let no man write a line that he would not have his daughter read. When a man begins to lust after the Muse instead of loving her, he may be sure that it is never the Muse that he embraces. But I have outlived many heresies, and shall outlive this new Adamite one of Swinburne. The true Church of poetry is founded on a rock, and I have no fear that these smutchy back-doors of hell shall prevail against her." [17] Lowell's extravagant language in reference to the works of these two new poets betrays more than a tincture of the squeamishness of contemporary Cambridge taste. Nevertheless, though he shared with the vast majority of New Englanders of his time a dislike for the introduction into literature of sexual passion unidealized and undisguised, he was mainly concerned with the ultimate impression which the introduction of sexual material conveyed. On that question he assumed a position of unexceptionable wholesomeness: "I certainly do *not* believe in the value of any literature that renders the relation between the sexes more ticklish than nature has already made it, or which paints self-indulgence as nobler than self-restraint." [18]

Even if Lowell's estimates of certain contemporary writers may leave something to be desired, still, he most among American critics of the nineteenth century revealed a fascinating discernment of the Olympians. His essays on the classic authors are not merely important historical specimens of American criticism; they are also illuminating excursions into the world of high art and human genius. Literary figures whose achievements and qualities have formed the time-worn topics of innumerable judges Lowell introduces with a vivacity which truly recreates the subjects. The freshness of his comment makes one unmindful of questions concerning the originality of his themes—the "gracious worldliness" of Chaucer, the "grand impersonality" of Shakespeare, the "innocency" of Walton, or the cosmopolitan humor of Cervantes. A mellifluous style enhances the delicate sensibility in these discourses. Lowell, when

---

[17] *Letters,* I, 377.
[18] *New Letters,* 207.

at his best, can cast unforgettable spells of appreciation, as in the essay on Spenser where he writes:

Spenser's is a magic glass in which we see few shadows cast back from actual life, but visionary shapes conjured up by the wizard's art from some confusedly remembered past or some impossible future; it is like one of those still pools of mediaeval legend which covers some sunken city of the antique world; a reservoir in which all our dreams seem to have been gathered. As we float upon it, we see that it pictures faithfully enough the summer-clouds that drift over it, the trees that grow about its margin, but in the midst of these shadowy echoes of actuality we catch faint tones of bells that seem blown to us from beyond the horizon of Time, and looking down into the clear depths, catch glimpses of towers and far-shining knights and peerless dames that waver and are gone. Is it a world that ever was, or shall be, or can be, or but a delusion? . . . It is the same kind of world that Petrarca's Laura has walked in for five centuries with all ears listening for the music of her footfall. The land of Spenser is the land of Dream, but it is also the land of Rest. To read him is like dreaming awake, without even the trouble of doing it yourself, but letting it be done for you by the finest dreamer that ever lived, who knows how to color his dreams like life and make them move before you in music.[19]

Lowell's voice in his critical pieces is not always, of course, enchanting. The music sometimes dies away, and the spell is broken by the prosaic tones of pedantic argument or historical digression. At intervals there intrudes also a superabundance of quotation. The form then betrays the commentator rather than the disciplined formal essayist. His procedure, he admitted, was often rather discursive.[20] He liked to browse along the path and allow both his mind and imagination to lead him where they so desired. It is therefore surprising that he did not more copiously express himself in the personal essay. Therein he could range with only the continuing thread of experience to preserve as it twists around the self. Such few informal compositions as Lowell did undertake—for example, *At Sea* or *Cambridge Thirty Years Ago*—allow him to chat engagingly within

_____
[19] *Works*, IV, 348–49.
[20] *Ibid.*, I, Prefatory Note.

the wide orbit of a reminiscent topic, and to interlard his reminiscences with acute observations on human destiny. But perhaps he appears to even better advantage in the loosest of his essay forms, the journal, for here he is able to build in mosaic pattern. Day by day, bits of changing color and varying substance are added in accordance with the imaginative fortunes of the moment. In *A Moosehead Journal* Lowell's whimsical mind seizes delightedly upon a tessellated literary structure in which it can depict a rich medley of scenes from the Maine back-country. There is dramatic interplay of Yankee humor and sensuous fancy, of deft characterizations in dialogue and sharp pictures of setting. And constantly these variegated tones and materials are blended into a pleasing mosaic harmony of "a little nature, a little human nature, and a great deal of I." Nowhere does Lowell show more versatility as a prose writer and as a critic of humanity than in this lively travelogue.

It is, however, in his letters that the genius of Lowell finds perhaps its ideal medium. In personal correspondence the utmost liberty may be granted to the habit of scintillating discursiveness—a habit preëminently characteristic of Lowell, who doted on all the allurements and provocations concealed in the coverts of language. Style, "the key which gives the pitch of the whole tune," [21] rather than Form, becomes the essential artistic element in letter-writing. Lowell's was a genius which best precipitated itself in perfect, if detached and unrelated, crystals, flashing back the light of our common day tinged with the diviner hue of his own recording powers. His epistolary comment reveals an energetic and richly stored mind seething with multitudinous associations. He wanders with discriminating judgment through human history and arts, and among the contemporary affairs of men—from the painting of the Italian Renaissance to the etymology of New England dialecticisms; from the problems of American democracy to the primitiveness of modern Spain. He dwells upon the homely incidents of daily living with a continual gusto, and relates them to the

---

[21] *Works,* VII, 147.

perennial courses of human experience. The gracious wisdom and the tonic style should secure for Lowell's letters a prominent place in American literature. They demonstrate their author's dictum that "the first lesson of literature, no less than of life, is the learning how to burn your own smoke; that the way to be original is to be healthy; that the fresh color, so delightful in all good writing, is won by escaping from the fixed air of self into the brisk atmosphere of universal sentiments; and that to make the common marvellous, as if it were a revelation, is the test of genius." [22]

6. A FIXED STAR IN THE NEW ENGLAND GALAXY

As a mechanized world with its consequent deflation of human values looms larger and larger on the horizon of history, men need more than ever to be reminded that that persuasive quality, style, may be quite as well exemplified in a character as in a work of art. No one of the brilliant galaxy of New England writers better illustrates this fact than James Russell Lowell. "Distinction marked him as her own, and he responded without effort to her election." [1]

Lowell possessed an invaluable stimulus to a high-minded life —a thirst for affection. "I would rather be loved than anything else in the world," he passionately avowed.[2] This craving led him into a multitude of close and enduring friendships, upon which he increasingly depended for the richer satisfactions of living. The devotion of friends was repaid by his deep concern for preserving the bonds of personal intimacy. The warmth throughout his correspondence testifies to the fine strain of loyalty which formed the keynote of his being.

That strong sense of loyalty did much to nurture Lowell's unshakable confidence in the "general common-sense and the honest intention of mankind." [3] He was far from blind to the

---

[22] *Ibid.*, III, 292–93.

[1] Agnes Repplier, *Eight Decades* (Boston, 1937), 14.
[2] *Letters*, II, 75–76.
[3] *Ibid.*, II, 51.

shortcomings in human nature, as the peroration to his address, *Democracy,* proves, but his faith in its fundamental intelligence and morality triumphed over all other considerations. "We have an instinct to prefer the good, other things being equal, and in exact proportion to our culture we know better what *is* good, and prefer it more habitually." [4] Obviously cynicism won no allegiance from Lowell; his writings lack all trace of this widespread twentieth-century disease.

Lowell indeed encouraged in himself a humorous sympathy with moral frailty. His letters show this characteristic rapidly predominating over the more censorious disposition of youth. He never allowed it, however, to degenerate into mawkish sentimentality, for he cherished a vehement scorn of compromise with base men or things. He rather turned toward kindliness of spirit and temperance in judgment. Although Abolitionism and the cause of the Union had received his ardent support both before and during the Civil War, the end of the struggle quite dissipated his prejudices and found him a leading proponent of mutual aid in the reconstruction of the South. The absence of rancor or of patronage in his attitude is best expressed by the following sentence written in 1868 to E. L. Godkin, the editor of the *Nation:* "I confess to a strong sympathy with men who sacrificed everything even to a bad cause which they could see only the good side of; and, now the war is over, I see no way to heal the old wounds but by frankly admitting this and acting upon it." [5] Thus in all his relations Lowell displayed himself a man of unfeigned good will. In that spirit he sought to deliver admonition and criticism. It made him the ideal diplomat. "Tell us the truth as much as you like, it will do us good; but tell it in a friendly way . . . ," he wrote once to Thomas Hughes.[6] Here is the epitome of his own manner of dealing.

Lowell's charitableness derived from both conscience and intellect. It was the choice blending of two cultural streams, the Hebraic and the Hellenic. The Hebraic through Puritan de-

---

[4] *Ibid.,* II, 15.
[5] *Ibid.,* II, 5.
[6] *Ibid.,* II, 42.

scent bred in Lowell moral enthusiasm and a passion for human equality. His earnest support of democracy, and his statement, "We value character more than any amount of talent," [7] bear witness to deep convictions. The Hellenic stream through classic art and literature contributed breadth of mind and respect for creative genius of all kinds. It caused Lowell to write to one young scholar: "What one wants is to enlarge his mind, to make it charitable, and capable of instruction and enjoyment from many sides." [8] More important still, the Hellenic influence implanted in Lowell the habit of seeking and seeing harmony, whether in human effort or in the universe. That habit became the perpetual spring of his lifelong optimism, an optimism which overlooked neither waste nor disorder nor evil, but yet took the long view of the inherent stability and goodness of man's earth. "The world has outlived much, and will outlive a great deal more, and men have contrived to be happy in it." [9]

The commingling of the Puritan and the Greek heritage also produced in Lowell a marked idealism. Yankee hardheadedness tempered, however, his ceaseless devotion to abstract principle. He believed in a much more equitable distribution of the good things of this world than has been achieved in the United States, but still he knew all too well man's eternal love of material possessions. "Property is always too much for communism in the long run," he observed sagely.[10] Nevertheless, his practicality of judgment was steadily counterbalanced by a heavenly vision, as his words in *Democracy* testify: "I am one of those who believe that the real will never find an irremovable basis till it rests on the ideal." [11]

Aspiration therefore suffused Lowell's entire life, both private and public. It caused him to be generous in impulse toward his fellows, and yet to be stern in opposition to all that appeared ugly and sordid in their enterprizes. Aspiration indeed gave the final admirable touch to his style of character. This style,

[7] *Works*, II, 257.
[8] *Letters*, II, 39.
[9] *Works*, VI, 37.
[10] *Letters*, II, 209.
[11] *Works*, VI, 21.

though stamped with the image and superscription of nine-teenth-century New England, bears a winsomeness which par-takes of no time or place and makes James Russell Lowell a figure of enduring influence to thoughtful men on both sides of the Atlantic. They find superlatively expressed in him that rich and wise humanity which must predominate if any genuinely democratic civilization is to survive in the modern world.

SELECTED BIBLIOGRAPHY

I. EDITIONS

The Writings of James Russell Lowell in Prose and Poetry,
Riverside edition, 11 vols., Boston [N.D.]. The definitive
text of the essays and poems, which Lowell himself prepared
for collected publication.

Letters of James Russell Lowell, edited by Charles Eliot Norton,
2 vols., New York, 1893.

Last Poems, Boston, 1895.

The Complete Poetical Works of James Russell Lowell, Cambridge edition, Boston, 1896. This work contains in one volume all the poems from both the Riverside edition and *Last
Poems.*

Lectures on English Poets, Cleveland, 1897. A private reprint
of the *Boston Advertiser* reports of Lowell's twelve lectures at
the Lowell Institute, Boston, in 1855.

Impressions of Spain, compiled by J. B. Gilder, with an introd.
by A. A. Adee, Boston, 1899. An undistinguished selection
of six letters written by Lowell as American Minister to Spain
and addressed to the Secretary of State.

Early Prose Writings of James Russell Lowell, with a pref. note
by Dr. E. E. Hale, and an introd. by Walter Littlefield, London and New York [1902]. A selection of ten minor prose
pieces first printed in the *Boston Miscellany and Pioneer.*

The Anti-Slavery Papers of James Russell Lowell, 2 vols., Boston, 1902. A collection of Lowell's periodical articles on the
slavery issue in the 1840's and early 1850's.

The Complete Writings of James Russell Lowell, Elmwood edition, 16 vols., Boston, 1904. The first thirteen volumes re-

1

print the text and the contents of the Riverside edition.   The
last three contain the Norton edition of Lowell's letters.

The Function of the Poet, and Other Essays, collected and edited
by Albert Mordell, Boston, 1920.   An important collection of
eighteen prose pieces: five lectures on *belles-lettres,* twelve
book-reviews on old and contemporary authors, and one humorous essay.

New Letters of James Russell Lowell, edited by M. A. DeWolfe
Howe, New York, 1932.

II. BIOGRAPHY AND CRITICISM

Beatty, Richmond C., *James Russell Lowell,* Nashville, Tenn.,
1942.   A biographical study based in part on fresh manuscript
sources and other little-examined material, and emphasizing
Lowell's relations to public affairs.   It is strongly critical of
both his political and literary comment.

Boynton, P. H., "Lowell in His Times," *New Republic,* XVIII
(1919), pp. 112–14.

Bremer, Fredrika, America of the Fifties: Letters of, selected and
edited by Adolph B. Benson, New York, 1924.   This volume
contains several brief but picturesque glimpses of the Lowell
family at Elmwood in 1849.

Brooks, Van Wyck, *The Flowering of New England: 1815–
1865,* New York, 1936.   The studies of Lowell the poet (pp.
311–22) and of Lowell the essayist (pp. 512–25) are vigorous
and dramatic in style, but unsympathetic.

Brownell, W. C., *American Prose Masters,* New York, 1909.
The chapter on Lowell (pp. 271–335) offers perspicuous, albeit cold and abstract, criticism on Lowell the essayist.

Clark, Harry Hayden, "Lowell—Humanitarian, Nationalist, or
Humanist?" *Studies in Philology,* XXVII (1930), pp. 411–41.

Clark, Harry Hayden, "Lowell's Mental Growth" in *James
Russell Lowell: Representative Selections,* Introd., Pt. I, New

York, 1946. This essay amplifies and modifies his 1930 study.

Commemoration of the Centenary of the Birth of James Russell Lowell, New York, 1919. A collection of interestingly varied tributes by prominent American and English men of letters.

Cooke, G. W., *A Bibliography of James Russell Lowell,* Boston, 1906. An invaluable reference work up to the date of its publication.

Foerster, Norman, *Nature in American Literature,* New York, 1923. Chapter V, on Lowell, discusses both the use of nature in his writing and its effect upon his philosophic attitude. Some repetition of Brownell.

Foerster, Norman, *American Criticism,* Boston, 1928. Chapter III, on Lowell, is a decidedly unfavorable analysis of his capacity as critic. The estimate is somewhat prejudiced by the author's evident desire to further a general theory of criticism.

Greenslet, Ferris, *James Russell Lowell,* Boston, 1905. A compact and readable biography with excellent final chapters on Lowell's poetry and prose.

Hale, Edward Everett, Jr., *James Russell Lowell and His Friends,* Boston, 1899. A biographical narrative with the emphasis upon historical associations and personages. Excellent illustrations.

Higginson, T. W., *Old Cambridge,* New York, 1900. Chapter I, on old Cambridge, presents the traditions and atmosphere of Lowell's birthplace. Chapter V, on Lowell, gives a significant personal portrait of Lowell as seen by a fellow townsman.

Howe, M. A. DeWolfe, *Memories of a Hostess: a Chronicle of Eminent Friendships Drawn Chiefly from the Diaries of Mrs. James T. Fields,* Boston [N.D.]. Some interesting and significant glimpses, *passim,* of Lowell with his social peers and intimates in Boston.

Howells, W. D., *Literary Friends and Acquaintance,* New York, 1902. Part VII, *Studies of Lowell,* portrays the personality of Lowell in the eyes of a younger literary friend. Elsewhere the

book includes interesting material on surroundings and personages connected with Lowell's later life.

James, Henry, *James Russell Lowell* in *Essays in London and
Elsewhere,* New York, 1893. Much personal reminiscence of
Lowell in England. An over-laudatory discussion of his
poetry.

James, Henry, "Conversations with Mr. Lowell," *Atlantic
Monthly,* LXXIX (1897), pp. 127–30.

James, Henry, *James Russell Lowell* in *Library of the World's
Best Literature,* XVI, New York [N.D.]. A comprehensive
and flattering estimate of Lowell as man of letters.

"Lowell's Temperament," *Atlantic Monthly,* XC (1902), pp.
862–64. A brief but penetrating analysis.

Parrington, Vernon L., "James Russell Lowell, Cambridge Brah-
min" in *The Romantic Revolution in America* (vol. II of
Main Currents in American Thought), New York, 1927,
p. 460 ff. A searching and, on the whole, an unfavorable
analysis of Lowell the intellectual.

Reilly, Joseph J., *James Russell Lowell as a Critic,* New York,
1915. An exhaustive and disparaging consideration of Lowell's critical attainments.

Scudder, Horace E., *James Russell Lowell: a Biography,* 2 vols.,
Boston, 1901. The standard life of Lowell. A thorough account, but inferior to Greenslet in its critical estimate of
achievement.

Smalley, George W., "Mr. Lowell in England," *Harper's Magazine,* XCII (1896), pp. 788–801. An intimate and anecdotal
memoir.

Stephen, Leslie, Letter to C. E. Norton with reminiscence and
appreciation of Lowell, printed as an appendix to vol. I of the
Letters edited by C. E. Norton.

Stillman, W. J., "A Few of Lowell's Letters" in *The Old Rome
and the New,* Boston, 1898. Miscellaneous reminiscences
chiefly of Lowell the man.

Stillman, W. J., *Autobiography of a Journalist,* 2 vols., Boston,

1901.   Chapter 14, on Lowell, contains somewhat more critical comment than the earlier essay.

Underwood, Francis H., *The Poet and the Man: Recollections
and Appreciations of James Russell Lowell,* Boston, 1893.
A memoir volume by a Cambridge intimate of Lowell's in the
1850's.

Wendell, Barrett, "Mr. Lowell as a Teacher" in *Stelligeri and
Other Essays,* New York, 1893. A portrait of the professor
by a distinguished pupil.

Wilkinson, W. C., "Mr. Lowell's Prose," *Scribner's Monthly,*
IV (1872), pp. 75–86, 227–37, 339–45. A prejudiced, but
none the less thorough, exposition of Lowell's shortcomings as
critic and stylist. The first important adverse commentary on
his writings.

Wurfl, George, "Lowell's Debt to Goethe," *The Pennsylvania
State College Studies,* vol. 1, no. 2 (1936). A significant
monograph on Lowell's great interest in and indebtedness to
Goethe.

ESSAYS

ESSAYS

A MOOSEHEAD JOURNAL [1]

Addressed to the Edelmann Storg [2] at the Bagni Di Lucca. [3]

Thursday, 11th August.—I knew as little yesterday of the interior of Maine as the least penetrating person knows of the inside of that great social millstone which, driven by the river Time, sets imperatively agoing the several wheels of our individual activities. Born while Maine was still a province of native Massachusetts,[4] I was as much a foreigner to it as yourself, my dear Storg. I had seen many lakes, ranging from that of Virgil's Cumaean [5] to that of Scott's Caledonian Lady; [6] but Moosehead, within two days of me, had never enjoyed the profit of being mirrored in my retina. At the sound of the name, no

---

[1] Written originally by installments as a journal for his wife during an excursion to Maine with his nephew, Charles Russell Lowell, in the summer of 1853. Revised slightly in September, 1853 (*Letters,* I, 202), for publication in the November issue of *Putnam's Magazine.* Reprinted in Lowell's first volume of collected essays, *Fireside Travels* (1864).

[2] Lowell's nickname for William W. Story (1819–95), a boyhood friend in Cambridge and a Harvard classmate. (See *infra* Lowell's letter to Story, November 10, 1855.) Story, a sculptor of considerable note, went to Rome in 1847 and took up residence there. He was naturally Lowell's boon companion while the latter sojourned in Italy during the winter of 1851–52. In token of their warm friendship Lowell dedicated his *Fireside Travels* to Story.

[3] The "Lucca Baths," a hot-springs resort about fifteen miles north of the city of Lucca in west-central Italy.

[4] Until 1820 Maine was recognized as a district of Massachusetts, but on March 15 of that year was admitted to the Union as the twenty-third state.

[5] Lake Avernus near Cumae, a Greek settlement on the Italian coast west of Naples. Aeneas visited the famous prophetess, the Cumaean Sibyl, at her grotto by the south shore of Avernus, and from there descended into the Underworld. See Virgil's *Aeneid,* Book VI.

[6] Loch Katrine in the Western Highlands of Scotland (Caledonia). In *The Lady of the Lake* by Sir Walter Scott (1771–1832) the heroine, Ellen, has as her favorite haunt an island in Loch Katrine.

reminiscential atoms (according to Kenelm Digby's Theory of Association,[7]—as good as any) stirred and marshalled themselves in my brain. The truth is, we think lightly of Nature's penny shows, and estimate what we see by the cost of the ticket. Empedocles gave his life for a pit-entrance to Ætna,[8] and no doubt found his account in it. Accordingly, the clean face of Cousin Bull[9] is imaged patronizingly in Lake George,[10] and Loch Lomond[11] glasses the hurried countenance of Jonathan,[12] diving deeper in the streams of European association (and coming up drier) than any other man. Or is the cause of our not caring to see what is equally within the reach of all our neighbors to be sought in that aristocratic principle so deeply implanted in human nature? I knew a pauper graduate who always borrowed a black coat, and came to eat the Commencement dinner, —not that it was better than the one which daily graced the board of the public institution in which he hibernated (so to speak) during the other three hundred and sixty-four days of the year, save in this one particular, that none of his eleemosynary[13] fellow-commoners could eat it. If there are unhappy men who wish that they were as the Babe Unborn, there are more who would aspire to the lonely distinction of being that other figurative personage, the Oldest Inhabitant. You remember the charming irresolution of our dear Esthwaite, (like Mac-

---

[7] Sir Kenelm Digby (1603–65), English author, diplomat, and amateur scientist, propounded the theory that every object or idea is stored away by the mind in the form of a group of inert atoms which can be set in motion by only one particular undulation of their liquid-like medium, the memory; and that when the proper undulation of the memory does set in motion these atoms of like sensitivity they assemble together and form an image in the mind. See Digby's treatise, a favorite of Lowell's, entitled *Of Bodies, and of Man's Soul* (London, 1645), chap. 33: "Of Memory."

[8] A Greek philosopher of the fifth century B.C., who, according to tradition, threw himself into the crater of the Sicilian volcano Aetna in order that his sudden disappearance might prove him a god.

[9] I.e., the Englishman.

[10] A lovely resort lake on the eastern edge of New York state.

[11] The largest and most beautiful lake in the Scottish Highlands, closely associated with the famous outlaw Rob Roy (1671–1734), and located near Loch Katrine.

[12] I.e., the American.

[13] Supported by charity.

heath between his two doxies,[14]) divided between his theory that
he is under thirty, and his pride at being the only one of us
who witnessed the September gale [15] and the rejoicings at the
Peace? [16] Nineteen years ago I was walking through the Fran-
conia Notch,[17] and stopped to chat with a hermit, who fed with
gradual logs the unwearied teeth of a saw-mill. As the strident
steel slit off the *slabs* of the log, so did the less willing machine
of talk, acquiring a steadier up-and-down motion, pare away
that outward bark of conversation which protects the core,
and which, like other bark, has naturally most to do with
the weather, the season, and the heat of the day. At length I
asked him the best point of view for the Old Man of the Mountain.

"Dunno,—never see it."

Too young and too happy either to feel or affect the Horatian
indifference, I was sincerely astonished, and I expressed it.

The log-compelling man attempted no justification, but after
a little asked, "Come from Baws'n?"

"Yes" (with peninsular pride).

"Goodle to see in the vycinity o' Baws'n."

"Oh, yes!" I said; and I thought,—see Boston and die! see the
State-Houses, old and new, the caterpillar wooden bridges
crawling with innumerable legs across the flats of Charles; see
the Common,—largest park, doubtless, in the world,—with its
files of trees planted as if by a drill-sergeant, and then for your
nunc dimittis! [18]

---

[14] Two sweethearts.—Macheath, the highwayman hero of the famous
Beggar's Opera (1728) by John Gay (1685–1732), continually wavers in
his affections between Polly Peachum, his lawful wife, and Lucy Lockit,
his mistress.

[15] The great New England hurricane, September 18–24, 1815.

[16] The Peace of Paris, November 20, 1815: the treaty, concluded by Great
Britain, Russia, and Prussia, with France, which brought the Napoleonic
wars to an end.

[17] The famous pass in the White Mountains of New Hampshire, on the
west side of which is situated "The Old Man of the Mountain," Hawthorne's
celebrated "Great Stone Face."

[18] Request to depart (lit., now thou lettest depart).—This Latin phrase is
the opening of Simeon's song of blessing as it is found in the Vulgate version
of the Bible, Luke ii: 29.

"I should like, 'awl, I *should* like to stan' on Bunker Hill. You've ben there offen, likely?"

"N-o-o," unwillingly, seeing the little end of the horn in clear vision at the terminus of this Socratic perspective.

" 'Awl, my young frien', you've larned neow thet wut a man *kin* see any day for nawthin', childern half price, he never *doos* see. Nawthin' pay, nawthin' vally."

With this modern instance of a wise saw, I departed, deeply revolving these things with myself, and convinced that, whatever the ratio of population, the average amount of human nature to the square mile differs little the world over. I thought of it when I saw people upon the Pincian [19] wondering at the alchemist sun, as if he never burned the leaden clouds to gold in sight of Charles Street.[20] I thought of it when I found eyes first discovering at Mont Blanc [21] how beautiful snow was. As I walked on, I said to myself, There is one exception, wise hermit, —it is just these *gratis* [22] pictures which the poet puts in his show-box, and which we all gladly pay Wordsworth and the rest for a peep at. The divine faculty is to see what everybody can look at.

While every well-informed man in Europe, from the barber down to the diplomatist, has his view of the Eastern Question,[23] why should I not go personally down East [24] and see for myself? Why not, like Tancred,[25] attempt my own solution of the Mys-

---

[19] I.e., the Pincian Walk, fashionable promenade in the Pincio, the lovely public gardens near the heart of Rome.

[20] At this time one of Boston's elite residential thoroughfares, running between the Public Gardens and the Common, and thence northward to the Charles River.

[21] The highest peak in the Swiss Alps.

[22] Free.

[23] That problem of nineteenth-century European politics which constantly threatened the so-called "balance of power" and revolved about two main points: (1) Mohammedan Turkey's authority over the Christian minorities within her empire; (2) Russia's ambition to gain, at Turkey's expense, control of the Balkan peninsula and access to the Mediterranean.

[24] I.e., down to Maine: a New England colloquialism.

[25] Tancred, a Norman nobleman and warrior, joined the First Crusade in 1096 and took part in the sieges of Antioch, Bethlehem, and Jerusalem. He later became governor of Antioch, and was holding that office when he died in 1112.

tery of the Orient,—doubly mysterious when you begin the two words with capitals? You know my way of doing things, to let them simmer in my mind gently for months, and at last do them *impromptu* [26] in a kind of desperation, driven by the Eumenides [27] of unfulfilled purpose. So, after talking about Moosehead till nobody believed me capable of going thither, I found myself at the Eastern Railway station. The only event of the journey hither (I am now at Waterville) was a boy hawking exhilaratingly the last great railroad smash,—thirteen lives lost,—and no doubt devoutly wishing there had been fifty. This having a mercantile interest in horrors, holding stock, as it were, in murder, misfortune, and pestilence, must have an odd effect on the human mind. The birds of ill-omen, at whose sombre flight the rest of the world turn pale, are the ravens which bring food to this little outcast in the wilderness. If this lad give thanks for daily bread, it would be curious to inquire what that phrase represents to his understanding. If there ever be a plum in it, it is Sin or Death that puts it in. Other details of my dreadful ride I will spare you. Suffice it that I arrived here in safety,—in complexion like an Ethiopian serenader half got-up, and so broiled and peppered that I was more like a devilled kidney than anything else I can think of.

10 P.M.—The civil landlord and neat chamber at the "Elmwood House" were very grateful, and after tea I set forth to explore the town. It has a good chance of being pretty; but, like most American towns, it is in a hobbledehoy [28] age, growing yet, and one cannot tell what may happen. A child with great promise of beauty is often spoiled by its second teeth. There is something agreeable in the sense of completeness which a walled town gives one. It is entire, like a crystal,—a work which man

---

[26] Offhand.

[27] An allusion to the unhappy situation of Orestes, whose mother Clytemnestra had had his father Agamemnon murdered. Orestes was pursued, after avenging the murder, by the Eumenides or Furies, the three goddesses who, according to Greek myth, sought out and punished evildoers that had avoided the penalties of the public justice. For the most dramatic version of this tale see *The Eumenides* by the Greek tragedian Aeschylus (525–456 B.C.).

[28] Awkwardly adolescent.

has succeeded in finishing. I think the human mind pines more or less where everything is new, and is better for a diet of stale bread. The number of Americans who visit the Old World, and the deep inspirations with which they breathe the air of antiquity, as if their mental lungs had been starved with too thin an atmosphere, is beginning to afford matter of speculation to observant Europeans. For my part, I never saw a house which I thought old enough to be torn down. It is too like that Scythian [29] fashion of knocking old people on the head. I cannot help thinking that the indefinable something which we call *character* is cumulative,—that the influence of the same climate, scenery, and associations for several generations is necessary to its gathering head, and that the process is disturbed by continual change of place. The American is nomadic in religion, in ideas, in morals, and leaves his faith and opinions with as much indifference as the house in which he was born. However, we need not bother: Nature takes care not to leave out of the great heart of society either of its two ventricles of hold-back and go-ahead.

It seems as if every considerable American town must have its one specimen of everything, and so there is a college [30] in Waterville, the buildings of which are three in number, of brick, and quite up to the average ugliness which seems essential in edifices of this description. Unhappily, they do not reach that extreme of ugliness where it and beauty come together in the clasp of fascination. We erect handsomer factories for cottons, woollens, and steam-engines, than for doctors, lawyers, and parsons. The truth is, that, till our struggle with nature is over, till this shaggy hemisphere is tamed and subjugated, the workshop will be the college whose degrees will be most valued. Moreover, steam has made travel so easy that the great university of the world is open to all comers, and the old cloister system is falling astern. Perhaps it is only the more needed, and, were I rich, I should like to found a few lazyships in my Alma Mater as a kind of counterpoise. The Anglo-Saxon race has accepted the primal

---

[29] The Scythians, a nomadic people of southeastern Europe, were noted for their primitive and cruel behavior.
[30] Colby College.

curse as a blessing, has deified work, and would not have thanked Adam for abstaining from the apple. They would have dammed the four rivers of Paradise,[31] substituted cotton for fig-leaves among the antediluvian [32] populations, and commended man's first disobedience [33] as a wise measure of political economy. But to return to our college. We cannot have fine buildings till we are less in a hurry. We snatch an education like a meal at a railroad-station. Just in time to make us dyspeptic, the whistle shrieks, and we must rush, or lose our places in the great train of life. Yet noble architecture is one element of patriotism, and an eminent one of culture, the finer portions of which are taken in by unconscious absorption through the pores of the mind from the surrounding atmosphere. I suppose we must wait, for we are a great bivouac as yet, rather than a nation on the march from the Atlantic to the Pacific, and pitch tents instead of building houses. Our very villages seem to be in motion, following westward the bewitching music of some Pied Piper of Hamelin.[34] We still feel the great push toward sundown given to the peoples somewhere in the gray dawn of history. The cliff-swallow alone of all animated nature emigrates eastward.

Friday, 12th.—The coach leaves Waterville at five o'clock in the morning, and one must breakfast in the dark at a quarter past four, because a train starts at twenty minutes before five,— the passengers by both conveyances being pastured gregariously. So one must be up at half past three. The primary geological formations contain no trace of man, and it seems to me that these eocene [35] periods of the day are not fitted for sustaining the hu-

---

[31] The rivers Pison, Gihon, Hiddekel, and Euphrates watered the Garden of Eden. See Genesis 2:11–14.

[32] Before the Deluge.

[33] I.e., Adam's in the Garden of Eden.

[34] According to old German legend, a certain piper, dressed in variegated colors (hence "pied"), came to Hamelin in Prussia and agreed for a monetary reward to rid the town of the rats which infested it. He proceeded with his piping to charm the rats into the Weser River, where they all drowned. Then when he found his reward withheld, he lured with his magic pipe the town's children into a cave which closed on them all forever.

[35] In geological time, the earliest period in the Tertiary era or Age of Mammals.

man forms of life. One of the Fathers held that the sun was created to be worshipped, at his rising, by the Gentiles. The more reason that Christians (except, perhaps, early Christians) should abstain from these heathenish ceremonials. As one arriving by an early train is welcomed by a drowsy maid with the sleep scarce brushed out of her hair, and finds empty grates and polished mahogany, on whose arid plains the pioneers of breakfast have not yet encamped, so a person waked thus unseasonably is sent into the world before his faculties are up and dressed to serve him. It might have been for this reason that my stomach resented for several hours a piece of fried beefsteak which I forced upon it, or, more properly speaking, a piece of that leathern conveniency which in these regions assumes the name. You will find it as hard to believe, my dear Storg, as that quarrel of the Sorbonists, whether one should say *ego amat* [36] or no, that the use of the gridiron is unknown hereabout, and so near a river named after St. Lawrence,[37] too!

To-day has been the hottest day of the season, yet our drive has not been unpleasant. For a considerable distance we followed the course of the Sebasticook River, a pretty stream with alternations of dark brown pools and wine-colored rapids. On each side of the road the land had been cleared, and little one-story farm-houses were scattered at intervals. But the stumps still held out in most of the fields, and the tangled wilderness closed in behind, striped here and there with the slim white trunks of the elm. As yet only the edges of the great forest have been nibbled away. Sometimes a root-fence stretched up its bleaching antlers, like the trophies of a giant hunter. Now and then the houses thickened into an unsocial-looking village, and we drove up to the grocery to leave and take a mail-bag, stopping again presently to water the horses at some pallid little tavern, whose one red-curtained eye (the bar-room) had been put out by the inexorable thrust of Maine Law. Had Shenstone

---

[36] Lit., I he loves: a humorous allusion to the petty scholastic quarrels at the Sorbonne in Paris during the thirteenth century.

[37] St. Lawrence the Deacon met his martyrdom in 258, when he was roasted to death on a gridiron at Rome for his refusal to turn over church treasures to the Emperor Valerian.

travelled this road, he would never have written that famous
stanza of his;[38] had Johnson, he would never have quoted it.[39]
They are to real inns as the skull of Yorick[40] to his face.
Where these villages occurred at a distance from the river, it
was difficult to account for them. On the river-bank, a saw-
mill or a tannery served as a logical premise, and saved them
from total inconsequentiality. As we trailed along, at the rate
of about four miles an hour, it was discovered that one of our
mail-bags was missing. "Guess somebody'll pick it up," said
the driver coolly; " 't any rate, likely there's nothin' in it." Who
knows how long it took some Elam D. or Zebulon K. to compose
the missive intrusted to that vagrant bag, and how much longer
to persuade Pamela Grace or Sophronia Melissa[41] that it had
really and truly been written? The discovery of our loss was
made by a tall man who sat next to me on the top of the coach,
every one of whose senses seemed to be prosecuting its several
investigation as we went along. Presently, sniffing gently, he
remarked: " 'Pears to me's though I smelt sunthin'. Ain't the
aix het, think?" The driver pulled up, and, sure enough, the
off fore-wheel was found to be smoking. In three minutes he
had snatched a rail from the fence, made a lever, raised the
coach, and taken off the wheel, bathing the hot axle and box
with water from the river. It was a pretty spot, and I was not
sorry to lie under a beech-tree (Tityrus-like,[42] meditating over
my pipe) and watch the operations of the fire-annihilator. I
could not help contrasting the ready helpfulness of our driver,

---

[38] The last stanza of *Written at an Inn at Henley,* by the English poet
William Shenstone (1714–63), reads:

> Whoe'er has travell'd Life's dull round,
> Where'er his stages may have been,
> May sigh to think he still has found
> The warmest welcome at an inn.

[39] See chap. xxxi (1776) of *The Life of Samuel Johnson,* L.L.D.
(1709–84) by James Boswell (1740–95).

[40] Yorick, the king's jester, whose skull is brought to light in the famous
gravedigging scene of *Hamlet.* See Act V, Sc. 1, l. 198ff.

[41] These odd-sounding names, both male and female, are actual New
England originals.

[42] Tityrus was a shepherd character in Virgil's *Eclogues.* The firs
eclogue opens with this line:

> O Tityrus, thou reclining under the shade of the spreading beech.

all of whose wits were about him, current, and redeemable in the specie of action on emergency, with an incident of travel in Italy, where, under a somewhat similar stress of circumstances, our *vetturino* [43] had nothing for it but to dash his hat on the ground and call on Sant' Antonio, the Italian Hercules.

There being four passengers for the Lake, a vehicle called a mud-wagon was detailed at Newport for our accommodation. In this we jolted and rattled along at a livelier pace than in the coach. As we got farther north, the country (especially the hills) gave evidence of longer cultivation. About the thriving town of Dexter we saw fine farms and crops. The houses, too, became prettier; hop-vines were trained about the doors, and hung their clustering thyrsi [44] over the open windows. A kind of wild rose (called by the country folk the primrose) and asters were planted about the door-yards, and orchards, commonly of natural fruit, added to the pleasant home-look. But everywhere we could see that the war between the white man and the forest was still fierce, and that it would be a long while yet before the axe was buried. The haying being over, fires blazed or smouldered against the stumps in the fields, and the blue smoke widened slowly upward through the quiet August atmosphere. It seemed to me that I could hear a sigh now and then from the immemorial pines, as they stood watching these campfires of the inexorable invader. Evening set in, and, as we crunched and crawled up the long gravelly hills, I sometimes began to fancy that Nature had forgotten to make the corresponding descent on the other side. But erelong we were rushing down at full speed; and, inspired by the dactylic beat of the horses' hoofs, I essayed to repeat the opening lines of Evangeline. At the moment I was beginning, we plunged into a hollow, where the soft clay had been overcome by a road of unhewn logs. I got through one line to this corduroy accompaniment, somewhat as a country choir stretches a short metre on the Procrustean [45] rack of a long-drawn tune. The result was like this:—

[43] Driver.
[44] Blossoms.
[45] Harsh and inflexible.—Procrustes was, in Greek legend, a notorious

Thihis ihis thehe fohorest prihihimeheval; thehe murhurmuring
   pihines hahand thehe hehemlohocks!

At a quarter past eleven, P.M., we reached Greenville, (a little
village which looks as if it had dripped down from the hills, and
settled in the hollow at the foot of the lake,) having accomplished seventy-two miles in eighteen hours. The tavern was
totally extinguished. The driver rapped upon the bar-room
window, and after a while we saw heat-lightnings of unsuccessful matches followed by a low grumble of vocal thunder, which
I am afraid took the form of imprecation. Presently there was
a great success, and the steady blur of lighted tallow succeeded
the fugitive brilliance of the pine. A hostler fumbled the door
open, and stood staring at but not seeing us, with the sleep sticking out all over him. We at last contrived to launch him, more
like an insensible missile than an intelligent or intelligible being,
at the slumbering landlord, who came out wide-awake, and welcomed us as so many half-dollars,—twenty-five cents each for
bed, *ditto* breakfast. O Shenstone, Shenstone! The only roost
was in the garret, which had been made into a single room, and
contained eleven double-beds, ranged along the walls. It was
like sleeping in a hospital. However, nice customs curtsy to
eighteen-hour rides, and we slept.

Saturday, 13th.—This morning I performed my toilet in the
bar-room, where there was an abundant supply of water, and a
halo of interested spectators. After a sufficient breakfast, we
embarked on the little steamer Moosehead, and were soon throbbing up the lake. The boat, it appeared, had been chartered by
a party, this not being one of her regular trips. Accordingly we
were mulcted in twice the usual fee, the philosophy of which I
could not understand. However, it always comes easier to us to
comprehend why we receive than why we pay. I dare say it
was quite clear to the captain. There were three or four clear-
ings on the western shore; but after passing these, the lake became wholly primeval, and looked to us as it did to the first
adventurous Frenchman who paddled across it. Sometimes a

---

highwayman of Attica, who bound his victims onto an iron bed and then
stretched or cut off their limbs so that they would fit the bed neatly.

cleared point would be pink with the blossoming willow-herb, "a cheap and excellent substitute" for heather, and, like all such, not *quite* so good as the real thing. On all sides rose deep-blue mountains, of remarkably graceful outline, and more fortunate than common in their names. There were the Big and Little Squaw, the Spencer and Lily-bay Mountains. It was debated whether we saw Katahdin [46] or not, (perhaps more useful as an intellectual exercise than the assured vision would have been), and presently Mount Kineo rose abruptly before us, in shape not unlike the island of Capri.[47] Mountains are called great natural features, and why they should not retain their names long enough for these also to become naturalized, it is hard to say. Why should every new surveyor rechristen them with the gubernatorial patronymics of the current year? They are geological noses, and as they are aquiline or pug, indicate terrestrial idiosyncrasies. A cosmical physiognomist, after a glance at them, will draw no vague inference as to the character of the country. The word *nose* is no better than any other word; but since the organ has got that name, it is convenient to keep it. Suppose we had to label our facial prominences every season with the name of our provincial governor, how should *we* like it? If the old names have no other meaning, they have that of age; and, after all, meaning is a plant of slow growth, as every reader of Shakespeare knows. It is well enough to call mountains after their discoverers, for Nature has a knack of throwing doublets, and somehow contrives it that discoverers have good names. Pike's Peak [48] is a curious hit in this way. But these surveyors' names have no natural *stick* in them. They remind one of the epithets of poetasters, which peel off like a badly gummed postage-stamp. The early settlers did better, and there is something pleasant in the sound of Graylock,[49] Saddleback,[50] and Great Haystack.[51]

---

[46] The highest peak in Maine.
[47] A famous rocky resort off the Italian coast opposite Naples.
[48] A noted summit in the Colorado Rockies.
[49] The highest peak of the Berkshire Hills in western Massachusetts.
[50] A peak of the Adirondack Mountains in eastern New York.
[51] Another and higher peak of the Adirondacks.

I love those names
Wherewith the exiled farmer tames
Nature down to companionship
　With his old world's more homely mood,
And strives the shaggy wild to clip
　In the arms of familiar habitude.

It is possible that Mount Marcy [52] and Mount Hitchcock [53] may sound as well hereafter as Hellespont [54] and Peloponnesus,[55] when the heroes, their namesakes, have become mythic with antiquity. But that is to look forward a great way. I am no fanatic for Indian nomenclature,—the name of my native district having been Pigsgusset,—but let us at least agree on names for ten years.

There were a couple of loggers on board, in red flannel shirts, and with rifles. They were the first I had seen, and I was interested in their appearance. They were tall, well-knit men, straight as Robin Hood, and with a quiet, self-contained look that pleased me. I fell into talk with one of them.

"Is there a good market for the farmers here in the woods?" I asked.

"None better. They can sell what they raise at their doors, and for the best of prices. The lumberers want it all, and more."

"It must be a lonely life. But then we all have to pay more or less life for a living."

"Well, it *is* lonesome. Shouldn't like it. After all, the best crop a man can raise is a good crop of society. We don't live none too long, anyhow; and without society a fellow couldn't tell more'n half the time whether he was alive or not."

This speech gave me a glimpse into the life of the lumberers' camp. It was plain that there a man would soon find out how much alive he was,—there he could learn to estimate his quality, weighed in the nicest self-adjusting balance. The best arm at

[52] The highest peak of the Adirondacks.
[53] A small peak in Wales township, southwestern Massachusetts.
[54] The celebrated strait, now called the Dardanelles, which separates Macedonia and Asia Minor.
[55] The great peninsula which forms the southern portion of Greece.

the axe or the paddle, the surest eye for a road or for the weak point of a *jam*, the steadiest foot upon the squirming log, the most persuasive voice to the tugging oxen,—all these things are rapidly settled, and so an aristocracy is evolved from this democracy of the woods, for good old mother Nature speaks Saxon still, and with her either Canning or Kenning means King.[56]

A string of five loons was flying back and forth in long, irregular zigzags, uttering at intervals their wild, tremulous cry, which always seems far away, like the last faint pulse of echo dying among the hills, and which is one of those few sounds that, instead of disturbing solitude, only deepen and confirm it. On our inland ponds they are usually seen in pairs, and I asked if it were common to meet five together. My question was answered by a queer-looking old man, chiefly remarkable for a pair of enormous cowhide boots, over which large blue trousers of frocking strove in vain to crowd themselves.

"Wahl, 't ain't ushil," said he, "and it's called a sign o' rain comin', that is."

"Do you think it will rain?"

With the caution of a veteran *auspex*,[57] he evaded a direct reply. "Wahl, they *du* say it's a sign o' rain comin'," said he.

I discovered afterward that my interlocutor was Uncle Zeb. Formerly, every New England town had its representative uncle. He was not a pawnbroker, but some elderly man who, for want of more defined family ties, had gradually assumed this avuncular [58] relation to the community, inhabiting the borderland between respectability and the almshouse, with no regular calling, but ready for odd jobs at haying, wood-sawing, whitewashing, associated with the demise of pigs and the ailments of cattle, and possessing as much patriotism as might be implied in

---

[56] Thomas Carlyle (1795–1881), renowned Scottish critic and historian, in *Sartor Resartus* (1833–34) stated a false etymology for the word "king," which received wide credence, and to which Lowell is here alluding. In Bk. III, Chap. VII, "Organic Filaments," Carlyle wrote: "König (King), anciently Könning, means Ken-ning (Cunning), or which is the same thing, Can-ning."

[57] Prognosticator.

[58] Uncle-like.

a devoted attachment to "New England"—with a good deal of sugar and very little water in it. Uncle Zeb was a good specimen of this palæozoic [59] class, extinct among us for the most part, or surviving, like the Dodo,[60] in the Botany Bays [61] of society. He was ready to contribute (somewhat muddily) to all general conversation; but his chief topics were his boots and the 'Roostick war.[62] Upon the lowlands and levels of ordinary palaver he would make rapid and unlooked-for incursions; but, provision failing, he would retreat to these two fastnesses, whence it was impossible to dislodge him, and to which he knew innumerable passes and short cuts quite beyond the conjecture of common woodcraft. His mind opened naturally to these two subjects, like a book to some favorite passage. As the ear accustoms itself to any sound recurring regularly, such as the ticking of a clock, and, without a conscious effort of attention, takes no impression from it whatever, so does the mind find a natural safeguard against this pendulum species of discourse, and performs its duties in the parliament by an unconscious reflex action, like the beating of the heart or the movement of the lungs. If talk seemed to be flagging, our Uncle would put the heel of one boot upon the toe of the other, to bring it within point-blank range, and say, "Wahl, I stump the Devil himself to make that 'ere boot hurt *my* foot," leaving us in doubt whether it were the virtue of the foot or its case which set at naught the wiles of the adversary; or, looking up suddenly, he would exclaim, "Wahl, we eat *some* beans to the 'Roostick war, I tell *you!*" When his poor old clay was wet with gin, his thoughts and words acquired a rank flavor from it, as from too strong a fertilizer. At such times, too, his fancy commonly reverted to a prehistoric period of his life, when he singly had settled all the

---

[59] The oldest geologic era.

[60] A fat and clumsy bird of the pigeon family, larger than a turkey but incapable of flying. It was found only on the African island of Mauritius and there exterminated late in the seventeenth century by European visitors.

[61] I.e., outcast regions.—Botany Bay, five miles south of Port Jackson (Sidney), New South Wales, Australia, became in 1787 the site of the first British overseas convict settlement, and soon attained world-wide notoriety.

[62] The question of the boundary between Maine and New Brunswick produced in 1837–38 a near outbreak of hostilities along the Aroostook River.

surrounding country, subdued the Injuns and other wild animals, and named all the towns.

We talked of the winter-camps and the life there. "The best
thing is," said our Uncle, "to hear a log squeal thru the snow.
Git a good, col', frosty mornin', in Febuary say, an' take an'
hitch the critters on to a log that'll scale seven thousan', an' it'll
squeal as pooty as an'thin' *you* ever hearn, I tell *you*."

A pause.

"Lessee,—seen Cal Hutchins lately?"

"No."

"Seems to me's though I hedn't seen Cal sence the 'Roostick
war. Wahl," &c., &c.

Another pause.

"To look at them boots you'd think they was too large; but
kind o' git your foot into 'em, and they're as easy's a glove."
(I observed that he never seemed really to get his foot in,—there
was always a qualifying *kind o'*.) "Wahl, my foot can play in
'em like a young hedgehog."

By this time we had arrived at Kineo,—a flourishing village
of one house, the tavern kept by 'Squire Barrows. The 'Squire
is a large, hearty man, with a voice as clear and strong as a northwest wind, and a great laugh suitable to it. His table is neat
and well supplied, and he waits upon it himself in the good old
landlordly fashion. One may be much better off here, to my
thinking, than in one of those gigantic Columbaria [63] which are
foisted upon us patient Americans for hotels, and where one is
packed away in a pigeon-hole so near the heavens that, if the
comet should flirt its tail (no unlikely thing in the month of
flies,) one would run some risk of being brushed away. Here
one does not pay his diurnal three dollars for an undivided five-
hundredth part of the pleasure of looking at gilt gingerbread.
Here one's relations are with the monarch himself, and one is
not obliged to wait the slow leisure of those "attentive clerks"
whose praises are sung by thankful deadheads, and to whom the
slave who pays may feel as much gratitude as might thrill the

---

[63] Pigeon houses.

heart of a brown-paper parcel toward the express-man who labels it and chucks it under his counter.

Sunday, 14th.—The loons were right. About midnight it began to rain in earnest, and did not hold up till about ten o'clock this morning. "This is a Maine dew," said a shaggy woodman cheerily, as he shook the water out of his wide-awake, "if it don't look out sharp, it'll begin to rain afore it thinks on't." The day was mostly spent within doors; but I found good and intelligent society. We should have to be shipwrecked on Juan Fernandez [64] not to find men who knew more than we. In these travelling encounters one is thrown upon his own resources, and is worth just what he carries about him. The social currency of home, the smooth-worn coin which passes freely among friends and neighbors, is of no account. We are thrown back upon the old system of barter; and, even with savages, we bring away only as much of the wild wealth of the woods as we carry beads of thought and experience, strung one by one in painful years, to pay for them with. A useful old jackknife will buy more than the daintiest Louis Quinze [65] paper-folder fresh from Paris. Perhaps the kind of intelligence one gets in these out-of-the-way places is the best,—where one takes a fresh man after breakfast instead of the damp morning paper, and where the magnetic telegraph of human sympathy flashes swift news from brain to brain.

Meanwhile, at a pinch, to-morrow's weather can be discussed. The augury from the flight of birds is favorable,—the loons no longer prophesying rain. The wind also is hauling round to the right quarter, according to some,—to the wrong, if we are to believe others. Each man has his private barometer of hope, the mercury in which is more or less sensitive, and the opinion vibrant with its rise or fall. Mine has an index which can be moved mechanically. I fixed it at *set fair,* and resigned myself.

---

[64] An island off the coast of Chile, on which Alexander Selkirk lived alone from 1704 to 1708. Selkirk's experience is supposed to have served as the basis for Defoe's story of Robinson Crusoe.

[65] I.e., style of the reign of Louis XV of France (1710–74).

I read an old volume of the Patent-Office Report on Agriculture, and stored away a beautiful pile of facts and observations for future use, which the current of occupation, at its first freshet, would sweep quietly off to blank oblivion. Practical application is the only mordant which will set things in the memory. Study, without it, is gymnastics, and not work, which alone will get intellectual bread. One learns more metaphysics from a single temptation than from all the philosophers. It is curious, though, how tyrannical the habit of reading is, and what shifts we make to escape thinking. There is no bore we dread being left alone with so much as our own minds. I have seen a sensible man study a stale newspaper in a country tavern, and husband it as he would an old shoe on a raft after shipwreck. Why not try a bit of hibernation? There are few brains that would not be better for living on their own fat a little while. With these reflections, I, notwithstanding, spent the afternoon over my Report. If our own experience is of so little use to us, what a dolt is he who recommends to man or nation the experience of others! Like the mantle in the old ballad,[66] it is always too short or too long, and exposes or trips us up. "Keep out of that candle," says old Father Miller, "or you'll get a singeing." "Pooh, pooh, father, I've been dipped in the new asbestos preparation," and *frozz!* it is all over with young Hopeful. How many warnings have been drawn from Pretorian bands,[67] and Janizaries,[68] and Mamelukes,[69] to make Napoleon III impossible in 1851![70] I found myself thinking the same thoughts over again,

---

[66] *The Boy and the Mantle,* which Lowell probably first read in Thomas Percy's *Reliques of Ancient English Poetry,* Bk. 7. The ballad tells of a magic cloak which in a public trial revealed the infidelity of several ladies of high station by exposing their persons in various ways.

[67] The Praetorian guard, the bodyguard of Roman emperors, was instituted by Augustus Caesar and finally dissolved in A.D. 312 by Constantine.

[68] The Janizaries, originally the personal slaves who guarded the Turkish sultan, became a body of conscript infantrymen who formed the main force of the Turkish army. On their revolt in 1826 from the authority of the sultanate the Janizary troops were permanently dispersed.

[69] The Mamelukes were a body of Egyptian soldiers recruited from Islam converts of the slave class, and constituted a powerful factor in the politics of Egypt from the fourteenth to the nineteenth centuries. In 1811 Mehemet Ali, the first Turkish viceroy, put an end to this military organization.

[70] On December 2, 1851, Louis Napoleon Bonaparte, President of the

when we walked later on the beach and picked up pebbles. The old time-ocean throws upon its shores just such rounded and polished results of the eternal turmoil, but we only see the beauty of those we have got the headache in stooping for ourselves, and wonder at the dull brown bits of common stone with which our comrades have stuffed their pockets. . . .[71]

Monday, 15th.—The morning was fine, and we were called at four o'clock. At the moment my door was knocked at, I was mounting a giraffe with that charming *nil admirari*[72] which characterizes dreams, to visit Prester John.[73] *Rat-tat-tat-tat!* upon my door and upon the horn gate of dreams also. I re-marked to my skowhegan (the Tâtar for giraffe-driver) that I was quite sure the animal had the *raps,* a common disease among them, for I heard a queer knocking noise inside him. It is the sound of his joints, O Tambourgi! (an Oriental term of reverence,) and proves him to be of the race of El Keirat. *Rat-tat-tat-too!* and I lost my dinner at the Prester's, embarking for a voyage to the Northwest Carry instead. Never use the word *canoe,* my dear Storg, if you wish to retain your self-respect. *Birch* is the term among us backwoodsmen. I never knew it till yesterday; but, like a true philosopher, I made it appear as if I had been intimate with it from childhood. The rapidity with which the human mind levels itself to the standard around it gives us the most pertinent warning as to the company we keep. It is as hard for most characters to stay at their own aver-age point in all companies, as for a thermometer to stay 65° for twenty-four hours together. I like this in our friend Johannes Taurus,[74] that he carries everywhere and maintains his insular temperature, and will have everything accommodate itself to

French Republic, by a violent *coup d'état* overthrew the existing government and set himself up as dictator of France. Exactly one year later he was proclaimed emperor of the French with the title of Napoleon III.

[71] There is omitted at this point a rhymed fable in the John Gay manner entitled *Doctor Lobster.*

[72] Nothing-to-be-wondered-at.

[73] A mythical Christian king of great power and wealth, whose realm was vaguely located in the interior of Asia and long sought by European travelers.

[74] John Bull: i.e., the Englishman.

that. Shall I confess that this morning I would rather have broken the moral law, than have endangered the equipoise of the birch by my awkwardness? that I should have been prouder of a compliment to my paddling, than to have had both my guides suppose me the author of Hamlet? Well, Cardinal Richelieu [75] used to jump over chairs.

We were to paddle about twenty miles; but we made it rather more by crossing and recrossing the lake. Twice we landed,— once at a camp, where we found the cook alone, baking bread and gingerbread. Monsieur Soyer [76] would have been startled a little by this shaggy professor,—this Pre-Raphaelite [77] of cookery. He represented the *salæratus* [78] period of the art, and his bread was of a brilliant yellow, like those cakes tinged with saffron, which hold out so long against time and the flies in little water-side shops of seaport towns,—dingy extremities of trade fit to moulder on Lethe [79] wharf. His water was better, squeezed out of ice-cold granite in the neighboring mountains, and sent through subterranean ducts to sparkle up by the door of the camp.

"There's nothin' so sweet an' hulsome as your *real* spring water," said Uncle Zeb, "git it pure. But it's dreffle hard to git it that ain't got sunthin' the matter of it. Snow-water'll burn a man's inside out,—I larned that to the 'Roostick war,—and the snow lays terrible long on some o'thes'ere hills. Me an' Eb Stiles was up old Ktahdn onct jest about this time o' year, an' we come

[75] Armand Jean du Plessis de Richelieu (1585–1642), French prime minister under Louis XIII, in his youth strengthened a weak physique by unconventional exercises.

[76] Alexis Benoît Soyer (1809–58), a French cook who came to England after the revolution of 1830, served as chef at the Reform Club, 1837–47, and then in the latter year was put in charge of the English governmental relief kitchens in Ireland, where he achieved a great success. He went with Florence Nightingale to the Crimea in 1855 and reformed the British military diet and hospital rations. He published a number of works on cookery and dietetics.

[77] I.e., one who practices a primitive style.—The Pre-Raphaelite school in nineteenth-century English art copied the primitive Italian painters, the predecessors of Raphael.

[78] Baking soda.

[79] According to Greek and Roman myth, a river of the Underworld, the water of which, if swallowed, caused forgetfulness of the past.

acrost a kind o' holler like, as full o' snow as your stockin's full
o' your foot. *I* see it fust, an' took an' rammed a settin'-pole—
wahl, it was all o' twenty foot into 't, an' couldn't fin' no bottom.
I dunno as there's snow-water enough in this to do no hurt. I
don't somehow seem to think that *real* spring-water's so plenty
as it used to be." And Uncle Zeb, with perhaps a little over-
refinement of scrupulosity, applied his lips to the Ethiop [80] ones
of a bottle of raw gin, with a kiss that drew out its very soul,—
a *basia* that Secundus [81] might have sung. He must have been
a wonderful judge of water, for he analyzed this, and detected
its latent snow simply by his eye, and without the clumsy process
of tasting. I could not help thinking that he had made the
desert his dwelling-place chiefly in order to enjoy the ministra-
tions of this one fair spirit unmolested.

We pushed on. Little islands loomed trembling between sky
and water, like hanging gardens. Gradually the filmy trees defined themselves, the aerial enchantment lost its potency, and we
came up with common prose islands that had so late been magical and poetic. The old story of the attained and unattained.
About noon we reached the head of the lake, and took possession
of a deserted *wongen*,[82] in which to cook and eat our dinner.
No Jew, I am sure, can have a more thorough dislike of salt pork
than I have in a normal state, yet I had already eaten it raw with
hard bread for lunch, and relished it keenly. We soon had our
tea-kettle over the fire, and before long the cover was chattering
with the escaping steam, which had thus vainly begged of all
men to be saddled and bridled, till James Watt [83] one day happened to overhear it. One of our guides shot three Canada
grouse, and these were turned slowly between the fire and a bit
of salt pork, which dropped fatness upon them as it fried. Al-

---

[80] I.e., black.—The Ethiopians in northeast Africa are negroes.

[81] *Basia* (= kisses) is the title of a volume of Latin love poems by a noted
Dutch poet of the Renaissance, Johannes Secundus or Jan Nicolai Everaerts
(1511–36).

[82] An accountant's shack in a lumber camp. "Wongen" is a variant of
the Algonquin "wanigan" or "wangan."

[83] Watt (1736–1819), a Scottish mechanical engineer, actually had the
idea of the modern condensing steam-engine flash across his mind while
on a Sunday afternoon walk at Glasgow Green in 1765.

though *my* fingers were certainly not made before knives and forks, yet they served as a convenient substitute for those more ancient inventions.   We sat round, Turk-fashion, and ate thankfully, while a party of aborigines of the Mosquito tribe, who had camped in the *wongen* before we arrived, dined upon us. I do not know what the British Protectorate of the Mosquitoes amounts to; but, as I squatted there at the mercy of these bloodthirsty savages, I no longer wondered that the classic Everett [84] had been stung into a willingness for war on the question.

"This 'ere'd be about a complete place for a camp, ef there was on'y a spring o' sweet water handy. Frizzled pork goes wal, don't it?   Yes, an' sets wal, too," said Uncle Zeb, and he again tilted his bottle, which rose nearer and nearer to an angle of forty-five at every gurgle.   He then broached a curious dietetic theory: "The reason we take salt pork along is cos it packs handy: you git the greatest amount o' board in the smallest compass,—let alone that it's more nourishin' than an'thin' else.   It kind o' don't disgest so quick, but stays by ye, anourishin' ye all the while.

"A feller can live wal on frizzled pork an' good spring-water, git it *good*. To the 'Roostick war we didn't ask for nothin' better,—on'y beans." (*Tilt, tilt, gurgle, gurgle.*) Then, with an apparent feeling of inconsistency, "But then, come to git used to a particular *kind* o' spring-water, an' it makes a feller hard to suit. Most all sorts o' water taste kind o' *in*sipid away from home. Now, I've gut a spring to my place that's as sweet— wahl, it's as sweet as maple sap. A feller acts about water jest as he doos about a pair o' boots. It's all on it in gittin' wonted. Now, *them* boots," &c., &c. (*Gurgle, gurgle, gurgle, smack!*)

All this while he was packing away the remains of the pork and hard bread in two large firkins. This accomplished, we re-embarked, our Uncle on his way to the birch essaying a kind of song in four or five parts, of which the words were hilarious and

---

[84] Edward Everett (1794–1865), while American Minister to Great Britain, 1841–45, carried on negotiations for the suppression of the slave trade on the West African coast. Incensed finally by British hypocrisy and procrastination, he urged extreme diplomatic measures.

the tune profoundly melancholy, and which was finished, and the rest of his voice apparently jerked out of him in one sharp falsetto note, by his tripping over the root of a tree. We paddled a short distance up a brook which came into the lake smoothly through a little meadow not far off. We soon reached the Northwest Carry, and our guide, pointing through the woods, said: "That's the Cannydy road. You can travel that clearn to Kebeck,[85] a hunderd an' twenty mile,"—a privilege of which I respectfully declined to avail myself. The offer, however, remains open to the public. The Carry is called two miles; but this is the estimate of somebody who had nothing to lug. I had a headache and all my baggage, which, with a traveller's instinct, I had brought with me. (P.S.—I did not even take the keys out of my pocket, and both my bags were wet through before I came back.) *My* estimate of the distance is eighteen thousand six hundred and seventy-four miles and three quarters, —the fraction being the part left to be travelled after one of my companions most kindly insisted on relieving me of my heaviest bag. I know very well that the ancient Roman soldiers used to carry sixty pounds' weight, and all that; but I am not, and never shall be, an ancient Roman soldier,—no, not even in the miraculous Thundering Legion.[86] Uncle Zeb slung the two provender firkins across his shoulder, and trudged along, grumbling that "he never see sech a contrairy pair as them." He had begun upon a second bottle of his "particular kind o' spring-water," and, at every rest, the gurgle of this peripatetic[87] fountain might be heard, followed by a smack, a fragment of mosaic song, or a confused clatter with the cowhide boots, being an arbitrary symbol, intended to represent the festive dance. Christian's[88] pack gave him not half so much trouble as the firkins gave Uncle Zeb. It grew harder and harder to sling them, and

---

[85] Quebec.
[86] A Roman legion, said to have been composed of Christians. When in 174 A.D. they were fighting the Quadi, a Germanic tribe, their prayers were believed to have brought on a thunderstorm that threw their enemies into confusion.
[87] Walking.
[88] The hero of John Bunyan's *Pilgrim's Progress* (1687).

with every fresh gulp of the Batavian elixir,[89] they got heavier.
Or rather, the truth was, that his hat grew heavier, in which he
was carrying on an extensive manufacture of bricks without
straw. At last affairs reached a crisis, and a particularly favorable pitch offering, with a puddle at the foot of it, even *the*
boots afforded no sufficient ballast, and away went our Uncle, the satel-
lite firkins accompanying faithfully his headlong flight. Did
ever exiled monarch or disgraced minister find the cause of his
fall in himself? Is there not always a strawberry at the bottom
of our cup of life, on which we can lay all the blame of our
deviations from the straight path? Till now Uncle Zeb had
contrived to give a gloss of volition to smaller stumblings and
gyrations, by exaggerating them into an appearance of playful
burlesque. But the present case was beyond any such subter-
fuges. He held a bed of justice where he sat, and then arose
slowly, with a stern determination of vengeance stiffening every
muscle of his face. But what would he select as the culprit?
"It's that cussed firkin," he mumbled to himself. "I never
knowed a firkin cair on so,—no, not in the 'Roostehicick war.
There, go long, will ye? and don't come back till you've larned
how to walk with a genelman!" And, seizing the unhappy
scapegoat by the bail, he hurled it into the forest. It is a curious
circumstance, that it was not the firkin containing the bottle
which was thus condemned to exile.

The end of the Carry was reached at last, and, as we drew
near it, we heard a sound of shouting and laughter. It came
from a party of men making hay of the wild grass in Seboomok
meadows, which lie around Seboomok pond, into which the
Carry empties itself. Their camp was near, and our two hunters set out for it, leaving us seated in the birch on the plashy
border of the pond. The repose was perfect. Another heaven
hallowed and deepened the polished lake, and through that
nether world the fish-hawk's double floated with balanced wings,
or, wheeling suddenly, flashed his whitened breast against the
sun. As the clattering king-fisher flew unsteadily across, and
seemed to push his heavy head along with ever-renewing effort,

---

[89] I.e., gin: so called because it was, and still is, extensively manufactured
in Holland, which the ancient Romans named Batavia.

a visionary mate flitted from downward tree to tree below.
Some tall alders shaded us from the sun, in whose yellow afternoon light the drowsy forest was steeped, giving out that wholesome resinous perfume, almost the only warm odor which it is
refreshing to breathe. The tame hay-cocks in the midst of the
wildness gave one a pleasant reminiscence of home, like hearing
one's native tongue in a strange country.

Presently our hunters came back, bringing with them a tall,
thin, active-looking man, with black eyes, that glanced unconsciously on all sides, like one of those spots of sunlight which a
child dances up and down the street with a bit of looking-glass.
This was M., the captain of the hay-makers, a famous river-
driver, and who was to have fifty men under him next winter.
I could now understand that sleepless vigilance of eye. He had
consented to take two of our party in his birch to seek for moose.
A quick, nervous, decided man, he got them into the birch, and
was off instantly, without a superfluous word. He evidently
looked upon them as he would upon a couple of logs which he
was to deliver at a certain place. Indeed, I doubt if life and the
world presented themselves to Napier [90] himself in a more loga-
rithmic way. His only thought was to do the immediate duty
well, and to pilot his particular raft down the crooked stream of
life to the ocean beyond. The birch seemed to feel him as an
inspiring soul, and slid away straight and swift for the outlet
of the pond. As he disappeared under the overarching alders
of the brook, our two hunters could not repress a grave and
measured applause. There is never any extravagance among
these woodmen; their eye, accustomed to reckoning the number
of feet which a tree will *scale,* is rapid and close in its guess of
the amount of stuff in a man. It was *laudari a laudato,*[91] however, for they themselves were accounted good men in a birch.
I was amused, in talking with them about him, to meet with an
instance of that tendency of the human mind to assign some
utterly improbable reason for gifts which seem unaccountable.
After due praise, one of them said, "I guess he's got some Injun
in him," although I knew very well that the speaker had a thor-

---

[90] John Napier (1550–1617), the Scottish inventor of logarithms.
[91] To be applauded by one who has been applauded.

ough contempt for the red-man, mentally and physically. Here was mythology in a small way,—the same that under more favorable auspices hatched Helen out of an egg [92] and gave Merlin an Incubus for his father.[93] I was pleased with all I saw of M. He was in his narrow sphere a true ἄναξ ἀνδρῶν,[94] and the ragged edges of his old hat seemed to become coronated as I looked at him. He impressed me as a man really educated,—that is, with his aptitudes *drawn out* and ready for use. He was A.M. and LL.D. in Woods College,—Axe-master and Doctor of Logs. Are not *our* educations commonly like a pile of books laid over a plant in a pot? The compressed nature struggles through at every crevice, but can never get the cramp and stunt out of it. We spend all our youth in building a vessel for our voyage of life, and set forth with streamers flying; but the moment we come nigh the great loadstone mountain of our proper destiny, out leap all our carefully-driven bolts and nails, and we get many a mouthful of good salt brine, and many a buffet of the rough water of experience, before we secure the bare right to live.

We now entered the outlet, a long-drawn aisle of alder, on each side of which spired tall firs, spruces, and white cedars. The motion of the birch reminded me of the gondola, and they represent among water-craft the *felidæ,* the cat tribe, stealthy, silent, treacherous, and preying by night. I closed my eyes, and strove to fancy myself in the dumb city,[95] whose only horses are the bronze ones of St. Mark [96] and that of Colleoni.[97] But

---

[92] Zeus, according to Greek myth, at one time fell in love with Leda, wife of King Tyndareus of Sparta, and visited her in the guise of a swan. She subsequently brought forth two eggs, from one of which the beautiful Helen was born.

[93] Merlin, the Welsh bard and enchanter in Arthurian romance, was said to be the offspring of a woman and an incubus or devil.

[94] A prince among men—Homer's common epithet for Agamemnon in the *Iliad*.

[95] Venice.

[96] The four gilded statues of horses stand over the main gateway to St. Mark's Cathedral. They originally decorated Nero's triumphal arch at Rome, then were taken by Constantine to Byzantium, and finally were brought to Venice in 1204, where they have remained except for a stay in Paris (1797–1815) under Napoleon.

[97] The most famous equestrian statue in the world is that of Bartolommeo

Nature would allow no rival, and bent down an alder-bough to brush my cheek and recall me. Only the robin sings in the emerald chambers of these tall sylvan palaces, and the squirrel leaps from hanging balcony to balcony.

The rain which the loons foreboded had raised the west branch of the Penobscot so much, that a strong current was setting back into the pond; and, when at last we brushed through into the river, it was full to the brim,—too full for moose, the hunters said. Rivers with low banks have always the compensation of giving a sense of entire fulness. The sun sank behind its horizon of pines, whose pointed summits notched the rosy west in an endless black *sierra*.[98] At the same moment the golden moon swung slowly up in the east, like the other scale of that Homeric balance in which Zeus weighed the deeds of men. Sunset and moonrise at once! Adam had no more in Eden—except the head of Eve upon his shoulder. The stream was so smooth, that the floating logs we met seemed to hang in a glowing atmosphere, the shadow-half being as real as the solid. And gradually the mind was etherized to a like dreamy placidity, till fact and fancy, the substance and the image, floating on the current of reverie, became but as the upper and under halves of one unreal reality.

In the west still lingered a pale-green light. I do not know whether it be from lifelong familiarity, but it always seems to me that the pinnacles of pine-trees make an edge to the landscape which tells better against the twilight, or the fainter dawn before the rising moon, than the rounded and cloud-cumulus outline of hard-wood trees.

After paddling a couple of miles, we found the arbored mouth of the little Malahoodus River, famous for moose. We had been on the lookout for it, and I was amused to hear one of the hunters say to the other, to assure himself of his familiarity with the spot, "You *drove* the West Branch last spring, didn't you?" as

---

Colleoni (1400–1475), the most respectable of the *condottieri,* who left money at his death for this statue. It was designed by Andrea del Verrocchio in 1488, and was unveiled in 1496 on the Piazzo SS. Giovanni e Paolo.

[98] Range of mountains.

one of us might ask about a horse. We did not explore the
Malahoodus far, but left the other birch to thread its cedared
solitudes, while we turned back to try our fortunes in the larger
stream. We paddled on about four miles farther, lingering
now and then opposite the black mouth of a moose-path. The
incidents of our voyage were few, but quite as exciting and
profitable as the *items* of the newspapers. A stray log com-
pensated very well for the ordinary run of accidents, and the
floating *carkiss* of a moose which we met could pass muster
instead of a singular discovery of human remains by workmen
in digging a cellar. Once or twice we saw what seemed ghosts
of trees; but they turned out to be dead cedars, in winding-sheets
of long gray moss, made spectral by the moonlight. Just as we
were turning to drift back down-stream, we heard a loud gnawing sound close by us on the bank. One of our guides thought
it a hedgehog, the other a bear. I inclined to the bear, as making the adventure more imposing. A rifle was fired at the
sound, which began again with the most provoking indifference,
ere the echo, flaring madly at first from shore to shore, died far
away in a hoarse sigh.

Half past Eleven, P.M.—No sign of a moose yet. The birch,
it seems, was strained at the Carry, or the pitch was softened as
she lay on the shore during dinner, and she leaks a little. If
there be any virtue in the *sitzbad*,[99] I shall discover it. If I cannot extract green cucumbers from the moon's rays, I get something quite as cool. One of the guides shivers so as to shake the
birch.

Quarter to Twelve.—*Later from the Freshet!*—The water in
the birch is about three inches deep, but the dampness reaches
already nearly to the waist. I am obliged to remove the matches
from the ground floor of my trousers into the upper story of a
breast-pocket. Meanwhile, we are to sit immovable,—for fear
of frightening the moose,—which induces cramps.

Half past Twelve.—A crashing is heard on the left bank.

---

[99] A bath in which the bather sits, immersing only the part of the body
around the hips.

This is a moose in good earnest. We are besought to hold our
breaths, if possible. My fingers so numb, I could not, if I tried.
Crash! crash! again, and then a plunge, followed by dead still-
ness. "Swimmin' crik," whispers guide, suppressing all un-
necessary parts of speech,—"don't stir." I, for one, am not likely
to. A cold fog which has been gathering for the last hour has
finished me. I fancy myself one of those naked pigs that seem
rushing out of market-doors in winter, frozen in a ghastly attitude of gallop. If I were to be shot myself, I should feel no
interest in it. As it is, I am only a spectator, having declined a
gun. *Splash!* again; this time the moose is in sight, and *click!
click!* one rifle misses fire after the other. The fog has quietly
spiked our batteries. The moose goes crashing up the bank,
and presently we can hear it chawing its cud close by. So we lie
in wait, freezing.

At one o'clock, I propose to land at a deserted *wongen* I had
noticed on the way up, where I will make a fire, and leave them
to refrigerate as much longer as they please. Axe in hand, I go
plunging through waist-deep weeds dripping with dew, haunted
by an intense conviction that the gnawing sound we had heard
was a bear, and a bear at least eighteen hands high. There is
something pokerish about a deserted dwelling, even in broad
daylight; but here in the obscure wood, and the moon filtering
unwillingly through the trees! Well, I made the door at last,
and found the place packed fuller with darkness than it ever had
been with hay. Gradually I was able to make things out a little,
and began to hack frozenly at a log which I groped out. I was
relieved presently by one of the guides. He cut at once into
one of the uprights of the building till he got some dry splinters,
and we soon had a fire like the burning of a whole wood-wharf
in our part of the country. My companion went back to the
birch, and left me to keep house. First I knocked a hole in the
roof (which the fire began to lick in a relishing way) for a chimney, and then cleared away a damp growth of "pison-elder," to
make a sleeping place. When the unsuccessful hunters returned, I had everything quite comfortable, and was steaming

at the rate of about ten horse-power a minute. Young Telemachus [100] was sorry to give up the moose so soon, and, with the
teeth chattering almost out of his head, he declared that he
would like to stick it out all night. However, he reconciled
himself to the fire, and, making our beds of some "splits" which
we poked from the roof, we lay down at half past two. I, who
have inherited a habit of looking into every closet before I go to
bed, for fear of fire, had become in two days such a stoic of the
woods, that I went to sleep tranquilly, certain that my bedroom
would be in a blaze before morning. And so, indeed, it was;
and the withes that bound it together being burned off, one of
the sides fell in without waking me.

Tuesday, 16th.—After a sleep of two hours and a half, so
sound that it was as good as eight, we started at half past four
for the haymakers' camp again. We found them just getting
breakfast. We sat down upon the *deacon-seat* before the fire
blazing between the bedroom and the *salle à manger*,[101] which
were simply two roofs of spruce-bark, sloping to the ground on
one side, the other three being left open. We found that we
had, at least, been luckier than the other party, for M. had
brought back his convoy without even seeing a moose. As
there was not room at the table for all of us to breakfast together,
these hospitable woodmen forced us to sit down first, although
we resisted stoutly. Our breakfast consisted of fresh bread,
fried salt pork, stewed whortleberries, and tea. Our kind hosts
refused to take money for it, nor would M. accept anything for
his trouble. This seemed even more open-handed when I remembered that they had brought all their stores over the Carry
upon their shoulders, paying an ache *extra* for every pound. If
their hospitality lacked anything of hard external polish, it had
all the deeper grace which springs only from sincere manliness.
I have rarely sat at a *table d'hôte* [102] which might not have taken

---

[100] This was my nephew, Charles Russell Lowell, who fell at the head
of his brigade in the battle of Cedar Creek. [Lowell's note.]
[101] Dining room.
[102] Hotel table.

a lesson from them in essential courtesy. I have never seen a finer race of men. They have all the virtues of the sailor, without that unsteady roll in the gait with which the ocean proclaims itself quite as much in the moral as in the physical habit of a man. They appeared to me to have hewn out a short northwest passage through wintry woods to those spicelands of character which we dwellers in cities must reach, if at all, by weary voyages in the monotonous track of the trades.

By the way, as we were embirching last evening for our moose-chase, I asked what I was to do with my baggage. "Leave it here," said our guide, and he laid the bags upon a platform of alders, which he bent down to keep them beyond reach of the rising water.

"Will they be safe here?"

"As safe as they would be locked up in your house at home."

And so I found them at my return; only the hay-makers had carried them to their camp for greater security against the chances of the weather.

We got back to Kineo in time for dinner; and in the afternoon, the weather being fine, went up the mountain. As we landed at the foot, our guide pointed to the remains of a red shirt and a pair of blanket trousers. "That," said he, "is the reason there's such a trade in ready-made clo'es. A suit gits pooty well wore out by the time a camp breaks up in the spring, and the lumberers want to look about right when they come back into the settlements, so they buy somethin' ready-made, and heave old bust-up into the bush." True enough, thought I, this is the Ready-made Age. It is quicker being covered than fitted. So we all go to the slop-shop [103] and come out uniformed, every mother's son with habits of thinking and doing cut on one pattern, with no special reference to his peculiar build.

Kineo rises 1750 feet above the sea, and 750 above the lake. The climb is very easy, with fine outlooks at every turn over lake and forest. Near the top is a spring of water, which even Uncle Zeb might have allowed to be wholesome. The little tin dipper

---

[103] A shop where slops, i.e., cheap ready-made clothes, are sold.

was scratched all over with names, showing that vanity, at least, is not put out of breath by the ascent. O Ozymandias,[104] King of kings! We are all scrawling on something of the kind. "My name is engraved on the institutions of my country," thinks the statesman. But alas! institutions are as changeable as tin-dippers; men are content to drink the same old water, if the shape of the cup only be new, and our friend gets two lines in the Biographical Dictionaries. After all, these inscriptions, which make us smile up here, are about as valuable as the Assyrian ones which Hincks and Rawlinson read at cross-purposes.[105] Have we not Smiths and Browns enough, that we must ransack the ruins of Nimroud[106] for more? Near the spring we met a Bloomer![107] It was the first chronic one I had ever seen. It struck me as a sensible costume for the occasion, and it will be the only wear in the Greek Kalends,[108] when women believe that sense is an equivalent for grace.

The forest primeval is best seen from the top of a mountain. It then impresses one by its extent, like an Oriental epic. To be in it is nothing, for then an acre is as good as a thousand square miles. You cannot see five rods in any direction, and the ferns, mosses, and tree trunks just around you are the best of it. As for solitude, night will make a better one with ten feet square of pitch dark; and mere size is hardly an element of grandeur,

---

[104] The vain monarch celebrated in Shelley's famous sonnet of the same name.

[105] Edward Hincks (1792–1866), Irish Protestant cleric, and Sir Henry Creswicke Rawlinson (1810–95), English military officer, were two leading Assyriologists of the nineteenth century. They worked independently on the deciphering of the cuneiform text of the famous Darius inscription at Behistun in Babylonia and produced somewhat varying readings, Hincks first publishing his in 1846–47 and Rawlinson his in 1851.

[106] An ancient Assyrian city about twenty miles south of Nineveh. Its ruins were excavated in 1848 and again in 1851.

[107] I.e., a woman wearing a "bloomer" costume of long, loose-fitting trousers tied at the ankles. The costume was named after Mrs. Amelia Jenks Bloomer (1818–94), American reformer and feminist, who introduced it to the United States about 1849.

[108] I.e., in the time which will never come.—The Greeks had no kalends; the kalend is the first day of the Roman month. The Roman emperor Augustus (63 B.C.–14 A.D.) is said to have coined the phrase. See Suetonius, *Life of Augustus,* chap. 87.

except in works of man,—as the Colosseum. It is through one or the other pole of vanity that men feel the sublime in mountains. It is either, How small great I am beside it! or, Big as you are, little I's soul will hold a dozen of you. The true idea of a forest is not a *selva selvaggia*,[109] but something humanized a little, as we imagine the forest of Arden,[110] with trees standing at royal intervals,—a commonwealth, and not a communism. To some moods it is congenial to look over endless leagues of unbroken savagery without a hint of man.

Wednesday.—This morning fished. Telemachus caught a *laker* of thirteen pounds and a half, and I an overgrown cusk, which we threw away, but which I found afterwards Agassiz [111] would have been glad of, for all is fish that comes to his net, from the fossil down. The fish, when caught, are straightway knocked on the head. A lad who went with us seeming to show an over-zeal in this operation, we remonstrated. But he gave a good, human reason for it,—"He no need to ha' gone and been a fish if he didn't like it,"—an excuse which superior strength or cunning has always found sufficient. It was some comfort, in this case, to think that St. Jerome believed in a limitation of God's providence, and that it did not extend to inanimate things or creatures devoid of reason.

Thus, my dear Storg, I have finished my Oriental adventures, and somewhat, it must be owned, in the diffuse Oriental manner. There is very little about Moosehead Lake in it, and not even the Latin name for moose, which I might have obtained by sufficient research. If I had killed one, I would have given you his name in that dead language. I did not profess to give you an account of the lake; but a journal, and, moreover, *my* journal, with a little nature, a little human nature, and a great deal of I in it, which last ingredient I take to be the true spirit of this species of writing; all the rest being so much water for tender throats which cannot take it neat.

---

[109] Wild woods.

[110] The fanciful setting of Shakespeare's *As You Like It*.

[111] Louis John Rudolph Agassiz (1807–73), eminent Swiss scientist, who became professor of zoölogy and geology at Harvard College in 1847.

AT SEA [1]

THE SEA was meant to be looked at from shore, as mountains
are from the plain. Lucretius made this discovery long ago,[2]
and was blunt enough to blurt it forth, romance and sentiment—
in other words, the pretence of feeling what we do not feel—
being inventions of a later day. To be sure, Cicero used to twaddle about Greek literature and philosophy, much as people do
about ancient art nowadays; but I rather sympathize with those
stout old Romans who despised both, and believed that to found
an empire was as grand an achievement as to build an epic or to
carve a statue. But though there might have been twaddle, (as
why not, since there was a Senate?) I rather think Petrarch [3]
was the first choragus of that sentimental dance which so long
led young folks away from the realities of life like the piper of
Hamelin, and whose succession ended, let us hope, with Chateaubriand.[4] But for them, Byron, whose real strength lay in
his sincerity, would never have talked about the "sea bounding
beneath him like a steed that knows his rider," [5] and all that
sort of thing. Even if it had been true, steam has been as fatal

---

[1] Written in reminiscence of his first Atlantic crossing, from Boston to
Naples via Malta, in July–August, 1851, and of the return voyage from
Liverpool to Boston in October, 1852. Published in *Graham's Magazine,*
April, 1854, as the first of three monthly installments entitled *Leaves from
My Journal in Italy.* Reprinted as one of the collected essays in *Fireside
Travels* (1864).

[2] Titus Lucretius Carus (96?–55 B.C.), renowned Roman philosophical
poet, opened Book II of his great work, *De Rerum Natura,* thus: "Pleasant
it is, when over a great sea the winds trouble the waters, to gaze from
shore upon another's great tribulation." (Trans. W. H. D. Rouse.)

[3] Francesco Petrarch (1302–74), an Italian poet particularly famous for
his sonnets in praise of Laura, a married woman whom he first saw in a
church at Avignon, France. See *Rousseau and the Sentimentalists,* p. 128,
for a more extended comment on Petrarch.

[4] Vicomte François René de Chateaubriand (1768–1848), French statesman, philosopher, and novelist. See *Thoreau,* p. 106, for further comment on Chateaubriand's sentimentalism.

[5]   And the waves bound beneath me as a steed
                    That knows his rider. . . .
                         George Gordon, Lord Byron (1788–1824), *Childe
                         Harold's Pilgrimage,* Canto III, stanza 2.

to that part of the romance of the sea as to hand-loom weaving. But what say you to a twelve days' calm such as we dozed through in mid-Atlantic and in mid-August? I know nothing so tedious at once and exasperating as that regular slap of the wilted sails when the ship rises and falls with the slow breathing of the sleeping sea, one greasy, brassy swell following another, slow, smooth, immitigable as the series of Wordsworth's Ecclesiastical Sonnets. Even at his best, Neptune, in a *tête-à-tête*, has a way of repeating himself, an obtuseness to the *ne quid nimis*,[6] that is stupefying. It reminds me of organ-music and my good friend Sebastian Bach.[7] A fugue or two will do very well; but a concert made up of nothing else is altogether too epic for me. There is nothing so desperately monotonous as the sea, and I no longer wonder at the cruelty of pirates. Fancy an existence in which the coming up of a clumsy finback whale, who says *Pooh!* to you solemnly as you lean over the taffrail, is an event as exciting as an election on shore! The dampness seems to strike into the wits as into the lucifer-matches, so that one may scratch a thought half a dozen times and get nothing at last but a faint sputter, the forlorn hope of fire, which only goes far enough to leave a sense of suffocation behind it. Even smoking becomes an employment instead of a solace. Who less likely to come to their wit's end than W.M.T. and A.H.C.?[8] Yet I have seen them driven to five meals a day for mental occupation. I sometimes sit and pity Noah; but even he had this advantage over all succeeding navigators, that, wherever he landed, he was sure to get no ill news from home. He should be canonized as the patron-saint of newspaper correspondents, being the only man who ever had the very last authentic intelligence from everywhere.

The finback whale recorded just above has much the look of a brown-paper parcel,—the whitish stripes that run across him

[6] Avoidance of excess (lit., nothing too much).

[7] John Sebastian Bach (1685–1750), the great German composer of organ fugues.

[8] William Makepeace Thackeray (1811–63) and Arthur Hugh Clough (1819–61), noted English writers who were fellow passengers on Lowell's return voyage.

answering for the packthread.   He has a kind of accidental hole
in the top of his head, through which he *pooh-poohs* the rest of
creation, and which looks as if it had been made by the chance
thrust of a chestnut rail.   He was our first event.   Our second
was harpooning a sunfish, which basked dozing on the lap of the
sea, looking so much like the giant turtle of an alderman's
dream, that I am persuaded he would have let himself be made
into mock-turtle soup rather than acknowledge his imposture.
But he broke away just as they were hauling him over the side,
and sank placidly through the clear water, leaving behind him
a crimson trail that wavered a moment and was gone.

The sea, though, has better sights than these.   When we were
up with the Azores, we began to meet flying-fish and Portuguese
men-of-war beautiful as the galley of Cleopatra, tiny craft that
dared these seas before Columbus.   I have seen one of the former rise from the crest of a wave, and, glancing from another
some two hundred feet beyond, take a fresh flight of perhaps as
far.   How Calderon [9] would have similized this pretty creature
had he ever seen it!   How he would have run him up and down
the gamut of simile!   If a fish, then a fish with wings; if a bird,
then a bird with fins; and so on, keeping up the light shuttle-
cock of a conceit as is his wont.   Indeed, the poor thing is the
most killing bait for a comparison, and I assure you I have three
or four in my inkstand;—but be calm, they shall stay there.
Moore,[10] who looked on all nature as a kind of *Gradus ad Par-
nassum*,[11] a *thesaurus* of similitude, and spent his life in a game
of What is my thought like? with himself, *did* the flying-fish on
his way to Bermuda.   So I leave him in peace.

The most beautiful thing I have seen at sea, all the more so
that I had never heard of it, is the trail of a shoal of fish through
the phosphorescent water.   It is like a flight of silver rockets, or

---

[9] Pedro Calderon de la Barca (1600–81), a leading Spanish poet and
dramatist.

[10] Thomas Moore (1779–1852), a well-known Irish poet, who made a
trip to Bermuda, the West Indies, and the United States in 1803–4.   He
published in his *Epistles, Odes and Other Poems* (1806) a poem entitled
"To the Flying Fish."

[11] Dictionary of prosody (lit., a step toward Parnassus).

the streaming of northern lights through that silent nether heaven. I thought nothing could go beyond that rustling star-foam which was churned up by our ship's bows, or those eddies and disks of dreamy flame that rose and wandered out of sight behind us.

> 'Twas fire our ship was plunging through,
> Cold fire that o'er the quarter flew;
> And wandering moons of idle flame
> Grew full and waned, and went and came,
> Dappling with light the huge sea-snake
> That slid behind us in the wake.

But there was something even more delicately rare in the apparition of the fish, as they turned up in gleaming furrows the latent moonshine which the ocean seemed to have hoarded against these vacant interlunar nights. In the Mediterranean one day, as we were lying becalmed, I observed the water freckled with dingy specks, which at last gathered to a pinkish scum on the surface. The sea had been so phosphorescent for some nights, that when the Captain gave me my bath, by dousing me with buckets from the house on deck, the spray flew off my head and shoulders in sparks. It occurred to me that this dirty-looking scum might be the luminous matter, and I had a pailful dipped up to keep till after dark. When I went to look at it after night-fall, it seemed at first perfectly dead; but when I shook it, the whole broke out into what I can only liken to milky flames, whose lambent silence was strangely beautiful, and startled me almost as actual projection might an alchemist. I could not bear to be the death of so much beauty; so I poured it all overboard again.

Another sight worth taking a voyage for is that of the sails by moonlight. Our course was "south and by east, half south," so that we seemed bound for the full moon as she rolled up over our wavering horizon. Then I used to go forward to the bow-sprit and look back. Our ship was a clipper, with every rag set, stunsails, skyscrapers, and all; nor was it easy to believe that such a wonder could be built of canvas as that white many-

storied pile of cloud that stooped over me or drew back as we
rose and fell with the waves.

These are all the wonders I can recall of my five weeks at sea,
except the sun. Were you ever alone with the sun? You think
it a very simple question; but I never was, in the full sense of the
word, till I was held up to him one cloudless day on the broad
buckler of the ocean. I suppose one might have the same feeling in the desert. I remember getting something like it years
ago, when I climbed alone to the top of a mountain, and lay face
up on the hot gray moss, striving to get a notion of how an Arab
might feel. It was my American commentary of the Koran,[12]
and not a bad one. In a New England winter, too, when everything is gagged with snow, as if some gigantic physical geographer were taking a cast of the earth's face in plaster, the bare
knob of a hill will introduce you to the sun as a comparative
stranger. But at sea you may be alone with him day after day,
and almost all day long. I never understood before that nothing short of full daylight can give the supremest sense of solitude. Darkness will not do so, for the imagination peoples it
with more shapes than ever were poured from the frozen loins
of the populous North. The sun, I sometimes think, is a little
grouty[13] at sea, especially at high noon, feeling that he wastes
his beams on those fruitless furrows. It is otherwise with the
moon. She "comforts the night," as Chapman[14] finely says,
and I always found her a companionable creature.

In the ocean-horizon I took untiring delight. It is the true
magic-circle of expectation and conjecture,—almost as good as
a wishing-ring. What will rise over that edge we sail towards
daily and never overtake? A sail? an island? the new shore of
the Old World? Something rose every day, which I need not
have gone so far to see, but at whose levee I was a much more
faithful courtier than on shore. A cloudless sunrise in mid-
ocean is beyond comparison for simple grandeur. It is like

[12] The Arab's "bible," the writings of the prophet Mohammed.
[13] Sullen.
[14] George Chapman (1559–1634), an important poet and dramatist of
Elizabethan England, wrote, "the moon hath comforted the night," in *The
Conspiracy of Charles Duke of Byron* (1608), III, i, 5.

Dante's style, bare and perfect. Naked sun meets naked sea, the true classic of nature. There may be more sentiment in morning on shore,—the shivering fairy-jewelry of dew, the silver point-lace of sparkling hoar-frost,—but there is also more complexity, more of the romantic. The one savors of the elder Edda,[15] the other of the Minnesingers.[16]

> And I thus floating, lonely elf,
> A kind of planet by myself,
> The mists draw up and furl away,
> And in the east a warming gray,
> Faint as the tint of oaken woods
> When o'er their buds May breathes and broods,
> Tells that the golden sunrise-tide
> Is lapsing up earth's thirsty side,
> Each moment purpling on the crest
> Of some stark billow farther west:
> And as the sea-moss droops and hears
> The gurgling flood that nears and nears,
> And then with tremulous content
> Floats out each thankful filament,
> So waited I until it came,
> God's daily miracle,—O shame
> That I had seen so many days
> Unthankful, without wondering praise,
> Not recking more this bliss of earth
> Than the cheap fire that lights my hearth!
> But now glad thoughts and holy pour
> Into my heart, as once a year
> To San Miniato's [17] open door,
> In long procession, chanting clear,
> Through slopes of sun, through shadows hoar,
> The coupled monks slow-climbing sing,
> And like a golden censer swing
> From rear to front, from front to rear
> Their alternating bursts of praise,
> Till the roof's fading seraphs gaze

[15] A collection of old Icelandic mythological and heroic poems, discovered in 1643.

[16] German court lyric poets of the twelfth and thirteenth centuries.

[17] An ancient church on a lovely height overlooking Florence, Italy.

Down through an odorous mist, that crawls
Lingeringly up the darkened walls,
And the dim arches, silent long,
Are startled with triumphant song.

I wrote yesterday that the sea still rimmed our prosy lives with mystery and conjecture. But one is shut up on shipboard like Montaigne [18] in his tower, with nothing to do but to review his own thoughts and contradict himself. *Dire, redire, et me contredire,*[19] will be the staple of my journal till I see land. I say nothing of such matters as the *montagna bruna* [20] on which Ulysses wrecked; but since the sixteenth century could any man reasonably hope to stumble on one of those wonders which were cheap as dirt in the days of St. Saga? Faustus,[21] Don Juan,[22] and Tannhäuser [23] are the last ghosts of legend, that lingered almost till the Gallic cockcrow of universal enlightenment and disillusion. The Public School has done for Imagination. What shall I see in Outre-Mer,[24] or on the way thither, but what can be seen with eyes? To be sure, I stick by the sea-serpent,

---

[18] Michel de Montaigne (1533–92), who wrote his famous *Essays* in the family castle at Périgord, France.

[19] To talk, to reply, and to contradict myself.

[20] Dark mountain.—Ulysses and his companions, according to the great Italian poet Dante (1265–1321) in his *Divine Comedy,* had voyaged beyond the straits of Gibraltar into the Atlantic for five days when a dark mountain appeared in the distance. Suddenly a whirlwind blowing from this peak struck Ulysses' ship, tossed it around three times, and then sank it with all on board. See "Inferno," Canto XXVI, l. 133ff.

[21] Dr. Johann Faust, celebrated German magician of the sixteenth century.

[22] The legendary prince of libertines. In Spanish tradition Don Juan de Tenorio, a profligate nobleman of Seville, killed the father of a lady whom he had tried to seduce. Later he visited the tomb of the slain man and mockingly invited to supper the statue erected over the latter's grave. The statue accepted the invitation, and, in the end, carried Don Juan off to hell.

[23] A Teutonic knight in love with a lady of Mantua, Italy, who was lured away from his ladylove by the promise that Venus should be his mistress if he would enter the mysterious precincts of Venusberg. He went thither and indulged his desires to the full. On his return to Italy he sought absolution of his sins from Pope Urban, but was refused and fled in despair back to Venusberg.

[24] Pilgrims and crusaders in the late Middle Ages called the Holy Land "Pays d'Outre-Mer," i.e., The Land Beyond the Sea. Then the term came to denote, in general, a distant, wonderful region.

and would fain believe that science has scotched, not killed him.
Nor is he to be lightly given up, for, like the old Scandinavian
snake,[25] he binds together for us the two hemispheres of Past
and Present, of Belief and Science. He is the link which knits
us seaboard Yankees with our Norse progenitors, interpreting
between the age of the dragon and that of the railroad-train.
We have made ducks and drakes of that large estate of wonder
and delight bequeathed to us by ancestral vikings, and this alone
remains to us unthrift Heirs of Linn.[26]

I feel an undefined respect for a man who has seen the sea-
serpent. He is to his brother-fishers what the poet is to his
fellow-men. Where they have seen nothing better than a
school of horse-mackerel, or the idle coils of ocean round Half-
way Rock, he has caught authentic glimpses of the withdrawing
mantle-hem of the Edda age. I care not for the monster himself. It is not the thing, but the belief in the thing, that is dear
to me. May it be long before Professor Owen [27] is comforted
with the sight of his unfleshed vertebræ, long before they stretch
many a rood behind Kimball's [28] or Barnum's [29] glass, reflected
in the shallow orbs of Mr. and Mrs. Public, which stare, but see
not! I speak of him in the singular number, for I insist on believing that there is but one left, without chance of duplicate.
When we read that Captain Spalding, of the pink-stern [30] *Three*

[25] The "huge kraken" of Norse mythology, to which Lowell refers in
Abraham Lincoln, p. 88.

[26] The Heir of Linne, the hero of an old ballad by the same name, spent
his money in riotous living, and then sold his estates to John o' the Scales
for a third of their value. He went to a lonely lodge and hung himself, but
the rope broke. On his fall he found three chests full of money. He then
bought back his estates.

[27] Richard Owen (1804–92), English zoölogist, carried on widely known
pioneering studies in the comparative anatomy of higher vertebrates and
attempted a systematic classification of these animals in his huge *Descriptive
and Illustrative Catalogue of the Physiological Series of Comparative Anatomy* (1833–40).

[28] Moses Kimball (1809–95) opened in 1841 the "Boston Museum," a
popular place of public amusement located on Tremont Street between
Court and School Streets, Boston.

[29] Phineas Taylor Barnum (1810–91), "the great American showman,"
in 1842 opened in New York City the "American Museum," where all sorts
of so-called marvels were exhibited.

[30] Narrow-stern: "pink" < Fr. *pinque.*

Pollies, has beheld him rushing through the brine like an infinite series of bewitched mackerel-casks, we feel that the mystery of old Ocean, at least, has not yet been sounded,—that Faith and Awe survive there unevaporate. I once ventured the horse-mackerel theory to an old fisherman, browner than a tomcod. "Hos-mackril!" he exclaimed indignantly, "hos-mackril be —" (here he used a phrase commonly indicated in laical literature by the same sign which serves for Doctorate in Divinity,) "don't yer spose *I* know a hos-mackril?" The intonation of that *"I"* would have silenced Professor Monkbarns Owen with his provoking *phoca* [31] forever. What if one should ask *him* if he knew a trilobite? [32]

The fault of modern travellers is, that they see nothing out of sight. They talk of eocene [33] periods and tertiary [34] formations, and tell us how the world looked to the plesiosaur.[35] They take science (or nescience) with them, instead of that soul of generous trust their elders had. All their senses are sceptics and doubters, materialists reporting things for other sceptics to doubt still further upon. Nature becomes a reluctant witness upon the stand, badgered with geologist hammers and phials of acid. There have been no travellers since those included in Hakluyt [36] and Purchas,[37] except Martin,[38] perhaps, who saw an inch or two into the invisible at the Western Islands. We have peripatetic lecturers, but no more travellers. Travellers' stories are

---

[31] Professor Owen in *The Times,* London, November 11, 1848, expressed the opinion that the sea-serpent sighted by Captain Peter M'Quhae of the Daedalus that year was a sea-elephant (*phocaproboscidea*). "Monkbarns" = antiquarian; Scott's Antiquary lived at Monkbarns.

[32] An extinct marine anthropod of the oldest geologic period.

[33] See note on p. 9.

[34] The Tertiary period, the earlier of the two divisions in the most recent geologic era, is that in which the great mountain ranges were formed and the land life became dominantly mammalian.

[35] An extinct marine lizard of large size.

[36] Richard Hakluyt (1552?–1616), first important English geographer, whose *Voyages,* first published in 1589, has become a widely read work.

[37] Samuel Purchas (1575?–1626), who published in 1625 a volume on sea voyages entitled *Hakluytus Posthumus, or Purchas his Pilgrimes.*

[38] Martin Martin (d. 1719), a native of the Isle of Skye, who wrote an interesting travel book popular in the eighteenth century, *A Description of the Western Islands of Scotland* (1703).

no longer proverbial. We have picked nearly every apple (wormy or otherwise) from the world's tree of knowledge, and that without an Eve to tempt us. Two or three have hitherto hung luckily beyond reach on a lofty bough shadowing the interior of Africa, but there is a German Doctor at this very moment pelting at them with sticks and stones. It may be only next week, and these too, bitten by geographers and geologists, will be thrown away.

Analysis is carried into everything. Even Deity is subjected to chemic tests. We must have exact knowledge, a cabinet stuck full of facts pressed, dried, or preserved in spirits, instead of the large, vague world our fathers had. With them science was poetry; with us, poetry is science. Our modern Eden is a *hortus siccus*.[39] Tourists defraud rather than enrich us. They have not that sense of æsthetic proportion which characterized the elder traveller. Earth is no longer the fine work of art it was, for nothing is left to the imagination. Job Hortop,[40] arrived at the height of the Bermudas, thinks it full time to indulge us in a merman. Nay, there is a story told by Webster, in his Witchcraft,[41] of a merman with a mitre, who, on being sent back to his watery diocese of finland, made what advances he could toward an episcopal benediction by bowing his head thrice. Doubtless he had been consecrated by St. Antony of Padua.[42] A dumb bishop would be sometimes no unpleasant phenomenon, by the way. Sir John Hawkins [43] is not satisfied with tell-

[39] Herbarium (lit., dry garden).

[40] An English seaman who in 1567 embarked with Captain John Hawkyns on his voyage to the Bermudas and the West Indies, but subsequently separated from that expedition in the West Indies, and suffered many adventures and hardships in the next twenty-five years. His travels are narrated by Hakluyt.

[41] An old and curious work entitled *"The displaying of supposed Witchcraft. . . .* By John Webster, Practitioner in Physick. . . . London, 1677."

[42] St. Antony of Padua (1195–1231), the most celebrated of the followers of St. Francis of Assisi, was reputed in medieval legend so eloquent a preacher that the fishes even leapt out of the water to listen to him.

[43] Sir John Hawkins or Hawkyns (1532–95), famous sea-captain, freebooter, and admiral of the English fleet in the battle against the Spanish Armada, 1588.

ing us about the merely sensual Canaries, but is generous enough
to throw us in a handful of "certain flitting islands" to boot.
Henry Hawkes describes the visible Mexican cities, and then is
not so frugal but that he can give us a few invisible ones.[44]
Thus do these generous ancient mariners make children of us
again.   Their successors show us an earth effete and in a double
sense past bearing, tracing out with the eyes of industrious fleas
every wrinkle and crowfoot.

The journals of the elder navigators are prose Odysseys. The
geographies of our ancestors were works of fancy and imagination. They read poems where we yawn over items. Their
world was a huge wonder-horn, exhaustless as that which Thor
strove to drain. Ours would scarce quench the small thirst of
a bee. No modern voyager brings back the magical foundation-
stones of a Tempest. No Marco Polo,[45] traversing the desert
beyond the city of Lok,[46] would tell of things able to inspire the
mind of Milton with

> Calling shapes and beckoning shadows dire,
> And airy tongues that syllable men's names
> On sands and shores and desert wildernesses.[47]

It was easy enough to believe the story of Dante,[48] when two
thirds of even the upper-world were yet untraversed and un-
mapped. With every step of the recent traveller our inheritance
of the wonderful is diminished. Those beautifully pictured
notes of the Possible are redeemed at a ruinous discount in the

---

[44] See "A relation of the commodities of Nova Hispania, and the manners of the inhabitants, written by Henry Hawks merchant, which lived
five yeeres in the sayd countrey, and drew the same at the request of Mr.
Rich. Hakluyt . . . , 1572," in *Hakluyt's Voyages*, IX, 378–97 (Hakluyt
Soc. series, Glasgow, 1903–05).

[45] Venetian merchant and traveler (1254?–?1324), whose story of his
Asiatic travels is world-renowned.

[46] The now vanished city of Lop or Lob (*not* Lok) was located on the
western edge of the Gobi desert in eastern Turkestan (Sinkiang). See *The
Book of Marco Polo*, Bk. I, chap. 39.

[47] *Comus*, ll. 207–9.

[48] I.e., his imaginary journey through Hell, Purgatory, and Paradise, as
related in the *Divine Comedy*.

hard and cumbrous coin of the Actual. How are we not defrauded and impoverished? Does California vie with El Do-
rado? or are Bruce's Abyssinian kings [49] a set-off for Prester
John? [50] A bird in the bush is worth two in the hand. And if
the philosophers have not even yet been able to agree whether
the world has any existence independent of ourselves, how do we
not gain a loss in every addition to the catalogue of Vulgar Errors? Where are the fishes which nidificated [51] in trees?
Where the monopodes [52] sheltering themselves from the sun beneath their single umbrella-like foot,—umbrella-like in everything but the fatal necessity of being borrowed? Where the
Acephali,[53] with whom Herodotus, in a kind of ecstasy, wound
up his climax of men with abnormal top-pieces? Where the
Roc [54] whose eggs are possibly boulders, needing no far-fetched
theory of glacier or iceberg to account for them? Where the
tails of the men of Kent? [55] Where the no legs of the bird
of paradise? Where the Unicorn, with that single horn of
his, sovereign against all manner of poisons? Where that
Thessalian spring, which, without cost to the country, con-
victed and punished perjurers? [56] Where the Amazons of

[49] James Bruce (1730–94), famous Scottish explorer in Africa, gave a remarkable account of the Abyssinian (Ethiopian) royalty and court in his
Travels to Discover the Sources of the Nile in the Years 1768–73, a work of
wide and long-standing popularity.

[50] See note on p. 21. In the fifteenth century a Portuguese traveler,
Pedro Covilham, returned from a journey to Abyssinia (Ethiopia) and
claimed that in the Christian king of that African country, whom he called
Negus, he had at last discovered Prester John.

[51] Made their nests.

[52] A legendary tribe of Ethiopians who possessed but one foot and used
it to shade themselves against the African sun.

[53] Fabulous creatures without heads, who, according to the Greek historian
Herodotus, dwelt in Libya.

[54] A mythical Arabian bird of enormous size and strength.

[55] It was for centuries a saying, especially on the Continent, that the men
of Kent were born with tails as a punishment for the murder of Archbishop
Thomas à Becket at Canterbury, the Kentish capital, in 1170. See, for example, Joseph Addison, *Spectator,* No. 173.

[56] Lowell here has fallen into error, for classical lore reports no such
Thessalian spring. Philostratus' *Life of Apollonius of Tyana,* Bk. I, chap. 6,
contains, however, the following account of the spring of Asbamaeum,

Orellana? [57] Where, in short, the Fountain of Youth? All these, and a thousand other varieties, we have lost, and have got nothing instead of them. And those who have robbed us of them have stolen that which not enriches themselves. It is so much wealth cast into the sea beyond all approach of diving-bells. We owe no thanks to Mr. J. E. Worcester, whose Geography we studied enforcedly at school. Yet even he had his relentings, and in some softer moment vouchsafed us a fine, inspiring print of the Maelstrom,[58] answerable to the twenty-four mile diameter of its suction. Year by year, more and more of the world gets disenchanted. Even the icy privacy of the arctic and antarctic circles is invaded. Our youth are no longer ingenuous, as indeed no ingenuity is demanded of them. Everything is accounted for, everything cut and dried, and the world may be put together as easily as the fragments of a dissected map. The Mysterious bounds nothing now on the North, South, East, or West. We have played Jack Horner with our earth, till there is never a plum left in it.

---

which was located near Tyana in Cappadocia, Asia Minor, and was sacred to Zeus, the god of oaths: "This water is favorable and sweet to those who keep their oaths, but to perjurers it brings hot-footed justice; for it attacks their eyes and hands and feet, and they fall the prey of dropsy and wasting disease; and they are not even able to go away, but are held on the spot and bemoan themselves at the edge of the spring, acknowledging their perjuries." (Loeb Library trans.) An identical account of the same spring appears in the pseudo-Aristotelian *De mirabilibus auscultationibus* (*Tales of Marvels*), par. 152. The immediately preceding paragraph (par. 151) tells of a deadly sacred serpent in *Thessaly*. Quite probably Lowell had read this pseudo-Aristotelian work too, did not recall the location of Tyana (the site of the spring), and assumed that the paragraph about the spring, like the preceding one about the serpent, dealt with Thessaly. Hence the miraculous spring got fixed in his mind as Thessalian.

[57] Francisco Orellana (d. 1550), a Spanish explorer who accompanied the Pizarro brothers to Peru, on his eastward descent of the Andes in 1541 encountered some fierce opposition from the female warriors among the Tapuya Indians and hence called these women "Amazons" out of respect for their military prowess.

[58] A famous whirlpool off the coast of Norway, which formerly was believed to possess amazing destructive power.

THE FUNCTION OF THE POET [1]

Whether, as some philosophers assume, we possess only the fragments of a great cycle of knowledge in whose centre stood the primeval man in friendly relation with the powers of the universe, and build our hovels out of the ruins of our ancestral palace; or whether, according to the development theory of others, we are rising gradually, and have come up out of an atom instead of descending from an Adam, so that the proudest pedigree might run up to a barnacle or a zoöphyte at last, are questions that will keep for a good many centuries yet. Confining myself to what little we can learn from history, we find tribes rising slowly out of barbarism to a higher or lower point of culture and civility, and everywhere the poet also is found, under one name or other, changing in certain outward respects, but essentially the same.

And however far we go back, we shall find this also—that the poet and the priest were united originally in the same person; which means that the poet was he who was conscious of the world of spirit as well as that of sense, and was the ambassador of the gods to men. This was his highest function, and hence his name of "seer." He was the discoverer and declarer of the perennial beneath the deciduous. His were the *epea pteroenta,* the true "winged words" that could fly down the unexplored future and carry the names of ancestral heroes, of the brave and wise and good. It was thus that the poet could reward virtue, and, by and by, as society grew more complex, could burn in the brand of shame. This is Homer's character of Demodocus, in the eighth book of the "Odyssey," "whom the Muse loved and gave the good and ill"—the gift of conferring good or evil im-

---

[1] This essay originally constituted the last in a series of twelve lectures delivered during January and February, 1855, at the Lowell Institute, Boston, on the general subject of the English poets. Abridged versions of the lectures appeared regularly in the *Boston Advertiser* of that period, but Lowell never saw fit subsequently to print any of them in their properly complete form. This concluding lecture, edited from the original manuscript, was posthumously published in the *Century Magazine,* January, 1894, with a prefatory note by Charles Eliot Norton.

mortality. The first histories were in verse; and sung as they were at feasts and gatherings of the people, they awoke in men the desire of fame, which is the first promoter of courage and self-trust, because it teaches men by degrees to appeal from the present to the future. We may fancy what the influence of the early epics was when they were recited to men who claimed the heroes celebrated in them for their ancestors, by what Bouchardon, the sculptor,[2] said, only two centuries ago: "When I read Homer, I feel as if I were twenty feet high."[3] Nor have poets lost their power over the future in modern times. Dante lifts up by the hair the face of some petty traitor, the Smith or Brown of some provincial Italian town, lets the fire of his Inferno glare upon it for a moment, and it is printed forever on the memory of mankind. The historians may iron out the shoulders of Richard the Third as smooth as they can, they will never get over the wrench that Shakespeare gave them.

The peculiarity of almost all early literature is that it seems to have a double meaning, that, underneath its natural, we find ourselves continually seeing or suspecting a supernatural meaning. In the older epics the characters seem to be half typical and only half historical. Thus did the early poets endeavor to make realities out of appearances; for, except a few typical men in whom certain ideas get embodied, the generations of mankind are mere apparitions who come out of the dark for a purposeless moment, and reënter the dark again after they have performed the nothing they came for.

Gradually, however, the poet as the "seer" became secondary to the "maker." His office became that of entertainer rather than teacher. But always something of the old tradition was kept alive. And if he has now come to be looked upon merely as the best expresser, the gift of seeing is implied as necessarily

---

[2] Edme Bouchardon (1698–1762), noted French sculptor, whose most famous work is the fountain in the Rue de Grenelle, Paris.

[3] According to the French critic, Victor Hugo (1802–85), the author of this saying was the Italian sculptor, Michelangelo Buonarroti (1475–1564). Hugo in his *William Shakespeare* (1864), Bk. II, Part II, Sec. I, quotes Michelangelo as follows: "When I read Homer, I look at myself to see if I am not twenty feet high."

antecedent to that, and of seeing very deep, too. If any man would seem to have written without any conscious moral, that man is Shakespeare. But that must be a dull sense, indeed, which does not see through his tragic—yes, and his comic—masks awful eyes that flame with something intenser and deeper than a mere scenic meaning—a meaning out of the great deep that is behind and beyond all human and merely personal character. Nor was Shakespeare himself unconscious of his place as a teacher and profound moralist: witness that sonnet in which he bewails his having neglected sometimes the errand that was laid upon him:

> Alas, 'tis true I have gone here and there,
> And made myself a motley to the view,
> Gored mine own thoughts, sold cheap what is most dear,
> Made old offences of affections new;
> Most true it is that I have look'd on truth
> Askance and strangely; [4]

the application of which is made clear by the next sonnet, in which he distinctly alludes to his profession.

There is this unmistakable stamp on all the great poets—that, however in little things they may fall below themselves, whenever there comes a great and noble thing to say, they say it greatly and nobly, and bear themselves most easily in the royalties of thought and language. There is not a mature play of Shakespeare's in which great ideas do not jut up in mountainous permanence, marking forever the boundary of provinces of thought, and known afar to many kindreds of men.

And it is for this kind of sight, which we call insight, and not for any faculty of observation and description, that we value the poet. It is in proportion as he has this that he is an adequate expresser, and not a juggler with words. It is by means of this that for every generation of man he plays the part of "namer." Before him, as before Adam, the creation passes to be named anew: first the material world; then the world of passions and emotions; then the world of ideas. But whenever a great imagi-

---

[4] Sonnet CX (1609 ed.).

nation comes, however it may delight itself with imagining the outward beauty of things, however it may seem to flow thoughtlessly away in music like a brook, yet the shadow of heaven lies also in its depth beneath the shadow of earth. Continually the visible universe suggests the invisible. We are forever feeling this in Shakespeare. His imagination went down to the very bases of things, and while his characters are the most natural that poet ever created, they are also perfectly ideal, and are more truly the personifications of abstract thoughts and passions than those of any allegorical writer whatever.

Even in what seems so purely a picturesque poem as the "Iliad," we feel something of this. Beholding as Homer did, from the tower of contemplation, the eternal mutability and nothing permanent but change, he must look underneath the show for the reality. Great captains and conquerors came forth out of the eternal silence, entered it again with their trampling hosts, and shoutings, and trumpet-blasts, and were as utterly gone as those echoes of their deeds which he sang, and which faded with the last sound of his voice and the last tremble of his lyre. History relating outward events alone was an unmeaning gossip, with the world for a village. This life could only become other than phantasmagoric, could only become real, as it stood related to something that was higher and permanent. Hence the idea of Fate, of a higher power unseen—that shadow, as of an eagle circling to its swoop, which flits stealthily and swiftly across the windy plains of Troy. In the "Odyssey" we find pure allegory.

Now, under all these names—praiser, seer, soothsayer—we find the same idea lurking. The poet is he who can best see and best say what is ideal—what belongs to the world of soul and of beauty. Whether he celebrate the brave and good man, or the gods, or the beautiful as it appears in man or nature, something of a religious character still clings to him; he is the revealer of Deity. He may be unconscious of his mission; he may be false to it; but in proportion as he is a great poet, he rises to the level of it the more often. He does not always directly rebuke what is bad and base, but indirectly by making us feel what delight there is in the good and fair. If he besiege evil, it is with such beautiful engines of war (as Plutarch tells us of Demetrius) that the besieged themselves are charmed with them. Whoever reads the great poets cannot but be made better by it, for they always introduce him to a higher society, to a greater style of manners and of thinking. Whoever learns to love what is beautiful is made incapable of the low and mean and bad. If Plato excludes the poets from his Republic, it is expressly on the ground that they speak unworthy things of the gods; that is, that they have lost the secret of their art, and use artificial types instead of speaking the true universal language of imagination. He who translates the divine into the vulgar, the spiritual into the sensual, is the reverse of a poet.

The poet, under whatever name, always stands for the same thing—imagination. And imagination in its highest form gives him the power, as it were, of assuming the consciousness of whatever he speaks about, whether man or beast, or rock or tree. It is the ring of Canace,[5] which whoso has on understands the language of all created things. And as regards expression, it seems to enable the poet to condense the whole of himself into a single word. Therefore, when a great poet has said a thing, it is finally and utterly expressed, and has as many meanings as there are men who read his verse. A great poet is something more than an interpreter between man and nature; he is also an interpreter between man and his own nature. It is he who gives us those key-words, the possession of which makes us masters of all the unsuspected treasure-caverns of thought, and feeling, and beauty which open under the dusty path of our daily life.

And it is not merely a dry lexicon that he compiles,—a thing which enables us to translate from one dead dialect into another as dead,—but all his verse is instinct with music, and his words open windows on every side to pictures of scenery and life. The difference between the dry fact and the poem is as great as that between reading the shipping news and seeing the actual coming

---

[5] The daughter of Cambuscan, king of Sarra in the land of Tartary, to whom the king of Araby gave a ring by which she could know the virtues of all the plants and understand the language of all the birds.

and going of the crowd of stately ships,—"the city on the inconstant billows dancing,"—as there is between ten minutes of happiness and ten minutes by the clock. Everybody remembers
the story of the little Montague who was stolen and sold to the
chimney-sweep: how he could dimly remember lying in a beautiful chamber; how he carried with him in all his drudgery the
vision of a fair, sad mother's face that sought him everywhere
in vain; how he threw himself one day, all sooty as he was from
his toil, on a rich bed and fell asleep, and how a kind person
woke him, questioned him, pieced together his broken recollections for him, and so at last made the visions of the beautiful
chamber and the fair, sad countenance real to him again. It
seems to me that the offices that the poet does for us are typified
in this nursery-tale. We all of us have our vague reminiscences
of the stately home of our childhood,—for we are all of us poets
and geniuses in our youth, while earth is all new to us, and the
chalice of every buttercup is brimming with the wine of poesy,—
and we all remember the beautiful, motherly countenance which
nature bent over us there. But somehow we all get stolen away
thence; life becomes to us a sooty taskmaster, and we crawl
through dark passages without end—till suddenly the word of
some poet redeems us, makes us know who we are, and of helpless orphans makes us the heir to a great estate. It is to our true
relations with the two great worlds of outward and inward nature that the poet reintroduces us.

But the imagination has a deeper use than merely to give poets
a power of expression. It is the everlasting preserver of the
world from blank materialism. It forever puts matter in the
wrong, and compels it to show its title to existence. Wordsworth tells us that in his youth he was sometimes obliged to
touch the walls to find if they were visionary or no, and such
experiences are not uncommon with persons who converse much
with their own thoughts. Dr. Johnson said that to kick one's
foot against a stone was a sufficient confutation of Berkeley,[6]

---

[6] George Berkeley (1684–1753), English bishop and philosopher, who
in *The Principles of Human Knowledge* (1710) asserted that there was no
proof of matter's existence except as a concept of the human mind.

and poor old Pyrrho [7] has passed into a proverb because, denying the objectivity of matter, he was run over by a cart and killed. But all that he affirmed was that to the soul the cart was no more real than its own imaginative reproduction of it, and perhaps the shade of the philosopher ran up to the first of his deriders who crossed the Styx with a triumphant "I told you so! The cart did not run over *me,* for here I am without a bone broken."

And, in another sense also, do those poets who deal with human character, as all the greater do, continually suggest to us the purely phantasmal nature of life except as it is related to the world of ideas. For are not their personages more real than most of those in history? Is not Lear more authentic and permanent than Lord Raglan? [8] Their realm is a purely spiritual one in which space and time and costume are nothing. What matters it that Shakespeare puts a seaport in Bohemia, and knew less geography than Tommy who goes to the district school? He understood eternal boundaries, such as are laid down on no chart, and are not defined by such transitory affairs as mountain chains, rivers, and seas.

No great movement of the human mind takes place without the concurrent beat of those two wings, the imagination and the understanding. It is by the understanding that we are enabled to make the most of this world, and to use the collected material of experience in its condensed form of practical wisdom; and it is the imagination which forever beckons toward that other world which is always future, and makes us discontented with this. The one rests upon experience; the other leans forward and listens after the *in*experienced, and shapes the features of that future with which it is forever in travail. The imagination might be defined as the common sense of the invisible world, as the understanding is of the visible; and as those are the finest individual characters in which the two moderate and rectify each other, so those are the finest eras where the same

[7] Pyrrho (*c.* 360–*c.* 270 B.C.), the founder of the Skeptic school in Greek philosophy.

[8] Fitzroy James Henry Somerset, Baron Raglan (1788–1855), as commander of the British forces in the Crimea, 1854–55, was a figure much in the public eye at the time of this lecture.

may be said of society. In the voyage of life, not only do we depend on the needle, true to its earthly instincts, but upon observation of the fixed stars, those beacons lighted upon the eternal promontories of heaven above the stirs and shiftings of our lower system.

But it seems to be thought that we have come upon the earth too late, that there has been a feast of imagination formerly, and all that is left for us is to steal the scraps. We hear that there is no poetry in railroads and steamboats and telegraphs, and especially none in Brother Jonathan.[9] If this be true, so much the worse for him. But because *he* is a materialist, shall there be no more poets? When we have said that we live in a materialistic age we have said something which meant more than we intended. If we say it in the way of blame, we have said a foolish thing, for probably one age is as good as another, and, at any rate, the worst is good enough company for us. The age of Shakespeare was richer than our own, only because it was lucky enough to have such a pair of eyes as his to see it, and such a gift of speech as his to report it. And so there is always room and occasion for the poet, who continues to be, just as he was in the early time, nothing more nor less than a "seer." He is always the man who is willing to take the age he lives in on trust, as the very best that ever was. Shakespeare did not sit down and cry for the water of Helicon to turn the wheels of his little private mill at the Bankside. He appears to have gone more quietly about his business than any other playwright in London, to have drawn off what water-power he needed from the great prosy current of affairs that flows alike for all and in spite of all, to have ground for the public what grist they wanted, coarse or fine, and it seems a mere piece of luck that the smooth stream of his activity reflected with such ravishing clearness every changing mood of heaven and earth, every stick and stone, every dog and clown and courtier that stood upon its brink. It is a

---

[9] A humorous, colloquial term for the United States. It is supposed to have arisen from Washington's jocular reference, early in the American Revolution, to Governor Jonathan Trumbull of Connecticut as "Brother Jonathan." Trumbull, noted for his practical-mindedness, was a trusted counselor in time of need.

curious illustration of the friendly manner in which Shakespeare received everything that came along,—of what a *present* man he was,—that in the very same year that the mulberry-tree was brought into England, he got one and planted it in his garden at Stratford.

It is perfectly true that this is a materialistic age, and for that very reason we want our poets all the more. We find that every generation contrives to catch its singing larks without the sky's falling. When the poet comes, he always turns out to be the man who discovers that the passing moment is the inspired one, and that the secret of poetry is not to have lived in Homer's day, or Dante's, but to be alive now. To be alive now, that is the great art and mystery. They are dead men who live in the past, and men yet unborn that live in the future. We are like Hans in Luck, forever exchanging the burdensome good we have for something else, till at last we come home empty-handed.

That pale-faced drudge of Time opposite me there, that weariless sexton whose callous hands bury our rosy hours in the irrevocable past, is even now reaching forward to a moment as rich in life, in character, and thought, as full of opportunity, as any since Adam. This little isthmus that we are now standing on is the point to which martyrs in their triumphant pain, prophets in their fervor, and poets in their ecstasy, looked forward as the golden future, as the land too good for them to behold with mortal eyes; it is the point toward which the faint-hearted and desponding hereafter will look back as the priceless past when there was still some good and virtue and opportunity left in the world.

The people who feel their own age prosaic are those who see only its costume. And that is what makes it prosaic—that we have not faith enough in ourselves to think our own clothes good enough to be presented to posterity in. The artists fancy that the court dress of posterity is that of Van Dyck's time, or Caesar's. I have seen the model of a statue of Sir Robert Peel,[10]— a statesman whose merit consisted in yielding gracefully to the

---

[10] Prominent English statesman (1788–1850), best known for his advocacy of the Catholic Emancipation Act.

present,—in which the sculptor had done his best to travesty the real man into a make-believe Roman. At the period when England produced its greatest poets, we find exactly the reverse of this, and we are thankful that the man who made the monument of Lord Bacon had genius to copy every button of his dress, everything down to the rosettes on his shoes, and then to write under his statue, "Thus sat Francis Bacon"—not "Cneius Pompeius"—"Viscount Verulam." Those men had faith even in their own shoe-strings.

After all, how is our poor scapegoat of a nineteenth century to blame? Why, for not being the seventeenth, to be sure! It is always raining opportunity, but it seems it was only the men two hundred years ago who were intelligent enough not to hold their cups bottom-up. We are like beggars who think if a piece of gold drop into their palm it must be counterfeit, and would rather change it for the smooth-worn piece of familiar copper. And so, as we stand in our mendicancy by the wayside, Time tosses carefully the great golden to-day into our hats, and we turn it over grumblingly and suspiciously, and are pleasantly surprised at finding that we can exchange it for beef and potatoes. Till Dante's time the Italian poets thought no language good enough to put their nothings into but Latin,—and indeed a dead tongue was the best for dead thoughts,—but Dante found the common speech of Florence, in which men bargained and scolded and made love, good enough for him, and out of the world around him made a poem such as no Roman ever sang.

In our day, it is said despairingly, the understanding reigns triumphant: it is the age of common sense. If this be so, the wisest way would be to accept it manfully. But, after all, what is the meaning of it? Looking at the matter superficially, one would say that a striking difference between our science and that of the world's gray fathers is that there is every day less and less of the element of wonder in it. What they saw written in light upon the great arch of heaven, and, by a magnificent reach of sympathy, of which we are incapable, associated with the fall of monarchs and the fate of man, is for us only a professor, a piece of chalk, and a blackboard. The solemn and unapproachable skies we have vulgarized; we have peeped and botanized [11] among the flowers of light, pulled off every petal, fumbled in every calyx, and reduced them to the bare stem of order and class. The stars can no longer maintain their divine reserves, but whenever there is a conjunction and congress of planets, every enterprising newspaper sends thither its special reporter with his telescope. Over those arcana of life where once a mysterious presence brooded, we behold scientific explorers skipping like so many incarnate notes of interrogation. We pry into the counsels of the great powers of nature, we keep our ears at the keyhole, and know everything that is going to happen. There is no longer any sacred inaccessibility, no longer any enchanting unexpectedness, and life turns to prose the moment there is nothing unattainable. It needs no more a voice out of the unknown proclaiming "Great Pan is dead!" We have found his tombstone, deciphered the arrowheaded inscription upon it, know his age to a day, and that he died universally regretted.

Formerly science was poetry. A mythology which broods over us in our cradle, which mingles with the lullaby of the nurse, which peoples the day with the possibility of divine encounters, and night with intimation of demonic ambushes, its something quite other, as the material for thought and poetry, from one that we take down from our bookshelves, as sapless as the shelf it stood on, as remote from all present sympathy with man or nature as a town history with its genealogies of Mr. Nobody's great-grandparents.

We have utilized everything. The Egyptians found a hint of the solar system in the concentric circles of the onion, and revered it as a symbol, while we respect it as a condiment in cookery, and can pass through all Wethersfield [12] without a thought of the stars. Our world is a museum of natural history; that of our forefathers was a museum of supernatural history. And the

---

[11] Cf. Wordsworth's *A Poet's Epitaph* (1799), ll. 19–20:
> One that would peep and botanize
> Upon his mother's grave?

[12] Wethersfield, Connecticut, one of the first settlements in the state, was early noted as a center of onion culture which rapidly spread throughout the lower Connecticut River valley.

rapidity with which the change has been going on is almost startling, when we consider that so modern and historical a personage as Queen Elizabeth was reigning at the time of the death
of Dr. John Faustus, out of whose story the Teutonic imagination built up a mythus that may be set beside that of Prometheus.

Science, looked at scientifically, is bare and bleak enough. On
those sublime heights the air is too thin for the lungs, and blinds
the eyes. It is much better living down in the valleys, where
one cannot see farther than the next farmhouse. Faith was
never found in the bottom of a crucible, nor peace arrived at by
analysis or synthesis. But all this is because science has become
too grimly intellectual, has divorced itself from the moral and
imaginative part of man. Our results are not arrived at in that
spirit which led Kepler [13] (who had his theory-traps set all along
the tracks of the stars to catch a discovery) to say, "In my opinion
the occasions of new discoveries have been no less wonderful
than the discoveries themselves."

But we are led back continually to the fact that science can
not, if it would, disengage itself from human nature and from
imagination. No two men have ever argued together without
at least agreeing in this, that something more than proof is required to produce conviction, and that a logic which is capable
of grinding the stubbornest facts to powder (as every man's *own*
logic always is) is powerless against so delicate a structure as the
brain. Do what we will, we cannot contrive to bring together
the yawning edges of proof and belief, to weld them into one.
When Thor strikes Skrymir with his terrible hammer, the giant
asks if a leaf has fallen.[14] I need not appeal to the Thors of argument in the pulpit, the senate, and the mass-meeting, if they
have not sometimes found the popular giant as provokingly insensible. The $\sqrt{-x}$ is nothing in comparison with the chance-

---

[13] Johann Kepler (1571–1630), the German astronomer who discovered
the laws which rule the motions of the planets.

[14] Skrymir, according to Norse myth, was awakened under an oak tree
by a furious blow on the head from his traveling companion, Thor the
thunder god, who was angry because the giant had tied a fast knot on their
food bag.

caught smell of a single flower which by the magic of association recreates for us the unquestioning day of childhood.
Demonstration may lead to the very gate of heaven, but there
she makes us a civil bow, and leaves us to make our way back
again to Faith, who has the key. That science which is of the
intellect alone steps with indifferent foot upon the dead body of
Belief, if only she may reach higher or see farther.

But we cannot get rid of our wonder—we who have brought
down the wild lightning, from writing fiery doom upon the
walls of heaven, to be our errand-boy and penny-postman.
Wonder is crude imagination; and it is necessary to us, for man
shall not live by bread alone, and exact knowledge is not enough.
Do we get nearer the truth or farther from it that we have got
a gas or an imponderable fluid instead of a spirit? We go on
exorcising one thing after another, but what boots it? The eva-
sive genius flits into something else, and defies us. The powers
of the outer and inner world form hand in hand a magnetic
circle for whose connection man is necessary. It is the imagination that takes his hand and clasps it with that other
stretched to him in the dark, and for which he was vainly groping. It is that which renews the mystery in nature, makes it
wonderful and beautiful again, and out of the gases of the man
of science remakes the old spirit. But we seem to have created
too many wonders to be capable of wondering any longer; as
Coleridge said, when asked if he believed in ghosts, that he had
seen too many of them. But nature all the more imperatively
demands it, and science can at best but scotch it, not kill it. In
this day of newspapers and electric telegraphs, in which common sense and ridicule can magnetize a whole continent between
dinner and tea, we say that such a phenomenon as Mahomet [15]
were impossible, and behold Joe Smith [16] and the State of Dese-
ret! [17] Turning over the yellow leaves of the same copy of

[15] This Arabian orphan shepherd boy, b. 570, became a prophet, taught
a new religion, and by the time of his death in 632 had established his
power and his principles of Islam over all Arabia.

[16] Joseph Smith (1805–44), the founder of the Mormon sect.

[17] The name of Utah in the early days of Mormon settlement, and the
one under which it first tried to enter the Union.

"Webster on Witchcraft" [18] which Cotton Mather [19] studied, I thought, "Well, that goblin is laid at last!"—and while I mused the tables were turning, and the chairs beating the devil's tattoo all over Christendom.[20] I have a neighbor who dug down through tough strata of clay to a spring pointed out by a witch-hazel rod in the hands of a seventh son's seventh son, and the water is the sweeter to him for the wonder that is mixed with it. After all, it seems that our scientific gas, be it never so brilliant, is not equal to the dingy old Aladdin's lamp.

It is impossible for men to live in a world without poetry of some sort or other. If they cannot get the best they will get some substitute for it, and thus seem to verify Saint Augustine's slur that it is wine of devils. The mind bound down too closely to what is practical either becomes inert, or revenges itself by rushing into the savage wilderness of "isms." The insincerity of our civilization has disgusted some persons so much that they have sought refuge in Indian wigwams and found refreshment in taking a scalp now and then. Nature insists above all things upon balance. She contrives to maintain a harmony between the material and spiritual, nor allows the cerebrum an expansion at the cost of the cerebellum. If the character, for example, run on one side into religious enthusiasm, it is not unlikely to develop on the other a counterpoise of worldly prudence. Thus the Shaker and the Moravian are noted for thrift, and mystics are not always the worst managers. Through all changes of condition and experience man continues to be a citizen of the world of idea as well as the world of fact, and the tax-gatherers of both are punctual.

And these antitheses which we meet with in individual character we cannot help seeing on the larger stage of the world also, a moral accompanying a material development. History, the great satirist, brings together Alexander and the blower of peas to hint to us that the tube of the one and the sword of the other

---

[18] See note on p. 45.

[19] Outstanding minister and author of Puritan Boston (1663–1728), notorious for his participation in the Salem witchcraft trials of 1691–92.

[20] An allusion to the widespread popularity of "Spiritualism." A Lowell letter of 1853 speaks of the "Rappers" and the "Tippers."

were equally transitory; but meanwhile Aristotle was conquering kingdoms out of the unknown, and establishing a dynasty of thought from whose hand the sceptre has not yet passed. So there are Charles V,[21] and Luther; the expansion of trade resulting from the Spanish and Portuguese discoveries, and the Elizabethan literature; the Puritans seeking spiritual El Dorados while so much valor and thought were spent in finding mineral ones. It seems to be the purpose of God that a certain amount of genius shall go to each generation, particular quantities being represented by individuals, and while no *one* is complete in himself, all collectively make up a whole ideal figure of a man. Nature is not like certain varieties of the apple that cannot bear two years in succession. It is only that her expansions are uniform in all directions, that in every age she completes her circle, and like a tree adds a ring to her growth be it thinner or thicker.

Every man is conscious that he leads two lives, the one trivial and ordinary, the other sacred and recluse; the one which he carries to the dinner-table and to his daily work, which grows old with his body and dies with it, the other that which is made up of the few inspiring moments of his higher aspiration and attainment, and in which his youth survives for him, his dreams, his unquenchable longings for something nobler than success. It is this life which the poets nourish for him, and sustain with their immortalizing nectar. Through them he feels once more the white innocence of his youth. His faith in something nobler than gold and iron and cotton comes back to him, not as an upbraiding ghost that wrings its pale hands and is gone, but beautiful and inspiring as a first love that recognizes nothing in him that is not high and noble. The poets are nature's perpetual pleaders, and protest with us against what is worldly. Out of their own undying youth they speak to ours. "Wretched is the man," says Goethe, "who has learned to despise the dreams of his youth!" It is from this misery that the imagination and the

---

[21] Charles V (1500–58), king of Spain and emperor of Germany, presided over the famous Diet of Worms in 1521 when Martin Luther (1483–1546) asserted his religious independence and set in motion the Protestant Reformation.

poets, who are its spokesmen, rescue us. The world goes to church, kneels to the eternal Purity, and then contrives to sneer at innocence and ignorance of evil by calling it green. Let every man thank God for what little there may be left in him of his vernal sweetness. Let him thank God if he have still the capacity for feeling an unmarketable enthusiasm, for that will make him worthy of the society of the noble dead, of the companionship of the poets. And let him love the poets for keeping youth young, woman womanly, and beauty beautiful.

There is as much poetry as ever in the world if we only knew how to find it out; and as much imagination, perhaps, only that it takes a more prosaic direction. Every man who meets with misfortune, who is stripped of material prosperity, finds that he has a little outlying mountain-farm of imagination, which did not appear in the schedule of his effects, on which his spirit is able to keep itself alive, though he never thought of it while he was fortunate. Job turns out to be a great poet as soon as his flocks and herds are taken away from him.

There is no reason why our continent should not sing as well as the rest. We have had the practical forced upon us by our position. We have had a whole hemisphere to clear up and put to rights. And we are descended from men who were hardened and stiffened by a downright wrestle with necessity. There was no chance for poetry among the Puritans. And yet if any people have a right to imagination, it should be the descendants of these very Puritans. They had enough of it, or they could never have conceived the great epic they did, whose books are States, and which is written on this continent from Maine to California.

But there seems to be another reason why we should not become a poetical people. Formerly the poet embodied the hopes and desires of men in visible types. He gave them the shoes of swiftness, the cap of invisibility and the purse of Fortunatus.[22] These were once stories for grown men, and not for the nursery

---

[22] The hero of a popular European tale, a peasant of Cyprus who is given an inexhaustible purse by Fortune and who later steals from the Sultan at Babylon a wishing hat which will carry him anywhere instantly.

as now. We are apt ignorantly to wonder how our forefathers could find satisfaction in fiction the absurdity of which any of our primary-school children could demonstrate. But we forget that the world's gray fathers were children themselves, and that in their little world, with its circle of the black unknown all about it, the imagination was as active as it is with people in the dark. Look at a child's toys, and we shall understand the matter well enough. Imagination is the fairy godmother (every child has one still), at the wave of whose wand sticks become heroes, the closet in which she has been shut fifty times for being naughty is turned into a palace, and a bit of lath acquires all the potency of Excalibur.

But nowadays it is the understanding itself that has turned poet. In her railroads she has given us the shoes of swiftness. Fine-Ear herself could not hear so far as she, who in her magnetic telegraph can listen in Boston and hear what is going on in New Orleans. And what need of Aladdin's lamp when a man can build a palace with a patent pill? The office of the poet seems to be reversed, and he must give back these miracles of the understanding to poetry again, and find out what there is imaginative in steam and iron and telegraph-wires. After all, there is as much poetry in the iron horses that eat fire as in those of Diomed that fed on men.[23] If you cut an apple across you may trace in it the lines of the blossom that the bee hummed around in May, and so the soul of poetry survives in things prosaic. Borrowing money on a bond does not seem the most promising subject in the world, but Shakespeare found the "Merchant of Venice" in it. Themes of song are waiting everywhere for the right man to sing them, like those enchanted swords which no one can pull out of the rock till the hero comes, and he finds no more trouble than in plucking a violet.

John Quincy Adams, making a speech at New Bedford, many years ago, reckoned the number of whale-ships (if I remember rightly) that sailed out of that port, and, comparing it with some

---

[23] In Greek myth, Diomedes, son of Mars and king of Thrace, possessed man-eating horses and was finally devoured by them after he had been killed in battle with Hercules.

former period, took it as a type of American success. But, alas! it is with quite other oil that those far-shining lamps of a nation's true glory which burn forever must be filled. It is not by any amount of material splendor or prosperity, but only by moral greatness, by ideas, by works of imagination, that a race can conquer the future. No voice comes to us from the once mighty Assyria but the hoot of the owl that nests amid her crumbling palaces. Of Carthage, whose merchant-fleets once furled their sails in every port of the known world, nothing is left but the deeds of Hannibal.[24] She lies dead on the shore of her once subject sea, and the wind of the desert only flings its handfuls of burial-sand upon her corpse. A fog can blot Holland or Switzerland out of existence. But how large is the space occupied in the maps of the soul by little Athens and powerless Italy! They were great by the soul, and their vital force is as indestructible as the soul.

Till America has learned to love art, not as an amusement, not as the mere ornament of her cities, not as a superstition of what is *comme il faut* [25] for a great nation, but for its humanizing and ennobling energy, for its power of making men better by arousing in them a perception of their own instincts for what is beautiful, and therefore sacred and religious, and an eternal rebuke of the base and worldly, she will not have succeeded in that high sense which alone makes a nation out of a people, and raises it from a dead name to a living power. Were our little mother-island sunk beneath the sea, or, worse, were she conquered by Scythian barbarians, yet Shakespeare would be an immortal England, and would conquer countries, when the bones of her last sailor had kept their ghastly watch for ages in unhallowed ooze beside the quenched thunders of her navy.

Old Purchas in his "Pilgrims" [26] tells of a sacred caste in India

---

[24] The famous general (B. C. 247–183) of the North African city once located near the site of modern Tunis.

[25] Proper.

[26] See note on p. 44.—*Purchas His Pilgrimes* (1625 ed., Pt. 4, p. 1767) reports: "As these *Nayros* [soldier-noblemen of the Malabar coast in India] goe in the streets, they use to cry *Po, Po,* which is to say, *Take heed, looke to yourselves,* or *I come, stand out of the way,* for that the other sort of [common] people . . . may not once touch or trouble one of them."

who, when they go out into the street, cry out, "Poo! Poo!" to warn all the world out of their way lest they should be defiled by something unclean. And it is just so that the understanding in its pride of success thinks to pooh-pooh all that it considers impractical and visionary. But whatever of life there is in man, except what comes of beef and pudding, is in the visionary and unpractical, and if it be not encouraged to find its activity or its solace in the production or enjoyment of art and beauty, if it be bewildered or thwarted by an outward profession of faith covering up a practical unbelief in anything higher and holier than the world of sense, it will find vent in such wretched holes and corners as table-tippings and mediums who sell news from heaven at a quarter of a dollar the item. Imagination cannot be banished out of the world. She may be made a kitchen-drudge, a Cinderella, but there are powers that watch over her. When her two proud sisters, the intellect and understanding, think her crouching over her ashes, she startles and charms by her splendid apparition, and Prince Soul will put up with no other bride.

The practical is a very good thing in its way—if it only be not another name for the worldly. To be absorbed in it is to eat of that insane root which the soldiers of Antonius found in their retreat from Parthia—which whoso tasted kept gathering sticks and stones as if they were some great matter till he died.[27]

One is forced to listen, now and then, to a kind of talk which makes him feel as if this was the after-dinner time of the world, and mankind were doomed hereafter forever to that kind of contented materialism which comes to good stomachs with the nuts and raisins. The dozy old world has nothing to do now but stretch its legs under the mahogany, talk about stocks, and get rid of the hours as well as it can till bedtime. The centuries before us have drained the goblet of wisdom and beauty, and all we have left is to cast horoscopes in the dregs. But divine beauty, and the love of it, will never be without apostles and messengers on earth, till Time flings his hour-glass into the abyss as having no need to turn it longer to number the indistinguish-

---

[27] For this anecdote about Mark Antony see Plutarch's *Lives* XLV: 5–6.

able ages of Annihilation. It was a favorite speculation with the learned men of the sixteenth century that they had come upon the old age and decrepit second childhood of creation, and while they maundered,[28] the soul of Shakespeare was just coming out of the eternal freshness of Deity, "trailing" such "clouds of glory"[29] as would beggar a Platonic year of sunsets.

No; morning and the dewy prime are born into the earth again with every child. It is our fault if drought and dust usurp the noon. Every age says to her poets, like the mistress to her lover, "Tell me what I am like"; and, in proportion as it brings forth anything worth seeing, has need of seers and will have them. Our time is not an unpoetical one. We are in our heroic age, still face to face with the shaggy forces of unsubdued Nature, and we have our Theseuses[30] and Perseuses,[31] though they may be named Israel Putnam[32] and Daniel Boone.[33] It is nothing against us that we are commercial people. Athens was a trading community; Dante and Titian[34] were the growth of great marts, and England was already commercial when she produced Shakespeare.

This lesson I learn from the past: that grace and goodness, the fair, the noble, and the true, will never cease out of the world till the God from whom they emanate ceases out of it; that they manifest themselves in an eternal continuity of change to every generation of men, as new duties and occasions arise; that the sacred duty and noble office of the poet is to reveal and justify them to men; that so long as the soul endures, endures also the theme of new and unexampled song; that while there is grace

---

[28] Grumbled.

[29] See Wordsworth's ode, *Intimations of Immortality from Recollections of Early Childhood,* ll. 64–5.

[30] Theseus, Greek hero who performed many exploits, of which the greatest was the destruction of the Minotaur, the Cretan monster.

[31] Perseus, the Greek hero who cut off the head of the snaky-locked Medusa.

[32] A noted American general (1718–1790), who had an adventurous career, first in the French and Indian War, and then in the Revolution.

[33] The famous explorer and pioneer (1735–1820) who opened up Kentucky for white settlement.

[34] A leading Italian painter (1477–1576), noted especially for his portraits and his mastery of color.

in grace, love in love, and beauty in beauty, God will still send
poets to find them and bear witness of them, and to hang their
ideal portraitures in the gallery of memory. God with us is forever the mystical name of the hour that is passing. The lives
of the great poets teach us that they were the men of their generation who felt most deeply the meaning of the present.

ABRAHAM LINCOLN [1]

THERE have been many painful crises since the impatient
vanity of South Carolina hurried ten prosperous Common-
wealths into a crime whose assured retribution was to leave them
either at the mercy of the nation they had wronged, or of the
anarchy they had summoned but could not control, when no
thoughtful American opened his morning paper without dread-
ing to find that he had no longer a country to love and honor.
Whatever the result of the convulsion whose first shocks were
beginning to be felt, there would still be enough square miles of
earth for elbow-room; but that ineffable sentiment made up
of memory and hope, of instinct and tradition, which swells
every man's heart and shapes his thought, though perhaps never
present to his consciousness, would be gone from it, leaving it
common earth and nothing more. Men might gather rich crops
from it, but that ideal harvest of priceless associations would be
reaped no longer; that fine virtue which sent up messages of
courage and security from every sod of it would have evaporated
beyond recall. We should be irrevocably cut off from our past,

---

[1] Written originally as a political article in anticipation of the presidential
election of 1864, and published in the *North American Review*, January,
1864, under the title of "The President's Policy." The "epilogue," so to
speak, in the present text was written shortly after Lincoln's assassination in
1865 and was added subsequently by Lowell to his original article. The
text of the latter, however, was never carefully revised by the author, so that
considerable confusion in tenses has resulted. This later enlarged version
Lowell entitled "Abraham Lincoln" and included in his *Political Essays*
(1888). The Lincoln article of 1864 drew a letter of appreciation from
the President to the publishers, and became a political tract of wide circulation. (H. E. Scudder, *J. R. Lowell*, II, 51n.)

and be forced to splice the ragged ends of our lives upon whatever new conditions chance might leave dangling for us.

We confess that we had our doubts at first whether the patriotism of our people were not too narrowly provincial to embrace the proportions of national peril. We felt an only too natural distrust of immense public meetings and enthusiastic cheers.

That a reaction should follow the holiday enthusiasm with which the war was entered on, that it should follow soon, and that the slackening of public spirit should be proportionate to the previous over-tension, might well be foreseen by all who had studied human nature or history. Men acting gregariously are always in extremes. As they are one moment capable of higher courage, so they are liable, the next, to baser depression, and it is often a matter of chance whether numbers shall multiply confidence or discouragement. Nor does deception lead more surely to distrust of men than self-deception to suspicion of principles. The only faith that wears well and holds its color in all weathers is that which is woven of conviction and set with the sharp mordant of experience. Enthusiasm is good material for the orator, but the statesman needs something more durable to work in,—must be able to rely on the deliberate reason and consequent firmness of the people, without which that presence of mind, no less essential in times of moral than of material peril, will be wanting at the critical moment. Would this fervor of the Free States hold out? Was it kindled by a just feeling of the value of constitutional liberty? Had it body enough to withstand the inevitable dampening of checks, reverses, delays? Had our population intelligence enough to comprehend that the choice was between order and anarchy, between the equilibrium of a government by law and the tussle of misrule by *pronunciamiento*? Could a war be maintained without the ordinary stimulus of hatred and plunder, and with the impersonal loyalty of principle? These were serious questions, and with no precedent to aid in answering them.

At the beginning of the war there was, indeed, occasion for the most anxious apprehension. A President known to be infected with the political heresies, and suspected of sympathy with the treason, of the Southern conspirators, had just surrendered the reins, we will not say of power, but of chaos, to a successor known only as the representative of a party whose leaders, with long training in opposition, had none in the conduct of affairs; an empty treasury was called on to supply resources beyond precedent in the history of finance; the trees were yet growing and the iron unmined with which a navy was to be built and armored; officers without discipline were to make a mob into an army; and, above all, the public opinion of Europe, echoed and reinforced with every vague hint and every specious argument of despondency by a powerful faction at home, was either contemptuously sceptical or actively hostile. It would be hard to over-estimate the force of this latter element of disintegration and discouragement among a people where every citizen at home, and every soldier in the field, is a reader of newspapers. The pedlers of rumor in the North were the most effective allies of the rebellion. A nation can be liable to no more insidious treachery than that of the telegraph, sending hourly its electric thrill of panic along the remotest nerves of the community, till the excited imagination makes every real danger loom heightened with its unreal double.

And even if we look only at more palpable difficulties, the problem to be solved by our civil war was so vast, both in its immediate relations and its future consequences; the conditions of its solution were so intricate and so greatly dependent on incalculable and uncontrollable contingencies; so many of the data, whether for hope or fear, were, from their novelty, incapable of arrangement under any of the categories of historical precedent, that there were moments of crisis when the firmest believer in the strength and sufficiency of the democratic theory of government might well hold his breath in vague apprehension of disaster. Our teachers of political philosophy, solemnly arguing from the precedent of some petty Grecian, Italian, or Flemish city, whose long periods of aristocracy were broken now and then by awkward parentheses of mob, had always taught us that democracies were incapable of the sentiment of loyalty, of concentrated and prolonged effort, of far-reaching conceptions; were absorbed in material interests; impatient of regular, and much more of exceptional restraint; had no natural nucleus of gravitation, nor any forces but centrifugal; were always on the verge of civil war, and slunk at last into the natural almshouse of bankrupt popular government, a military despotism. Here was indeed a dreary outlook for persons who knew democracy, not by rubbing shoulders with it lifelong, but merely from books, and America only by the report of some fellow-Briton, who, having eaten a bad dinner or lost a carpet-bag here, had written to the "Times" demanding redress, and drawing a mournful inference of democratic instability. Nor were men wanting among ourselves who had so steeped their brains in London literature as to mistake Cockneyism for European culture, and contempt of their country for cosmopolitan breadth of view, and who, owing all they had and all they were to democracy, thought it had an air of high-breeding to join in the shallow epicedium [2] that our bubble had burst.

But beside any disheartening influences which might affect the timid or the despondent, there were reasons enough of settled gravity against any over-confidence of hope. A war—which, whether we consider the expanse of the territory at stake, the hosts brought into the field, or the reach of the principles involved, may fairly be reckoned the most momentous of modern times—was to be waged by a people divided at home, unnerved by fifty years of peace, under a chief magistrate without experience and without reputation, whose every measure was sure to be cunningly hampered by a jealous and unscrupulous minority, and who, while dealing with unheard-of complications at home, must soothe a hostile neutrality abroad, waiting only a pretext to become war. All this was to be done without warning and without preparation, while at the same time a social revolution was to be accomplished in the political condition of four millions of people, by softening the prejudices, allaying the fears, and gradually obtaining the coöperation, of their unwilling liberators. Surely, if ever there were an occasion when the height-

[2] Funeral song.

ened imagination of the historian might see Destiny visibly intervening in human affairs, here was a knot worthy of her shears. Never, perhaps, was any system of government tried by so continuous and searching a strain as ours during the last three years; never has any shown itself stronger; and never could that strength be so directly traced to the virtue and intelligence of the people,—to that general enlightenment and prompt efficiency of public opinion possible only under the influence of a political framework like our own. We find it hard to understand how even a foreigner should be blind to the grandeur of the combat of ideas that has been going on here,—to the heroic energy, persistency, and self-reliance of a nation proving that it knows how much dearer greatness is than mere power; and we own that it is impossible for us to conceive the mental and moral condition of the American who does not feel his spirit braced and heightened by being even a spectator of such qualities and achievements. That a steady purpose and a definite aim have been given to the jarring forces which, at the beginning of the war, spent themselves in the discussion of schemes which could only become operative, if at all, after the war was over; that a popular excitement has been slowly intensified into an earnest national will; that a somewhat impracticable moral sentiment has been made the unconscious instrument of a practical moral end; that the treason of covert enemies, the jealousy of rivals, the unwise zeal of friends, have been made not only useless for mischief, but even useful for good; that the conscientious sensitiveness of England to the horrors of civil conflict has been prevented from complicating a domestic with a foreign war;—all these results, any one of which might suffice to prove greatness in a ruler, have been mainly due to the good sense, the good-humor, the sagacity, the large-mindedness, and the unselfish honesty of the unknown man whom a blind fortune, as it seemed, had lifted from the crowd to the most dangerous and difficult eminence of modern times. It is by presence of mind in untried emergencies that the native metal of a man is tested; it is by the sagacity to see, and the fearless honesty to admit, whatever of truth there may be in an adverse opinion, in order more convincingly to expose the fallacy that lurks behind it, that a reasoner at length gains for his mere statement of a fact the force of argument; it is by a wise forecast which allows hostile combinations to go so far as by the inevitable reaction to become elements of his own power, that a politician proves his genius for state-craft; and especially it is by so gently guiding public sentiment that he seems to follow it, by so yielding doubtful points that he can be firm without seeming obstinate in essential ones, and thus gain the advantages of compromise without the weakness of concession; by so instinctively comprehending the temper and prejudices of a people as to make them gradually conscious of the superior wisdom of his freedom from temper and prejudice,—it is by qualities such as these that a magistrate shows himself worthy to be chief in a commonwealth of freemen. And it is for qualities such as these that we firmly believe History will rank Mr. Lincoln among the most prudent of statesmen and the most successful of rulers. If we wish to appreciate him, we have only to conceive the inevitable chaos in which we should now be weltering, had a weak man or an unwise one been chosen in his stead.

"Bare is back," says the Norse proverb, "without brother behind it"; and this is, by analogy, true of an elective magistracy. The hereditary ruler in any critical emergency may reckon on the inexhaustible resources of *prestige,* of sentiment, of superstition, of dependent interest, while the new man must slowly and painfully create all these out of the unwilling material around him, by superiority of character, by patient singleness of purpose, by sagacious presentiment of popular tendencies and instinctive sympathy with the national character. Mr. Lincoln's task was one of peculiar and exceptional difficulty. Long habit had accustomed the American people to the notion of a party in power, and of a President as its creature and organ, while the more vital fact, that the executive for the time being represents the abstract idea of government as a permanent principle superior to all party and all private interest, had gradually become unfamiliar. They had so long seen the public policy more or less directed by views of party, and often even of personal advantage, as to be ready to suspect the motives of a chief magistrate compelled, for the first time in our history, to feel himself the head and hand of a great nation, and to act upon the fundamental maxim, laid down by all publicists, that the first duty of a government is to defend and maintain its own existence. Accordingly, a powerful weapon seemed to be put into the hands of the opposition by the necessity under which the administration found itself of applying this old truth to new relations. Nor were the opposition his only nor his most dangerous opponents.

The Republicans had carried the country upon an issue in which ethics were more directly and visibly mingled with politics than usual. Their leaders were trained to a method of oratory which relied for its effect rather on the moral sense than the understanding. Their arguments were drawn, not so much from experience as from general principles of right and wrong. When the war came, their system continued to be applicable and effective, for here again the reason of the people was to be reached and kindled through their sentiments. It was one of those periods of excitement, gathering, contagious, universal, which, while they last, exalt and clarify the minds of men, giving to the mere words *country, human rights, democracy,* a meaning and a force beyond that of sober and logical argument. They were convictions, maintained and defended by the supreme logic of passion. That penetrating fire ran in and roused those primary instincts that make their lair in the dens and caverns of the mind. What is called the great popular heart was awakened, that indefinable something which may be, according to circumstances, the highest reason or the most brutish unreason. But enthusiasm, once cold, can never be warmed over into anything better than cant,—and phrases, when once the inspiration that filled them with beneficent power has ebbed away, retain only that semblance of meaning which enables them to supplant reason in hasty minds. Among the lessons taught by the French Revolution there is none sadder or more striking than this, that you may make everything else out of the passions of men except a political system that will work, and that there is nothing so pitilessly and unconsciously cruel as sincerity formulated into dogma. It is always demoralizing to extend the domain of sentiment over questions where it has no legitimate jurisdiction; and perhaps the severest strain upon Mr. Lincoln was in resisting a tendency of his own supporters which chimed with his own private desires, while wholly opposed to his convictions of what would be wise policy.

The change which three years have brought about is too remarkable to be passed over without comment, too weighty in its lesson not to be laid to heart. Never did a President enter upon office with less means at his command, outside his own strength of heart and steadiness of understanding, for inspiring confidence in the people, and so winning it for himself, than Mr. Lincoln. All that was known of him was that he was a good stump-speaker, nominated for his *availability,*—that is, because he had no history,—and chosen by a party with whose more extreme opinions he was not in sympathy. It might well be feared that a man past fifty, against whom the ingenuity of hostile partisans could rake up no accusation, must be lacking in manliness of character, in decision of principle, in strength of will; that a man who was at best only the representative of a party, and who yet did not fairly represent even that, would fail of political, much more of popular, support. And certainly no one ever entered upon office with so few resources of power in the past, and so many materials of weakness in the present, as Mr. Lincoln. Even in that half of the Union which acknowledged him as President, there was a large and at that time dangerous minority, that hardly admitted his claim to the office, and even in the party that elected him there was also a large minority that suspected him of being secretly a communicant with the church of Laodicea.[3] All that he did was sure to be virulently attacked as ultra by one side; all that he left undone, to be stigmatized as proof of lukewarmness and backsliding by the other. Meanwhile, he was to carry on a truly colossal war by means of both; he was to disengage the country from diplomatic entanglements of unprecedented peril undisturbed by the

---

[3] The early Christian church of Laodicea in the province of Phrygia, Asia Minor, became notorious for its lukewarmness. See Revelations iii: 14–22.

help or the hindrance of either, and to win from the crowning dangers of his administration, in the confidence of the people, the means of his safety and their own. He has contrived to do it, and perhaps none of our Presidents since Washington has stood so firm in the confidence of the people as he does after three years of stormy administration.

Mr. Lincoln's policy was a tentative one, and rightly so. He laid down no programme which must compel him to be either inconsistent or unwise, no cast-iron theorem to which circumstances must be fitted as they rose, or else be useless to his ends. He seemed to have chosen Mazarin's motto, *Le temps et moi.*[4] The *moi*, to be sure, was not very prominent at first; but it has grown more and more so, till the world is beginning to be persuaded that it stands for a character of marked individuality and capacity for affairs. Time was his prime-minister, and, we began to think, at one period, his general-in-chief also. At first he was so slow that he tired out all those who see no evidence of progress but in blowing up the engine; then he was so fast, that he took the breath away from those who think there is no getting on safely while there is a spark of fire under the boilers. God is the only being who has time enough; but a prudent man, who knows how to seize occasion, can commonly make a shift to find as much as he needs. Mr. Lincoln, as it seems to us in reviewing his career, though we have sometimes in our impatience thought otherwise, has always waited, as a wise man should, till the right moment brought up all his reserves. *Semper nocuit differre paratis*[5] is a sound axiom, but the really efficacious man will also be sure to know when he is *not* ready, and be firm against all persuasion and reproach till he is.

One would be apt to think, from some of the criticisms made on Mr. Lincoln's course by those who mainly agree with him in principle, that the chief object of a statesman should be rather to proclaim his adhesion to certain doctrines, than to achieve their triumph by quietly accomplishing his ends. In our opin-

[4] The time and I. Cardinal Jules Mazarin (1602–61), a distinguished French statesman, prime minister of King Louis XIV.

[5] To postpone has always been injurious to those who are ready.

ion, there is no more unsafe politician than a conscientiously rigid *doctrinaire,* nothing more sure to end in disaster than a theoretic scheme of policy that admits of no pliability for contingencies. True, there is a popular image of an impossible He, in whose plastic hands the submissive destinies of mankind become as wax, and to whose commanding necessity the toughest facts yield with the graceful pliancy of fiction; but in real life we commonly find that the men who control circumstances, as it is called, are those who have learned to allow for the influence of their eddies, and have the nerve to turn them to account at the happy instant. Mr. Lincoln's perilous task has been to carry a rather shaky raft through the rapids, making fast the unrulier logs as he could snatch opportunity, and the country is to be congratulated that he did not think it his duty to run straight at all hazards, but cautiously to assure himself with his setting-pole where the main current was, and keep steadily to that. He is still in wild water, but we have faith that his skill and sureness of eye will bring him out right at last.

A curious, and, as we think, not inapt parallel might be drawn between Mr. Lincoln and one of the most striking figures in modern history,—Henry IV. of France.[6] The career of the latter may be more picturesque, as that of a daring captain always is; but in all its vicissitudes there is nothing more romantic than that sudden change, as by a rub of Aladdin's lamp, from the attorney's office in a country town of Illinois to the helm of a great nation in times like these. The analogy between the characters and circumstances of the two men is in many respects singularly close. Succeeding to a rebellion rather than a crown, Henry's chief material dependence was the Huguenot party, whose doctrines sat upon him with a looseness distasteful certainly, if not suspicious, to the more fanatical among them. King only in name over the greater part of France, and with his capital barred against him, it yet gradually became clear to the more far-seeing even of the Catholic party that he was the only centre of order and legitimate authority round which France

6 The founder of the Bourbon monarchy, he ruled from 1589 till his assassination in 1610.

could reorganize itself. While preachers who held the divine right of kings made the churches of Paris ring with declamations in favor of democracy rather than submit to the heretic dog of a Béarnois,[7]—much as our *soi-disant* [8] Democrats have lately been preaching the divine right of slavery, and denouncing the heresies of the Declaration of Independence,—Henry bore both parties in hand till he was convinced that only one course of action could possibly combine his own interests and those of France. Meanwhile the Protestants believed somewhat doubtfully that he was theirs, the Catholics hoped somewhat doubtfully that he would be theirs, and Henry himself turned aside remonstrance, advice, and curiosity alike with a jest or a proverb (if a little *high,* he liked them none the worse), joking continually as his manner was. We have seen Mr. Lincoln contemptuously compared to Sancho Panza by persons incapable of appreciating one of the deepest pieces of wisdom in the profoundest romance ever written; namely, that, while Don Quixote was incomparable in theoretic and ideal statesmanship, Sancho, with his stock of proverbs, the ready money of human experience, made the best possible practical governor. Henry IV. was as full of wise saws and modern instances as Mr. Lincoln, but beneath all this was the thoughtful, practical, humane, and thoroughly earnest man, around whom the fragments of France were to gather themselves till she took her place again as a planet of the first magnitude in the European system. In one respect Mr. Lincoln was more fortunate than Henry. However some may think him wanting in zeal, the most fanatical can find no taint of apostasy in any measure of his, nor can the most bitter charge him with being influenced by motives of personal interest. The leading distinction between the policies of the two is one of circumstances. Henry went over to the nation; Mr. Lincoln has steadily drawn the nation over to him. One left a united France; the other, we hope and believe, will

[7] Henry IV was so called because he was suzerain of the province of Béarn in the south of France near the Pyrenees. This province, which he inherited from the Bourbon line, did not become an integral part of the French kingdom until 1620.

[8] Self-styled.

leave a reunited America. We leave our readers to trace the
further points of difference and resemblance for themselves,
merely suggesting a general similarity which has often occurred
to us. One only point of melancholy interest we will allow
ourselves to touch upon. That Mr. Lincoln is not handsome
nor elegant, we learn from certain English tourists who would
consider similar revelations in regard to Queen Victoria as thoroughly American in their want of *bienséance*.[9] It is no concern
of ours, nor does it affect his fitness for the high place he so
worthily occupies; but he is certainly as fortunate as Henry in
the matter of good looks, if we may trust contemporary evidence.
Mr. Lincoln has also been reproached with Americanism by
some not unfriendly British critics; but, with all deference, we
cannot say that we like him any the worse for it, or see in it any
reason why he should govern Americans the less wisely.

People of more sensitive organizations may be shocked, but
we are glad that in this our true war of independence, which is
to free us forever from the Old World, we have had at the head
of our affairs a man whom America made, as God made Adam,
out of the very earth, unancestried, unprivileged, unknown, to
show us how much truth, how much magnanimity, and how
much state-craft await the call of opportunity in simple manhood
when it believes in the justice of God and the worth of man.
Conventionalities are all very well in their proper place, but they
shrivel at the touch of nature like stubble in the fire. The genius that sways a nation by its arbitrary will seems less august
to us than that which multiplies and reinforces itself in the instincts and convictions of an entire people. Autocracy may
have something in it more melodramatic than this, but falls far
short of it in human value and interest.

Experience would have bred in us a rooted distrust of improvised statesmanship, even if we did not believe politics to be a
science, which, if it cannot always command men of special
aptitude and great powers, at least demands the long and steady
application of the best powers of such men as it can command
to master even its first principles. It is curious, that, in a coun-

---

[9] Propriety.

try which boasts of its intelligence, the theory should be so generally held that the most complicated of human contrivances, and one which every day becomes more complicated, can be worked at sight by any man able to talk for an hour or two without stopping to think.

Mr. Lincoln is sometimes claimed as an example of a ready-made ruler. But no case could well be less in point; for, besides that he was a man of such fair-mindedness as is always the raw material of wisdom, he had in his profession a training precisely the opposite of that to which a partisan is subjected. His experience as a lawyer compelled him not only to see that there is a principle underlying every phenomenon in human affairs, but that there are always two sides to every question, both of which must be fully understood in order to understand either, and that it is of greater advantage to an advocate to appreciate the strength than the weakness of his antagonist's position. Nothing is more remarkable than the unerring tact with which, in his debate with Mr. Douglas, he went straight to the reason of the question; nor have we ever had a more striking lesson in political tactics than the fact, that, opposed to a man exceptionally adroit in using popular prejudice and bigotry to his purpose, exceptionally unscrupulous in appealing to those baser motives that turn a meeting of citizens into a mob of barbarians, he should yet have won his case before a jury of the people. Mr. Lincoln was as far as possible from an impromptu politician. His wisdom was made up of a knowledge of things as well as of men; his sagacity resulted from a clear perception and honest acknowledgment of difficulties, which enabled him to see that the only durable triumph of political opinion is based, not on any abstract right, but upon so much of justice, the highest attainable at any given moment in human affairs, as may be had in the balance of mutual concession. Doubtless he had an ideal, but it was the ideal of a practical statesman,—to aim at the best, and to take the next best, if he is lucky enough to get even that. His slow, but singularly masculine, intelligence taught him that precedent is only another name for embodied experience, and that it counts for even more in the guidance of communities of men than in that of the individual life. He was not a man who held it good public economy to pull down on the mere chance of rebuilding better. Mr. Lincoln's faith in God was qualified by a very well-founded distrust of the wisdom of man. Perhaps it was his want of self-confidence that more than anything else won him the unlimited confidence of the people, for they felt that there would be no need of retreat from any position he had deliberately taken. The cautious, but steady, advance of his policy during the war was like that of a Roman army. He left behind him a firm road on which public confidence could follow; he took America with him where he went; what he gained he occupied, and his advanced posts became colonies. The very homeliness of his genius was its distinction. His kingship was conspicuous by its workday homespun. Never was ruler so absolute as he, nor so little conscious of it; for he was the incarnate common-sense of the people. With all that tenderness of nature whose sweet sadness touched whoever saw him with something of its own pathos, there was no trace of sentimentalism in his speech or action. He seems to have had but one rule of conduct, always that of practical and successful politics, to let himself be guided by events, when they were sure to bring him out where he wished to go, though by what seemed to unpractical minds, which let go the possible to grasp at the desirable, a longer road.

Undoubtedly the highest function of statesmanship is by degrees to accommodate the conduct of communities to ethical laws, and to subordinate the conflicting self-interests of the day to higher and more permanent concerns. But it is on the understanding, and not on the sentiment, of a nation that all safe legislation must be based. Voltaire's saying, that "a consideration of petty circumstances is the tomb of great things," may be true of individual men, but it certainly is not true of governments. It is by a multitude of such considerations, each in itself trifling, but all together weighty, that the framers of policy can alone divine what is practicable and therefore wise. The imputation of inconsistency is one to which every sound politician and every honest thinker must sooner or later subject himself. The foolish and the dead alone never change their opinion.

The course of a great statesman resembles that of navigable rivers, avoiding immovable obstacles with noble bends of concession, seeking the broad levels of opinion on which men soonest settle and longest dwell, following and marking the almost imperceptible slopes of national tendency, yet always aiming at direct advances, always recruited from sources nearer heaven, and sometimes bursting open paths of progress and fruitful human commerce through what seem the eternal barriers of both. It is loyalty to great ends, even though forced to combine the small and opposing motives of selfish men to accomplish them; it is the anchored cling to solid principles of duty and action, which knows how to swing with the tide, but is never carried away by it,—that we demand in public men, and not obstinacy in prejudice, sameness of policy, or a conscientious persistency in what is impracticable. For the impracticable, however theoretically enticing, is always politically unwise, sound statesmanship being the application of that prudence to the public business which is the safest guide in that of private men.

No doubt slavery was the most delicate and embarrassing question with which Mr. Lincoln was called on to deal, and it was one which no man in his position, whatever his opinions, could evade; for, though he might withstand the clamor of partisans, he must sooner or later yield to the persistent importunacy of circumstances, which thrust the problem upon him at every turn and in every shape.

It has been brought against us as an accusation abroad, and repeated here by people who measure their country rather by what is thought of it than by what it is, that our war has not been distinctly and avowedly for the extinction of slavery, but a war rather for the preservation of our national power and greatness, in which the emancipation of the negro has been forced upon us by circumstances and accepted as a necessity. We are very far from denying this; nay, we admit that it is so far true that we were slow to renounce our constitutional obligations even toward those who had absolved us by their own act from the letter of our duty. We are speaking of the government which, legally installed for the whole country, was bound, so long as it was possible, not to overstep the limits of orderly prescription, and could not, without abnegating its own very nature, take the lead in making rebellion an excuse for revolution.   There were, no doubt, many ardent and sincere persons who seemed to think this as simple a thing to do as to lead off a Virginia reel.   They forgot what should be forgotten least of all in a system like ours, that the administration for the time being represents not only the majority which elects it, but the minority as well,—a minority in this case powerful, and so little ready for emancipation that it was opposed even to war.   Mr. Lincoln had not been chosen as general agent of an antislavery society, but President of the United States, to perform certain functions exactly defined by law.   Whatever were his wishes, it was no less duty than policy to mark out for himself a line of action that would not further distract the country, by raising before their time questions which plainly would soon enough compel attention, and for which every day was making the answer more easy.

Meanwhile he must solve the riddle of this new Sphinx, or be devoured.   Though Mr. Lincoln's policy in this critical affair has not been such as to satisfy those who demand an heroic treatment for even the most trifling occasion, and who will not cut their coat according to their cloth, unless they can borrow the scissors of Atropos,[10] it has been at least not unworthy of the long-headed king of Ithaca.[11]   Mr. Lincoln had the choice of Bassanio[12] offered him.   Which of the three caskets held the prize that was to redeem the fortunes of the country?   There was the golden one whose showy speciousness might have tempted a vain man; the silver of compromise, which might have decided the choice of a merely acute one; and the leaden,—

[10] Atropos, one of the three Fates in Greek myth, was the fate that can- not be avoided, and was sometimes represented as a maiden with a cutting instrument in her hand.

[11] Odysseus, the cunning and wise warrior among the Greeks in their war against Troy.   He it was who suggested the stratagem of the wooden horse, by which the Greeks were enabled to get inside Troy and invest the city.

[12] Bassanio, the suitor of Portia in *The Merchant of Venice*, was shown three caskets, of gold, silver, and lead respectively, in one of which reposed a portrait of Portia.   Choice of the casket with the portrait therein would win him the lady's hand.   See *The Merchant of Venice*, III, ii.

dull and homely looking, as prudence always is,—yet with something about it sure to attract the eye of practical wisdom. Mr. Lincoln dallied with his decision perhaps longer than seemed needful to those on whom its awful responsibility was not to rest, but when he made it, it was worthy of his cautious but sure-footed understanding. The moral of the Sphinx-riddle,[13] and it is a deep one, lies in the childish simplicity of the solution. Those who fail in guessing it, fail because they are over-ingenious, and cast about for an answer that shall suit their own notion of the gravity of the occasion and of their own dignity, rather than the occasion itself.

In a matter which must be finally settled by public opinion, and in regard to which the ferment of prejudice and passion on both sides has not yet subsided to that equilibrium of compromise from which alone a sound public opinion can result, it is proper enough for the private citizen to press his own convictions with all possible force of argument and persuasion; but the popular magistrate, whose judgment must become action, and whose action involves the whole country, is bound to wait till the sentiment of the people is so far advanced toward his own point of view, that what he does shall find support in it, instead of merely confusing it with new elements of division. It was not unnatural that men earnestly devoted to the saving of their country, and profoundly convinced that slavery was its only real enemy, should demand a decided policy round which all patriots might rally,—and this might have been the wisest course for an absolute ruler. But in the then unsettled state of the public mind, with a large party decrying even resistance to the slaveholders' rebellion as not only unwise, but even unlawful; with a majority, perhaps, even of the would-be loyal so long accustomed to regard the Constitution as a deed of gift conveying to the South their

---

[13] The Sphinx, a monster with the body of a lion and with the upper part of a woman, crouched on a rock near Thebes and killed all travelers who came that way, because they could not solve the riddle which it proposed, namely, "A being with four feet has two feet and three feet, and only one voice; but its feet vary, and when it has most, it is weakest." Oedipus, son of Laius, the king of Thebes, finally gave the correct answer, "Man," and thus put an end to the scourge of the Sphinx.

own judgment as to policy and instinct as to right, that they were in doubt at first whether their loyalty were due to the country or to slavery; and with a respectable body of honest and influential men who still believed in the possibility of conciliation, —Mr. Lincoln judged wisely, that, in laying down a policy in deference to one party, he should be giving to the other the very fulcrum for which their disloyalty had been waiting.

It behooved a clear-headed man in his position not to yield so far to an honest indignation against the brokers of treason in the North as to lose sight of the materials for misleading which were their stock in trade, and to forget that it is not the falsehood of sophistry which is to be feared, but the grain of truth mingled with it to make it specious,—that it is not the knavery of the leaders so much as the honesty of the followers they may seduce, that gives them power for evil. It was especially his duty to do nothing which might help the people to forget the true cause of the war in fruitless disputes about its inevitable consequences.

The doctrine of state rights can be so handled by an adroit demagogue as easily to confound the distinction between liberty and lawlessness in the minds of ignorant persons, accustomed always to be influenced by the sound of certain words, rather than to reflect upon the principles which give them meaning. For, though Secession involves the manifest absurdity of denying to a State the right of making war against any foreign power while permitting it against the United States; though it supposes a compact of mutual concessions and guaranties among States without any arbiter in case of dissension; though it contradicts common-sense in assuming that the men who framed our government did not know what they meant when they substituted Union for Confederation; though it falsifies history, which shows that the main opposition to the adoption of the Constitution was based on the argument that it did not allow that independence in the several States which alone would justify them in seceding; —yet, as slavery was universally admitted to be a reserved right, an inference could be drawn from any direct attack upon it (though only in self-defence) to a natural right of resistance, logical enough to satisfy minds untrained to detect fallacy, as the majority of men always are, and now too much disturbed by the disorder of the times to consider that the order of events had any legitimate bearing on the argument. Though Mr. Lincoln was too sagacious to give the Northern allies of the Rebels the occasion they desired and even strove to provoke, yet from the beginning of the war the most persistent efforts have been made to confuse the public mind as to its origin and motives, and to drag the people of the loyal States down from the national position they had instinctively taken to the old level of party squabbles and antipathies. The wholly unprovoked rebellion of an oligarchy proclaiming negro slavery the corner-stone of free institutions, and in the first flush of over-hasty confidence venturing to parade the logical sequence of their leading dogma, "that slavery is right in principle, and has nothing to do with difference of complexion," has been represented as a legitimate and gallant attempt to maintain the true principles of democracy. The rightful endeavor of an established government, the least onerous that ever existed, to defend itself against a treacherous attack on its very existence, has been cunningly made to seem the wicked effort of a fanatical clique to force its doctrines on an oppressed population.

Even so long ago as when Mr. Lincoln, not yet convinced of the danger and magnitude of the crisis, was endeavoring to persuade himself of Union majorities at the South, and to carry on a war that was half peace in the hope of a peace that would have been all war,—while he was still enforcing the Fugitive Slave Law, under some theory that Secession, however it might absolve States from their obligations, could not escheat them of their claims under the Constitution, and that slaveholders in rebellion had alone among mortals the privilege of having their cake and eating it at the same time,—the enemies of free government were striving to persuade the people that the war was an Abolition crusade. To rebel without reason was proclaimed as one of the rights of man, while it was carefully kept out of sight that to suppress rebellion is the first duty of government. All the evils that have come upon the country have been attributed to the Abolitionists, though it is hard to see how any party can become permanently powerful except in one of two ways,—either by the greater truth of its principles, or the extravagance of the party opposed to it. To fancy the ship of state, riding safe at her constitutional moorings, suddenly engulfed by a huge kraken [14] of Abolitionism, rising from unknown depths and grasping it with slimy tentacles, is to look at the natural history of the matter with the eyes of Pontoppidan.[15] To believe that the leaders in the Southern treason feared any danger from Abolitionism would be to deny them ordinary intelligence, though there can be little doubt that they made use of it to stir the passions and excite the fears of their deluded accomplices. They rebelled, not because they thought slavery weak, but because they believed it strong enough, not to overthrow the government, but to get possession of it; for it becomes daily clearer that they used rebellion only as a means of revolution, and if they got revolution, though not in the shape they looked for, is the American people to save them from its consequences at the cost of its own existence? The election of Mr. Lincoln, which it was clearly in their power to prevent had they wished, was the occasion merely, and not the cause, of their revolt. Abolitionism, till within a year or two, was the despised heresy of a few earnest persons, without political weight enough to carry the election of a parish constable; and their cardinal principle was disunion, because they were convinced that within the Union the position of slavery was impregnable. In spite of the proverb, great effects do not follow from small causes,—that is, disproportionately small,—but from adequate causes acting under certain required conditions. To contrast the size of the oak with that of the parent acorn, as if the poor seed had paid all costs from its slender strongbox, may serve for a child's wonder; but the real miracle lies in that divine league which bound all the forces of nature to the service of the tiny germ in fulfilling its destiny. Everything has been at work for the past ten years in the cause of anti-

---

[14] A fabulous Scandinavian sea-monster.

[15] Erik Pontoppidan (1698–1764), Danish author and bishop of Bergen, related remarkable tales of the "kraken" in his *Natural History of Norway* (Eng. trans., 1755).

slavery, but Garrison [16] and Phillips [17] have been far less successful propagandists than the slaveholders themselves, with the
constantly growing arrogance of their pretensions and encroachments. They have forced the question upon the attention of
every voter in the Free States, by defiantly putting freedom and
democracy on the defensive. But, even after the Kansas out-
rages, there was no wide-spread desire on the part of the North
to commit aggressions, though there was a growing determination to resist them. The popular unanimity in favor of the war
three years ago was but in small measure the result of anti-slavery
sentiment, far less of any zeal for abolition. But every month
of the war, every movement of the allies of slavery in the Free
States, has been making Abolitionists by the thousand. The
masses of any people, however intelligent, are very little moved
by abstract principles of humanity and justice, until those principles are interpreted for them by the stinging commentary of
some infringement upon their own rights, and then their instincts and passions, once aroused, do indeed derive an incalculable reinforcement of impulse and intensity from those higher
ideas, those sublime traditions, which have no motive political
force till they are allied with a sense of immediate personal
wrong or imminent peril. Then at last the stars in their courses
begin to fight against Sisera.[18] Had any one doubted before
that the rights of human nature are unitary, that oppression is
of one hue the world over, no matter what the color of the oppressed,—had any one failed to see what the real essence of the
contest was,—the efforts of the advocates of slavery among ourselves to throw discredit upon the fundamental axioms of the
Declaration of Independence and the radical doctrines of Christianity could not fail to sharpen his eyes.

[16] William Lloyd Garrison (1804–79), newspaper editor and leader of
the Abolitionists.

[17] Wendell Phillips (1811–84), eminent American orator and participant
in many reform movements.

[18] Sisera, captain of the army of Jabin, king of Canaan, was defeated by
the Israelites in a great battle by the river Kishon. Deborah, a prophetess
of Israel, sang a song in honor of the victory. In her song occurs the
famous line, "The stars in their courses fought against Sisera." See
Judges v: 20.

While every day was bringing the people nearer to the conclusion which all thinking men saw to be inevitable from the beginning, it was wise in Mr. Lincoln to leave the shaping of his policy to events. In this country, where the rough and ready understanding of the people is sure at last to be the controlling power, a profound common-sense is the best genius for statesmanship. Hitherto the wisdom of the President's measures has been justified by the fact that they have always resulted in more firmly uniting public opinion. One of the things particularly admirable in the public utterances of President Lincoln is a certain tone of familiar dignity, which, while it is perhaps the most difficult attainment of mere style, is also no doubtful indication of personal character. There must be something essentially noble in an elective ruler who can descend to the level of confidential ease without forfeiting respect, something very manly in one who can break through the etiquette of his conventional rank and trust himself to the reason and intelligence of those who have elected him. No higher compliment was ever paid to a nation than the simple confidence, the fireside plainness, with which Mr. Lincoln always addresses himself to the reason of the American people. This was, indeed, a true democrat, who grounded himself on the assumption that a democracy can think. "Come, let us reason together about this matter," has been the tone of all his addresses to the people; and accordingly we have never had a chief magistrate who so won to himself the love and at the same time the judgment of his countrymen. To us, that simple confidence of his in the right-mindedness of his fellow-men is very touching, and its success is as strong an argument as we have ever seen in favor of the theory that men can govern themselves. He never appeals to any vulgar sentiment, he never alludes to the humbleness of his origin; it probably never occurred to him, indeed, that there was anything higher to start from than manhood; and he put himself on a level with those he addressed, not by going down to them, but only by taking it for granted that they had brains and would come up to a common ground of reason. In an article lately printed in "The

Nation," Mr. Bayard Taylor [19] mentions the striking fact, that in the foulest dens of the Five Points [20] he found the portrait of Lincoln. The wretched population that makes its hive there threw all its votes and more against him, and yet paid this instinctive tribute to the sweet humanity of his nature. Their ignorance sold its vote and took its money, but all that was left of manhood in them recognized its saint and martyr.

Mr. Lincoln is not in the habit of saying, "This is *my* opinion, or *my* theory," but, "This is the conclusion to which, in my judgment, the time has come, and to which, accordingly, the sooner we come the better for us." His policy has been the policy of public opinion based on adequate discussion and on a timely recognition of the influence of passing events in shaping the features of events to come.

One secret of Mr. Lincoln's remarkable success in captivating the popular mind is undoubtedly an unconsciousness of self which enables him, though under the necessity of constantly using the capital *I,* to do it without any suggestion of egotism. There is no single vowel which men's mouths can pronounce with such difference of effect. That which one shall hide away, as it were, behind the substance of his discourse, or, if he bring it to the front, shall use merely to give an agreeable accent of individuality to what he says, another shall make an offensive challenge to the self-satisfaction of all his hearers, and an unwarranted intrusion upon each man's sense of personal importance, irritating every pore of his vanity, like a dry northeast wind, to a goose-flesh of opposition and hostility. Mr. Lincoln has never studied Quintilian; [21] but he has, in the earnest simplicity and unaffected Americanism of his own character, one art of oratory worth all the rest. He forgets himself so entirely in his object

---

[19] American traveler, journalist, and man of letters (1825–78).

[20] A district of lower Manhattan, New York City, which in the nineteenth century was a notorious resort for "hard cases" and criminals.

[21] Marcus Fabius Quintilianus (A.D. 35–c. 97), the leading Roman rhetorician, whose famous work, *De Institutione Oratoria,* a complete compendium of Latin rhetoric in twelve books, was studied commonly as a basic text in oratory until within the last century.

as to give his *I* the sympathetic and persuasive effect of *We* with the great body of his countrymen. Homely, dispassionate, showing all the rough-edged process of his thought as it goes along, yet arriving at his conclusions with an honest kind of every-day logic, he is so eminently our representative man, that, when he speaks, it seems as if the people were listening to their own thinking aloud. The dignity of his thought owes nothing to any ceremonial garb of words, but to the manly movement that comes of settled purpose and an energy of reason that knows not what rhetoric means. There has been nothing of Cleon,[22] still less of Strepsiades [23] striving to underbid him in demagogism, to be found in the public utterances of Mr. Lincoln. He has always addressed the intelligence of men, never their prejudice, their passion, or their ignorance.

On the day of his death, this simple Western attorney, who according to one party was a vulgar joker, and whom the *doctrinaires* [24] among his own supporters accused of wanting every element of statesmanship, was the most absolute ruler in Christendom, and this solely by the hold his good-humored sagacity had laid on the hearts and understandings of his countrymen. Nor was this all, for it appeared that he had drawn the great majority, not only of his fellow-citizens, but of mankind also, to his side. So strong and so persuasive is honest manliness without a single quality of romance or unreal sentiment to help it! A civilian during times of the most captivating military achievement, awkward, with no skill in the lower technicalities of manners, he left behind him a fame beyond that of any conqueror, the memory of a grace higher than that of outward person, and

---

[22] An Athenian demagogue (d. 422 B.C.), who championed the continuance of the Peloponnesian War, and was unmercifully lampooned therefor by the playwright Aristophanes in *The Knights* (424 B.C.) and *The Wasps* (422 B.C.).

[23] One of the leading characters in Aristophanes' comedy *The Clouds* (423 B.C.). He is a wealthy country gentleman, who, involved in debt by the extravagance of his son, comes to Athens and seeks to learn the new art of argument as taught by Socrates at the thinking shop of the Sophists. Thus, by skill in humbug, he thinks to turn the tables on his creditors.

[24] Dogmatic theorists.

of a gentlemanliness deeper than mere breeding.   Never before
that startled April morning did such multitudes of men shed
tears for the death of one they had never seen, as if with him a
friendly presence had been taken away from their lives, leaving
them colder and darker.   Never was funeral panegyric so eloquent as the silent look of sympathy which strangers exchanged
when they met on that day.   Their common manhood had lost
a kinsman.

THOREAU [1]

WHAT contemporary, if he was in the fighting period of his
life, (since Nature sets limits about her conscription for spiritual
fields, as the state does in physical warfare,) will ever forget
what was somewhat vaguely called the "Transcendental Movement" of thirty years ago?   Apparently set astir by Carlyle's
essays on the "Signs of the Times," and on "History," the final
and more immediate impulse seemed to be given by "Sartor
Resartus." [2]   At least the republication in Boston of that wonderful Abraham à Sancta Clara sermon on Falstaff's text of the
miserable forked radish [3] gave the signal for a sudden men-

---

[1] Written originally as a review of the volume of Thoreau's letters which
Ralph Waldo Emerson (1803–82) edited and published in 1865 under the
title, *Letters to Various Persons.*   Lowell's review was entitled "Thoreau's
Letters" when published in the *North American Review,* October, 1865.
The essay was somewhat revised for inclusion in *My Study Windows* (1871),
and the title changed to "Thoreau."   Lowell had earlier ventured an estimate of Thoreau, more largely concerned with stylistic matters, in a review
of *A Week on the Concord and Merrimack Rivers* for the *Massachusetts
Quarterly Review,* December, 1849.   Therein occurs his oft-quoted comment on Thoreau's style—"the language has an antique purity like wine
grown colorless with age."

[2] For Carlyle see note on p. 16.   *Signs of the Times* appeared in the
Edinburgh Review, June, 1829; *Thoughts on History* in *Fraser's Magazine,*
November, 1830.   *Sartor Resartus,* after appearing in *Fraser's Magazine,*
1833–34, was republished as a book in 1836 at Boston through the interest
of Emerson, who wrote a preface.

[3] Abraham à Sancta Clara (1644–1709), Augustinian friar and later court
preacher in Vienna, was noted for his eloquent sermons.   Falstaff opens
a long diatribe on Justice Shallow by saying: "When he was naked, he was,
for all the world, like a forked radish, with a head fantastically carved upon
it with a knife."   (2 *Henry IV,* III, ii, 334.   Globe ed., 1891.)

tal and moral mutiny. *Ecce nunc tempus acceptabile!* [4] was
shouted on all hands with every variety of emphasis, and by
voices of every conceivable pitch, representing the three sexes of
men, women, and Lady Mary Wortley Montagues.[5] The nameless eagle of the tree Ygdrasil [6] was about to sit at last, and wild-
eyed enthusiasts rushed from all sides, each eager to thrust under
the mystic bird that chalk egg from which the new and fairer
Creation was to be hatched in due time. *Redeunt Saturnia
regna,*[7]—so far was certain, though in what shape, or by what
methods, was still a matter of debate. Every possible form of
intellectual and physical dyspepsia brought forth its gospel.
Bran had its prophets, and the presartorial simplicity of Adam
its martyrs, tailored impromptu from the tar-pot by incensed
neighbors, and sent forth to illustrate the "feathered Mercury,"
as defined by Webster and Worcester. Plainness of speech was
carried to a pitch that would have taken away the breath of
George Fox; [8] and even swearing had its evangelists, who answered a simple inquiry after their health with an elaborate
ingenuity of imprecation that might have been honorably mentioned by Marlborough [9] in general orders. Everybody had a
mission (with a capital M) to attend to everybody-else's business.
No brain but had its private maggot, which must have found
pitiably short commons sometimes. Not a few impecunious
zealots abjured the use of money (unless earned by other people), professing to live on the internal revenues of the spirit.
Some had an assurance of instant millennium so soon as hooks
and eyes should be substituted for buttons. Communities were
established where everything was to be common but common-
sense. Men renounced their old gods, and hesitated only

---

[4] Behold, now is the acceptable time.

[5] Lady Mary Wortley Montagu(e) (1689–1762), a colorful lady of wide
reputation in the eighteenth century, was one of the earliest English femi-
nists.

[6] A huge tree which, according to Norse myth, supports the universe, and
in the top of which sits a wise eagle.

[7] The Golden Age (lit., reign of Saturn) returns.

[8] George Fox (1624–91), the founder of the Society of Friends.

[9] John Churchill, Duke of Marlborough (1650–1722), English general
famous for his victory at Blenheim (1704) over the French.

whether to bestow their furloughed allegiance on Thor or Budh. Conventions were held for every hitherto inconceivable purpose. The belated gift of tongues, as among the Fifth Monarchy men,[10] spread like a contagion, rendering its victims incomprehensible to all Christian men; whether equally so to the most distant possible heathen or not was unexperimented, though many would have subscribed liberally that a fair trial might be made. It was the pentecost of Shinar.[11] The day of utterances reproduced the day of rebuses and anagrams, and there was nothing so simple that uncial letters [12] and the style of Diphilus the Labyrinth [13] could not turn it into a riddle. Many foreign revolutionists out of work added to the general misunderstanding their contribution of broken English in every most ingenious form of fracture. All stood ready at a moment's notice to reform everything but themselves. The general motto was:—

> "And we'll *talk* with them, too,
> And take upon's the mystery of things
> As if we were God's spies." [14]

Nature is always kind enough to give even her clouds a humorous lining. I have barely hinted at the comic side of the affair, for the material was endless. This was the whistle and trailing fuse of the shell, but there was a very solid and serious kernel, full of the most deadly explosiveness. Thoughtful men divined it, but the generality suspected nothing. The word

---

[10] A fanatical sect in England during the Commonwealth. The adherents believed that a fifth monarchy under Christ's rule—to continue for 1000 years—was near at hand and that they should assist its coming by the use of force.

[11] I.e., it was a field day of confused and unintelligible speechmaking.— On the first Day of Pentecost which the early Christians observed at Jerusalem the apostles suddenly and involuntarily began to preach in various foreign languages. (See Acts ii: 1–13.) The Tower of Babel, famous for the confusion of tongues which resulted from its erection, was located in Shinar, i.e., Babylonia. (See Genesis xi: 2–9.)

[12] The large, rounded style of lettering used in classical manuscripts up to the tenth century A.D.

[13] Diphilus of Sinope (342–291 B.C.), a famous author of the Greek New Comedy, was noted for his simple and natural dialogue. Hence Lowell's appellation here is a bit of ironic witticism.

[14] *King Lear*, V, iii, 14–16.

"transcendental" then was the maid of all work for those who could not think, as "Pre-Raphaelite" has been more recently for people of the same limited housekeeping. The truth is, that there was a much nearer metaphysical relation and a much more distant æsthetic and literary relation between Carlyle and the Apostles of the Newness, as they were called in New England, than has commonly been supposed. Both represented the reaction and revolt against *Philisterei*,[15] a renewal of the old battle begun in modern times by Erasmus and Reuchlin,[16] and continued by Lessing, Goethe,[17] and, in a far narrower sense, by Heine [18] in Germany, and of which Fielding, Sterne, and Wordsworth [19] in different ways have been the leaders in England. It was simply a struggle for fresh air, in which, if the windows could not be opened, there was danger that panes would be broken, though painted with images of saints and martyrs. Light, colored by these reverend effigies, was none the more respirable for being picturesque. There is only one thing better than tradition, and that is the original and eternal life out of which all tradition takes its rise. It was this life which the reformers demanded, with more or less clearness of consciousness and expression, life in politics, life in literature, life in religion. Of what use to import a gospel from Judæa, if we leave behind

---

[15] Philistinism, i.e., unintelligence in mind combined with coarseness in feeling.

[16] Desiderius Erasmus (1467–1536), outstanding Dutch scholar of the Renaissance.

Johann Reuchlin (1455–1522), eminent German scholar of the Renaissance, a leader in the revival of classical learning and a staunch defender of Hebraic culture.

[17] Gotthold Ephraim Lessing (1729–81), the first great German dramatist and critic.

Johann Wolfgang von Goethe (1749–1832), Germany's greatest man of letters.

[18] Heinrich Heine (1799–1856), a leading German poet of the Romantic Movement.

[19] Henry Fielding (1707–54), English playwright and novelist, whose masterpiece is *Tom Jones* (1749), a picaresque narrative of contemporary life.

Laurence Sterne (1713–68), English novelist best known for his *Tristram Shandy* (1760–67), a work of eccentric humor and unique literary method.

William Wordsworth (1770–1850), dean of the English Romantic poets.

the soul that made it possible, the God who keeps it forever real and present? Surely Abana and Pharpar *are* better than Jordan,[20] if a living faith be mixed with those waters and none with these.

Scotch Presbyterianism as a motive of spiritual progress was dead; New England Puritanism was in like manner dead; in other words, Protestantism had made its fortune and no longer protested; but till Carlyle spoke out in the Old World and Emerson in the New, no one had dared to proclaim, *Le roi est mort: vive le roi!* [21] The meaning of which proclamation was essentially this: the vital spirit has long since departed out of this form once so kingly, and the great seal has been in commission long enough; but meanwhile the soul of man, from which all power emanates and to which it reverts, still survives in undiminished royalty; God still survives, little as you gentlemen of the Commission seem to be aware of it,—nay, will possibly outlive the whole of you, incredible as it may appear. The truth is, that both Scotch Presbyterianism and New England Puritanism made their new avatar in Carlyle and Emerson, the heralds of their formal decease, and the tendency of the one toward Authority and of the other toward Independency might have been prophesied by whoever had studied history. The necessity was not so much in the men as in the principles they represented and the traditions which overruled them. The Puritanism of the past found its unwilling poet in Hawthorne, the rarest creative imagination of the century, the rarest in some ideal respects since Shakespeare; but the Puritanism that cannot die, the Puritanism that made New England what it is, and is destined to make America what it should be, found its voice in Emerson. Though holding himself aloof from all active partnership in movements of reform, he has been a sleeping partner who has supplied a great part of their capital.

The artistic range of Emerson is narrow, as every well-read

---

[20] When Elisha told Naaman, the Syrian captain, to wash in the Jordan seven times and thus be healed of his leprosy, Naaman retorted peevishly: "Are not Abana and Pharpar, rivers of Damascus, better than all the waters of Israel?" (II Kings v: 12.)

[21] The king is dead: long live the king!

critic must feel at once; and so is that of Æschylus, so is that of Dante, so is that of Montaigne, so is that of Schiller, so is that of nearly everyone except Shakespeare; but there is a gauge of height no less than of breadth, of individuality as well as of comprehensiveness, and, above all, there is the standard of genetic power, the test of the masculine as distinguished from the receptive minds. There are staminate plants in literature, that make no fine show of fruit, but without whose pollen, quintessence of fructifying gold, the garden had been barren. Emerson's mind is emphatically one of these, and there is no man to whom our æsthetic culture owes so much. The Puritan revolt had made us ecclesiastically and the Revolution politically independent, but we were still socially and intellectually moored to English thought, till Emerson cut the cable and gave us a chance at the dangers and the glories of blue water. No man young enough to have felt it can forget or cease to be grateful for the mental and moral *nudge* which he received from the writings of his high-minded and brave-spirited countryman. That we agree with him, or that he always agrees with himself, is aside from the question; but that he arouses in us something that we are the better for having awakened, whether that something be of opposition or assent, that he speaks always to what is highest and least selfish in us, few Americans of the generation younger than his own would be disposed to deny. His oration before the Phi Beta Kappa Society at Cambridge, some thirty years ago, was an event without any former parallel in our literary annals, a scene to be always treasured in the memory for its picturesqueness and its inspiration. What crowded and breathless aisles, what windows clustering with eager heads, what enthusiasm of approval, what grim silence of foregone dissent! It was our Yankee version of a lecture by Abelard,[22] our Harvard parallel to the last public appearances of Schelling.[23]

I said that the Transcendental Movement was the protestant

---

[22] A great scholar and teacher (1079–1142) in medieval Paris.

[23] Friedrich Wilhelm Joseph von Schelling (1775–1854), distinguished German metaphysician, who closed his public career by lecturing on philosophy at the University of Berlin, 1841–46.

spirit of Puritanism seeking a new outlet and an escape from
forms and creeds which compressed rather than expressed it.
In its motives, its preaching, and its results, it differed radically
from the doctrine of Carlyle. The Scotchman, with all his genius, and his humor gigantesque as that of Rabelais,[24] has grown
shriller and shriller with years, degenerating sometimes into a
common scold, and emptying very unsavory vials of wrath on
the head of the sturdy British Socrates of worldly common-
sense. The teaching of Emerson tended much more exclusively
to self-culture and the independent development of the individual man. It seemed to many almost Pythagorean [25] in its
voluntary seclusion from commonwealth affairs. Both Carlyle
and Emerson were disciples of Goethe, but Emerson in a far
truer sense; and while the one, from his bias toward the eccentric, has degenerated more and more into mannerism, the other
has clarified steadily toward perfection of style,—exquisite fine-
ness of material, unobtrusive lowness of tone and simplicity of
fashion, the most high-bred garb of expression. Whatever may
be said of his thought, nothing can be finer than the delicious
limpidness of his phrase. If it was ever questionable whether
democracy could develop a gentleman, the problem has been
affirmatively solved at last. Carlyle, in his cynicism and his
admiration of force in and for itself, has become at last positively
inhuman; Emerson, reverencing strength, seeking the highest
outcome of the individual, has found that society and politics
are also main elements in the attainment of the desired end, and
has drawn steadily manward and worldward. The two men
represent respectively those grand personifications in the drama
of Æschylus, Βία and Κράτος.[26]

Among the pistillate plants kindled to fruitage by the Emer-
sonian pollen, Thoreau is thus far the most remarkable; and it

---

[24] François Rabelais (1494?–1553), outstanding French satirist, whose
fame rests on two novels of racy humor and grotesque plot, *Pantagruel*
(1533) and *Gargantua* (1535).

[25] Pythagoras was a Greek mathematician and philosopher of the sixth
century B.C., who finally settled in southern Italy and inspired the forma-
tion of clubs devoted to philosophical and religious contemplation.

[26] Force and Strength, two characters in *Prometheus Bound*.

is something eminently fitting that his posthumous works should be offered us by Emerson, for they are strawberries from his own garden. A singular mixture of varieties, indeed, there is;—alpine, some of them, with the flavor of rare mountain air; others wood, tasting of sunny roadside banks or shy openings in the forest; and not a few seedlings swollen hugely by culture, but lacking the fine natural aroma of the more modest kinds. Strange books these are of his, and interesting in many ways,—instructive chiefly as showing how considerable a crop may be raised on a comparatively narrow close of mind, and how much a man may make of his life if he will assiduously follow it, though perhaps never truly finding it at last.

I have just been renewing my recollection of Mr. Thoreau's writings, and have read through his six volumes in the order of their production. I shall try to give an adequate report of their impression upon me both as critic and as mere reader. He seems to me to have been a man with so high a conceit of himself that he accepted without questioning, and insisted on our accepting, his defects and weaknesses of character as virtues and powers peculiar to himself. Was he indolent, he finds none of the activities which attract or employ the rest of mankind worthy of him. Was he wanting in the qualities that make success, it is success that is contemptible, and not himself that lacks persistency and purpose. Was he poor, money was an unmixed evil. Did his life seem a selfish one, he condemns doing good as one of the weakest of superstitions. To be of use was with him the most killing bait of the wily tempter Uselessness. He had no faculty of generalization from outside of himself, or at least no experience which would supply the material of such, and he makes his own whim the law, his own range the horizon of the universe. He condemns a world, the hollowness of whose satisfactions he had never had the means of testing, and we recognize Apemantus behind the mask of Timon.[27] He had little

---

[27] Apemantus is the churlish philosopher and cynic in Shakespeare's *Timon of Athens,* who out of privation in early life has come to despise mankind. Timon, though a man of high place and plentiful means, is by temperament essentially a cynic and a misanthrope also, hence, beneath his royal mask, akin to Apemantus.

active imagination; of the receptive he had much. His appreciation is of the highest quality; his critical power, from want of
continuity of mind, very limited and inadequate. He somewhere cites a simile from Ossian,[28] as an example of the superiority of the old poetry to the new, though, even were the his-
toric evidence less convincing, the sentimental melancholy of
those poems should be conclusive of their modernness. He had
none of the artistic mastery which controls a great work to the
serene balance of completeness, but exquisite mechanical skill in
the shaping of sentences and paragraphs, or (more rarely) short
bits of verse for the expression of a detached thought, sentiment,
or image. His works give one the feeling of a sky full of stars,—
something impressive and exhilarating certainly, something high
overhead and freckled thickly with spots of isolated brightness;
but whether these have any mutual relation with each other, or
have any concern with our mundane matters, is for the most
part matter of conjecture,—astrology as yet, and not astronomy.

It is curious, considering what Thoreau afterwards became,
that he was not by nature an observer. He only saw the things
he looked for, and was less poet than naturalist. Till he built
his Walden shanty, he did not know that the hickory grew in
Concord. Till he went to Maine, he had never seen phosphorescent wood, a phenomenon early familiar to most country boys.
At forty he speaks of the seeding of the pine as a new discovery,
though one should have thought that its gold dust of blowing
pollen might have earlier drawn his eye. Neither his attention
nor his genius was of the spontaneous kind. He discovered
nothing. He thought everything a discovery of his own, from
moonlight to the planting of acorns and nuts by squirrels. This
is a defect in his character, but one of his chief charms as a writer.
Everything grows fresh under his hand. He delved in his mind

---

[28] A legendary Celtic hero, son of Fingal. James MacPherson (1736–96),
a Scottish antiquarian and author, claimed to have discovered some old
manuscripts containing poems by Ossian in Gaelic, and proceeded to pub-
lish in the early 1760's several volumes of English translations of this
purported Ossianic poetry. The whole proceeding was soon proved a
literary hoax, but the so-called Ossian poems continued famous for close to
a century.

and nature; he planted them with all manner of native and foreign seeds, and reaped assiduously. He was not merely solitary, he would be isolated, and succeeded at last in almost persuading himself that he was autochthonous. He valued everything in proportion as he fancied it to be exclusively his own. He complains in "Walden" that there is no one in Concord with whom he could talk of Oriental literature, though the man was living within two miles of his hut who had introduced him to it.[29] This intellectual selfishness becomes sometimes almost painful in reading him. He lacked that generosity of "communication" which Johnson admired in Burke. De Quincey[30] tells us that Wordsworth was impatient when any one else spoke of mountains, as if he had a peculiar property in them. And we can readily understand why it should be so: no one is satisfied with another's appreciation of his mistress. But Thoreau seems to have prized a lofty way of thinking (often we should be inclined to call it a remote one) not so much because it was good in itself as because he wished few to share it with him. It seems now and then as if he did not seek to lure others up "above our lower region of turmoil," but to leave his own name cut on the mountain peak as the first climber. This itch of originality infects his thought and style. To be misty is not to be mystic. He turns commonplaces end for end, and fancies it makes something new of them. As we walk down Park Street, our eye is caught by Dr. Winship's[31] dumb-bells, one of which bears an inscription testifying that it is the heaviest ever put up at arm's length by any athlete; and in reading Mr. Thoreau's books we cannot help feeling as if he sometimes invited our attention to a particular

---

[29] Emerson, late in 1838.

[30] For Johnson see note on p. 11.
Edmund Burke (1730–97), distinguished Irish statesman and author. Thomas DeQuincey (1785–1859), English Romantic critic and essayist.

[31] George Barker Windship (1834–76), a Boston physician who at this date had his office in the basement of the Park Street Church on the corner of Tremont Street across from the Common, and advertised a "strength doubling health process." In 1859 he gave lectures on physical training, illustrated by prodigious feats of strength with dumb-bells and barrels, and was generally believed to be the strongest man of his weight in the world.

sophism or paradox as the biggest yet maintained by any single writer. He seeks, at all risks, for perversity of thought, and revives the age of *concetti* [32] while he fancies himself going back to a pre-classical nature. "A day," he says, "passed in the society of those Greek sages, such as described in the Banquet of Xenophon, would not be comparable with the dry wit of decayed cranberry-vines and the fresh Attic salt of the moss-beds." [33] It is not so much the True that he loves as the Out-of-the-Way. As the Brazen Age shows itself in other men by exaggeration of phrase, so in him by extravagance of statement. He wishes always to trump your suit and to *ruff* [34] when you least expect it. Do you love Nature because she is beautiful? He will find a better argument in her ugliness. Are you tired of the artificial man? He instantly dresses you up an ideal in a Penobscot Indian, [35] and attributes to this creature of his otherwise-mindedness as peculiarities things that are common to all woodsmen, white or red, and this simply because he has not studied the pale-faced variety.

This notion of an absolute originality, as if one could have a patent-right in it, is an absurdity. A man cannot escape in thought, any more than he can in language, from the past and the present. As no one ever invents a word, and yet language somehow grows by general contribution and necessity, so it is with thought. Mr. Thoreau seems to me to insist in public on going back to flint and steel, when there is a match-box in his pocket which he knows very well how to use at a pinch. Originality consists in power of digesting and assimilating thoughts, so that they become part of our life and substance. Montaigne, [36] for example, is one of the most original of authors,

---

[32] Conceits, i.e., fanciful or witty turns of expression.

[33] The quotation is from Thoreau's *A Week on the Concord and Merrimack Rivers:* "Thursday" (*Writings*, Walden ed., I, 319).

Xenophon (434?–355? B.C.), the Athenian historian, wrote a dialogue entitled the *Symposium,* in which he pictured Socrates and other philosophers discoursing with one another at a banquet.

[34] To play a trump card on a plain suit lead.

[35] An Indian of the Algonquin tribe which has long lived in the vicinity of the Penobscot River in northern Maine.

[36] See note on p. 42.

though he helped himself to ideas in every direction. But they turn to blood and coloring in his style, and give a freshness of complexion that is forever charming. In Thoreau much seems yet to be foreign and unassimilated, showing itself in symptoms of indigestion. A preacher-up of Nature, we now and then detect under the surly and stoic garb something of the sophist and the sentimentalizer. I am far from implying that this was conscious on his part. But it is much easier for a man to impose on himself when he measures only with himself. A greater familiarity with ordinary men would have done Thoreau good, by showing him how many fine qualities are common to the race. The radical vice of his theory of life was that he confounded physical with spiritual remoteness from men. A man is far enough withdrawn from his fellows if he keep himself clear of their weaknesses. He is not so truly withdrawn as exiled, if he refuse to share in their strength. "Solitude," says Cowley,[37] "can be well fitted and set right but upon a very few persons. They must have enough knowledge of the world to see the vanity of it, and enough virtue to despise all vanity." It is a morbid self-consciousness that pronounces the world of men empty and worthless before trying it, the instinctive evasion of one who is sensible of some innate weakness, and retorts the accusation of it before any has made it but himself. To a healthy mind, the world is a constant challenge of opportunity. Mr. Thoreau had not a healthy mind, or he would not have been so fond of prescribing. His whole life was a search for the doctor. The old mystics had a wiser sense of what the world was worth. They ordained a severe apprenticeship to law, and even ceremonial, in order to the gaining of freedom and mastery over these. Seven years of service for Rachel were to be rewarded at last with Leah.[38] Seven other years of faithfulness

---

[37] Abraham Cowley (1618–67), English poet and essayist, in his essay *Of Solitude* (1668).

[38] Jacob served Laban seven years in order to secure as his wife Rachel, Laban's youngest daughter, but on the wedding night Laban secretly placed in Jacob's tent his elder daughter, Leah. In the morning Jacob discovered the substitution and remonstrated, only to find that he must serve Laban seven more years to win Rachel outright. See Genesis XXIX.

with her were to win them at last the true bride of their souls.
Active Life was with them the only path to the Contemplative.

Thoreau had no humor, and this implies that he was a sorry
logician. Himself an artist in rhetoric, he confounds thought
with style when he undertakes to speak of the latter. He was
forever talking of getting away from the world, but he must be
always near enough to it, nay, to the Concord corner of it, to feel
the impression he makes there. He verifies the shrewd remark
of Sainte-Beuve,[39] *"On touche encore à son temps et très-fort,
même quand on le repousse."* [40] This egotism of his is a Stylites
pillar [41] after all, a seclusion which keeps him in the public eye.
The dignity of man is an excellent thing, but therefore to hold
one's self too sacred and precious is the reverse of excellent.
There is something delightfully absurd in six volumes addressed
to a world of such "vulgar fellows" as Thoreau affirmed his
fellowmen to be. I once had a glimpse of a genuine solitary
who spent his winters one hundred and fifty miles beyond all
human communication, and there dwelt with his rifle as his only
confidant. Compared with this, the shanty on Walden Pond
has something the air, it must be confessed, of the Hermitage of
La Chevrette.[42] I do not believe that the way to a true cosmo-
politanism carries one into the woods or the society of musquashes. Perhaps the narrowest provincialism is that of Self;
that of Kleinwinkel [43] is nothing to it. The natural man, like
the singing birds, comes out of the forest as inevitably as the

---

[39] Charles Augustin Sainte-Beuve (1804–69), eminent French critic and
biographer.

[40] One is still related to his time, and very much so, even when one
rejects it.

[41] St. Simon, or Simeon, Stylites (born *c.* 500 A.D.), a member of a
Christian monastery near Antioch, spent thirty-seven years on the top of
a pillar as a means of self-torture.

[42] A little châlet in the park of the Château de la Chevrette at Mont-
morency, France. The châlet, which belonged to Madame d'Épinay
(1726–83), a well-known patron of literary men, was in 1756–57 the
residence of Jean Jacques Rousseau (1712–78), noted French philosopher
and novelist.

[43] Lit., Little Corner, i.e., Podunk or a one-horse town. The word apparently is of Lowell's coinage, for the usual German term is *Krahwinkel*,
i.e., Crow's Corner.

natural bear and the wildcat stick there. To seek to be natural implies a consciousness that forbids all naturalness forever. It is as easy—and no easier—to be natural in a *salon* as in a swamp, if one do not aim at it, for what we call unnaturalness always has its spring in a man's thinking too much about himself. "It is impossible," said Turgot,[44] "for a vulgar man to be simple."

I look upon a great deal of the modern sentimentalism about Nature as a mark of disease. It is one more symptom of the general liver-complaint. To a man of wholesome constitution the wilderness is well enough for a mood or a vacation, but not for a habit of life. Those who have most loudly advertised their passion for seclusion and their intimacy with nature, from Petrarch[45] down, have been mostly sentimentalists, unreal men, misanthropes on the spindle side, solacing an uneasy suspicion of themselves by professing contempt for their kind. They make demands on the world in advance proportioned to their inward measure of their own merit, and are angry that the world pays only by the visible measure of performance. It is true of Rousseau,[46] the modern founder of the sect, true of Saint-Pierre,[47] his intellectual child, and of Chateaubriand,[48] his grandchild, the inventor, we might almost say, of the primitive forest, and who first was touched by the solemn falling of a tree from natural decay in the windless silence of the woods. It is a very shallow view that affirms trees and rocks to be healthy, and cannot see that men in communities are just as true to the laws of their organization and destiny; that can tolerate the puffin and the fox, but not the fool and the knave; that would shun politics because of its demagogues, and snuff up the stench of the obscene fungus. The divine life of Nature is more wonderful,

---

[44] Anne Robert Jacques Turgot (1727–81), French scholar, economist, and financier.

[45] See note on p. 36.

[46] See note 42 and, for Lowell's detailed estimate of the man, his essay *Rousseau and the Sentimentalists*.

[47] Jacques Henri Bernardin de Saint-Pierre (1737–1814), chiefly known for his poetic romance of naive and virtuous love, entitled *Paul et Virginie*.

[48] See note on p. 36. In 1801 Chateaubriand published *Atala,* the highly romantic story of an Indian maid, Atala, and her lover, Chactas, amid the forests and prairies of North America.

more various, more sublime in man than in any other of her works, and the wisdom that is gained by commerce with men, as Montaigne and Shakespeare gained it, or with one's own soul among men, as Dante, is the most delightful, as it is the most precious, of all.   In outward nature it is still man that interests us, and we care far less for the things seen than the way in which they are seen by poetic eyes like Wordsworth's or Thoreau's, and the reflections they cast there.   To hear the to-do that is often made over the simple fact that a man sees the image of himself in the outward world, one is reminded of a savage when he for the first time catches a glimpse of himself in a looking-glass. "Venerable child of Nature," we are tempted to say, "to whose science in the invention of the tobacco-pipe, to whose art in the tattooing of thine undegenerate hide not yet enslaved by tailors, we are slowly striving to climb back, the miracle thou beholdest is sold in my unhappy country for a shilling!"   If matters go on as they have done, and everybody must needs blab of all the favors that have been done him by roadside and riverbrink and woodland walk, as if to kiss and tell were no longer treachery, it will be a positive refreshment to meet a man who is as superbly indifferent to Nature as she is to him.   By and by we shall have John Smith, of No. 12–12th Street, advertising that he is not the J.S. who saw a cowlily on Thursday last, as he never saw one in his life, would not see one if he could, and is prepared to prove an alibi on the day in question.

Solitary communion with Nature does not seem to have been sanitary or sweetening in its influence on Thoreau's character. On the contrary, his letters show him more cynical as he grew older.   While he studied with respectful attention the minks and woodchucks, his neighbors, he looked with utter contempt on the august drama of destiny of which his country was the scene, and on which the curtain had already risen.   He was converting us back to a state of nature "so eloquently," as Voltaire said of Rousseau, "that he almost persuaded us to go on all fours," [49] while the wiser fates were making it possible for us to

---

[49] On August 30, 1755, the renowned French philosopher and satirist Voltaire (1694–1778) wrote a letter to Rousseau, in which he remarked:

walk erect for the first time. Had he conversed more with his
fellows, his sympathies would have widened with the assurance
that his peculiar genius had more appreciation, and his writings
a larger circle of readers, or at least a warmer one, than he
dreamed of. We have the highest testimony [50] to the natural
sweetness, sincerity, and nobleness of his temper, and in his
books an equally irrefragable one to the rare quality of his mind.
He was not a strong thinker, but a sensitive feeler. Yet his
mind strikes us as cold and wintry in its purity. A light snow
has fallen everywhere in which he seems to come on the track
of the shier sensations that would elsewhere leave no trace. We
think greater compression would have done more for his fame.
A feeling of sameness comes over us as we read so much. Trifles
are recorded with an over-minute punctuality and conscientious-
ness of detail. He registers the state of his personal thermometer thirteen times a day. We cannot help thinking sometimes of
the man who

> "Watches, starves, freezes, and sweats
> To learn but catechisms and alphabets
> Of unconcerning things, matters of fact," [51]

and sometimes of the saying of the Persian poet, that "when the
owl would boast, he boasts of catching mice at the edge of a
hole." We could readily part with some of his affectations. It
was well enough for Pythagoras to say, once for all, "When I
was Euphorbus at the siege of Troy"; not so well for Thoreau
to travesty it into "When I was a shepherd on the plains of

"On n'a jamais employé tant d'esprit à vouloir nous rendre bêtes; il prend
envie de marcher à quatre pattes, quand on lit votre ouvrage." ("No one
has ever employed so much passion in wishing to turn us into animals;
it produces a deep desire to go on all fours, when one reads your work.")
Lowell obviously did not quote with text in hand.

[50] Mr. Emerson, in the Biographical Sketch prefixed to the *Excursions*.
[Lowell's note.]

[51] These lines are slightly misquoted from *Of the Progresse of the Soule
The Second Anniversarie*, ll. 284–86, by John Donne (1573–1631), the first
of the so-called "metaphysical poets," and later Dean of St. Paul's, London.
The second line should read:
> To know but catechisms and alphabets

Assyria." [52]   A naïve thing said over again is anything but
naïve.   But with every exception, there is no writing comparable with Thoreau's in kind, that is comparable with it in degree
where it is best; where it disengages itself, that is, from the tangled roots and dead leaves of a second-hand Orientalism, and
runs limpid and smooth and broadening as it runs, a mirror for
whatever is grand and lovely in both worlds.

George Sand says neatly, that "Art is not a study of positive
reality," (*actuality* were the fitter word,) "but a seeking after
ideal truth." [53]   It would be doing very inadequate justice to
Thoreau if we left it to be inferred that this ideal element did
not exist in him, and that too in larger proportion, if less obtrusive, than his nature-worship.   He took nature as the mountain-
path to an ideal world.   If the path wind a good deal, if he record too faithfully every trip over a root, if he botanize somewhat wearisomely, he gives us now and then superb outlooks
from some jutting crag, and brings us out at last into an illimit-
able ether, where the breathing is not difficult for those who
have any true touch of the climbing spirit.   His shanty-life was
a mere impossibility, so far as his own conception of it goes, as
an entire independency of mankind.   The tub of Diogenes [54]
had a sounder bottom.   Thoreau's experiment actually presup-
posed all that complicated civilization which it theoretically abjured.   He squatted on another man's land; he borrows an axe;
his boards, his nails, his bricks, his mortar, his books, his lamp,

---

[52] For Pythagoras see note on p. 99.   Lowell here is not quoting his
sources exactly.—Pythagoras, who believed in the transmigration of souls,
is described in the *Metamorphoses* (xv, 158–60) of the Latin poet Ovid
(43 B.C.–17? A.D.) as saying, "I myself (for I have remembered) in the
time of the Trojan War was Euphorbus, son of Panthous."   This Euphorbus, a Trojan warrior, was slain by the Spartan Menelaus.—Thoreau in a
letter to Harrison Blake (February 27, 1853) declared, "As the stars looked
to me when I was a shepherd in Assyria, they look to me now, a New-
Englander."   (*Writings,* Walden ed., VI, 210.)

[53] An exact translation from the novel, *La Mare au Diable* (1846),
Chap. I, p. 11 (ed. Paris, 1884).   George Sand is the pseudonym of the
French novelist, Amandine Lucile Aurore Dupin, Baronne Dudevant
(1804–76), whose works were extremely popular among American readers
in the middle of the nineteenth century.

[54] A famous Greek philosopher (*c.* 412–*c.* 323 B.C.) who made his home
at Athens in a large tub.

his fish-hooks, his plough, his hoe, all turn state's evidence
against him as an accomplice in the sin of that artificial civilization which rendered it possible that such a person as Henry D.
Thoreau should exist at all. *Magnis tamen excidit ausis.*[55] His
aim was a noble and a useful one, in the direction of "plain living and high thinking." [56] It was a practical sermon on Emerson's text that "things are in the saddle and ride mankind," [57]
an attempt to solve Carlyle's problem (condensed from Johnson)
of "lessening your denominator." [58] His whole life was a rebuke of the waste and aimlessness of our American luxury,
which is an abject enslavement to tawdry upholstery. He had
"fine translunary things" [59] in him. His better style as a writer
is in keeping with the simplicity and purity of his life. We
have said that his range was narrow, but to be a master is to be
a master. He had caught his English at its living source, among
the poets and prose-writers of its best days; his literature was extensive and recondite; his quotations are always nuggets of the
purest ore: there are sentences of his as perfect as anything in the
language, and thoughts as clearly crystallized; his metaphors and
images are always fresh from the soil; he had watched Nature
like a detective who is to go upon the stand; as we read him, it
seems as if all-out-of-doors had kept a diary and become its own
Montaigne; we look at the landscape as in a Claude Lorraine
glass; [60] compared with his, all other books of similar aim, even

---

[55] Yet, though he dared great things, he failed (Ovid, *Metamorphoses,* ii,
328).

[56] From Wordsworth's sonnet, "O Friend! I know not which way I
must look," l. 11.

[57] *Ode, Inscribed to W. H. Channing,* ll. 50–1.

[58] "The Fraction of Life can be increased in value not so much by increasing your Numerator as by lessening your Denominator." (*Sartor
Resartus,* Bk. II, chap. 9: "Everlasting Yea.")

[59] A slight misquotation from the tribute by Michael Drayton (1563–
1637) to his fellow-poet, Christopher Marlowe (1564–93):

> Neat Marlowe, bathed in the Thespian springs,
> Had in him those brave translunary things
> That the first poets had . . .

> > *To . . . Henry Reynolds, . . . Of Poets and Poesy,* ll. 105–7.

[60] A blackened convex glass designed to show the effect of a landscape
reflected in somewhat exaggerated perspective—a glass therefore similar

White's "Selborne," [61] seem dry as a country clergyman's me-
teorological journal in an old almanac. He belongs with
Donne [62] and Browne [63] and Novalis; [64] if not with the originally creative men, with the scarcely smaller class who are peculiar, and whose leaves shed their invisible thought-seed like ferns.

ROUSSEAU AND THE SENTIMENTALISTS [1]

"WE HAVE had the great professor and founder of the philosophy of Vanity in England. As I had good opportunities of
knowing his proceedings almost from day to day, he left no
doubt in my mind that he entertained no principle either to influence his heart or to guide his understanding but vanity; with
this vice he was possessed to a degree little short of madness.
Benevolence to the whole species, and want of feeling for every
individual with whom the professors come in contact, form the
character of the new philosophy. Setting up for an unsocial
independence, this their hero of vanity refuses the just price of

in its effects to the landscape work of Claude Lorrain (1600–82), a French
painter noted for his unusual handling of shadow and light.

[61] Gilbert White (1720–93), a curate of Selborne in Hampshire, England,
who raised natural history into the region of literature by his celebrated
Natural History and Antiquities of Selborne (1789).

[62] See note on p. 108.

[63] Sir Thomas Browne (1605–82), noted English physician, antiquarian,
and writer.

[64] Pseudonym of Friedrich Leopold, Freiherr von Hardenburg (1772–
1801), German poet and novelist, who was one of the leading pioneers in
the Romantic Movement and exerted a considerable influence on Thomas
Carlyle, by whom he was introduced to the English and American public.

[1] Written originally as a review of M. Jules Barni's *Histoire des idées
morales et politiques en France au XVIIIme siècle* with the admixture, according to Lowell, of material from five or six Harvard lectures, and printed
in the *North American Review*, July, 1867. Lowell himself seems never
to have attached a very high value to this article. In June, 1867, he wrote:
"You must not expect much from the 'Rousseau.' I am always bothered
when I try to do anything with old material. I never do anything good
unless it keep me awake of nights, and Rousseau lets me sleep to my heart's
content." (*Letters*, I, 385.) Again, in the fall of 1869, when he was
about to revise the article very slightly for publication in the volume
Among My Books (1870), he made a disparaging comment: "It is not one
of my best." (*Letters*, II, 47.)

common labor, as well as the tribute which opulence owes to genius, and which, when paid, honors the giver and the receiver, and then pleads his beggary as an excuse for his crimes. He melts with tenderness for those only who touch him by the remotest relation, and then, without one natural pang, casts away, as a sort of offal and excrement, the spawn of his disgustful amours, and sends his children to the hospital of foundlings. The bear loves, licks, and forms her young; but bears are not philosophers."

This was Burke's [2] opinion of the only contemporary who can be said to rival him in fervid and sustained eloquence, to surpass him in grace and persuasiveness of style. Perhaps we should have been more thankful to him if he had left us instead a record of those "proceedings almost from day to day" which he had such "good opportunities of knowing," but it probably never entered his head that posterity might care as much about the doings of the citizen of Geneva as about the sayings of even a British Right Honorable. Vanity eludes recognition by its victims in more shapes, and more pleasing, than any other passion, and perhaps had Mr. Burke been able imaginatively to translate Swiss Jean Jacques into Irish Edmund, he would have found no juster equivalent for the obnoxious trisyllable than "righteous self-esteem." For Burke was himself also, in the subtler sense of the word, a sentimentalist, that is, a man who took what would now be called an æsthetic view of morals and politics. No man who ever wrote English, except perhaps Mr. Ruskin, [3] more habitually mistook his own personal likes and dislikes, tastes and distastes, for general principles, and this, it may be suspected, is the secret of all merely eloquent writing. He hints at madness as an explanation of Rousseau, and it is curious enough that Mr. Buckle [4] was fain to explain *him* in the

---

[2] See note on p. 102.—These remarks on Rousseau are quoted, with unnoted excisions, from *A Letter to a Member of the* [French] *National Assembly*. See *Works* (Bohn's Library, London, 1886), II, 536–37.

[3] John Ruskin (1819–1900), an important English critic of art and society.

[4] Henry Thomas Buckle (1821–62), an English historian who achieved considerable fame for his unfinished work in two volumes, *The History of Civilization in England* (1857–62).

same way. It is not, I confess, a solution that we find very satisfactory in this latter case. Burke's fury against the French
Revolution was nothing more than was natural to a desperate
man in self-defence. It was his own life, or, at least, all that
made life dear to him, that was in danger. He had all that
abstract political wisdom which may be naturally secreted by a
magnanimous nature and a sensitive temperament, absolutely
none of that rough-and-tumble kind which is so needful for the
conduct of affairs. Fastidiousness is only another form of egotism; and all men who know not where to look for truth save
in the narrow well of self will find their own image at the bottom, and mistake it for what they are seeking. Burke's hatred
of Rousseau was genuine and instinctive. It was so genuine
and so instinctive as no hatred can be but that of self, of our own
weaknesses as we see them in another man. But there was also
something deeper in it than this. There was mixed with it the
natural dread in the political diviner of the political logician,—
in the empirical, of the theoretic statesman. Burke, confound-
ing the idea of society with the form of it then existing, would
have preserved that as the only specific against anarchy. Rousseau, assuming that society as it then existed was but another
name for anarchy, would have reconstituted it on an ideal basis.
The one has left behind him some of the profoundest aphorisms
of political wisdom; the other, some of the clearest principles of
political science. The one, clinging to Divine right, found in
the fact that things were, a reason that they ought to be; the
other, aiming to solve the problem of the Divine order, would
deduce from that abstraction alone the claim of anything to be
at all. There seems a mere oppugnancy of nature between the
two, and yet both were, in different ways, the dupes of their own
imaginations.

Now let us hear the opinion of a philosopher who *was* a bear,
whether bears be philosophers or not. Boswell [5] had a genuine
relish for what was superior in any way, from genius to claret,
and of course he did not let Rousseau escape him. "One evening at the Mitre, Johnson said sarcastically to me, 'It seems, sir,

<hr>

[5] See note on p. 11.

you have kept very good company abroad,—Rousseau and
Wilkes!' I answered with a smile, 'My dear sir, you don't call
Rousseau bad company; do you really think *him* a bad man?'—
JOHNSON. 'Sir, if you are talking jestingly of this, I don't talk
with you. If you mean to be serious, I think him one of the
worst of men, a rascal who ought to be hunted out of society, as
he has been. Three or four nations have expelled him, and it
is a shame that he is protected in this country. Rousseau, sir, is
a very bad man. I would sooner sign a sentence for his transportation, than that of any felon who has gone from the Old
Bailey these many years. Yes, I should like to have him work in
the plantations.' " [6] *We* were the plantations then, and Rousseau was destined to work there in another and much more wonderful fashion than the gruff old Ursa Major [7] imagined. However, there is always a refreshing heartiness in his growl, a
masculine bass with no snarl in it. The Doctor's logic is of
that fine old crusted Port sort, the native manufacture of the
British conservative mind. Three or four nations *have,* therefore England ought. A few years later, had the Doctor been
living, if three or four nations had treated their kings as France
did hers, would he have thought the *ergo* [8] a very stringent one
for England?

Mr. Burke, who could speak with studied respect of the Prince
of Wales, and of his vices with that charity which thinketh no
evil and can afford to think no evil of so important a living member of the British Constitution, surely could have had no unmixed moral repugnance for Rousseau's "disgustful amours."
It was because they were *his* that they were so loathsome. Mr.
Burke was a snob, though an inspired one. Dr. Johnson, the

---

[6] Quoted with unnoted excisions from Boswell's *Life of Johnson,* chap.
XVI (1766–67).

[7] Big Bear.—Dr. Johnson was nicknamed by his contemporaries "the
Bear" or "the Big Bear." Lowell's humor, always quick for a play on
words, seized upon the Latin form of the latter nickname, because that
form coincides with the astronomical name of the constellation more
familiarly known as "the Big Dipper."

[8] The "therefore."

friend of that wretchedest of lewd fellows, Richard Savage,[9] and of that gay man about town, Topham Beauclerk,[10]—himself sprung from an amour that would have been disgustful had it not been royal,—must also have felt something more in respect of Rousseau than the mere repugnance of virtue for vice. We must sometimes allow to personal temperament its right of peremptory challenge. Johnson had not that fine sensitiveness to the political atmosphere which made Burke presageful of coming tempest, but both of them felt that there was something dangerous in this man. Their dislike has in it somewhat of the energy of fear. Neither of them had the same feeling toward Voltaire, the man of supreme talent, but both felt that what Rousseau was possessed by was genius, with its terrible force either to attract or repel.

> "By the pricking of my thumbs,
> Something wicked this way comes." [11]

Burke and Johnson were both of them sincere men, both of them men of character as well as of intellectual force; and I cite their opinions of Rousseau with the respect due to an honest conviction which has apparent grounds for its adoption, whether we agree with it or no. But it strikes me as a little singular that one whose life was so full of moral inconsistency, whose character is so contemptible in many ways, in some one might almost say so revolting, should yet have exercised so deep and lasting an influence, and on minds so various, should still be an object of minute and earnest discussion,—that he should have had such vigor in his intellectual loins as to have been the father of Cha-

---

[9] Richard Savage (1697–1743), a hack-writer whose superficial learning and extreme indigence drew Johnson to him. Johnson many a night walked the London streets with Savage when both men were without lodgings, and in 1744 he published *An Account of the Life of Mr. Richard Savage*.

[10] The only son of Lord Sidney Beauclerk and the great-grandson of Charles II and Nell Gwynn, he was an intimate acquaintance of Johnson from 1752 until his death in 1780, and was called most appropriately "Beau" by Johnson.

[11] *Macbeth*, IV, i, 44–45. The lines are uttered by the Second Witch just before the entrance of Macbeth to the witches' cavern.

teaubriand,[12] Byron, Lamartine,[13] George Sand,[14] and many
more in literature, in politics of Jefferson and Thomas Paine,[15]—
that the spots he had haunted should draw pilgrims so unlike
as Gibbon [16] and Napoleon, nay, should draw them still, after
the lapse of near a century. Surely there must have been a basis
of sincerity in this man seldom matched, if it can prevail against
so many reasons for repugnance, aversion, and even disgust.
He could not have been the mere sentimentalist and rhetorician
for which the rough-and-ready understanding would at first
glance be inclined to condemn him. In a certain sense he was
both of these, but he was something more. It will bring us a
little nearer the point I am aiming at if I quote one other and
more recent English opinion of him.

Mr. Thomas Moore,[17] returning pleasantly in a travelling-
carriage from a trip to Italy, in which he had never forgotten the
poetical shop at home, but had carefully noted down all the
pretty images that occurred to him for future use,—Mr. Thomas
Moore, on his way back from a visit to his noble friend Byron, at
Venice, who had there been leading a life so gross as to be talked
about, even amid the crash of Napoleon's fall, and who was just
writing "Don Juan" for the improvement of the world,—
Mr. Thomas Moore, fresh from the reading of Byron's Memoirs,
which were so scandalous that, by some hocus-pocus, three
thousand guineas afterward found their way into his own pocket
for consenting to suppress them,—Mr. Thomas Moore, the *ci-
devant* [18] friend of the Prince Regent, and the author of Little's
Poems, among other objects of pilgrimage visits *Les Charmettes,*

---

[12] See note on p. 36.

[13] Alphonse de Lamartine (1790–1869), French statesman and man of
letters, a leading figure of the Romantic revival in France.

[14] See note on p. 109.

[15] Paine (1737–1809), an Englishman sometime resident in America,
was a prominent pamphleteer in defense of the American and French Revo-
lutions.

[16] Edward Gibbon (1737–94), English historian celebrated for his
History of the Decline and Fall of the Roman Empire (1776–88).

[17] See note on p. 38.

[18] Former.—Moore dedicated his first book (see note 20) to the Prince
Regent, later George IV (1762–1830), but subsequently attacked him as

where Rousseau had lived with Madame de Warens. So good
an opportunity for occasional verses was not to be lost, so good
a text for a little virtuous moralizing not to be thrown away; and
accordingly Mr. Moore pours out several pages of octosyllabic
disgust at the sensuality of the dead man of genius. There was
no horror for Byron. Toward him all was suavity and decorous *bienséance*.[19] That lively sense of benefits to be received
made the Irish Anacreon [20] wink with both his little eyes. In
the judgment of a liberal like Mr. Moore, were not the errors
of a lord excusable? But with poor Rousseau the case was very
different. The son of a watchmaker, an outcast from boyhood
up, always on the perilous edge of poverty,—what right had he
to indulge himself in any immoralities? So it is always with
the sentimentalists. It is never the thing in itself that is bad or
good, but the thing in its relation to some conventional and
mostly selfish standard. Moore could be a moralist, in this
case, without any trouble, and with the advantage of winning
Lord Lansdowne's [21] approval; he could write some graceful
verses which everybody would buy, and for the rest it is not hard
to be a stoic in eight-syllable measure and in a travelling-carriage.
The next dinner at Bowood [22] will taste none the worse. Accordingly he speaks of

> The mire, the strife
> And vanities of this man's life,
> Who more than all that e'er have glowed
> With fancy's flame (and it was his
> In fullest warmth and radiance) showed
> What an impostor Genius is;
> How, with that strong mimetic art
> Which forms its life and soul, it takes

a political foe. Moore's second book, *Poems of the Late Thomas Little*
(1801), caused a mild sensation.

[19] Propriety.

[20] Greek lyric poet of the sixth century B.C. In 1800 Moore published
a translation of Anacreon's odes.

[21] Henry Petty Fitzmaurice (1780–1863), third marquess of Lansdowne,
an English statesman of note.

[22] Lord Lansdowne's country seat in Wiltshire, near which Moore was
residing in 1817.

All shapes of thought, all hues of heart,
Nor feels itself one throb it wakes;
How, like a gem, its light may shine,
O'er the dark path by mortals trod,
Itself as mean a worm the while
As crawls at midnight o'er the sod,

.   .   .   .

How, with the pencil hardly dry
From colouring up such scenes of love
And beauty as make young hearts sigh,
And dream and think through heaven they rove,[23] &c.

Very spirited, is it not? One has only to overlook a little
threadbareness in the similes, and it is very good oratorical verse.
But would we believe in it, we must never read Mr. Moore's own
journal, and find out how thin a piece of veneering his own life
was,—how he lived in sham till his very nature had become subdued to it, till he could persuade himself that a sham could be
written into a reality, and actually made experiment thereof in
his Diary.

One verse in this diatribe deserves a special comment,—

What an impostor Genius is!

In two respects there is nothing to be objected to in it. It is of
eight syllables, and "is" rhymes unexceptionably with "his."
But is there the least filament of truth in it? I venture to assert,
not the least. It was not Rousseau's genius that was an impostor. It was the one thing in him that was always true. We
grant that, in allowing that a man has genius. Talent is that
which is in a man's power; genius is that in whose power a man
is. That is the very difference between them. We might turn
the tables on Moore, the man of talent, and say truly enough,
What an impostor talent is! Moore talks of the mimetic power
with a total misapprehension of what it really is. The mimetic
power had nothing whatever to do with the affair. Rousseau
had none of it; Shakespeare had it in excess; but what difference

---

[23] These lines are to be found in Moore's *Rhymes on the Road,* VIII,
but Lowell has quoted by no means accurately.

would it make in our judgment of Hamlet or Othello if a manuscript of Shakespeare's memoirs should turn up, and we should find out that he had been a pitiful fellow? None in the world; for he is not a professed moralist, and his life does not give the warrant to his words. But if Demosthenes, after all his Philippics, throws away his shield and runs, we feel the contemptibleness of the contradiction. With genius itself we never find any fault. It would be an over-nicety that would do that. We do not get invited to nectar and ambrosia so often that we think of grumbling and saying we have better at home. No; the same genius that mastered him who wrote the poem masters us in reading it, and we care for nothing outside the poem itself. How the author lived, what he wore, how he looked,—all that is mere gossip, about which we need not trouble ourselves. Whatever he was or did, somehow or other God let him be worthy to write *this,* and that is enough for us. We forgive everything to the genius; we are inexorable to the man. Shakespeare, Goethe, Burns,—what have their biographies to do with us? Genius is not a question of character. It may be sordid, like the lamp of Aladdin, in its externals; what care we, while the touch of it builds palaces for us, makes us rich as only men in dream-land are rich, and lords to the utmost bound of imagination? So, when people talk of the ungrateful way in which the world treats its geniuses, they speak unwisely. There is no work of genius which has not been the delight of mankind, no word of genius to which the human heart and soul have not, sooner or later, responded. But the man whom the genius takes possession of for its pen, for its trowel, for its pencil, for its chisel, *him* the world treats according to his deserts. Does Burns drink? It sets him to gauging casks of gin. For, remember, it is not to the practical world that the genius appeals; it *is* the practical world which judges of the man's fitness for its uses, and has a right so to judge. No amount of patronage could have made distilled liquors less toothsome to Robbie Burns, as no amount of them could make a Burns of the Ettrick Shepherd.[24]

---

[24] James Hogg (1770–1835), the Scottish poet, became so called because he was born in Ettrick Forest and in early life was a shepherd.

There is an old story in the *Gesta Romanorum* [25] of a priest who was found fault with by one of his parishioners because his life was in painful discordance with his teaching. So one day he takes his critic out to a stream, and, giving him to drink of it, asks him if he does not find it sweet and pure water. The parishioner, having answered that it was, is taken to the source, and finds that what had so refreshed him flowed from between the jaws of a dead dog. "Let this teach thee," said the priest, "that the very best doctrine may take its rise in a very impure and disgustful spring, and that excellent morals may be taught by a man who has no morals at all." It is easy enough to see the fallacy here. Had the man known beforehand from what a carrion fountain-head the stream issued, he could not have drunk of it without loathing. Had the priest merely bidden him to *look* at the stream and see how beautiful it was, instead of tasting it, it would have been quite another matter. And this is precisely the difference between what appeals to our æsthetic or to our moral sense, between what is judged of by the taste or by the conscience.

It is when the sentimentalist turns preacher of morals that we investigate his character, and are justified in so doing. He may express as many and as delicate shades of feeling as he likes,—for this the sensibility of his organization perfectly fits him and no other person could do it so well,—but the moment he undertakes to establish his feeling as a rule of conduct, we ask at once how far are his own life and deed in accordance with what he preaches? For every man feels instinctively that all the beautiful sentiments in the world weigh less than a single lovely action; and that while tenderness of feeling and susceptibility to generous emotions are accidents of temperament, goodness is an achievement of the will and a quality of the life. Fine words, says our homely old proverb, butter no parsnips; and if the question be how to render those vegetables palatable, an ounce of butter would be worth more than all the orations of Cicero. The

---

[25] A famous collection of short Latin tales, which was much current in the late Middle Ages and often used as a source by later poets and playwrights.

only conclusive evidence of a man's sincerity is that he give *himself* for a principle. Words, money, all things else, are comparatively easy to give away; but when a man makes a gift of his daily life and practice, it is plain that the truth, whatever it may be, has taken possession of him. From that sincerity his words gain the force and pertinency of deeds, and his money is no longer the pale drudge 'twixt man and man, but, by a beautiful magic, what erewhile bore the image and superscription of Caesar seems now to bear the image and superscription of God. It is thus that there is a genius for goodness, for magnanimity, for self-sacrifice, as well as for creative art; and it is thus that by a more refined sort of Platonism the Infinite Beauty dwells in and shapes to its own likeness the soul which gives it body and individuality. But when Moore charges genius with being an impostor, the confusion of his ideas is pitiable. There is nothing so true, so sincere, so downright and forthright, as genius. It is always truer than the man himself is, greater than he. If Shakespeare the man had been as marvellous a creature as the genius that wrote his plays, that genius so comprehensive in its intelligence, so wise even in its play that its clowns are moralists and philosophers, so penetrative that a single one of its phrases reveals to us the secret of our own character, would his contemporaries have left us so wholly without record of him as they have done, distinguishing him in no wise from his fellow-players?

Rousseau, no doubt, was weak, nay, more than that, was sometimes despicable, but yet is not fairly to be reckoned among the herd of sentimentalists. It is shocking that a man whose preaching made it fashionable for women of rank to nurse their children should have sent his own, as soon as born, to the foundling hospital, still more shocking that, in a note to his *Discours sur l'inégalité,*[26] he should speak of this crime as one of the consequences of our social system. But for all that there was a faith and an ardor of conviction in him that distinguish him from most of the writers of his time. Nor were his practice and his preaching always inconsistent. He contrived to pay regularly,

---

[26] *Discourse on Inequality* (1753), one of his earliest writings.

whatever his own circumstances were, a pension of one hundred *livres* [27] a year to a maternal aunt who had been kind to him in childhood. Nor was his asceticism a sham. He might have turned his gift into laced coats and *châteaux* [28] as easily as Voltaire, had he not held it too sacred to be bartered away in any such losing exchange.

But what is worthy of especial remark is this,—that in nearly all that he wrote his leading object was the good of his kind, and that, through all the vicissitudes of a life which illness, sensibility of temperament, and the approaches of insanity rendered wretched,—the associate of infidels, the foundling child, as it were, of an age without belief, least of all with any belief in itself, —he professed and evidently felt deeply a faith in the goodness both of man and of God. There is no such thing as scoffing in his writings. On the other hand, there is no stereotyped morality. He does not ignore the existence of scepticism; he recognizes its existence in his own nature, meets it frankly face to face, and makes it confess that there are things in the teaching of Christ that are deeper than its doubt. The influence of his early education at Geneva is apparent here. An intellect so acute as his, trained in the school of Calvin [29] in a republic where theological discussion was as much the amusement of the people as the opera was at Paris, could not fail to be a good logician. He had the fortitude to follow his logic wherever it led him. If the very impressibility of character which quickened his perception of the beauties of nature, and made him alive to the charm of music and musical expression, prevented him from being in the highest sense an original writer, and if his ideas were mostly suggested to him by books, yet the clearness, consecutiveness, and eloquence with which he stated and enforced them made them his own. There was at least that original fire in him which could fuse them and run them in a novel mould. His power lay in this very ability of manipulating the thoughts of

---

[27] Pounds.

[28] Castles, i.e., large French country houses.

[29] John Calvin (1509–64), eminent French theologian and preacher who settled in Geneva, Switzerland, and became a leader in the Protestant Reformation.

others. Fond of paradox he doubtless was, but he had a way of putting things that arrested attention and excited thought.

It was, perhaps, this very sensibility to the surrounding atmosphere of feeling and speculation, which made Rousseau more directly influential on contemporary thought (or perhaps we should say sentiment) than any writer of his time. And this is rarely consistent with enduring greatness in literature. It forces us to remember, against our will, the oratorical character of his works. They were all pleas, and he a great advocate, with Europe in the jury-box. Enthusiasm begets enthusiasm, eloquence produces conviction for the moment, but it is only by truth to nature and the everlasting intuitions of mankind that those abiding influences are won that enlarge from generation to generation. Rousseau was in many respects—as great pleaders always are—a man of the day, who must needs become a mere name to posterity, yet he could not but have had in him some not inconsiderable share of that principle by which man eternizes himself. For it is only to such that the night cometh not in which no man shall work, and he is still operative both in politics and literature by the principles he formulated or the emotions to which he gave a voice so piercing and so sympathetic.

In judging Rousseau, it would be unfair not to take note of the malarious atmosphere in which he grew up. The constitution of his mind was thus early infected with a feverish taint that made him shiveringly sensitive to a temperature which hardier natures found bracing. To him this rough world was but too literally a rack. Good-humored Mother Nature commonly imbeds the nerves of her children in a padding of self-conceit that serves as a buffer against the ordinary shocks to which even a life of routine is liable, and it would seem at first sight as if Rousseau had been better cared for than usual in this regard. But as his self-conceit was enormous, so was the reaction from it proportionate, and the fretting suspiciousness of temper, sure mark of an unsound mind, which rendered him incapable of intimate friendship, while passionately longing for it, became inevitably, when turned inward, a tormenting self-

distrust. To dwell in unrealities is the doom of the sentimentalist; but it should not be forgotten that the same fitful intensity
of emotion which makes them real as the means of elation, gives
them substance also for torture. Too irritably jealous to endure the rude society of men, he steeped his senses in the ener-
vating incense that women are only too ready to burn. If their
friendship be a safeguard to the other sex, their homage is fatal
to all but the strongest, and Rousseau was weak both by inheritance and early training. His father was one of those feeble
creatures for whom a fine phrase could always satisfactorily fill
the void that non-performance leaves behind it. If he neglected
duty, he made up for it by that cultivation of the finer sentiments
of our common nature which waters flowers of speech with the
brineless tears of a flabby remorse, without one fibre of resolve in
it, and which impoverishes the character in proportion as it enriches the vocabulary. He was a very Apicius [30] in that digest-
ible kind of woe which makes no man leaner, and had a favorite
receipt for cooking you up a sorrow *à la douleur inassouvie* [31]
that had just enough delicious sharpness in it to bring tears into
the eyes by tickling the palate. "When he said to me, 'Jean
Jacques, let us speak of thy mother,' I said to him, 'Well, father,
we are going to weep, then,' and this word alone drew tears from
him. 'Ah!' said he, groaning, 'give her back to me, console me
for her, fill the void she has left in my soul!' " [32] Alas! in such
cases, the void she leaves is only that she found. The grief that
seeks any other than its own society will erelong want an object.
This admirable parent allowed his son to become an outcast at
sixteen, without any attempt to reclaim him, in order to enjoy
unmolested a petty inheritance to which the boy was entitled in
right of his mother. "This conduct," Rousseau tells us, "of
a father whose tenderness and virtue were so well known to me,
caused me to make reflections on myself which have not a little

---

[30] Marcus Gavius Apicius, a prodigious glutton in the reign of the
Roman emperor Tiberius, who spent some four million dollars, so it is
said, in securing from all over the world new delicacies and new recipes
for cooking.

[31] With unsatiated anguish.

[32] Rousseau's *Confessions*, Bk. I (1712–19).

contributed to make my heart sound. I drew from it this great maxim of morals, the only one perhaps serviceable in practice, to avoid situations which put our duties in opposition to our interest, and which show us our own advantage in the wrong of another, sure that in such situations, *however sincere may be one's love of virtue,* it sooner or later grows weak without our perceiving it, *and that we become unjust and wicked in action without having ceased to be just and good in soul.*" [33]

This maxim may do for that "fugitive and cloistered virtue, unexercised and unbreathed, that never sallies out and seeks its adversary," [34] which Milton could not praise,—that is, for a manhood whose distinction it is not to be manly,—but it is chiefly worth notice as being the characteristic doctrine of sentimentalism. This disjoining of deed from will, of practice from theory, is to put asunder what God has joined by an indissoluble sacrament. The soul must be tainted before the action become corrupt; and there is no self-delusion more fatal than that which makes the conscience dreamy with the anodyne of lofty sentiments, while the life is grovelling and sensual,—witness Coleridge. In his case we feel something like disgust. But where, as in his son Hartley,[35] there is hereditary infirmity, where the man sees the principle that might rescue him slip from the clutch of a nerveless will, like a rope through the fingers of a drowning man, and the confession of faith is the moan of despair, there is room for no harsher feeling than pity. Rousseau showed through life a singular proneness for being convinced by his own eloquence; he was always his own first convert; and this reconciles his power as a writer with his weakness as a man. He and all like him mistake emotion for conviction, velleity [36] for resolve, the brief eddy of sentiment for the mid-current of ever-gathering faith in duty that draws to itself all the affluents of conscience

---

[33] Ibid., Bk. II (1728–31).

[34] Quoted from Milton's *Areopagitica* (1644).

[35] David Hartley Coleridge (1796–1849), son of Samuel Taylor Coleridge (1772–1834), noted English Romantic poet and critic, was a minor literary figure whose career came to an early end through intemperance. The elder Coleridge early became addicted to opium as a relief from intense neuralgia.

[36] Weak and vague purposing.

and will, and gives continuity of purpose to life. They are like men who love the stimulus of being under conviction,[37] as it is called, who, forever getting religion, never get capital enough to retire upon and to spend for their own need and the common service.

The sentimentalist is the spiritual hypochondriac, with whom fancies become facts, while facts are a discomfort because they will not be evaporated into fancy. In his eyes, Theory is too fine a dame to confess even a country-cousinship with coarse-handed Practice, whose homely ways would disconcert her artificial world. The very susceptibility that makes him quick to feel, makes him also incapable of deep and durable feeling. He loves to think he suffers, and keeps a pet sorrow, a blue-devil familiar, that goes with him everywhere, like Paracelsus's black dog.[38] He takes good care, however, that it shall not be the true sulphurous article that sometimes takes a fancy to fly away with his conjurer. René[39] says: "In my madness I had gone so far as even to wish I might experience a misfortune, so that my suffering might at least have a real object." But no; selfishness is only active egotism, and there is nothing and nobody, with a single exception, which this sort of creature will not sacrifice, rather than give any other than an imaginary pang to his idol. Vicarious pain he is not unwilling to endure, nay, will even commit suicide by proxy, like the German poet who let his wife kill herself to give him a sensation.[40] Had young Jerusa-

---

[37] Strong awareness of sin.

[38] Philippus Aureolus Paracelsus Theophrastus Bombastus von Hohenheim (c. 1490–1541), a German scientist and physician, who after becoming a professor of medicine at Basel in 1526 denounced the practices of Arabian medical science, the accepted authority in Europe at the time, and therefore soon lost his post. He then wandered about in Switzerland and Germany for the next fifteen years, preaching here and there his iconoclastic doctrines and also presenting experiments in magic and alchemy, in which he had dabbled somewhat during earlier years.

[39] René is the hero of a romantic episode of the same name in Chateaubriand's *Génie du christianisme* (1802). The episode contains much morbid reflection out of René's melancholy, dissatisfied soul, and is largely autobiographic in its delineation.

[40] On December 29, 1834, Charlotte (née Willhoft), the wife of Heinrich Stieglitz (1801–49), one of the minor writers in the "Young German" movement, committed suicide of her own free will in the hope that the

lem [41] been anything like Goethe's portrait of him in Werther,[42] he would have taken very good care not to blow out the brains which he would have thought only too precious. Real sorrows are uncomfortable things, but purely æsthetic ones are by no means unpleasant, and I have always fancied the handsome young Wolfgang [43] writing those distracted letters to Auguste Stolberg [44] with a looking-glass in front of him to give back an image of his desolation, and finding it rather pleasant than otherwise to shed the tear of sympathy with self that would seem so bitter to his fair correspondent. The tears that have real salt in them will keep; they are the difficult, manly tears that are shed in secret; but the pathos soon evaporates from that fresh-water with which a man can bedew a dead donkey in public,[45] while his wife is having a good cry over his neglect of her at home. We do not think the worse of Goethe for hypothetically desolating himself in the fashion aforesaid, for with many constitutions it is as purely natural a crisis as dentition,[46] which the stronger worry through, and turn out very sensible, agreeable fellows. But where there is an arrest of development, and the heartbreak of the patient is audibly prolonged through life, we have a spectacle which the toughest heart would wish to get as far away from as possible.

I would not be supposed to overlook the distinction, too often lost sight of, between sentimentalism and sentiment, the latter

---

deep sorrow caused by her death would exert a healing influence on her husband, and revive his lagging creative urge.

[41] Jerusalem, a young student whom Goethe knew well at Leipzig and Wetzlar, committed suicide in 1772 because he found himself in love with a friend's wife.

[42] The hero of Goethe's romance *Die Leiden des jungen Werthers* (1774), whose character and fate were to a considerable degree derived from the example of Jerusalem.

[43] Goethe's middle name.

[44] Countess Auguste Stolberg (1753–1835), sister of the poets Christian and Friedrich Stolberg, became acquainted with Goethe through her brothers, with whom in May, 1775, Goethe took a trip to Switzerland. During 1774 and 1775 Goethe corresponded copiously and warmly with the Countess.

[45] See the episode of the dead ass in the chapters "The Bidet" and "Nampont" of Sterne's *Sentimental Journey* (1768).

[46] The cutting of teeth.

being a very excellent thing in its way, as genuine things are apt to be. Sentiment is intellectualized emotion, emotion precipitated, as it were, in pretty crystals by the fancy. This is the delightful staple of the poets of social life like Horace and Béranger,[47] or Thackeray, when he too rarely played with verse. It puts into words for us that decorous average of feeling to the expression of which society can consent without danger of being indiscreetly moved. It is excellent for people who are willing to save their souls alive to any extent that shall not be discomposing. It is even satisfying till some deeper experience has given us a hunger which what we so glibly call "the world" cannot sate, just as a water-ice is nourishment enough to a man who has had his dinner. It is the sufficing lyrical interpreter of those lighter hours that should make part of every healthy man's day, and is noxious only when it palls men's appetite for the truly profound poetry which is very passion of very soul sobered by afterthought and embodied in eternal types by imagination. True sentiment is emotion ripened by a slow ferment of the mind and qualified to an agreeable temperance by that taste which is the conscience of polite society. But the sentimentalist always insists on taking his emotion neat, and, as his sense gradually deadens to the stimulus, increases his dose till he ends in a kind of moral deliquium. At first the debaucher, he becomes at last the victim of his sensations.

Among the ancients we find little or no trace of sentimentalism, though Euripides [48] and still more Ovid give hints of it. Their masculine mood both of body and mind left no room for it, and hence the bracing quality of their literature compared with that of recent times, its tonic property, that seems almost too astringent to palates relaxed by a daintier diet. The first great example of the degenerate modern tendency was Petrarch,[49] who may be said to have given it impulse and direction. A more perfect specimen of the type has not since appeared. An

---

[47] Pierre Jean de Béranger (1780–1857), a French lyric poet of considerable fame in the early nineteenth century.

[48] Greek tragedian (480–406 B.C.)

[49] See note on p. 36.

intellectual voluptuary, a moral *dilettante,* the first instance of that character, since too common, the gentleman in search of a sensation, seeking a solitude at Vaucluse because it made him more likely to be in demand at Avignon,[50] praising philosophic poverty with a sharp eye to the next rich benefice in the gift of his patron, commending a good life but careful first of a good living, happy only in seclusion but making a dangerous journey to enjoy the theatrical show of a coronation in the Capitol,[51] cherishing a fruitless passion which broke his heart three or four times a year and yet could not make an end of him till he had reached the ripe age of seventy and survived his mistress a quarter of a century,—surely a more exquisite perfection of inconsistency would be hard to find.

When Petrarch returned from his journey into the North of Europe in 1332, he balanced the books of his unrequited passion, and, finding that he had now been in love seven years, thought the time had at last come to call deliberately on Death. Had Death taken him at his word, he would have protested that he was only in fun. For we find him always taking good care of an excellent constitution, avoiding the plague with commendable assiduity, and in the very year when he declares it absolutely essential to his peace of mind to die for good and all, taking refuge in the fortress of Capranica, from a wholesome dread of having his throat cut by robbers. There is such a difference between dying in a sonnet with a cambric handkerchief at one's eyes, and the prosaic reality of demise certified in the parish register! Practically it is inconvenient to be dead. Among other things, it puts an end to the manufacture of sonnets. But there seems to have been an excellent understanding between Petrarch and Death, for he was brought to that grisly monarch's door so often, that, otherwise, nothing short of a miracle or the nine lives of that animal whom love also makes lyrical could have saved him. "I consent," he cries, "to live and die in Africa

---

[50] A city in southern France, the residence of the "French" popes, 1309–77. Vaucluse was a nearby village, to which Petrarch retired in 1337.
[51] In 1341 the Roman senate bestowed upon Petrarch at the Capitol the laurel crown for excellence in poetry.

among its serpents, upon Caucasus, or Atlas, if, while I live, to breathe a pure air, and after my death a little corner of earth where to bestow my body, may be allowed me. This is all I ask, but this I cannot obtain. Doomed always to wander, and to be a stranger everywhere, O Fortune, Fortune, fix me at last to some one spot! I do not covet thy favors. Let me enjoy a tranquil poverty, let me pass in this retreat the few days that remain to me!" [52] The pathetic stop of Petrarch's poetical organ was one he could pull out at pleasure,—and indeed we soon learn to distrust literary tears, as the cheap subterfuge for want of real feeling with natures of this quality. Solitude with him was but the pseudonym of notoriety. Poverty was the archdeaconry of Parma, with other ecclesiastical pickings. During his retreat at Vaucluse, in the very height of that divine sonneteering love of Laura, of that sensitive purity which called Avignon Babylon, and rebuked the sinfulness of Clement,[53] he was himself begetting that kind of children which we spell with a *b*. We believe that, if Messer Francesco had been present when the woman was taken in adultery, he would have flung the first stone without the slightest feeling of inconsistency, nay, with a sublime sense of virtue.[54] The truth is, that it made very little difference to him what sort of proper sentiment he expressed, provided he could do it elegantly and with unction. And with supreme elegance he knew how to express it, thereby conferring an incalculable benefit on the literature of Italy and of Europe.

Would any one feel the difference between his faint abstractions and the Platonism of a powerful nature fitted alike for the withdrawal of ideal contemplation and for breasting the storms of life,—would any one know how wide a depth divides a noble

---

[52] A loosely translated passage from his fifth Latin epistle to Marco Barbato da Sulmona.

[53] Pope Clement VI (1291–1352), who refused to return the papal seat to Rome and in 1348 purchased Avignon, France, for the papacy.

[54] A woman taken in adultery was brought before Jesus for judgment on one of his visits to Jerusalem, but he refused to condemn her and suggested that any guiltless person among the bystanders might cast the first stone at her. See John viii: 1–11.

friendship based on sympathy of pursuit and aspiration, on that mutual help which souls capable of self-sustainment are the readiest to give or to take, and a simulated passion, true neither to the spiritual nor the sensual part of man,—let him compare the sonnets of Petrarch with those which Michel Angelo addressed to Vittoria Colonna.[55] In them the airiest pinnacles of sentiment and speculation are buttressed with solid mason-work of thought, of an actual, not fancied experience, and the depth of feeling is measured by the sobriety and reserve of expression, while in Petrarch's all ingenuousness is frittered away into ingenuity. Both are cold, but the coldness of the one is self-restraint, while the other chills with pretence of warmth. In Michel Angelo's, you feel the great architect; in Petrarch's the artist who can best realize his conception in the limits of a cherry-stone.[56] And yet this man influenced literature longer and more widely than almost any other in modern times. So great is the charm of elegance, so unreal is the larger part of what is written!

Certainly I do not mean to say that a work of art should be looked at by the light of the artist's biography, or measured by our standard of his character. Nor do I reckon what was genuine in Petrarch—his love of letters, his refinement, his skill in the superficial graces of language, that rhetorical art by which the music of words supplants their meaning, and the verse moulds the thought instead of being plastic to it—after any such fashion. I have no ambition for that character of *valet de chambre* [57] which is said to disenchant the most heroic figures into mere every-day personages, for it implies a mean soul no less than a servile condition. But we have a right to demand a certain amount of reality, however small, in the emotion of a man who makes it his business to endeavor at exciting our own. We have a privilege of nature to shiver before a painted flame, how

---

[55] Vittoria Colonna (1490–1547), Marchioness of Pescara, a distinguished Italian writer of deeply religious poetry.

[56] An echo of Dr. Johnson's remark about Milton: "a genius that could cut a Colossus from a rock, but could not carve heads upon cherry-stones." See Boswell's *Life of Johnson,* June 13, 1784.

[57] Gentleman-in-waiting.

cunningly soever the colors be laid on. Yet our love of minute biographical detail, our desire to make ourselves spies upon the men of the past, seems so much of an instinct in us, that we must look for the spring of it in human nature, and that somewhat deeper than mere curiosity or love of gossip. It should seem to arise from what must be considered on the whole a creditable feeling, namely, that we value character more than any amount of talent,—the skill to *be* something, above that of doing anything but the best of its kind. The highest creative genius, and that only, is privileged from arrest by this personality, for there the thing produced is altogether disengaged from the producer. But in natures incapable of this escape from themselves, the author is inevitably mixed with his work, and we have a feeling that the amount of his sterling character is the security for the notes he issues. Especially we feel so when truth to self, which is always self-forgetful, and not truth to nature, makes an essential part of the value of what is offered us; as where a man undertakes to narrate personal experience or to enforce a dogma. This is particularly true as respects sentimentalists, because of their intrusive self-consciousness; for there is no more universal characteristic of human nature than the instinct of men to apologize to themselves for themselves, and to justify personal failings by generalizing them into universal laws. A man would be the keenest devil's advocate against himself, were it not that he has always taken a retaining fee for the defence; for I think that the indirect and mostly unconscious pleas in abatement which we read between the lines in the works of many authors are oftener written to set themselves right in their own eyes than in those of the world. And in the real life of the sentimentalist it is the same. He is under the wretched necessity of keeping up, at least in public, the character he has assumed, till he at last reaches that last shift of bankrupt self-respect, to play the hypocrite with himself. Lamartine,[58] after passing round the hat in Europe and America, takes to his bed from wounded pride when the French Senate votes him a subsidy, and sheds tears of humiliation. Ideally, he resents it; in practical coin, he will

---

[58] See note on p. 116.

accept the shame without a wry face, he will "impeticos the gra-
tillity." [59]

George Sand, speaking of Rousseau's "Confessions," says that
an autobiographer always makes himself the hero of his own
novel, and cannot help idealizing, even if he would. But the
weak point of all sentimentalists is that they always have been,
and always continue under every conceivable circumstance to
be, their own ideals, whether they are writing their own lives or
no. Rousseau opens his book with the statement: "I am not
made like any of those I have seen; I venture to believe myself
unlike any that exists. If I am not worth more, at least I am
different." [60] O exquisite cunning of self-flattery! It is this very
imagined difference that makes us worth more in our own foolish sight. For while all men are apt to think, or to persuade
themselves that they think, all other men their accomplices in
vice or weakness, they are not difficult of belief that they are
singular in any quality or talent on which they hug themselves.
More than this; people who are truly original are the last to find
it out, for the moment we become conscious of a virtue, it has
left us or is getting ready to go. Originality does not consist in
a fidgety assertion of selfhood, but in the faculty of getting rid
of it altogether, that the truer genius of the man, which com-
merces with universal nature and with other souls through a
common sympathy with that, may take all his powers wholly to
itself,—and the truly original man could no more be jealous of
his peculiar gift, than the grass could take credit to itself for
being green. What is the reason that all children are geniuses,
(though they contrive so soon to outgrow that dangerous quality,) except that they never cross-examine themselves on the
subject? The moment that process begins, their speech loses its
gift of unexpectedness, and they become as tediously impertinent
as the rest of us.

If there never was any one like him, if he constituted a genus
in himself, to what end write confessions in which no other

---

[59] I.e., "pocket the gratuity." This bit of drunken jargon was addressed
by the Clown to Sir Andrew Aguecheek in *Twelfth Night*, II, iii, 27.
[60] Not the opening, but the second paragraph of the *Confessions*.

human being could ever be in a condition to take the least possible interest? All men are interested in Montaigne [61] in proportion as all men find more of themselves in him, and all men see but one image in the glass which the greatest of poets holds up to nature, an image which at once startles and charms them with its familiarity. Fabulists always endow their animals with the passions and desires of men. But if an ox could dictate his confessions, what glimmer of understanding should we find in those bovine confidences, unless on some theory of preëxistence, some blank misgiving of a creature moving about in worlds not realized? [62] The truth is, that we recognize the common humanity of Rousseau in the very weakness that betrayed him into this conceit of himself; we find he is just like the rest of us in this very assumption of essential difference, for among all animals man is the only one who tries to pass for more than he is, and so involves himself in the condemnation of seeming less.

Benvenuto Cellini [63] was right in his *dictum* about autobiographies; and so was Dr. Kitchener, [64] in his about hares. First catch your perfectly sincere and unconscious man. He is even more uncommon than a genius of the first order. Most men dress themselves for their autobiographies, as Machiavelli [65] used to do for reading the classics, in their best clothes; they receive us, as it were, in a parlor chilling and awkward from its unfa-

---

[61] See note on p. 42.

[62] From Wordsworth's ode, *Intimations of Immortality,* ll. 144–45.

[63] Cellini (1500–71), renowned Italian craftsman, inventor, sculptor, began his *Autobiography* with the following *dictum:* "All men of whatsoever quality they be, who have done anything of excellence, or which may properly resemble excellence, ought, if they are persons of truth and honesty, to describe their life with their own hand; but they ought not to attempt so fine an enterprize till they have passed the age of forty." (Symonds trans.)

[64] William Kitchener, M.D. (1775?–1827), a famous London epicure of his day, experimented in cookery in his own house. Out of his gastronomic experience he published a long-popular recipe book, *Apicius Redivivus, or the Cook's Oracle* (1817), "a culinary code for the rational epicure." To him is attributed the saying: "To make rabbit soup you must first catch your rabbit."

[65] Niccolo Machiavelli (1469–1527), distinguished Italian statesman and author.

miliarity with man, and keep us carefully away from the kitchen-chimney-corner, where they would feel at home, and would not look on a lapse into nature as the unpardonable sin. But what do we want of a hospitality that makes strangers of us, or of confidences that keep us at arm's-length? Better the tavern and the newspaper; for in the one we can grumble, and from the other learn more of our neighbors than we care to know. John Smith's autobiography is commonly John Smith's design for an equestrian statue of himself,—very fine, certainly, and as much like him as like Marcus Aurelius.[66] Saint Augustine,[67] kneeling to confess, has an eye to the picturesque, and does it *in pontificalibus*,[68] resolved that Domina Grundy [69] shall think all the better of him. Rousseau cries, "I will bare my heart to you!" and, throwing open his waistcoat, makes us the confidants of his dirty linen. Montaigne, indeed, reports of himself with the impartiality of a naturalist, and Boswell, in his letters to Temple,[70] shows a maudlin irretentiveness; but is not old Samuel Pepys,[71] after all, the only man who spoke to himself of himself with perfect simplicity, frankness, and unconsciousness? a creature unique as the dodo, a solitary specimen, to show that it was possible for Nature to indulge in so odd a whimsey! An autobiography is good for nothing, unless the author tell us in it precisely what he meant not to tell. A man who can say what he thinks of another to his face is a disagreeable rarity; but one who could

---

[66] Marcus Aurelius Antoninus (A.D. 121–80), Roman emperor and author of a widely known book called *Meditations*.

[67] Aurelius Augustinus (A.D. 354–430), early Christian Church father and philosopher, who began his autobiography *c.* 397 under the title of *Confessions*.

[68] With priestly robes and ceremony.

[69] Mistress Grundy: a proverbial term of personification for that body of public opinion which emphasizes strict observance of the social proprieties. The term gained currency from the widely popular English comedy *Speed the Plough* (1798), wherein the judgment of a certain Mrs. Grundy is constantly felt, though she never appears on the stage.

[70] The Reverend William Johnson Temple (d. 1796), friend of Boswell at the University of Edinburgh, and later vicar of St. Gluvias, Mamhead, Cornwall.

[71] Samuel Pepys (1633–1703), an English gentleman celebrated for his delightful and invaluable diary, 1660–69.

look his own Ego straight in the eye, and pronounce unbiased judgment, were worthy of Sir Thomas Browne's Museum.[72] Had Cheiron [73] written his autobiography, the consciousness of his equine crupper would have ridden him like a nightmare; should a mermaid write hers, she would sink the fish's tail, nor allow it to be put into the scales, in weighing her character. The mermaid, in truth, is the emblem of those who strive to see themselves; her mirror is too small to reflect anything more than the *mulier formosa supernè*.[74]

But it would be sheer waste of time to hunt Rousseau through all his doublings of inconsistency, and run him to earth in every new paradox. His first two books attacked, one of them literature, and the other society.[75] But this did not prevent him from being diligent with his pen, nor from availing himself of his credit with persons who enjoyed all the advantages of that inequality whose evils he had so pointedly exposed. Indeed, it is curious how little practical communism there has been, how few professors it has had who would not have gained by a general dividend. It is perhaps no frantic effort of generosity in a philosopher with ten crowns in his pocket when he offers to make common stock with a neighbor who has ten thousand of yearly income, nor is it an uncommon thing to see such theories knocked clean out of a man's head by the descent of a thumping legacy. But, consistent or not, Rousseau remains permanently interesting as the highest and most perfect type of the sentimentalist of genius. His was perhaps the acutest mind that

---

[72] See note on p. 111. Browne's famous museum was at his home in Norwich. Pepys, who visited Browne's house and garden in October, 1671, described them as "a paradise and cabinet of rarities," which included books, metals, plants, art objects, and specimens of natural history.

[73] Cheiron, grandfather of Peleus, who in turn was father of Achilles, was the wisest of the Centaurs and the tutor of Achilles. He was exceptionally skilled in medicine, music, and hunting.

[74] The beauteous maid above. See Horace, *Ars. Poetica*, 4: "*Desinat in piscem mulier formosa superne* (That a beauteous maid above should end in a fish!)."

[75] *Discourse against Arts and Letters* (1749), arguing that the increase of learning causes the degeneration of society; *Discourse on the Origin of Inequality* (1753).

was ever mated with an organization so diseased,[76] the brain most far-reaching in speculation that ever kept itself steady and worked out its problems amid such disordered tumult of the nerves. His letter to the Archbishop of Paris, admirable for its lucid power and soberness of tone, and his *Rousseau juge de Jean Jacques,* which no man can read and believe him to have been sane, show him to us in his strength and weakness, and give us a more charitable, let us hope therefore a truer, notion of him than his own apology for himself. That he was a man of genius appears unmistakably in his impressibility by the deeper meaning of the epoch in which he lived. Before an eruption, clouds steeped through and through with electric life gather over the crater, as if in sympathy and expectation. As the mountain heaves and cracks, these vapory masses are seamed with fire, as if they felt and answered the dumb agony that is struggling for utterance below. Just such flashes of eager sympathetic fire break continually from the cloudy volumes of Rousseau, the result at once and the warning of that convulsion of which Paris was to be the crater and all Europe to feel the spasm. There are symptoms enough elsewhere of that want of faith in the existing order which made the Revolution inevitable,—even so shallow an observer as Horace Walpole [77] could forebode it so early as 1765,—but Rousseau more than all others is the unconscious expression of the groping after something radically new, the instinct for a change that should be organic and pervade every fibre of the social and political body. Freedom of thought owes far more to the jester Voltaire, who also had his solid kernel of earnest, than to the sombre Genevese,[78] whose earnestness is of the deadly kind. Yet, for good or evil, the latter was the foster-father of modern democracy, and without him our Declaration of Independence would have wanted some of

---

[76] Perhaps we should except Newton. [Lowell's note.]

[77] An English aristocrat (1717–1797), famed for his patronage of art, his collecting of curios, and for his Gothic novel, *The Castle of Otranto* (1764). He wrote to his cousin, the Hon. Henry S. Conway, from Paris Oct. 28, 1765, that the French philosophers were attacking both religion and monarchy.

[78] John Calvin. See note on p. 122.

those sentences in which the immemorial longings of the poor
and the dreams of solitary enthusiasts were at last affirmed as
axioms in the manifesto of a nation, so that all the world might
hear.

Though Rousseau, like many other fanatics, had a remarkable
vein of common sense in him, (witness his remarks on duelling,
on landscape-gardening, on French poetry, and much of his
thought on education,) we cannot trace many practical results
to his teaching, least of all in politics. For the great difficulty
with his system, if system it may be called, is, that, while it pro-
fesses to follow nature, it not only assumes as a starting-point
that the individual man may be made over again, but proceeds to
the conclusion that man himself, that human nature, must be
made over again, and governments remodelled on a purely theoretic basis. But when something like an experiment in this
direction was made in 1789, not only did it fail as regarded man
in general, but even as regards the particular variety of man
that inhabited France. The Revolution accomplished many
changes, and beneficent ones, yet it left France peopled, not by
a new race without traditions, but by Frenchmen. Still, there
must have been a wonderful force in the words of a man who,
above all others, had the secret of making abstractions glow with
his own fervor; and his ideas, dispersed now in the atmosphere
of thought, have influenced, perhaps still continue to influence,
speculative minds, which prefer swift and sure generalization to
hesitating and doubtful experience.

Rousseau has, in one respect, been utterly misrepresented and
misunderstood. Even Chateaubriand most unfilially classes
him and Voltaire together.[79] It appears to me that the inmost
core of his being was religious. Had he remained in the Catholic Church, he might have been a saint. Had he come earlier,
he might have founded an order. His was precisely the nature
on which religious enthusiasm takes the strongest hold, a temperament which finds sensuous delight in spiritual things, and
satisfies its craving for excitement with celestial debauch. He

---

[79] Bk. IV, chap. 5, of Chateaubriand's *Genius of Christianity* (1802)
brands Rousseau as an anti-Christian writer.

had not the iron temper of a great reformer and organizer like Knox,[80] who, true Scotchman that he was, found a way to weld this world and the other together in a cast-iron creed; but he had as much as any man ever had that gift of a great preacher to make the oratorical fervor which persuades himself while it lasts into the abiding conviction of his hearers. That very persuasion of his, that the soul could remain pure while the life was corrupt, is not unexampled among men who have left holier names than he. His "Confessions," also, would assign him to that class with whom the religious sentiment is strong and the moral nature weak. They are apt to believe that they may, as special pleaders say, confess and avoid. Hawthorne has admirably illustrated this in the penance of Mr. Dimmesdale.[81] With all the soil that is upon Rousseau, I cannot help looking on him as one capable beyond any in his generation of being divinely possessed; and if it happened otherwise, when we remember the much that hindered and the little that helped in a life and time like his, we shall be much readier to pity than to condemn. It was his very fitness for being something better that makes him able to shock us so with what in too many respects he unhappily was. Less gifted, he had been less hardly judged. More than any other of the sentimentalists, except possibly Sterne,[82] he had in him a staple of sincerity. Compared with Chateaubriand, he is honesty, compared with Lamartine, he is manliness, itself. His nearest congener [83] in our own tongue is Cowper.[84]

In the whole school there is a sickly taint. The strongest mark which Rousseau has left upon literature is a sensibility to the picturesque in Nature, not with Nature as a strengthener

---

[80] John Knox (1505–72), the leader of the Protestant Reformation in Scotland.

[81] Arthur Dimmesdale, the Boston minister who plays the leading role in the tragic drama of *The Scarlet Letter,* tries for long to conceal from public knowledge and opprobrium his sinful relationship with Hester Prynne, and to practice private expiation for his secret fall from grace.

[82] See note on p. 96.

[83] One allied in nature.

[84] William Cowper (1731–1800), English poet whose lyric writings foreshadowed in some respects the romanticism of Wordsworth. His chief achievement is *The Task* (1785).

and consoler, a wholesome tonic for a mind ill at ease with itself, but with Nature as a kind of feminine echo to the mood, flattering it with sympathy rather than correcting it with rebuke or lifting it away from its unmanly depression, as in the wholesomer fellow-feeling of Wordsworth. They seek in her an accessory, and not a reproof. It is less a sympathy with Nature than a sympathy with ourselves as we compel her to reflect us. It is solitude, Nature for her estrangement from man, not for her companionship with him; it is desolation and ruin, Nature as she has triumphed over man, with which this order of mind seeks communion and in which it finds solace. It is with the hostile and destructive power of matter, and not with the spirit of life and renewal that dwells in it, that they ally themselves. And in human character it is the same. St. Preux,[85] René,[86] Werther,[87] Manfred,[88] Quasimodo,[89] they are all anomalies, distortions, ruins,—so much easier is it to caricature life from our own sickly conception of it than to paint it in its noble simplicity; so much cheaper is unreality than truth.

Every man is conscious that he leads two lives, the one trivial and ordinary, the other sacred and recluse; one which he carries to society and the dinner-table, the other in which his youth and aspiration survive for him, and which is a confidence between himself and God. Both may be equally sincere, and there need be no contradiction between them, any more than in a healthy man between soul and body. If the higher life be real and earnest, its result, whether in literature or affairs, will be real and earnest too. But no man can produce great things who is not thoroughly sincere in dealing with himself, who would not

---

[85] The lover of Julie in Rousseau's *La Nouvelle Héloise* (1761).

[86] The hero of Chateaubriand's *René* (1802), a man of secret sorrows who flees to the wilds of America.

[87] The hero and the lover of Charlotte in *Die Leiden des jungen Werthers* (1774) by Goethe.

[88] The hero of Lord Byron's autobiographic dramatic poem *Manfred* (1817), a social outcast who lives in the Alps.

[89] The deformed bell-ringer of Notre Dame Cathedral in the novel *Notre Dame de Paris* (1831) by Victor Hugo (1802–85), French Romantic critic, novelist, and playwright.

exchange the finest show for the poorest reality, who does not so love his work that he is not only glad to give himself for it, but finds rather a gain than a sacrifice in the surrender. The sentimentalist does not think of what he does so much as of what the world will think of what he does. He translates should into would, looks upon the spheres of duty and beauty as alien to each other, and can never learn how life rounds itself to a noble completeness between these two opposite but mutually sustaining poles of what we long for and what we must.

Did Rousseau, then, lead a life of this quality? Perhaps, when we consider the contrast which every man who looks backward must feel between the life he planned and the life which circumstance within him and without him has made for him, we should rather ask, Was this the life he meant to lead? Perhaps, when we take into account his faculty of self-deception, —it may be no greater than our own,—we should ask, Was this the life he believed he led? Have we any right to judge this man after our blunt English fashion, and condemn him, as we are wont to do, on the finding of a jury of average householders? Is French reality precisely our reality? Could we tolerate trag-edy in rhymed alexandrines,[90] instead of blank verse? The whole life of Rousseau is pitched on this heroic key, and for the most trivial occasion he must be ready with the sublime senti-ments that are supposed to suit him rather than it. It is one of the most curious features of the sentimental ailment, that, while it shuns the contact of men, it courts publicity. In proportion as solitude and communion with self lead the sentimentalist to exaggerate the importance of his own personality, he comes to think that the least event connected with it is of consequence to his fellow-men. If he change his shirt, he would have mankind aware of it. Victor Hugo, the greatest living representative of the class, considers it necessary to let the world know by letter from time to time his opinion on every conceivable subject about which it is not asked nor is of the least value unless we concede to him an immediate inspiration. We men of colder

_____
[90] Verse with lines of six feet, used in classical French tragedy.

blood, in whom self-consciousness takes the form of pride, and who have deified *mauvaise honte* [91] as if our defect were our virtue, find it especially hard to understand that artistic impulse of more southern races to *pose* themselves properly on every occasion, and not even to die without some tribute of deference to the taste of the world they are leaving. Was not even mighty Caesar's last thought of his drapery? Let us not condemn Rousseau for what seems to us the indecent exposure of himself in his "Confessions."

Those who allow an oratorical and purely conventional side disconnected with our private understanding of the facts and with life, in which everything has a wholly parliamentary sense where truth is made subservient to the momentary exigencies of eloquence, should be charitable to Rousseau. While we encourage a distinction which establishes two kinds of truth, one for the world and another for the conscience, while we take pleasure in a kind of speech that has no relation to the real thought of speaker or hearer, but to the rostrum only, we must not be hasty to condemn a sentimentalism which we do our best to foster. We listen in public with the gravity of augurs to what we smile at when we meet a brother adept. France is the native land of eulogy, of truth padded out to the size and shape demanded by *comme-il-faut*.[92] The French Academy has, perhaps, done more harm by the vogue it has given to this style, than it has done good by its literary purism; for the best purity of a language depends on the limpidity of its source in veracity of thought. Rousseau was in many respects a typical Frenchman, and it is not to be wondered at if he too often fell in with the fashion of saying what was expected of him, and what he thought due to the situation, rather than what would have been true to his inmost consciousness. Perhaps we should allow something to the influence of a Calvinistic training, which certainly helps men who have the least natural tendency towards it to set faith above works, and to persuade themselves of the efficacy of an inward grace to offset an outward and visible defec-

---

[91] Bashfulness (lit., false shame).
[92] Good-breeding.

tion from it; perhaps something also to the Jewish descent which his name seems to imply.

As the sentimentalist always takes a fanciful, sometimes an unreal, life for an ideal one, it would be too much to say that Rousseau was a man of earnest convictions. But he was a man of fitfully intense ones, as suited so mobile a temperament, and his writings, more than those of any other of his tribe, carry with them that persuasion that was in him while he wrote. In them at least he is as consistent as a man who admits new ideas can ever be. The children of his brain he never abandoned, but clung to them with paternal fidelity. Intellectually he was true and fearless; constitutionally, timid, contradictory, and weak; but never, if I understand him rightly, false. He was a little too credulous of sonorous sentiment, but he was never, like Chateaubriand or Lamartine, the mere lackey of fine phrases. If, as some fanciful physiologists have assumed, there be a masculine and feminine lobe of the brain, it should seem that in men of sentimental turn the masculine half fell in love with and made an idol of the other, obeying and admiring all the pretty whims of this *folle du logis*.[93] In Rousseau the mistress had some noble elements of character, and less taint of the *demi-monde* [94] than is visible in more recent cases of the same illicit relation.

DEMOCRACY [1]

HE MUST be a born leader or misleader of men, or must have been sent into the world unfurnished with that modulating and restraining balance-wheel which we call a sense of humor, who, in old age, has as strong a confidence in his opinions and in the

---

[93] Fancy.

[94] The courtesan or kept woman.

[1] Lowell's inaugural address on assuming the presidency of the Birmingham and Midland Institute, Birmingham, England, on October 6, 1884. Three days later he wrote to Mrs. W. K. Clifford: "My address would have been far better if I had been plain J.R.L. and not His Excellency." (*Letters,* II, 280.) To C. E. Norton, on October 17, he wrote about the address: "It has made a kind of (mildish) sensation, greatly to my surprise. I

necessity of bringing the universe into conformity with them as he had in youth. In a world the very condition of whose being is that it should be in perpetual flux, where all seems mirage, and the one abiding thing is the effort to distinguish realities from appearances, the elderly man must be indeed of a singularly tough and valid fibre who is certain that he has any clarified residuum of experience, any assured verdict of reflection, that deserves to be called an opinion, or who, even if he had, feels that he is justified in holding mankind by the button while he is expounding it. And in a world of daily—nay, almost hourly—journalism, where every clever man, every man who thinks himself clever, or whom anybody else thinks clever, is called upon to deliver his judgment point-blank and at the word of command on every conceivable subject of human thought, or, on what sometimes seems to him very much the same thing, on every inconceivable display of human want of thought, there is such a spendthrift waste of all those commonplaces which furnish the permitted staple of public discourse that there is little chance of beguiling a new tune out of the one-stringed instrument on which we have been thrumming so long. In this desperate necessity one is often tempted to think that, if all the words of the dictionary were tumbled down in a heap and then all those fortuitous juxtapositions and combinations that made tolerable sense were picked out and pieced together, we might

couldn't conceive . . . that I had made so great a splash with so small a pebble." (Ibid., II, 281.) Upon sending Norton a corrected copy of the address early in December, 1884, he remarks: "Of course you must read between the lines. I couldn't speak my mind freely whether for this latitude or that. I see our blots only too plainly, and have not forborne my commentary on them in time past." (Ibid., II, 287.) Some four years later he commented publicly concerning the famous Birmingham speech: "In that place I felt it incumbent on me to dwell on the good points and favorable aspects of democracy as I had seen them practically illustrated in my native land." (Speech before the Reform Club of New York, April 13, 1888.) On the date of its delivery the address appeared in brochure form for private circulation with the title "On Democracy." Lowell made a few revisions in the text very shortly afterward for the reprinting of the address in the Pall Mall Budget, of London, October 10, 1884. The inclusion of the address in Democracy and Other Addresses (1887) with a shorter title marked its first American publication. This American text was still further altered and enlarged by Lowell.

find among them some poignant suggestions towards novelty of thought or expression. But, alas! it is only the great poets who seem to have this unsolicited profusion of unexpected and incalculable phrase, this infinite variety of topic. For everybody else everything has been said before, and said over again after. He who has read his Aristotle will be apt to think that observation has on most points of general applicability said its last word, and he who has mounted the tower of Plato to look abroad from it will never hope to climb another with so lofty a vantage of speculation. Where it is so simple if not so easy a thing to hold one's peace, why add to the general confusion of tongues? There is something disheartening, too, in being expected to fill up not less than a certain measure of time, as if the mind were an hourglass, that need only be shaken and set on one end or the other, as the case may be, to run its allotted sixty minutes with decorous exactitude. I recollect being once told by the late eminent naturalist, Agassiz,[2] that when he was to deliver his first lecture as professor (at Zürich, I believe,) [3] he had grave doubts of his ability to occupy the prescribed three quarters of an hour. He was speaking without notes, and glancing anxiously from time to time at the watch that lay before him on the desk. "When I had spoken a half hour," he said, "I had told them everything I knew in the world, everything! Then I began to repeat myself," he added, roguishly, "and I have done nothing else ever since." Beneath the humorous exaggeration of the story I seemed to see the face of a very serious and improving moral. And yet if one were to say only what he had to say and then stopped, his audience would feel defrauded of their honest measure. Let us take courage by the example of the French, whose exportation of Bordeaux wines increases as the area of their land in vineyards is diminished.

To me, somewhat hopelessly revolving these things, the undelayable year has rolled round, and I find myself called upon to say something in this place, where so many wiser men have

---

[2] See note on p. 35.
[3] His first lecture as professor was not at Zürich, but at Neuchâtel, Switzerland, where he was appointed professor of natural history in 1838.

spoken before me. Precluded, in my quality of national guest, by motives of taste and discretion, from dealing with any question of immediate and domestic concern, it seemed to me wisest, or at any rate most prudent, to choose a topic of comparatively abstract interest, and to ask your indulgence for a few somewhat generalized remarks on a matter concerning which I had some experimental knowledge, derived from the use of such eyes and ears as Nature had been pleased to endow me withal, and such report as I had been able to win from them. The subject which most readily suggested itself was the spirit and the working of those conceptions of life and polity which are lumped together, whether for reproach or commendation, under the name of Democracy. By temperament and education of a conservative turn, I saw the last years of that quaint Arcadia which French travellers saw with delighted amazement a century ago,[4] and have watched the change (to me a sad one) from an agricultural to a proletary population. The testimony of Balaam [5] should carry some conviction. I have grown to manhood and am now growing old with the growth of this system of government in my native land; have watched its advances, or what some would call its encroachments, gradual and irresistible as those of a glacier; have been an ear-witness to the forebodings of wise and good and timid men, and have lived to see those forebodings belied by the course of events, which is apt to show itself humorously careless of the reputation of prophets. I recollect hearing a sagacious old gentleman say in 1840 that the doing away with the property qualification for suffrage twenty years before had been the ruin of the State of Massachusetts; that it had put public credit and private estate alike at the mercy of demagogues. I lived to see that Commonwealth twenty odd years later paying the interest on her bonds in gold, though it cost her sometimes nearly three for one to keep her faith, and that while suffering

---

[4] For example, J. H. St. Jean de Crèvecoeur (1735?–1813), who wrote *Letters from an American Farmer* (1782).

[5] Barak, king of Moab, tried earnestly to persuade the prophet Balaam to curse Israel, but Balaam found that the spirit of God forced him to bless rather than curse. "How shall I curse, whom God hath not cursed?" he cried out before Barak. See Numbers xxii, xxiii, xxiv, for the whole story.

an unparalleled drain of men and treasure in helping to sustain the unity and self-respect of the nation.

If universal suffrage has worked ill in our larger cities, as it certainly has, this has been mainly because the hands that wielded it were untrained to its use. There the election of a majority of the trustees of the public money is controlled by the most ignorant and vicious of a population which has come to us from abroad, wholly unpracticed in self-government and incapable of assimilation by American habits and methods. But the finances of our towns, where the native tradition is still dominant and whose affairs are discussed and settled in a public assembly of the people, have been in general honestly and prudently administered. Even in manufacturing towns, where a majority of the voters live by their daily wages, it is not so often the recklessness as the moderation of public expenditure that surprises an old-fashioned observer. "The beggar is in the saddle at last," cries Proverbial Wisdom. "Why, in the name of all former experience, doesn't he ride to the Devil?" Because in the very act of mounting he ceased to be a beggar and became part owner of the piece of property he bestrides. The last thing we need be anxious about is property. It always has friends or the means of making them. If riches have wings to fly away from their owner, they have wings also to escape danger.

I hear America sometimes playfully accused of sending you all your storms, and am in the habit of parrying the charge by alleging that we are enabled to do this because, in virtue of our protective system, we can afford to make better bad weather than anybody else. And what wiser use could we make of it than to export it in return for the paupers which some European countries are good enough to send over to us who have not attained to the same skill in the manufacture of them? But bad weather is not the worst thing that is laid at our door. A French gentleman, not long ago, forgetting Burke's monition of how unwise it is to draw an indictment against a whole people,[6] has

---

[6] Edmund Burke in his famous speech on Conciliation with America (March 22, 1775) remarked: "I do not know the method of drawing up an indictment against a whole people."

charged us with the responsibility of whatever he finds disagreeable in the morals or manners of his countrymen. If M. Zola [7] or some other competent witness would only go into the box and tell us what those morals and manners were before our example corrupted them! But I confess that I find little to interest and less to edify me in these international bandyings of "You're another."

I shall address myself to a single point only in the long list of offences of which we are more or less gravely accused, because that really includes all the rest. It is that we are infecting the Old World with what seems to be thought the entirely new disease of Democracy. It is generally people who are in what are called easy circumstances who can afford the leisure to treat themselves to a handsome complaint, and these experience an immediate alleviation when once they have found a sonorous Greek name to abuse it by. There is something consolatory also, something flattering to their sense of personal dignity, and to that conceit of singularity which is the natural recoil from our uneasy consciousness of being commonplace, in thinking ourselves victims of a malady by which no one had ever suffered before. Accordingly they find it simpler to class under one comprehensive heading whatever they find offensive to their nerves, their tastes, their interests, or what they suppose to be their opinions, and christen it Democracy, much as physicians label every obscure disease gout, or as cross-grained fellows lay their ill-temper to the weather. But is it really a new ailment, and, if it be, is America answerable for it? Even if she were, would it account for the phylloxera,[8] and hoof-and-mouth disease, and bad harvests, and bad English, and the German bands,[9] and the Boers,[10] and all the other discomforts with which these later days

---

[7] Emile Zola (1840–1902) led the way in French fiction toward an extreme naturalism.

[8] An insect disease which destroys grapevines.

[9] Bands of German musicians played about the streets of English cities in the 1880's. Lowell in his letters complained of their noise on more than one occasion.

[10] The Dutch settlers in Transvaal, South Africa, who after British annexation of the territory in 1879 rebelled and defeated the British in turn. They then gained a measure of self-government by the Pretoria Convention

have vexed the souls of them that go in chariots? Yet I have seen the evil example of Democracy in America cited as the source and origin of things quite as heterogeneous and quite as little connected with it by any sequence of cause and effect. Surely this ferment is nothing new. It has been at work for centuries, and we are more conscious of it only because in this age of publicity, where the newspapers offer a rostrum to whoever has a grievance, or fancies that he has, the bubbles and scum thrown up by it are more noticeable on the surface than in those dumb ages when there was a cover of silence and suppression on the cauldron. Bernardo Navagero, speaking of the Provinces of Lower Austria in 1546, tells us that "in them there are five sorts of persons, Clergy, Barons, Nobles, Burghers, and Peasants. Of these last no account is made, *because they have no voice in the Diet.*" [11]

Nor was it among the people that subversive or mistaken doctrines had their rise. A Father of the Church [12] said that property was theft many centuries before Proudhon [13] was born. Bourdaloue [14] reaffirmed it. Montesquieu [15] was the inventor of national workshops, and of the theory that the State owed every man a living. Nay, was not the Church herself the first

of 1881, but they continued occasional hostilities to secure more political freedom, and in 1884, the year of this address, they obtained British recognition of their South African Republic.

[11] Below the Peasants, it should be remembered, was still another, even more helpless, class, the servile farm-laborers. The same witness informs us that of the extraordinary imposts the Peasants paid nearly twice as much in proportion to their estimated property as the Barons, Nobles, and Burghers together. Moreover, the upper classes were assessed at their own valuation, while they arbitrarily fixed that of the Peasants, who had no voice. (*Relazioni degli Ambasciatori, Veneti*, Serie I., tomo i., pp. 378, 379, 389.) [Lowell's note.]

[12] The Father meant is probably St. Augustine, though St. Ambrose and St. Jerome also opposed the acquisition of private property.

[13] Pierre Joseph Proudhon (1809–65), French economist and revolutionary socialist, asserted in his treatise of 1840, *Qu'est-ce que la propriété?* (*What is Property?*) that *"la propriété, c'est la vol* (property is theft)."

[14] Louis Bourdaloue (1632–1704), a celebrated French divine and preacher of the reign of Louis XIV.

[15] Charles Louis de Secondat de Montesquieu (1689–1755), noted French political philosopher, who wrote *L'Esprit des lois* (*The Spirit of the Laws*), 1748.

organized Democracy? A few centuries ago the chief end of man was to keep his soul alive, and then the little kernel of leaven that sets the gases at work was religious, and produced the Reformation. Even in that, far-sighted persons like the Emperor Charles V [16] saw the germ of political and social revolution. Now that the chief end of man seems to have become the keeping of the body alive, and as comfortably alive as possible, the leaven also has become wholly political and social. But there had also been social upheavals before the Reformation and contemporaneously with it, especially among men of Teutonic race. The Reformation gave outlet and direction to an unrest already existing. Formerly the immense majority of men—our brothers—knew only their sufferings, their wants, and their desires. They are beginning now to know their opportunity and their power. All persons who see deeper than their plates are rather inclined to thank God for it than to bewail it, for the sores of Lazarus have a poison in them against which Dives has no antidote.[17]

There can be no doubt that the spectacle of a great and prosperous Democracy on the other side of the Atlantic must react powerfully on the aspirations and political theories of men in the Old World who do not find things to their mind; but, whether for good or evil, it should not be overlooked that the acorn from which it sprang was ripened on the British oak. Every successive swarm that has gone out from this *officina gentium* [18] has, when left to its own instincts—may I not call them hereditary instincts?—assumed a more or less thoroughly democratic form. This would seem to show, what I believe to be the fact, that the British Constitution, under whatever disguises of prudence or decorum, is essentially democratic. England, indeed, may be called a monarchy with democratic tendencies, the United States a democracy with conservative instincts. People

---

[16] See note on p. 63.

[17] Lazarus, a beggar, lay at the gate to the house of Dives, a rich man, and fed on the crumbs from the rich man's table. The dogs came and licked the sores which covered the body of Lazarus. After death, the beggar went to heaven, while Dives suffered torment in hell. See Luke xvi: 19–31.

[18] Manufactory of nations.

are continually saying that America is in the air, and I am glad
to think it is, since this means only that a clearer conception of
human claims and human duties is beginning to be prevalent.
The discontent with the existing order of things, however, pervaded the atmosphere wherever the conditions were favorable,
long before Columbus, seeking the back door of Asia, found
himself knocking at the front door of America. I say wherever
the conditions were favorable, for it is certain that the germs of
disease do not stick or find a prosperous field for their development and noxious activity unless where the simplest sanitary
precautions have been neglected. "For this effect defective
comes by cause," as Polonius said long ago.[19] It is only by instigation of the wrongs of men that what are called the Rights
of Man [20] become turbulent and dangerous. It is then only that
they syllogize unwelcome truths. It is not the insurrections of
ignorance that are dangerous, but the revolts of intelligence:—

> The wicked and the weak rebel in vain,
> Slaves by their own compulsion.[21]

Had the governing classes in France during the last century paid
as much heed to their proper business as to their pleasures or
manners, the guillotine need never have severed that spinal mar-
row of orderly and secular tradition through which in a nor-
mally constituted state the brain sympathizes with the extremities and sends will and impulsion thither. It is only when the
reasonable and practicable are denied that men demand the unreasonable and impracticable; only when the possible is made
difficult that they fancy the impossible to be easy. Fairy tales
are made out of the dreams of the poor. No; the sentiment

---

[19] Polonius, the aged royal counselor, makes this remark in *Hamlet,* II,
ii, 103.

[20] Thomas Paine (see also note on p. 116) wrote in 1791 an influential
revolutionary work, *The Rights of Man.* This book caused him to be out-
lawed from England and then to be imprisoned in France, whither he had
gone for asylum.

[21] These two lines are misquoted from Coleridge's *France: An Ode*
(1798), ll. 85–6. The correct version is:

> The Sensual and the Dark rebel in vain,
> Slaves by their own compulsion! . . .

which lies at the root of democracy is nothing new. I am speaking always of a sentiment, a spirit, and not of a form of government; for this was but the outgrowth of the other and not its cause. This sentiment is merely an expression of the natural wish of people to have a hand, if need be a controlling hand, in the management of their own affairs. What is new is that they are more and more gaining that control, and learning more and more how to be worthy of it. What we used to call the tendency or drift—what we are being taught to call more wisely the evolution of things—has for some time been setting steadily in this direction. There is no good in arguing with the inevitable. The only argument available with an east wind is to put on your overcoat. And in this case, also, the prudent will prepare themselves to encounter what they cannot prevent. Some people advise us to put on the brakes, as if the movement of which we are conscious were that of a railway train running down an incline. But a metaphor is no argument, though it be sometimes the gunpowder to drive one home and imbed it in the memory. Our disquiet comes of what nurses and other experienced persons call growing-pains, and need not seriously alarm us. They are what every generation before us—certainly every generation since the invention of printing—has gone through with more or less good fortune. To the door of every generation there comes a knocking, and unless the household, like the Thane of Cawdor and his wife,[22] have been doing some deed without a name,[23] they need not shudder. It turns out at worst to be a poor relation who wishes to come in out of the cold.[24] The porter always grumbles and is slow to open. "Who's there, in the name of Beelzebub?" he mutters. Not a change for the better in our human housekeeping has ever taken place that wise and good men have not opposed it,—have not prophesied with the alderman that the world would wake up to find its throat cut in con-

---

[22] Macbeth and Lady Macbeth.

[23] In *Macbeth*, IV, i, the witches reply to Macbeth's question, "What is't you do?" by saying, "A deed without a name."

[24] In this and the next sentence Lowell has reference to the remarks of the porter in the impressive scene of the knocking at the castle gate, *Macbeth*, II, iii.

sequence of it. The world, on the contrary, wakes up, rubs its eyes, yawns, stretches itself, and goes about its business as if nothing had happened. Suppression of the slave trade, abolition of slavery, trade unions,—at all of these excellent people shook their heads despondingly, and murmured "Ichabod." [25] But the trade unions are now debating instead of conspiring, and we all read their discussions with comfort and hope, sure that they are learning the business of citizenship and the difficulties of practical legislation.

One of the most curious of these frenzies of exclusion was that against the emancipation of the Jews. All share in the government of the world was denied for centuries to perhaps the ablest, certainly the most tenacious, race that had ever lived in it—the race to whom we owed our religion and the purest spiritual stimulus and consolation to be found in all literature—a race in which ability seems as natural and hereditary as the curve of their noses, and whose blood, furtively mingling with the bluest bloods in Europe, has quickened them with its own indomitable impulsion. We drove them into a corner, but they had their revenge, as the wronged are always sure to have it sooner or later. They made their corner the counter and banking-house of the world, and thence they rule it and us with the ignobler sceptre of finance. Your grandfathers mobbed Priestley [26] only that you might set up his statue and make Birmingham the headquarters of English Unitarianism. We hear it said sometimes that this is an age of transition, as if that made matters clearer; but can any one point us to an age that was not? If he could, he would show us an age of stagnation. The question for us, as it has been for all before us, is to make the transition gradual and easy, to see that our points are right so that the train may not come to grief. For we should remember that nothing is

---

[25] A Hebrew word meaning "The glory has departed." See I Samuel iv: 21.

[26] Joseph Priestley (1733–1804), an English dissenting clergyman, who in 1791 was attacked by a Birmingham mob and had his house burned, on account of his sympathy with the French Revolution. The statue to honor his memory was erected at Birmingham in 1874 and is one of the chief monuments in the city.

more natural for people whose education has been neglected than to spell evolution with an initial "r." A great man struggling with the storms of fate has been called a sublime spectacle; but surely a great man wrestling with these new forces that have come into the world, mastering them and controlling them to beneficent ends, would be a yet sublimer. Here is not a danger, and if there were it would be only a better school of manhood, a nobler scope for ambition. I have hinted that what people are afraid of in democracy is less the thing itself than what they conceive to be its necessary adjuncts and consequences. It is supposed to reduce all mankind to a dead level of mediocrity in character and culture, to vulgarize men's conceptions of life, and therefore their code of morals, manners, and conduct—to endanger the rights of property and possession. But I believe that the real gravamen of the charges lies in the habit it has of making itself generally disagreeable by asking the Powers that Be at the most inconvenient moment whether they are the powers that ought to be. If the powers that be are in a condition to give a satisfactory answer to this inevitable question, they need feel in no way discomfited by it.

Few people take the trouble of trying to find out what democracy really is. Yet this would be a great help, for it is our lawless and uncertain thoughts, it is the indefiniteness of our impressions, that fill darkness, whether mental or physical, with spectres and hobgoblins. Democracy is nothing more than an experiment in government, more likely to succeed in a new soil, but likely to be tried in all soils, which must stand or fall on its own merits as others have done before it. For there is no trick of perpetual motion in politics any more than in mechanics. President Lincoln defined democracy to be "the government of the people by the people for the people." This is a sufficiently compact statement of it as a political arrangement. Theodore Parker [27] said that "Democracy meant not 'I'm as good as you are,' but 'You're as good as I am.'" And this is the ethical conception of it, necessary as a complement of the other; a con-

---

[27] Theodore Parker (1810–60), a leading Unitarian minister and Abolitionist of Boston.

ception which, could it be made actual and practical, would easily solve all the riddles that the old sphinx of political and social economy who sits by the roadside has been proposing to mankind from the beginning, and which mankind have shown such a singular talent for answering wrongly. In this sense Christ was the first true democrat that ever breathed, as the old dramatist Dekker [28] said he was the first true gentleman. The characters may be easily doubled, so strong is the likeness between them. A beautiful and profound parable of the Persian poet Jellaladeen [29] tells us that "One knocked at the Beloved's door, and a voice asked from within 'Who is there?' and he answered 'It is I.' Then the voice said, 'This house will not hold me and thee'; and the door was not opened. Then went the lover into the desert and fasted and prayed in solitude, and after a year he returned and knocked again at the door; and again the voice asked 'Who is there?' and he said 'It is thyself'; and the door was opened to him." But that is idealism, you will say, and this is an only too practical world. I grant it; but I am one of those who believe that the real will never find an irremovable basis till it rests on the ideal. It used to be thought that a democracy was possible only in a small territory, and this is doubtless true of a democracy strictly defined, for in such all the citizens decide directly upon every question of public concern in a general assembly. An example still survives in the tiny Swiss canton of Appenzell.[30] But this immediate intervention of the people in their own affairs is not of the essence of democracy; it is not necessary, nor indeed, in most cases, practicable. Democracies to which Mr. Lincoln's definition would fairly enough apply have existed, and now exist, in which, though the supreme authority reside in the people, yet they can act only indirectly on the national policy. This generation has seen a democracy with

---

[28] Thomas Dekker (c. 1572–c. 1632), one of Shakespeare's fellow playwrights, in *The Honest Whore,* Pt. I, Sc. 15, l. 600.

[29] Jalal-uddin Rumi (1207–73), a translation of whose poetry appeared in 1881.

[30] With a total area of 162 square miles, it is divided into two separate half-cantons, Protestant and Catholic respectively. Appenzell joined the Swiss Confederation in 1513.

an imperial figurehead,[31] and in all that have ever existed the body politic has never embraced all the inhabitants included within its territory, the right to share in the direction of affairs has been confined to citizens, and citizenship has been further restricted by various limitations, sometimes of property, sometimes of nativity, and always of age and sex.

The framers of the American Constitution were far from wishing or intending to found a democracy in the strict sense of the word, though, as was inevitable, every expansion of the scheme of government they elaborated has been in a democratical direction. But this has been generally the slow result of growth, and not the sudden innovation of theory; in fact, they had a profound disbelief in theory, and knew better than to commit the folly of breaking with the past. They were not seduced by the French fallacy that a new system of government could be ordered like a new suit of clothes. They would as soon have thought of ordering a new suit of flesh and skin. It is only on the roaring loom of time [32] that the stuff is woven for such a vesture of their thought and experience as they were meditating. They recognized fully the value of tradition and habit as the great allies of permanence and stability. They all had that distaste for innovation which belonged to their race, and many of them a distrust of human nature derived from their creed. The day of sentiment was over, and no dithyrambic affirmations or fine-drawn analyses of the Rights of Man would serve their present turn. This was a practical question, and they addressed themselves to it as men of knowledge and judgment should. Their problem was how to adapt English principles and precedents to the new conditions of American life, and they solved it with singular discretion. They put as many obstacles as they could contrive, not in the way of the people's will, but of their whim. With few exceptions they probably admitted the logic of the then accepted syllogism,—democracy, anarchy, despotism.

---

[31] An allusion to Napoleon III (1808–73), commonly called Louis Napoleon, who was proclaimed Emperor of France in 1852 at the close of the Second Republic.

[32] This phrase, Carlyle's translation of a line from Goethe's *Faust*, comes from *Sartor Resartus*, Bk. I, chap. 8.

But this formula was framed upon the experience of small cities shut up to stew within their narrow walls, where the number of citizens made but an inconsiderable fraction of the inhabitants, where every passion was reverberated from house to house and from man to man with gathering rumor till every impulse became gregarious and therefore inconsiderate, and every popular assembly needed but an infusion of eloquent sophistry to turn it into a mob, all the more dangerous because sanctified with the formality of law.[33]

Fortunately their case was wholly different. They were to legislate for a widely scattered population and for States already practised in the discipline of a partial independence. They had an unequalled opportunity and enormous advantages. The material they had to work upon was already democratical by instinct and habitude. It was tempered to their hands by more than a century's schooling in self-government. They had but to give permanent and conservative form to a ductile mass. In giving impulse and direction to their new institutions, especially in supplying them with checks and balances, they had a great help and safeguard in their federal organization. The different, sometimes conflicting, interests and social systems of the several States made existence as a Union and coalescence into a nation conditional on a constant practice of moderation and compromise. The very elements of disintegration were the best guides in political training. Their children learned the lesson of compromise only too well, and it was the application of it to a question of fundamental morals that cost us our civil war. We learned once for all that compromise makes a good umbrella but a poor roof; that it is a temporary expedient, often wise in party politics, almost sure to be unwise in statesmanship.

Has not the trial of democracy in America proved, on the whole, successful? If it had not, would the Old World be vexed with any fears of its proving contagious? This trial would have

---

[33] The effect of the electric telegraph in reproducing this trooping of emotion and perhaps of opinion is yet to be measured. The effect of Darwinism as a disintegrator of humanitarianism is also to be reckoned with. [Lowell's note.]

been less severe could it have been made with a people homogeneous in race, language, and traditions, whereas the United States have been called on to absorb and assimilate enormous masses of foreign population, heterogeneous in all these respects, and drawn mainly from that class which might fairly say that the world was not their friend, nor the world's law. The previous condition too often justified the traditional Irishman, who, landing in New York and asked what his politics were, inquired if there was a Government there, and on being told that there was, retorted, "Thin I'm agin it!" We have taken from Europe the poorest, the most ignorant, the most turbulent of her people, and have made them over into good citizens, who have added to our wealth, and who are ready to die in defence of a country and of institutions which they know to be worth dying for. The exceptions have been (and they are lamentable exceptions) where these hordes of ignorance and poverty have coagulated in great cities. But the social system is yet to seek which has not to look the same terrible wolf in the eyes. On the other hand, at this very moment Irish peasants are buying up the worn-out farms of Massachusetts, and making them productive again by the same virtues of industry and thrift that once made them profitable to the English ancestors of the men who are deserting them. To have achieved even these prosaic results (if you choose to call them so), and that out of materials the most discordant,—I might say the most recalcitrant,—argues a certain beneficent virtue in the system that could do it, and is not to be accounted for by mere luck. Carlyle said scornfully that America meant only roast turkey every day for everybody.[34] He forgot that States, as Bacon said of wars, go on their bellies.[35] As for the security of property, it should be tolerably well

---

[34] Lowell has here altered very considerably a passage in Carlyle's *Latter-Day Pamphlets*, No. 1 (1850), where he says: "Hitherto she [i.e., America] but ploughs and hammers, in a very successful manner; hitherto, in spite of her 'roast-goose with apple-sauce,' she is not much."

[35] Francis Bacon (1561–1626), first Baron Verulam, English statesman, philosopher and writer never made a statement to this effect. Lowell apparently had in mind the famous saying, "An army, like a serpent, goes on its belly," generally attributed to Frederick the Great, King of Prussia (1740–86).

secured in a country where every other man hopes to be rich, even though the only property qualification be the ownership of two hands that add to the general wealth. Is it not the best security for anything to interest the largest possible number of persons in its preservation and the smallest in its division? In point of fact, far-seeing men count the increasing power of wealth and its combinations as one of the chief dangers with which the institutions of the United States are threatened in the not distant future. The right of individual property is no doubt the very corner-stone of civilization as hitherto understood, but I am a little impatient of being told that property is entitled to exceptional consideration because it bears all the burdens of the State. It bears those, indeed, which can most easily be borne, but poverty pays with its person the chief expenses of war, pestilence, and famine. Wealth should not forget this, for poverty is beginning to think of it now and then. Let me not be misunderstood. I see as clearly as any man possibly can, and rate as highly, the value of wealth, and of hereditary wealth, as the security of refinement, the feeder of all those arts that ennoble and beautify life, and as making a country worth living in. Many an ancestral hall here in England has been a nursery of that culture which has been of example and benefit to all. Old gold has a civilizing virtue which new gold must grow old to be capable of secreting.

I should not think of coming before you to defend or to criticise any form of government. All have their virtues, all their defects, and all have illustrated one period or another in the history of the race, with signal services to humanity and culture. There is not one that could stand a cynical cross-examination by an experienced criminal lawyer, except that of a perfectly wise and perfectly good despot, such as the world has never seen, except in that white-haired king of Browning's, who

> Lived long ago
> In the morning of the world,
> When Earth was nearer Heaven than now.[36]

---

[36] Lines 1-3 from Pippa's lyric in *Pippa Passes*, Scene 3 (Evening).

The English race, if they did not invent government by discussion, have at least carried it nearest to perfection in practice. It seems a very safe and reasonable contrivance for occupying the attention of the country, and is certainly a better way of settling questions than by push of pike. Yet, if one should ask it why it should not rather be called government by gabble, it would have to fumble in its pocket a good while before it found the change for a convincing reply. As matters stand, too, it is beginning to be doubtful whether Parliament and Congress sit at Westminster and Washington or in the editors' rooms of the leading journals, so thoroughly is everything debated before the authorized and responsible debaters get on their legs. And what shall we say of government by a majority of voices? To a person who in the last century would have called himself an Impartial Observer, a numerical preponderance seems, on the whole, as clumsy a way of arriving at truth as could well be devised, but experience has apparently shown it to be a convenient arrangement for determining what may be expedient or advisable or practicable at any given moment. Truth, after all, wears a different face to everybody, and it would be too tedious to wait till all were agreed. She is said to lie at the bottom of a well, for the very reason, perhaps, that whoever looks down in search of her sees his own image at the bottom, and is persuaded not only that he has seen the goddess, but that she is far better-looking than he had imagined.

The arguments against universal suffrage are equally unanswerable. "What," we exclaim, "shall Tom, Dick, and Harry have as much weight in the scale as I?" Of course, nothing could be more absurd. And yet universal suffrage has not been the instrument of greater unwisdom than contrivances of a more select description. Assemblies could be mentioned composed entirely of Masters of Arts and Doctors in Divinity which have sometimes shown traces of human passion or prejudice in their votes. Have the Serene Highnesses and Enlightened Classes carried on the business of Mankind so well, then, that there is no use in trying a less costly method? The democratic theory is that those Constitutions are likely to prove steadiest which have the broadest base, that the right to vote makes a safety-valve of every voter, and that the best way of teaching a man how to vote is to give him the chance of practice. For the question is no longer the academic one, "Is it wise to give every man the ballot?" but rather the practical one, "Is it prudent to deprive whole classes of it any longer?" It may be conjectured that it is cheaper in the long run to lift men up than to hold them down, and that the ballot in their hands is less dangerous to society than a sense of wrong in their heads. At any rate this is the dilemma to which the drift of opinion has been for some time sweeping us, and in politics a dilemma is a more unmanageable thing to hold by the horns than a wolf by the ears. It is said that the right of suffrage is not valued when it is indiscriminately bestowed, and there may be some truth in this, for I have observed that what men prize most is a privilege, even if it be that of chief mourner at a funeral. But is there not danger that it will be valued at more than its worth if denied, and that some illegitimate way will be sought to make up for the want of it? Men who have a voice in public affairs are at once affiliated with one or other of the great parties between which society is divided, merge their individual hopes and opinions in its safer, because more generalized, hopes and opinions, are disciplined by its tactics, and acquire, to a certain degree, the orderly qualities of an army. They no longer belong to a class, but to a body corporate. Of one thing, at least, we may be certain, that, under whatever method of helping things to go wrong man's wit can contrive, those who have the divine right to govern will be found to govern in the end, and that the highest privilege to which the majority of mankind can aspire is that of being governed by those wiser than they. Universal suffrage has in the United States sometimes been made the instrument of inconsiderate changes, under the notion of reform, and this from a misconception of the true meaning of popular government. One of these has been the substitution in many of the States of popular election for official selection in the choice of judges. The same system applied to military officers was the source of much evil during our civil war, and, I believe, had to be aban-

doned. But it has been also true that on all great questions of
national policy a reserve of prudence and discretion has been
brought out at the critical moment to turn the scale in favor of a
wiser decision. An appeal to the reason of the people has never
been known to fail in the long run. It is, perhaps, true that, by
effacing the principle of passive obedience, democracy, ill understood, has slackened the spring of that ductility to discipline
which is essential to "the unity and married calm of States." [37]
But I feel assured that experience and necessity will cure this
evil, as they have shown their power to cure others. And under
what frame of policy have evils ever been remedied till they became intolerable, and shook men out of their indolent indifference through their fears?

We are told that the inevitable result of democracy is to sap
the foundations of personal independence, to weaken the principle of authority, to lessen the respect due to eminence, whether
in station, virtue, or genius. If these things were so, society
could not hold together. Perhaps the best forcing-house of robust individuality would be where public opinion is inclined to
be most overbearing, as he must be of heroic temper who should
walk along Piccadilly at the height of the season in a soft hat.[38]
As for authority, it is one of the symptoms of the time that the
religious reverence for it is declining everywhere, but this is due
partly to the fact that state-craft is no longer looked upon as a
mystery, but as a business, and partly to the decay of superstition, by which I mean the habit of respecting what we are told
to respect rather than what is respectable in itself. There is
more rough and tumble in the American democracy than is
altogether agreeable to people of sensitive nerves and refined
habits, and the people take their political duties lightly and
laughingly, as is, perhaps, neither unnatural nor unbecoming in
a young giant. Democracies can no more jump away from

---

[37] See Ulysses' speech on rank in Shakespeare's *Troilus and Cressida*, I,
iii, 100.

[38] English fashion at this time decreed the high silk hat for town wear.
Piccadilly in London's West End was then one of the most fashionable
streets in the city.

their own shadows than the rest of us can. They no doubt some-times make mistakes and pay honor to men who do not deserve it. But they do this because they believe them worthy of it, and though it be true that the idol is the measure of the worshipper, yet the worship has in it the germ of a nobler religion. But is it democracies alone that fall into these errors? I, who have seen it proposed to erect a statue to Hudson,[39] the railway king, and have heard Louis Napoleon hailed as the saviour of society by men who certainly had no democratic associations or leanings, am not ready to think so. But democracies have likewise their finer instincts. I have also seen the wisest statesman and most pregnant speaker of our generation, a man of humble birth and ungainly manners, of little culture beyond what his own genius supplied, become more absolute in power than any monarch of modern times through the reverence of his countrymen for his honesty, his wisdom, his sincerity, his faith in God and man, and the nobly humane simplicity of his character. And I remember another whom popular respect enveloped as with a halo, the least vulgar of men, the most austerely genial, and the most independ-ent of opinion. Wherever he went he never met a stranger, but everywhere neighbors and friends proud of him as their orna-ment and decoration. Institutions which could bear and breed such men as Lincoln and Emerson had surely some energy for good. No, amid all the fruitless turmoil and miscarriage of the world, if there be one thing steadfast and of favorable omen, one thing to make optimism distrust its own obscure distrust, it is the rooted instinct in men to admire what is better and more beautiful than themselves. The touchstone of political and social institutions is their ability to supply them with worthy objects of this sentiment, which is the very tap-root of civilization and progress. There would seem to be no readier way of feeding it

---

[39] George Hudson (1800–71) was a leading English promoter and specu-lator in railway-building. His fame reached its zenith about 1844–45, when he was given £16,000 by admiring friends, but by 1849 his star had fallen as his wild speculations became known. Meanwhile a proposal to raise £25,000 for a statue in his honor had been made, but was soon dropped. See Carlyle's scathing essay, *Hudson's Statue* (1850).

with the elements of growth and vigor than such an organization of society as will enable men to respect themselves, and so to justify them in respecting others.

Such a result is quite possible under other conditions than those of an avowedly democratical Constitution. For I take it that the real essence of democracy was fairly enough defined by the First Napoleon when he said that the French Revolution meant *"la carrière ouverte aux talents"*—a clear pathway for merit of whatever kind.[40] I should be inclined to paraphrase this by calling democracy that form of society, no matter what its political classification, in which every man had a chance and knew that he had it. If a man can climb, and feels himself encouraged to climb, from a coalpit to the highest position for which he is fitted, he can well afford to be indifferent what name is given to the government under which he lives. The Bailli of Mirabeau,[41] uncle of the more famous tribune of that name,[42] wrote in 1771: "The English are, in my opinion, a hundred times more agitated and more unfortunate than the very Algerines themselves, because they do not know and will not know till the destruction of their overswollen power, which I believe very near, whether they are monarchy, aristocracy, or democracy, and wish to play the part of all three."[43] England has not been obliging enough to fulfil the Bailli's prophecy, and perhaps it was this very carelessness about the name, and concern about the substance of popular government, this skill in

---

[40] Lowell has changed somewhat the application of Napoleon's words. The phrase comes from *Napoleon in Exile* (1822) by O'Meara, Napoleon's surgeon at St. Helena. Napoleon was speaking of his own policy and was reported to have said: *"La carrière ouverte aux talents, voilà mon principe!* (The career open to talents, that is my principle!)."

[41] Jean-Antoine-Joseph-Charles-Elzear de Riquetti (1717–94), a French naval officer of some distinction.

[42] Gabriel-Honoré de Riquetti, comte de Mirabeau (1749–91), famous writer and statesman, who was leader of the Jacobins in the first years of the French Revolution. Lowell calls him "tribune" in the Roman sense, tribune of the people, because, though an aristocrat by birth, he became a leader of the popular cause.

[43] This quotation is from the well-known collected memoirs of the Mirabeau family, first published at Paris in 1834, and then printed in English at London in 1835–36.

getting the best out of things as they are, in utilizing all the motives which influence men, and in giving one direction to many impulses, that has been a principal factor of her greatness and power. Perhaps it is fortunate to have an unwritten Constitution, for men are prone to be tinkering the work of their own hands, whereas they are more willing to let time and circumstance mend or modify what time and circumstance have made. All free governments, whatever their name, are in reality governments by public opinion, and it is on the quality of this public opinion that their prosperity depends. It is, therefore, their first duty to purify the element from which they draw the breath of life. With the growth of democracy grows also the fear, if not the danger, that this atmosphere may be corrupted with poisonous exhalations from lower and more malarious levels, and the question of sanitation becomes more instant and pressing. Democracy in its best sense is merely the letting in of light and air. Lord Sherbrooke,[44] with his usual epigrammatic terseness, bids you educate your future rulers. But would this alone be a sufficient safeguard? To educate the intelligence is to enlarge the horizon of its desires and wants. And it is well that this should be so. But the enterprise must go deeper and prepare the way for satisfying those desires and wants in so far as they are legitimate. What is really ominous of danger to the existing order of things is not democracy (which, properly understood, is a conservative force), but the Socialism which may find a fulcrum in it. If we cannot equalize conditions and fortunes any more than we can equalize the brains of men—and a very sagacious person has said that "where two men ride of a horse one must ride behind"—we can yet, perhaps, do something to correct those methods and influences that lead to enormous inequalities, and to prevent their growing more enormous. It is all very well to pooh-pooh Mr. George [45] and to prove him mis-

---

[44] Robert Lowe, Viscount Sherbrooke (1811–92), who served as vice-president of the committee of the council of education during the Palmerston ministry of 1859–65, and instituted a number of reforms in the state-supported system of schools.

[45] Henry George (1839–97), noted political economist and leading advocate of the "single tax," wrote *Progress and Poverty* (1879) and *The*

taken in his political economy. I do not believe that land should be divided because the quantity of it is limited by nature. Of what may this not be said? *A fortiori*,[46] we might on the same principle insist on a division of human wit, for I have observed that the quantity of this has been even more inconveniently limited. Mr. George himself has an inequitably large share of it. But he is right in his impelling motive; right, also, I am convinced, in insisting that humanity makes a part, by far the most important part, of political economy; and in thinking man to be of more concern and more convincing than the longest columns of figures in the world. For unless you include human nature in your addition, your total is sure to be wrong and your deductions from it fallacious. Communism means barbarism, but Socialism means, or wishes to mean, coöperation and community of interests, sympathy, the giving to the hands not so large a share as to the brains, but a larger share than hitherto in the wealth they must combine to produce—means, in short, the practical application of Christianity to life, and has in it the secret of an orderly and benign reconstruction. State Socialism would cut off the very roots in personal character—self-help, forethought, and frugality—which nourish and sustain the trunk and branches of every vigorous Commonwealth.

I do not believe in violent changes, nor do I expect them. Things in possession have a very firm grip. One of the strongest cements of society is the conviction of mankind that the state of things into which they are born is a part of the order of the universe, as natural, let us say, as that the sun should go round the earth. It is a conviction that they will not surrender except on compulsion, and a wise society should look to it that this compulsion be not put upon them. For the individual man there is no radical cure, outside of human nature itself, for the evils to which human nature is heir. The rule will always hold good that you must

---

Land Question (1883), in which latter work he argued for the nationalization of land.

[46] With stronger reason.

Be your own palace or the world's your gaol.[47]

But for artificial evils, for evils that spring from want of thought, thought must find a remedy somewhere. There has been no period of time in which wealth has been more sensible of its duties than now. It builds hospitals, it establishes missions among the poor, it endows schools. It is one of the advantages of accumulated wealth, and of the leisure it renders possible, that people have time to think of the wants and sorrows of their fellows. But all these remedies are partial and palliative merely. It is as if we should apply plasters to a single pustule of the smallpox with a view of driving out the disease. The true way is to discover and to extirpate the germs. As society is now constituted these are in the air it breathes, in the water it drinks, in things that seem, and which it has always believed, to be the most innocent and healthful. The evil elements it neglects corrupt these in their springs and pollute them in their courses. Let us be of good cheer, however, remembering that the misfortunes hardest to bear are those which never come. The world has outlived much, and will outlive a great deal more, and men have contrived to be happy in it. It has shown the strength of its constitution in nothing more than in surviving the quack medicines it has tried. In the scales of the destinies brawn will never weigh so much as brain. Our healing is not in the storm or in the whirlwind, it is not in monarchies, or aristocracies, or democracies, but will be revealed by the still small voice [48] that speaks to the conscience and the heart, prompting us to a wider and wiser humanity.

---

[47] This line from John Donne's *To Sir Henry Wotton,* the first of the verse letters addressed to Wotton, has been modernized by Lowell. Line 52 of the original reads:
　　　　Bee thine owne Palace, or the world's thy gaole.
[48] See I Kings XIX:11–12.

DON QUIXOTE [1]

IN EVERY literature which can be in any sense called national there is a flavor of the soil from which it sprang, in which it grew, and from which its roots drew nourishment. This flavor, at first, perhaps, the cause of distaste, gives a peculiar relish when we have once learned to like it. It is a limitation, no doubt, and when artificially communicated, or in excess, incurs the reproach of provincialism, just as there are certain national dishes that are repugnant to every foreign palate. But it has the advantage of giving even to second-class writers in a foreign language that strangeness which in our own tongue is possible only to originality either of thought or style. When this savor of nationality is combined with original genius, as in such a writer as Calderon,[2] for example, the charm is incalculably heightened.

Spanish literature, if it have nothing that for height and depth can be compared with the "Divina Commedia" of Dante (as indeed what other modern literature has?), is rich in works that will repay study, and evolved itself by natural processes out of the native genius, the history, and the mingled races of the country more evidently, perhaps, than that of any other modern people. It was of course more or less modified from time to time by foreign, especially by French, influences in its earlier period, by Italian in the sixteenth century, and in later times again by French and German influences more or less plainly marked, but through all and in spite of all, by virtue of the vigor of its native impulse, it has given an essentially Spanish character to all its productions. Its earliest monument, the

---

[1] Notes read at the Workingmen's College, Great Ormond Street, London, sometime during Lowell's term as American Minister to Great Britain. This informal address was first printed, without any clue as to its date, in *Democracy and Other Addresses* (1887). The subject was one upon which, with great delight, Lowell had often lectured at Harvard. Evidently the copious notes in the margin of his pet volume of the much-beloved Cervantes masterpiece formed the basis for the lecture in London.

[2] See note on p. 38.

"Song of the Cid," is in form a reproduction of the French "Chanson de Geste," a song of action or of what has been acted, but the spirit which animates it is very different from that which animates the "Song of Roland," its nearest French parallel in subject and form. The Spanish Romances, very much misrepresented in the spirited and facile reproductions of Lockhart,[3] are beyond question the most original and fascinating popular poetry of which we know anything. Their influence upon the form of Heine's verse is unmistakable. In the Drama, also, Spain has been especially abundant and inventive. She has supplied all Europe with plots, and has produced at least one dramatist who takes natural rank with the greatest in any language by his depth of imagination and fertility of resource. For fascination of style and profound suggestion, it would be hard to name another author superior to Calderon, if indeed equal to him. His charm was equally felt by two minds as unlike each other as those of Goethe and Shelley. These in themselves are sufficient achievements, and the intellectual life of a nation could maintain itself on the unearned increment of these without further addition to its resources. But Spain has also had the good fortune to produce one book which by the happiness of its conception, by the variety of its invention, and the charm of its style, has been adopted into the literature of mankind, and has occupied a place in their affection to which few other books have been admitted.

We have no word in English so comprehensive as the *Dichtung* of the Germans, which includes every exercise of the creative faculty, whether in the line of pathos or humor, whether in the higher region of imagination or on the lower levels of fancy where the average man draws easier breath. It is about a work whose scene lies on this inferior plane, but whose vividness of intuition and breadth of treatment rank it among the highest achievements of imaginative literature, that I shall say a few words this evening, and I trust that I shall see nothing in it that

---

[3] John Gibson Lockhart (1794–1854), Scottish editor and writer, noted especially for his *Life of Sir Walter Scott* (1837–38), published in 1823 *Ancient Spanish Ballads, Historical and Romantic. Translated, with Notes.*

in the author's intention, at least, is not honestly to be found there; certainly that I shall not pretend to see anything which others have professed to discover there, but to which nature has made me color-blind.

I ask your attention not to an essay on "Don Quixote," still less to an essay on Cervantes, but rather to a few illustrative comments on his one immortal book (drawn almost wholly from notes written on its margin in repeated readings), which may tend to throw a stronger light on what I shall not scruple to call its incomparable originality both as a conception and a study of character. It is one of the few books that can lay undisputed claim to the distinction of being universal and cosmopolitan, equally at home in all languages and welcome to all kindreds and conditions of men; a *human* book in the fullest sense of the word; a kindly book, whether we take that adjective in its original meaning of *natural,* or in its present acceptation, which would seem to imply that at some time or other, not too precisely specified in history, to be kindly and to be natural had been equivalent terms. I can think of no book so thoroughly good-natured and good-humored; and this is the more remarkable because it shows that the optimism of its author had survived more misfortune and disenchantment than have fallen to the lot of many men, even the least successful. I suspect that Cervantes, with his varied experience, maimed at the battle of Lepanto, a captive in Algiers, pinched with poverty all his life, and writing his great book in a debtor's prison, might have formed as just an estimate of the vanity of vanities as the author of the Book of Ecclesiastes. But the notion of *Weltschmerz,* or the misery of living and acting in this beautiful world, seems never to have occurred to him, or, if it did, never to have embittered him. Had anybody suggested the thought to him, he would probably have answered, "Well, perhaps it is not the best of all possible worlds, but it is the best we have, or are likely to get in *my* time. Had I been present at its creation, I might, perhaps, as Alfonso the Learned thought *he* might, have given some useful advice for its improvement, and, were I consulted even now, could suggest some amendments in my own condition therein. But after all, it is not a bad world, as worlds go, and the wisest plan, if the luck go against us, is to follow the advice of Durandarte in the Cave of Montesinos, 'Patience, and shuffle the cards.' [4]   A new deal may give us better hands." His sense of humor kept his nature sweet and fresh, and made him capable of seeing that there are two sides to every question, even to a question in which his own personal interest was directly involved. In his dedication of the Second Part of "Don Quixote" to the Conde de Lemos, written in old age and infirmity, he smiles cheerfully on Poverty as on an old friend and lifelong companion. St. Francis could not have looked with more benignity on her whom he chose, as Dante tells us, for his bride.

I have called "Don Quixote" a cosmopolitan book, and I know of none other that can compete with it in this respect unless it be "Robinson Crusoe." But "Don Quixote," if less verisimilar as a narrative, and I am not sure that it is, appeals to far higher qualities of mind and demands a far subtler sense of appreciation than the masterpiece of Defoe. If the latter represent in simplest prose what interests us because it *might* happen to any man, the other, while seeming never to leave the low level of fact and possibility, constantly suggests the loftier region of symbol, and sets before us that eternal contrast between the ideal and the real, between the world as it might be and the world as it is, between the fervid completeness of conception and the chill inadequacy of fulfilment, which life sooner or later, directly or indirectly, forces upon the consciousness of every man who is more than a patent digester. There is a moral in "Don Quixote," and a very profound one, whether Cervantes consciously put it there or not, and it is this: that whoever quarrels with the Nature of Things, wittingly or unwittingly, is certain to get the worst of it. The great difficulty lies in finding out what the Nature of Things really and perdurably is, and the great wisdom, after we have

---

[4] For more than five hundred years Montesinos and his cousin Durandarte had been kept enchanted in the cave by Merlin. When Don Quixote visited them, Montesinos expressed to his cousin the hope that at last, through Don Quixote's aid, they might be disenchanted. In reply Durandarte remarked wearily, "If that may not be, then, O my cousin, I say 'patience and shuffle.'" (*Don Quixote,* Part II, Chap. xxiii.)

made this discovery, or persuaded ourselves that we have made it, is in accommodating our lives and actions to it as best we may or can. And yet, though all this be true, there is another and deeper moral in the book than this. The pathos which underlies its seemingly farcical turmoil,[5] the tears which sometimes tremble under our lids after its most poignant touches of humor, the sympathy with its hero which survives all his most ludicrous defeats and humiliations and is only deepened by them, the feeling that he is after all the one noble and heroic figure in a world incapable of comprehending him, and to whose inhabitants he is distorted and caricatured by the crooked panes in those windows of custom and convention through which they see him, all this seems to hint that only he who has the imagination to conceive and the courage to attempt a trial of strength with what foists itself on our senses as the Order of Nature for the time being, can achieve great results or kindle the coöperative and efficient enthusiasm of his fellowmen. The Don Quixote of one generation may live to hear himself called the savior of society by the next. How exalted was Don Quixote's own conception of his mission is clear from what is said of his first sight of the inn,[6] that "it was as if he had seen a star which guided him not to the portals, but to the fortress of his redemption," where the allusion were too daring were he not persuaded that he is going forth to redeem the world. Cervantes, of course, is not so much speaking in his own person, as telling what passed in the mind of his hero. But he would not have ventured such an allusion in jest.

Am I forcing upon Cervantes a meaning alien to the purpose of his story and anachronistic to the age in which he lived? I do not think so, and if I err I do so in good company. I admit that there is a kind of what is called constructive criticism, which is

---

[5] I can think of no better instance to show how thin is the partition that divides humor from pathos than the lustration of the two vulgar Laises (*distraidas mozas*) by the pure imagination of Don Quixote. (Part I, Chap. ii.) The sentiment is more natural and truer than that which Victor Hugo puts into the mouth of Marion Delorme when she tells her lover that "his love has given her back her maidenhood." To *him* it might, but it would rather have reproached her with the loss of it. [Lowell's note.]

[6] Part I, Chap. iii.

sometimes pushed so far beyond its proper limits as to deserve rather the name of destructive, as sometimes, in the so-called restoration of an ancient building, the materials of the original architect are used in the erection of a new edifice of which he had never dreamed, or, if he had dreamed of it, would have fancied himself the victim of some horrible nightmare. I would not willingly lay myself open to the imputation of applying this method to Cervantes, and attribute to him a depth of intention which, could he be asked about it, would call up in his eyes the meditative smile that must habitually have flickered there. Spaniards have not been wanting who protested against what they consider to be the German fashion of interpreting their national author. Don Juan Valera, in particular, one of the best of contemporary Spanish men of letters, both as critic and novelist, has argued the negative side of the question with force and acumen in a discourse pronounced on his admission to the Spanish Academy. But I must confess that, while he interested, he did not convince me. I could quite understand his impatience at what he considered the supersubtleties of interpretation to which our Teutonic cousins, who have taught us so much, are certainly somewhat prone. We have felt it ourselves when the obvious meaning of Shakespeare has been rewritten into Hegelese,[7] by some Doctor of Philosophy desperate with the task of saying something when everything had been already said, and eager to apply his new theory of fog as an illuminating medium. But I do not think that transcendental criticism can be charged with indiscretion in the case of "Don Quixote." After reading all that can be said against the justice of its deductions, or divinations if you choose to call them so, I am inclined to say, as Turner[8] did to the lady who, after looking at one of his pictures, declared that she could not see all this in nature, "Madam, don't you wish to heaven you could?" I believe that in all really great imaginative work we are aware, as in nature, of something far more deeply interfused with our consciousness, underlying

---

[7] I.e., wordy and abstruse language, such as was used by the well-known German philosopher George William Friedrich Hegel (1770–1831).
[8] Joseph M. W. Turner (1775–1851), a leading English landscape painter.

the obvious and familiar, as the living spirit of them, and accessible only to a heightened sense and a more passionate sympathy. He reads most wisely who thinks everything into a book that it is capable of holding, and it is the stamp and token of a great book so to incorporate itself with our own being, so to quicken our insight and stimulate our thought, as to make us feel as if we helped to create it while we read. Whatever we can find in a book that aids us in the conduct of life, or to a truer interpretation of it, or to a franker reconcilement with it, we may with a good conscience believe is not there by accident, but that the author meant that we should find it there. Cervantes certainly intended something of far wider scope than a mere parody on the Romances of Chivalry, which before his day had ceased to have any vitality as motives of human conduct, or even as pictures of a life that anybody believed to have ever existed except in dreamland. That he *did* intend his book as a good-humored criticism on *doctrinaire* reformers who insist, in spite of all history and experience, on believing that society is a device of human wit or an imposture of human cunning, and not a growth, an evolution from natural causes, is clear enough in more than one passage to the thoughtful reader. It is also a satire on all attempts to remake the world by the means and methods of the past, and on the humanity of impulse which looks on each fact that rouses its pity or its sense of wrong as if it was or could be complete in itself, and were not indissolubly bound up with myriads of other facts both in the past and the present. When we say that we are all of us the result of the entire past, we perhaps are not paying the past a very high compliment; but it is no less true that whatever happens is in some sense, more or less strict, the result of all that has happened before. As with all men of heated imaginations, a near object of compassion occupies the whole mind of Don Quixote; the figure of the present sufferer looms gigantic and shuts out all perception of remoter and more general considerations. Don Quixote's quarrel is with the structure of society, and it is only by degrees, through much mistake and consequent suffering, that he finds out how strong that structure is; nay, how strong it must be in order that the world may go smoothly and the course of events not be broken by a series of cataclysms. The French Revolutionists with the sincerest good intentions set about reforming in Don Quixote's style, and France has been in commotion ever since. They carefully grubbed up every root that drew its sustenance from the past, and have been finding out ever since to their sorrow that nothing with roots can be made to order. "Do right though the heavens fall" is an admirable precept so long as the heavens do not take you at your word and come down about your ears—still worse about those of your neighbors. It is a rule rather of private than public obligation—for indeed it is the doing of right that *keeps* the heavens from falling. After Don Quixote's temporary rescue of the boy Andrés from his master's beating,[9] the manner in which he rides off and discharges his mind of consequences is especially characteristic of reform by theory without study of circumstances. It is a profound stroke of humor that the reformer Don Quixote should caution Sancho not to attempt making the world over again, and to adapt himself to things as he finds them.

In one of his adventures, it is in perfect keeping that he should call on all the world to stop "till *he* was satisfied." It is to be noted that in both Don Quixote's attempts at the redress of particular wrong (Andrés, and the galley-slaves [10]) the objects (I might call them victims) of his benevolence come back again to his discomfiture. In the case of Andrés, Don Quixote can only blush, but Sancho (the practical man without theories) gives the poor fellow a hunch of bread and a few pennies, which are very much to the purpose.[11] Cervantes gives us a plain hint here that all our mistakes sooner or later surely come home to roost. It is remarkable how independent of time and circumstance the satire of the great humorists always is. Aristophanes, Rabelais, Shakespeare, Molière, seem to furnish side-lights to what we read in our morning paper. As another instance of this in Cervantes, who is continually illustrating it, read the whole scene of the

---

[9] Part I, Chap. iv.
[10] Part I, Chap. xxii.
[11] Part I, Chap. xxxi.

liberation of the galley-slaves. How perfectly does it fit those humanitarians who cannot see the crime because the person of the criminal comes between them and it! That Cervantes knew perfectly well what he was about in *his* satire and saw beneath the surface of things is shown by the apparition of the police and of the landlord with the bill in his hand, for it was these that brought the Good Old Times to their forlorn *Hic Jacet*.[12]

Coleridge, who in reach and range of intelligence, in penetration of insight, and in comprehensiveness of sympathy ranks among the first of critics, says, "Don Quixote is not a man out of his senses, but a man in whom the imagination and the pure reason are so powerful as to make him disregard the evidence of sense when it opposed their conclusions. Sancho is the common sense of the social man-animal unenlightened and unsanctified by the reason. You see how he reverences his master at the very time he is cheating him." [13]   W. S. Landor [14] thought that Coleridge took the hint for this enlargement of the scope of the book from him, but if I remember rightly it was Bouterwek [15] who first pointed criticism in the right direction. Down to his time "Don Quixote" had been regarded as a burlesque, a farcical satire on the Romances of Chivalry, just as Shylock was so long considered a character of low comedy.

But "Don Quixote," whatever its deeper meanings may be, has a literary importance almost without parallel, and it is time that we should consider it briefly. It would be hard to find a book more purely original and without precedent. Cervantes himself says in the preface to the First Part that he knows not what book he is following in it. Indeed, he follows none, though we find traces of his having read the "Golden Ass" [16]

---

[12] "Here lies."—The beginning of many inscriptions on old tombstones.

[13] Samuel Taylor Coleridge, *Table Talk*, Aug. 11, 1832.

[14] Walter Savage Landor (1775–1864), English poet and critic, celebrated particularly for his *Imaginary Conversations* written from 1824 onwards. Lowell met Landor just once, when he spent a day with the latter at Bath in the late summer of 1852.

[15] Friedrich Bouterwek (1765–1828), German philosopher and critic, whose *Geschichte der neuern Poesie und Beredsamkeit* (1801–19) included the first scholarly history of Spanish literature.

[16] *Metamorphosis, or the Golden Ass,* a fable or romance satirizing magi-

and the Greek Romances. It was the first time that characters had been drawn from real life with such nicety and discrimination of touch, with such minuteness in particulars, and yet with such careful elimination of whatever was unessential that the personages are idealized to a proper artistic distance from mere actuality. With all this, how perfectly life-like they are! As Don Quixote tells us that he was almost ready to say he had seen Amadis,[17] and proceeds to describe his personal appearance minutely, so we could affirm of the Knight of La Mancha and his Squire. They are real not because they are portraits, not because they are drawn from actual personages, but rather because of their very abstraction and generalization. They are not so much taken from life as informed with it. They are conceptions, not copies from any model; creations as no other characters but those of Shakespeare are in so full and adequate a manner; developed out of a seminal idea like the creatures of nature, not the matter-of-fact work of a detective's watchfulness, products of a quick eye and a faithful memory, but the true children of the imaginative faculty from which all the dregs of observation and memory have been distilled away, leaving only what is elementary and universal. I confess that in the productions of what is called the realistic school I too often find myself in company that is little to my taste, dragged back into a commonplace world from which I was only too glad to escape, and set to grind in the prison-house of the Philistines.[18] I walk about in a nightmare, the supreme horror of which is that my coat is all buttonholes for bores to thrust their fingers through and bait me to their heart's content. Give me the writers who take me for a while out of myself and (with pardon be it spoken) away from my neighbors! I do not ask that characters should be real; I need but go into the street to find such in abundance. I ask only that they should be possible, that they should be typical, because these I find in myself, and with these can sympathize. Hector

cians, priests, and debauchees, and written by Apuleius, a Latin philosopher and author (b. 150 A.D.).

[17] Amadis de Gaul, the legendary Welsh hero of a famous Spanish romance by Montalvo (c. 1500).

[18] An allusion to Samson's punishment. See Judges xvi: 21.

and Achilles,[19] Clytemnestra and Antigone,[20] Roland and Oliver,[21] Macbeth and Lear, move about, if not in worlds not realized, at least in worlds not realized to any eye but that of imagination, a world far from the police reports, a world into which it is a privilege, I might almost call it an achievement, to enter. Don Quixote and his Squire are inhabitants of this world, in spite of the prosaic and often vulgar stage on which their tragicomedy is acted, because they are symbolical, because they represent the two great factors of human character and springs of human action—the Imagination and the Understanding. If you would convince yourself how true this is, compare them with Sir Hudibras and Ralpho [22]—or still better with Roderick Random and Strap.[23] There can be no better proof that Cervantes meant to contrast the ideal with the matter-of-fact in the two characters than his setting side by side images of the same woman as reflected in the eyes of Sancho and of his master; in other words, as seen by common-sense and by passion.[24]

I shall not trouble you with any labored analysis of humor. If you wish to know what humor is, I should say read "Don Quixote." It is the element in which the whole story lives and moves and has its being, and it wakens and flashes round the course of the narrative like a phosphorescent sea in the track of a ship. It is nowhere absent; it is nowhere obtrusive; it lightens and plays about the surface for a moment and is gone. It is everywhere by suggestion, it is nowhere with emphasis and insistence. There is infinite variety, yet always in harmony with the characters and the purpose of the fable. The impression it produces

---

[19] The Trojan and Greek champions, respectively, in the celebrated Trojan War described by Homer's *Iliad*.

[20] Famous heroines in the Greek tragic drama: the former, the wife of Agamemnon, who was king of Argos and leader of the Greeks in the Trojan War; the latter, the daughter of Oedipus and his mother Jocasta.

[21] Boon friends and leading figures in the French medieval epic, *The Song of Roland*.

[22] The knight and his squire in *Hudibras* (1664), a notable satiric poem by Samuel Butler (1613-80).

[23] The young Scottish hero and his simple, faithful companion in *Roderick Random* (1748), a picaresque novel by Tobias Smollett (1721-71).

[24] Part I, Chap. x, xxxi.

is cumulative, not sudden or startling. It is unobtrusive as the tone of good conversation. I am not speaking of the *fun* of the book, of which there is plenty, and sometimes boisterous enough, but of that deeper and more delicate quality, suggestive of remote analogies and essential incongruities, which alone deserves the name of humor.

This quality is so diffused in "Don Quixote," so thoroughly permeates every pore and fibre of the book, that it is difficult to exemplify it by citation. Take as examples the scene with the goatherds, where Don Quixote, after having amply supped, discourses so eloquently of that Golden Age which was happy in having nothing to eat but acorns or to drink but water; where, while insisting that Sancho should assume equality as a man, he denies it to him as Sancho, by reminding him that it is granted by one who is his natural lord and master,[25]—there is such a difference, alas, between universal and particular Brotherhood! Take the debate of Don Quixote (already mad) as to what form of madness he should assume;[26] the quarrel of the two madmen, Don Quixote and Cardénio, about the good fame of Queen Madásima, a purely imaginary being;[27] the resolution of Don Quixote, when forced to renounce knight-errantry, that he will become a shepherd of the kind known to poets, thus exchanging one unreality for another.[28] Nay, take the whole book, if you would learn what humor is, whether in its most obvious or its most subtle manifestations. The highest and most complete illustration is the principal character of the story. I do not believe that a character so absolutely perfect in conception and delineation, so psychologically true, so full of whimsical inconsistencies, all combining to produce an impression of perfect coherence, is to be found in fiction. He was a monomaniac, all of whose faculties, his very senses themselves, are subjected by one overmastering prepossession, and at last conspire with it, almost against their will, in spite of daily disillusion and of the

[25] Part I, Chap. xi.
[26] Part I, Chap. xviii.
[27] Part I, Chap. xxiv.
[28] Part II, Chap. lxvii.

uniform testimony of facts and events to the contrary. The key
to Don Quixote's character is given in the first chapter where he
is piecing out his imperfect helmet with a new visor. He makes
one of pasteboard, and then, testing it with his sword, shatters it
to pieces. He proceeds to make another strengthened with
strips of iron, and "without caring to make a further trial of it,
commissioned and held it for the finest possible visor." Don
Quixote always sees what he wishes to see, and yet always sees
things as they are unless the necessities of his hallucination compel him to see them otherwise, and it is wonderful with what ingenuity he makes everything bend to those necessities. Cervantes calls him the sanest madman and the maddest reasonable
man in the world. Sancho says that he was fitter to be preacher
than knight-errant. He *makes* facts curtsy to his prepossessions.
At the same time, with exact truth to nature, he is never perfectly
convinced himself except in moments of exaltation, and when
the bee in his bonnet buzzes so loudly as to prevent his hearing
the voice of reason. Cervantes takes care to tell us that he was
never convinced that he was really a knight-errant till his cere-
monious reception at the castle of the Duke.

Sancho, on the other hand, sees everything in the dry light of
common sense, except when beguiled by cupidity or under the
immediate spell of his master's imagination. Grant the imagination its premises, and its logic is irresistible. Don Quixote
always takes these premises for granted, and Sancho, despite his
natural shrewdness, is more than half tempted to admit them,
or at any rate to run the risk of their being sound, partly out of
habitual respect for his master's superior rank and knowledge,
partly on the chance of the reward which his master perpetually
dangled before him. This reward was that island of which
Don Quixote confesses he cannot tell the name because it is not
down on any map. With delightful humor, it begins as *some*
island, then becomes *the* island, and then one of those islands.
And how much more probable does this vagueness render the
fulfilment of the promise than if Don Quixote had locked himself up in a specific *one!* A line of retreat is thus always kept
open, while Sancho's eagerness is held at bay by this seemingly

chance suggestion of a choice in these hypothetical lordships. This vague potentiality of islands eludes the thrust of any definite objection. And when Sancho is inclined to grumble, his master consoles him by saying, "I have already told thee, Sancho, to give thyself no care about it; for even should the island fail us, there are the kingdoms of Dinamarca and Sobradisa that would fit you as the ring fits the finger, and since they are on *terra firma,* you should rejoice the more." [29] As if these were more easily to be come at, though all his *terra firma* was in dreamland too. It should seem that Sancho was too shrewd for such a bait, and that here at least was an exception to that probability for which I have praised the story. But I think it rather a justification of it. We must remember how near the epoch of the story was to that of the *Conquistadores,*[30] when men's fancies were still glowing with the splendid potentialities of adventure. And when Don Quixote suggests the possibility of creating Sancho a marquis, it is remarkable that he mentions the title conferred upon Cortés.[31] The conscience of Don Quixote is in loyalty to his ideal; he prizes desert as an inalienable possession of the soul. The conscience of Sancho is in the eyes of his neighbors, and he values repute for its worldly advantages. When Sancho tries to divert his master from the adventure of the Fulling Mills by arguing that it was night, and that none could see them, so that they might well turn out of the way to avoid the danger, and begs him rather to take a little sleep, Don Quixote answers indignantly: "Sleep thou, who wast born for sleep. As for me, I shall do whatever I see to be most becoming to my profession." [32] With equal truth to nature in both cases, Sancho is represented as inclined to believe the extravagant delusions of his master because he has seen and known him all his life, while he obstinately refuses to believe that a barber's basin is the helmet of Mambrino because he sees and knows that it is a basin.[33]

---

[29] Part I, Chap. x.

[30] The title given to the Spanish adventurers and colonial conquerors during the Renaissance.

[31] Hernando Cortés (1485–1547), the Spanish conqueror of Mexico.

[32] Part I, Chap. xx.

[33] Part I, Chap. xxi.

Don Quixote says of him to the Duke, "He doubts everything and believes everything." [34] Cervantes was too great an artist to make him wholly vulgar and greedy and selfish, though he makes him all these. He is witty, wise according to his lights, affectionate, and faithful. When he takes leave of his imaginary governorship he is not without a certain manly dignity that is almost pathetic. [35]

The ingenuity of the story, the probability of its adventures, the unwearied fecundity of invention shown in devising and interlacing them, in giving variety to a single theme and to a plot so perfectly simple in its conception, are all wonderful. The narrative flows on as if unconsciously, and our fancies are floated along upon it. It is noticeable, too, in passing, what a hypæthral [36] story it is, how much of it passes in the open air, how the sun shines, the birds sing, the brooks dance, and the leaves murmur in it. This is peculiarly touching when we recollect that it was written in prison. In the First Part Cervantes made the mistake (as he himself afterwards practically admits) of introducing unprofitable digressions, and in respect to the propriety and congruousness of the adventures which befall Don Quixote I must also make one exception. I mean the practical jokes played upon him at the Duke's castle, in which his delusion is forced upon him instead of adapting circumstances to itself or itself to circumstances, according to the necessity of the occasion. [37] These tend to degrade him in the eyes of the reader, who resents rather than enjoys them, and feels the essential vulgarity of his tormentors through all their fine clothes. It is quite otherwise with the cheats put upon Sancho, for we feel that either he will be shrewd enough to be more than even with the framers of them, or that he is of too coarse a fibre to feel them keenly. But Don Quixote is a gentleman and a monomaniac,—qualities, the one of which renders such rudeness incongruous, and the other unfeeling. He is, moreover, a guest. It is curious that Shakespeare makes the same mistake with Fal-

---

[34] Part II, Chap. xxxii.
[35] Part II, Chap. liii.
[36] Open-air.
[37] Part II, Chap. xliv, xlvi, xlviii,

staff in the "Merry Wives of Windsor," and Fielding with Parson Adams,[38] and in both cases to our discomfort. The late Mr. Edward Fitzgerald [39] (*quis desiderio sit pudor aut modus tam cari capitis!* [40]) preferred the Second Part to the First, and, but for these scenes, which always pain and anger me, I should agree with him. For it is plain that Cervantes became slowly conscious as he went on how rich was the vein he had hit upon, how full of various and profound suggestion were the two characters he had conceived and who together make a complete man. No doubt he at first proposed to himself a parody of the Romances of Chivalry, but his genius soon broke away from the leading-strings of a plot that denied free scope to his deeper conception of life and men.

Cervantes is the father of the modern novel, in so far as it has become a study and delineation of character instead of being a narrative seeking to interest by situation and incident. He has also more or less directly given impulse and direction to all humoristic literature since his time. We see traces of him in Molière, in Swift,[41] and still more clearly in Sterne [42] and Richter.[43] Fielding assimilated and Smollett [44] copied him. Scott was his disciple in the "Antiquary," that most delightful of his delightful novels. Irving imitated him in his "Knickerbocker," and Dickens in his "Pickwick Papers." I do not mention this as detracting from *their* originality, but only as showing the wonderful virility of *his*. The pedigrees of books are as interesting and instructive as those of men. It is also good for us to remember that this man whose life was outwardly a failure restored to Spain the universal empire she had lost.

---

[38] A main character in *Joseph Andrews* (1741). For Fielding see note on p. 96.

[39] Fitzgerald (1809–83) is now famous chiefly for his translation of Omar Khayyam's *Rubaiyat*.

[40] What restraint or limit should there be to grief for one so dear! (Horace, *Odes*, I, 24: 1.)

[41] Jonathan Swift (1667–1745), English satirist celebrated for his *Gulliver's Travels* (1726).

[42] See note on p. 96.

[43] Johann Paul Friedrich Richter (1763–1825), a noted German writer of the Romantic Movement.

[44] See note 23.

POEMS

POEMS

READER! *walk up at once (it will soon be too late)*
and buy at a perfectly ruinous rate

A

FABLE FOR CRITICS;

OR, BETTER,

(I like, as a thing that the reader's first fancy may strike,
an old-fashioned title-page,
such as presents a tabular view of the volume's contents,)

A GLANCE

AT A FEW OF OUR LITERARY PROGENIES

(Mrs. Malaprop's word)

FROM

THE TUB OF DIOGENES;

A VOCAL AND MUSICAL MEDLEY,

THAT IS,

A SERIES OF JOKES

By a Wonderful Quiz,

who accompanies himself with a rub-a-dub-dub, full of spirit and
grace, on the top of the tub.

Set forth in October, the 31st day,
In the year '48, G. P. Putnam, Broadway.

It being the commonest mode of procedure, I premise a few
candid remarks

To THE READER:—
   This trifle, begun to please only myself and my own private
fancy, was laid on the shelf.   But some friends, who had seen it,
induced me, by dint of saying they liked it, to put it in print.
That is, having come to that very conclusion, I asked their advice

when 't would make no confusion. For though (in the gentlest of ways) they had hinted it was scarce worth the while, I should doubtless have printed it.

I began it, intending a Fable, a frail, slender thing, rhyme-ywinged, with a sting in its tail. But, by addings and alterings not previously planned, digressions chance-hatched, like birds' eggs in the sand, and dawdlings to suit every whimsey's demand (always freeing the bird which I held in my hand, for the two perched, perhaps out of reach, in the tree),—it grew by degrees to the size which you see. I was like the old woman that carried the calf, and my neighbors, like hers, no doubt, wonder and laugh; and when, my strained arms with their grown burthen full, I call it my Fable, they call it a bull.

Having scrawled at full gallop (as far as that goes) in a style that is neither good verse nor bad prose, and being a person whom nobody knows, some people will say I am rather more free with my readers than it is becoming to be, that I seem to expect them to wait on my leisure in following wherever I wander at pleasure, that, in short, I take more than a young author's lawful ease, and laugh in a queer way so like Mephistopheles, that the public will doubt, as they grope through my rhythm, if in truth I am making fun *of* them or *with* them.

So the excellent Public is hereby assured that the sale of my book is already secured. For there is not a poet throughout the whole land but will purchase a copy or two out of hand, in the fond expectation of being amused in it, by seeing his betters cut up and abused in it. Now, I find, by a pretty exact calculation, there are something like ten thousand bards in the nation, of that special variety whom the Review and Magazine critics call *lofty* and *true,* and about thirty thousand (*this* tribe is increasing) of the kinds who are termed *full of promise* and *pleasing.* The Public will see by a glance at this schedule, that they cannot expect me to be oversedulous about courting *them,* since it seems I have got enough fuel made sure of for boiling my pot.

As for such of our poets as find not their names mentioned once in my pages, with praises or blames, let them SEND IN THEIR CARDS, without further DELAY, to my friend G. P. PUTNAM, Esquire, in Broadway, where a LIST will be kept with the strictest regard to the day and the hour of receiving the card. Then, taking them up as I chance to have time (that is, if their names can be twisted in rhyme), I will honestly give each his PROPER POSITION,

at the rate of ONE AUTHOR to each NEW EDITION. Thus a PRE-
MIUM is offered sufficiently HIGH (as the magazines say when
they tell their best lie) to induce bards to CLUB their resources
and buy the balance of every edition, until they have all of them
fairly been run through the mill.

One word to such readers (judicious and wise) as read books
with something behind the mere eyes, of whom in the country,
perhaps, there are two, including myself, gentle reader, and you.
All the characters sketched in this slight *jeu d'esprit*,[1] though,
it may be, they seem, here and there, rather free, and drawn from
a somewhat too cynical standpoint, are *meant* to be faithful, for
that is the grand point, and none but an owl would feel sore at
a rub from a jester who tells you, without any subterfuge, that he
sits in Diogenes' tub.[2]

A FABLE FOR CRITICS [3]

PHŒBUS, sitting one day in a laurel-tree's shade,
Was reminded of Daphne, of whom it was made,
For the god being one day too warm in his wooing,
She took to the tree to escape his pursuing;
Be the cause what it might, from his offers she shrunk,   5
And, Ginevra [4]-like, shut herself up in a trunk;

---

[1] Humorous trifle.

[2] See note on p. 109.

[3] This satirical piece was begun by Lowell for his own amusement in the
autumn of 1847 and occupied him off and on for almost a year. He sent
a copy of the first half of the poem as a New Year's present to C. F. Briggs,
of New York, who was instructed, if he so desired, to have it printed for
his own benefit (*Letters,* I, 120). The satire reached completion in late
August, 1848 (*Ibid.,* I, 137), and under Briggs' direction was published
anonymously on October 25. Popular demand quickly exhausted the first
edition of one thousand copies. A second, with an added prefatory note,
was issued at the opening of 1849. By February of the same year the poem
had gone into a third edition. The more immediate inspiration for the
general scheme and the versification of his Fable Lowell derived from
Leigh Hunt's *The Feast of the Poets,* which in 1844 had been brought to
his especial attention by its publication in a Boston edition, but he no doubt
also had in mind the various "sessions of the poets" so well known in the
satirical literature of the seventeenth and early eighteenth centuries.

[4] A young Italian bride, who during a game of hide-and-seek hid herself in a large trunk. The lid suddenly fell and was held fast by a spring-
lock. The lady's skeleton came to light many years later when the trunk
was sold and opened.

And, though 'twas a step into which he had driven her,
He somehow or other had never forgiven her;
Her memory he nursed as a kind of a tonic,
Something bitter to chew when he'd play the Byronic,   10
And I can't count the obstinate nymphs that he brought over
By a strange kind of smile he put on when he thought of her.
"My case is like Dido's," [5] he sometimes remarked:
"When I last saw my love, she was fairly embarked
In a laurel, as *she* thought—but (ah, how Fate mocks!)   15
She has found it by this time a very bad box;
Let hunters from me take this saw when they need it,—
You're not always sure of your game when you've treed it.
Just conceive such a change taking place in one's mistress!
What romance would be left?—who can flatter or kiss trees?   20
And, for mercy's sake, how could one keep up a dialogue
With a dull wooden thing that will live and will die a log,—
Not to say that the thought would forever intrude
That you've less chance to win her the more she is wood?
Ah! it went to my heart, and the memory still grieves,   25
To see those loved graces all taking their leaves;
Those charms beyond speech, so enchanting but now,
As they left me forever, each making its bough!
If her tongue *had* a tang sometimes more than was right,
Her new bark is worse than ten times her old bite."   30

Now, Daphne—before she was happily treeified—
Over all other blossoms the lily had deified,
And when she expected the god on a visit
('Twas before he had made his intentions explicit),
Some buds she arranged with a vast deal of care,   35
To look as if artlessly twined in her hair,
Where they seemed, as he said, when he paid his addresses,
Like the day breaking through the long night of her tresses;
So whenever he wished to be quite irresistible,
Like a man with eight trumps in his hand at a whist-table   40
(I feared me at first that the rhyme was untwistable,
Though I might have lugged in an allusion to Cristabel [6]),—

---

[5] Princess of Carthage, Africa, who fell in love with the Trojan hero,
Aeneas. He refused to marry her and sailed away to Italy.
[6] The heroine of Coleridge's unfinished narrative poem *Christabel* (1798).

He would take up a lily, and gloomily look in it,
As I shall at the ——, when they cut up my book in it.

Well, here, after all the bad rhyme I've been spinning,   45
I've got back at last to my story's beginning:
Sitting there, as I say, in the shade of his mistress,
As dull as a volume of old Chester mysteries,[7]
Or as those puzzling specimens which, in old histories,
We read of his verses—the Oracles, namely,—   50
(I wonder the Greeks should have swallowed them tamely,
For one might bet safely whatever he has to risk,
They were laid at his door by some ancient Miss Asterisk,
And so dull that the men who retailed them out-doors
Got the ill name of augurs, because they were bores,—)   55
First, he mused what the animal substance or herb is
Would induce a mustache, for you know he's *imberbis;* [8]
Then he shuddered to think how his youthful position
Was assailed by the age of his son the physician;
At some poems he glanced, had been sent to him lately,   60
And the metre and sentiment puzzled him greatly;
"Mehercle! I'd make such proceeding felonious,—
Have they all of them slept in the cave of Trophonius? [9]
Look well to your seat, 'tis like taking an airing
On a corduroy road, and that out of repairing;   65
It leads one, 'tis true, through the primitive forest,
Grand natural features, but then one has no rest;
You just catch a glimpse of some ravishing distance,
When a jolt puts the whole of it out of existence,—
Why not use their ears, if they happen to have any?"   70
—Here the laurel-leaves murmured the name of poor Daphne.

"Oh, weep with me, Daphne," he sighed, "for you know it's
A terrible thing to be pestered with poets!
But, alas, she is dumb, and the proverb holds good,
She never will cry till she's out of the wood!   75
What wouldn't I give if I never had known of her?

---

[7] The religious, or miracle, plays given in Chester, England, from the
fourteenth to the sixteenth century.
[8] Beardless.
[9] Jupiter Trophonius, a god who delivered oracles from a cave in Bœotia,
Greece.

'Twere a kind of relief had I something to groan over:
If I had but some letters of hers, now, to toss over,
I might turn for the nonce a Byronic philosopher,
And bewitch all the flats by bemoaning the loss of her.   80
One needs something tangible, though, to begin on,—
A loom, as it were, for the fancy to spin on;
What boots all your grist? it can never be ground
Till a breeze makes the arms of the windmill go round;
(Or, if 'tis a water-mill, alter the metaphor,   85
And say it won't stir, save the wheel be well wet afore,
Or lug in some stuff about water 'so dreamily,'—
It is not a metaphor, though, 'tis a simile);
A lily, perhaps, would set *my* mill a-going,
For just at this season, I think, they are blowing.   90
Here, somebody, fetch one; not very far hence
They're in bloom by the score, 'tis but climbing a fence;
There's a poet hard by, who does nothing but fill his
Whole garden, from one end to t' other, with lilies;
A very good plan, were it not for satiety,   95
One longs for a weed here and there, for variety;
Though a weed is no more than a flower in disguise,
Which is seen through at once, if love give a man eyes."

Now there happened to be among Phœbus's followers,
A gentleman, one of the omnivorous swallowers,   100
Who bolt every book that comes out of the press,
Without the least question of larger or less,
Whose stomachs are strong at the expense of their head,—
For reading new books is like eating new bread,
One can bear it at first, but by gradual steps he   105
Is brought to death's door of a mental dyspepsy.
On a previous stage of existence, our Hero
Had ridden outside, with the glass below zero;
He had been, 'tis a fact you may safely rely on,
Of a very old stock a most eminent scion,—   110
A stock all fresh quacks their fierce boluses ply on,
Who stretch the new boots Earth's unwilling to try on,
Whom humbugs of all shapes and sorts keep their eye on,
Whose hair's in the mortar of every new Zion,
Who, when whistles are dear, go directly and buy one,   115
Who think slavery a crime that we must not say fie on,

Who hunt, if they e'er hunt at all, with the lion
(Though they hunt lions also, whenever they spy one),
Who contrive to make every good fortune a wry one,
And at last choose the hard bed of honor to die on,   120
Whose pedigree, traced to earth's earliest years,
Is longer than anything else but their ears;—
In short, he was sent into life with the wrong key,
He unlocked the door, and stept forth a poor donkey.
Though kicked and abused by his bipedal betters   125
Yet he filled no mean place in the kingdom of letters;
Far happier than many a literary hack,
He bore only paper-mill rags on his back
(For it makes a vast difference which side the mill
One expends on the paper his labor and skill);   130
So, when his soul waited a new transmigration,
And Destiny balanced 'twixt this and that station,
Not having much time to expend upon bothers,
Remembering he'd had some connection with authors,
And considering his four legs had grown paralytic,—   135
She set him on two, and he came forth a critic.

   Through his babyhood no kind of pleasure he took
In any amusement but tearing a book;
For him there was no intermediate stage
From babyhood up to straight-laced middle age;   140
There were years when he didn't wear coat-tails behind,
But a boy he could never be rightly defined;
Like the Irish Good Folk, though in length scarce a span,
From the womb he came gravely, a little old man;
While other boys' trousers demanded the toil   145
Of the motherly fingers on all kinds of soil,
Red, yellow, brown, black, clayey, gravelly, loamy,
He sat in the corner and read Viri Romæ.[10]
He never was known to unbend or to revel once
In base, marbles, hockey, or kick up the devil once;   150
He was just one of those who excite the benevolence
Of your old prigs who sound the soul's depths with a ledger,
And are on the lookout for some young men to "edger-
cate," as they call it, who won't be too costly,

---

[10] Heroes of Rome; probably a reference to Plutarch's *Lives* of famous
Greeks and Romans.

And who'll afterward take to the ministry mostly;   155
Who always wear spectacles, always look bilious,
Always keep on good terms with each *mater-familias* [11]
Throughout the whole parish, and manage to rear
Ten boys like themselves, on four hundred a year:
Who, fulfilling in turn the same fearful conditions,   160
Either preach through their noses, or go upon missions.

In this way our Hero got safely to college,
Where he bolted alike both his commons and knowledge;
A reading-machine, always wound up and going,
He mastered whatever was not worth the knowing,   165
Appeared in a gown, with black waistcoat of satin,
To spout such a Gothic oration in Latin
That Tully [12] could never have made out a word in it
(Though himself was the model the author preferred in it),
And grasping the parchment which gave him in fee   170
All the mystic and-so-forths contained in A.B.,
He was launched (life is always compared to a sea)
With just enough learning, and skill for the using it,
To prove he'd a brain, by forever confusing it.
So worthy St. Benedict, [13] piously burning   175
With the holiest zeal against secular learning,
Nesciensque scienter, as writers express it,
Indoctusque sapienter a Roma recessit. [14]

'Twould be endless to tell you the things that he knew,
All separate facts, undeniably true,   180
But with him or each other they'd nothing to do;
No power of combining, arranging, discerning,
Digested the masses he learned into learning;
There was one thing in life he had practical knowledge for
(And this, you will think, he need scarce go to college for),—
Not a deed would he do, nor a word would he utter,   186

---

[11] Female head of the house.

[12] Marcus Tullius Cicero (B.C. 106–43), a distinguished Roman orator
and statesman.

[13] An Italian monk (480–543) noted for his piety, the founder of the
Benedictine order.

[14] Knowingly ignorant, as writers express it, and wisely unlearned he
departed from Rome.

Till he'd weighed its relations to plain bread and butter.
When he left Alma Mater, he practised his wits
In compiling the journals' historical bits,—
Of shops broken open, men falling in fits,   190
Great fortunes in England bequeathed to poor printers,
And cold spells, the coldest for many past winters,—
Then, rising by industry, knack, and address,
Got notices up for an unbiased press,
With a mind so well poised, it seemed equally made for   195
Applause or abuse, just which chanced to be paid for:
From this point his progress was rapid and sure,
To the post of a regular heavy reviewer.

  And here I must say he wrote excellent articles
On Hebraical points, or the force of Greek particles;   200
They filled up the space nothing else was prepared for,
And nobody read that which nobody cared for;
If any old book reached a fiftieth edition,
He could fill forty pages with safe erudition:
He could gauge the old books by the old set of rules,   205
And his very old nothings pleased very old fools;
But give him a new book, fresh out of the heart,
And you put him at sea without compass or chart,—
His blunders aspired to the rank of an art;
For his lore was engraft, something foreign that grew in him,
Exhausting the sap of the native and true in him,   211
So that when a man came with a soul that was new in him,
Carving new forms of truth out of Nature's old granite,
New and old at their birth, like Le Verrier's planet,[15]
Which, to get a true judgment, themselves must create   215
In the soul of their critic the measure and weight,
Being rather themselves a fresh standard of grace,
To compute their own judge, and assign him his place,
Our reviewer would crawl all about it and round it,
And, reporting each circumstance just as he found it,   220
Without the least malice,—his record would be
Profoundly æsthetic as that of a flea,
Which, supping on Wordsworth, should print, for our sakes,

---

[15] I.e., Neptune, discovered in 1846 by the great French astronomer,
Urbain Jean Joseph Leverrier (1811-72).

Recollections of nights with the Bard of the Lakes,
Or, lodged by an Arab guide, ventured to render a   225
Comprehensive account [16] of the ruins at Denderah.[17]

   As I said, he was never precisely unkind,
The defect in his brain was just absence of mind;
If he boasted, 'twas simply that he was self-made,
A position which I, for one, never gainsaid,   230
My respect for my Maker supposing a skill
In his works which our Hero would answer but ill;
And I trust that the mould which he used may be cracked, or he,
Made bold by success, may enlarge his phylactery,[18]
And set up a kind of a man-manufactory,—   235
An event which I shudder to think about, seeing
That Man is a moral, accountable being.

   He meant well enough, but was still in the way,
As dunces still are, let them be where they may;
Indeed, they appear to come into existence   240
To impede other folks with their awkward assistance;
If you set up a dunce on the very North pole
All alone with himself, I believe, on my soul,
He'd manage to get betwixt somebody's shins,
And pitch him down bodily, all in his sins,   245
To the grave polar bears sitting round on the ice,
All shortening their grace, to be in for a slice;
Or, if he found nobody else there to pother,
Why, one of his legs would just trip up the other,
For there's nothing we read of in torture's inventions,   250
Like a well-meaning dunce, with the best of intentions.

   A terrible fellow to meet in society,
Not the toast that he buttered was ever so dry at tea;
There he'd sit at the table and stir in his sugar,
Crouching close for a spring, all the while, like a cougar;   255
Be sure of your facts, of your measures and weights,
Of your time,—he's as fond as an Arab of dates;

---

[16] First edition reads "general view."
[17] An Egyptian village, located on the Upper Nile and noted for its brick
temple to Hathor, the cow-goddess of love and joy.
[18] Acts of religious observance.

You'll be telling, perhaps, in your comical way,
Of something you've seen in the course of the day;
And, just as you're tapering out the conclusion,   260
You venture an ill-fated classic allusion,—
The girls have all got their laughs ready, when, whack!
The cougar comes down on your thunderstruck back!
You had left out a comma,—your Greek's put in joint,
And pointed at cost of your story's whole point.   265
In the course of the evening, you find chance for certain
Soft speeches to Anne, in the shade of the curtain:
You tell her your heart can be likened to *one* flower,
"And that, O most charming of women, 's the sunflower,
Which turns"—here a clear nasal voice, to your terror,   270
From outside the curtain, says, "That's all an error."
As for him, he's—no matter, he never grew tender,
Sitting after a ball, with his feet on the fender,
Shaping somebody's sweet features out of cigar smoke
(Though he'd willingly grant you that such doings are smoke);
All women he damns with *mutabile semper*,[19]   276
And if ever he felt something like love's distemper,
'Twas tow'rds a young lady who spoke ancient Mexican,
And assisted her father in making a lexicon;
Though I recollect hearing him get quite ferocious   280
About Mary Clausum,[20] the mistress of Grotius,[21]
Or something of that sort,—but, no more to bore ye
With character-painting, I'll turn to my story.

Now, Apollo, who finds it convenient sometimes
To get his court clear of the makers of rhymes,   285
The *genus,* I think it is called, *irritabile,*[22]
Every one of whom thinks himself treated most shabbily,
And nurses a—what is it?—*immedicabile,*[23]
Which keeps him at boiling-point, hot for a quarrel,
As bitter as wormwood, and sourer than sorrel,   290

---

[19] Constantly changeable.—An allusion to Virgil's famous phrase (*Aeneid,* IV, 569-70) *varium et mutabile semper femina* (different and constantly changeable is woman).

[20] A humorous garbling of the Latin phrase, *mare clausum* (closed sea).

[21] Hugo de Groot, or Grotius (1583-1645), a Dutch jurist who drew up a code of international law on the freedom of the seas.

[22] Excitable.

[23] Incurable [grudge].

If any poor devil but look at a laurel;—
Apollo, I say, being sick of their rioting
(Though he sometimes acknowledged their verse had a quieting
Effect after dinner, and seemed to suggest a
Retreat to the shrine of a tranquil siesta),   295
Kept our Hero at hand, who, by means of a bray,
Which he gave to the life, drove the rabble away;
And if that wouldn't do, he was sure to succeed,
If he took his review out and offered to read;
Or, failing in plans of this milder description,   300
He would ask for their aid to get up a subscription,
Considering that authorship wasn't a rich craft,
To print the "American drama of Witchcraft."
"Stay, I'll read you a scene,"—but he hardly began,
Ere Apollo shrieked "Help!" and the authors all ran: 305
And once, when these purgatives acted with less spirit,
And the desperate case asked a remedy desperate,
He drew from his pocket a foolscap epistle
As calmly as if 'twere a nine-barrelled pistol,
And threatened them all with the judgment to come,   310
Of "A wandering Star's first impressions of Rome."
"Stop! stop!" with their hands o'er their ears, screamed the
          Muses,
"He may go off and murder himself, if he chooses,
'Twas a means self-defence only sanctioned his trying,
'Tis mere massacre now that the enemy's flying;   315
If he's forced to 't again, and we happen to be there,
Give us each a large handkerchief soaked in strong ether."

    I called this a "Fable for Critics"; you think it's
More like a display of my rhythmical trinkets;
My plot, like an icicle, 's slender and slippery,   320
Every moment more slender, and likely to slip awry,
And the reader unwilling *in loco desipere* [24]
Is free to jump over as much of my frippery
As he fancies, and, if he's a provident skipper, he
May have like Odysseus control of the gales,   325
And get safe to port, ere his patience quite fails;
Moreover, although 'tis a slender return
For your toil and expense, yet my paper will burn,

---

[24] To play the fool on occasion (Horace, *Odes,* IV, 12: 28).

And, if you have manfully struggled thus far with me,
You may e'en twist me up, and just light your cigar with me: 330
If too angry for that, you can tear me in pieces,
And my *membra disjecta* [25] consign to the breezes,
A fate like great Ratzau's, [26] whom one of those bores,
Who beflead with bad verses poor Louis Quatorze,
Describes (the first verse somehow ends with *victoire*),   335
As *dispersant partout et ses membres et sa gloire;* [27]
Or, if I were over-desirous of earning
A repute among noodles for classical learning,
I could pick you a score of allusions, I wis,
As new as the jests of *Didaskalos tis;* [28]   340
Better still, I could make out a good solid list
From authors recondite who do not exist,—
But that would be naughty: at least, I could twist
Something out of Absyrtus, [29] or turn your inquiries
After Milton's prose metaphor, drawn from Osiris; [30]—   345
But, as Cicero says he won't say this or that
(A fetch, I must say, most transparent and flat),
After saying whate'er he could possibly think of,—
I simply will state that I pause on the brink of
A mire, ankle-deep, of deliberate confusion,   350
Made up of old jumbles of classic allusion:
So, when you were thinking yourselves to be pitied,
Just conceive how much harder your teeth you'd have gritted,
An 'twere not for the dulness I've kindly omitted.

I'd apologize here for my many digressions,   355
Were it not that I'm certain to trip into fresh ones

---

[25] Scattered limbs.

[26] Lowell probably has made a mistake in name. He seems to be referring to Josias, Comte de Rantzau (1609–50), maréchal de France. An extraordinary warrior, he lost an arm and a leg at the siege of Arras (1640), and at the time of his death was also minus an eye and an ear from battling in the service of King Louis XIV (Quatorze).

[27] Scattering everywhere both his limbs and his glory.

[28] Any teacher.

[29] Not an author at all, but a character in Greek myth. He was the brother of Medea, and the son of Æëtes, king of Colchis. When Medea fled from her father's kingdom with Jason, after helping the latter to secure the Golden Fleece, she slew Absyrtus to delay pursuit and scattered his limbs on the sea.

[30] Not an author, but an Egyptian god of the underworld.

('Tis so hard to escape if you get in their mesh once);
Just reflect, if you please, how 'tis said by Horatius,
That Mæonides [31] nods now and then, and, my gracious!
It certainly does look a little bit ominous   360
When he gets under way with *ton d'apameibomenos*.[32]
(Here a something occurs which I'll just clap a rhyme to,
And say it myself, ere a Zoilus [33] have time to,—
Any author a nap like Van Winkle's may take,
If he only contrive to keep readers awake,   365
But he'll very soon find himself laid on the shelf,
If *they* fall a-nodding when he nods himself.)

    Once for all, to return, and to stay, will I, nill I—
When Phœbus expressed his desire for a lily,
Our Hero, whose homœopathic [34] sagacity   370
With an ocean of zeal mixed his drop of capacity,
Set off for the garden as fast as the wind
(Or, to take a comparison more to my mind,
As a sound politician leaves conscience behind),
And leaped the low fence, as a party hack jumps   375
O'er his principles, when something else turns up trumps.

    He was gone a long time, and Apollo, meanwhile,
Went over some sonnets of his with a file,
For, of all compositions, he thought that the sonnet
Best repaid all the toil you expended upon it;   380
It should reach with one impulse the end of its course,
And for one final blow collect all of its force;
Not a verse should be salient, but each one should tend
With a wave-like up-gathering to break [35] at the end;
So, condensing the strength here, there smoothing a wry
    kink,   385

---

[31] I.e., Homer, the Greek poet, so called because he was reputed to be a
native of Mæonia, later known as Lydia, in Asia Minor.

[32] His speech-and-answer style.—This French-Greek phrase is of Lowell's
coining. Homer's *Iliad* frequently uses *apameibomenos* as a connective
word between one speech and the next.

[33] A Greek critic of about the time of Demosthenes, who made himself
notorious by assailing Homer for fabulous and incredible stories. Hence
the name has come to denote a captious and malignant critic.

[34] Homœopathy is the treatment of disease by drugs which in healthy
persons would produce symptoms like those of the disease in question.

[35] First edition reads "burst."

He was killing the time, when up walked Mr. D[uyckinck]; [36]
At a few steps behind him, a small man in glasses
Went dodging about, muttering, "Murderers! asses!"
From out of his pocket a paper he'd take,
With the proud look of martyrdom tied to its stake,   390
And, reading a squib at himself, he'd say, "Here I see
'Gainst American letters a bloody conspiracy,
They are all by my personal enemies written;
I must post an anonymous letter to Britain,
And show that this gall is the merest suggestion   395
Of spite at my zeal on the Copyright question,
For, on this side the water, 'tis prudent to pull
O'er the eyes of the public their national wool,
By accusing of slavish respect to John Bull
All American authors who have more or less   400
Of that anti-American humbug—success,
While in private we're always embracing the knees
Of some twopenny editor over the seas,
And licking his critical shoes, for you know 'tis
The whole aim of our lives to get one English notice;   405
My American puffs I would willingly burn all
(They're all from one source, monthly, weekly, diurnal)
To get but a kick from a transmarine journal!"

   So, culling the gibes of each critical scorner
As if they were plums, and himself were Jack Horner,   410
He came cautiously on, peeping round every corner,
And into each hole where a weasel might pass in,
Expecting the knife of some critic assassin,
Who stabs to the heart with a caricature,
Not so bad as those daubs of the Sun, to be sure,   415
Yet done with a dagger-o'-type, whose vile portraits
Disperse all one's good and condense all one's poor traits.

   Apollo looked up, hearing footsteps approaching,
And slipped out of sight the new rhymes he was broaching,—
"Good day, Mr. D[uyckinck], I'm happy to meet   420
With a scholar so ripe, and a critic so neat,

---

[36] E. A. Duyckinck (1816–78), critic and editor, who sponsored *Arcturus, a Journal of Books and Opinion*, published monthly from 1840 to 1842 in New York City. His home was for years the resort of eminent literary men.

Who through Grub Street the soul of a gentleman carries;
What news from that suburb of London and Paris
Which latterly makes such shrill claims to monopolize
The credit of being the New World's metropolis?"   425

     "Why, nothing of consequence, save this attack
On my friend there, behind, by some pitiful hack,
Who thinks every national author a poor one,
That isn't a copy of something that's foreign,
And assaults the American Dick—"   430

                                        "Nay, 'tis clear
That your Damon there's fond of a flea in his ear,
And, if no one else furnished them gratis, on tick
He would buy some himself, just to hear the old click;
Why, I honestly think, if some fool in Japan   435
Should turn up his nose at the 'Poems on Man,' . . .
Your friend there by some inward instinct would know it,
Would get it translated, reprinted, and show it;
As a man might take off a high stock to exhibit
The autograph round his own neck of the gibbet;   440
Nor would let it rest so, but fire column after column,
Signed Cato, or Brutus, or something as solemn,
By way of displaying his critical crosses,
And tweaking that poor transatlantic proboscis,
His broadsides resulting (this last there's no doubt of)   445
In successively sinking the craft they're fired out of.
Now nobody knows when an author is hit,
If he have not a public hysterical fit;
Let him only keep close in his snug garret's dim ether,
And nobody'd think of his foes—or him either;   450
If an author have any least fibre of worth in him,
Abuse would but tickle the organ of mirth in him;
All the critics on earth cannot crush with their ban
One word that's in tune with the nature of man."

     "Well, perhaps so; meanwhile I have brought you a book,   455
Into which if you'll just have the goodness to look,
You may feel so delighted (when once you are through it)
As to deem it not unworth your while to review it,

And I think I can promise your thoughts, if you do,
A place in the next Democratic Review." [37]   460

  "The most thankless of gods you must surely have thought me,
For this is the forty-fourth copy you've brought me;
I have given them away, or at least I have tried,
But I've forty-two left, standing all side by side
(The man who accepted that one copy died),—   465
From one end of a shelf to the other they reach,
'With the author's respects' neatly written in each.
The publisher, sure, will proclaim a Te Deum,
When he hears of that order the British Museum
Has sent for one set of what books were first printed   470
In America, little or big,—for 'tis hinted
That this is the first truly tangible hope he
Has ever had raised for the sale of a copy.
I've thought very often 'twould be a good thing
In all public collections of books, if a wing   475
Were set off by itself, like the seas from the dry lands,
Marked *Literature suited to desolate islands,*
And filled with such books as could never be read
Save by readers of proofs, forced to do it for bread,—
Such books as one's wrecked on in small country taverns,   480
Such as hermits might mortify over in caverns,
Such as Satan, if printing had then been invented,
As the climax of woe, would to Job have presented,
Such as Crusoe might dip in, although there are few so
Outrageously cornered by fate as poor Crusoe;   485
And since the philanthropists just now are banging
And gibbeting all who're in favor of hanging
(Though Cheever [38] has proved that the Bible and Altar
Were let down from Heaven at the end of a halter,
And that vital religion would dull and grow callous,   490
Unrefreshed, now and then, with a sniff of the gallows),—
And folks are beginning to think it looks odd,

---

[37] A monthly periodical published in New York from 1840 to 1859. It contained literary pieces and articles on current affairs, and numbered Whittier, Longfellow, Lowell, Hawthorne and Whitman among its contributors.

[38] George Barrell Cheever (1807–90), a Presbyterian pastor of the old New England Calvinist school, in 1841 started a public agitation over capital punishment. He strongly advocated its use on biblical grounds.

To choke a poor scamp for the glory of God;
And that He who esteems the Virginia reel
A bait to draw saints from their spiritual weal,   495
And regards the quadrille as a far greater knavery
Than crushing His African children with slavery,—
Since all who take part in a waltz or cotillion
Are mounted for hell on the Devil's own pillion,
Who, as every true orthodox Christian well knows,   500
Approaches the heart through the door of the toes,—
That He, I was saying, whose judgments are stored
For such as take steps in despite of His word,
Should look with delight on the agonized prancing
Of a wretch who has not the least ground for his dancing,   505
While the State, standing by, sings a verse from the Psalter
About offering to God on His favorite halter,
And, when the legs droop from their twitching divergence,
Sells the clothes to a Jew, and the corpse to the surgeons;—
Now, instead of all this, I think I can direct you all   510
To a criminal code both humane and effectual;—
I propose to shut up every doer of wrong
With these desperate books, for such term, short or long,
As, by statute in such cases made and provided,
Shall be by your wise legislators decided: 515
Thus: Let murderers be shut, to grow wiser and cooler,
At hard labor for life on the works of Miss [Fuller]; [39]
Petty thieves, kept from flagranter crimes by their fears,
Shall peruse Yankee Doodle a blank term of years,—
That American Punch, like the English, no doubt,—   520
Just the sugar and lemons and spirit left out.

"But stay, here comes Tityrus [40] Griswold,[41] and leads on
The flocks whom he first plucks alive, and then feeds on,—
A loud-cackling swarm, in whose feathers warm-drest,
He goes for as perfect a—swan as the rest.   525

---

[39] Margaret Fuller Ossoli (1810–50), a colorful and vigorous figure among the Boston Transcendentalists and literati, as well as a critic and essayist of more enthusiasm than ability.

[40] Common Greek name for a shepherd.

[41] Rufus Wilmot Griswold (1815–57), a leading advocate of Americanism in literature, edited *The Poets and Poetry of America* (1842) and played the role of patron to a large group of minor poets.

"There comes Emerson first, whose rich words, every one,
Are like gold nails in temples to hang trophies on,
Whose prose is grand verse, while his verse, the Lord knows,
Is some of it pr— No, 'tis not even prose;
I'm speaking of metres; some poems have welled   530
From those rare depths of soul that have ne'er been excelled;
They're not epics, but that doesn't matter a pin,
In creating, the only hard thing's to begin;
A grass-blade's no easier to make than an oak;
If you've once found the way, you've achieved the grand stroke;
In the worst of his poems are mines of rich matter,   536
But thrown in a heap with a crash and a clatter;
Now it is not one thing nor another alone
Makes a poem, but rather the general tone,
The something pervading, uniting the whole,   540
The before unconceived, unconceivable soul,
So that just in removing this trifle or that, you
Take away, as it were, a chief limb of the statue;
Roots, wood, bark, and leaves singly perfect may be,
But, clapt hodge-podge together, they don't make a tree.   545

"But, to come back to Emerson (whom, by the way,
I believe we left waiting),—his is, we may say,
A Greek head on right Yankee shoulders, whose range
Has Olympus for one pole, for t'other the Exchange;
He seems, to my thinking (although I'm afraid   550
The comparison must, long ere this, have been made),
A Plotinus-Montaigne, where the Egyptian's gold mist
And the Gascon's shrewd wit cheek-by-jowl coexist;
All admire, and yet scarcely six converts he's got
To I don't (nor they either) exactly know what;   555
For though he builds glorious temples, 'tis odd
He leaves never a doorway to get in a god.
'Tis refreshing to old-fashioned people like me
To meet such a primitive Pagan as he,
In whose mind all creation is duly respected   560
As parts of himself—just a little projected;
And who's willing to worship the stars and the sun,
A convert to—nothing but Emerson.
So perfect a balance there is in his head,
That he talks of things sometimes as if they were dead;   565

Life, nature, love, God, and affairs of that sort,
He looks at as merely ideas; in short,
As if they were fossils stuck round in a cabinet,
Of such vast extent that our earth's a mere dab in it;
Composed just as he is inclined to conjecture her,   570
Namely, one part pure earth, ninety-nine parts pure lecturer;
You are filled with delight at his clear demonstration,
Each figure, word, gesture, just fits the occasion,
With the quiet precision of science he'll sort 'em,
But you can't help suspecting the whole a *post mortem*.[42]   575

    "There are persons, mole-blind to the soul's make and style,
Who insist on a likeness 'twixt him and Carlyle;
To compare him with Plato would be vastly fairer,
Carlyle's the more burly, but E. is the rarer;
He sees fewer objects, but clearlier, truelier,   580
If C.'s as original, E.'s more peculiar;
That he's more of a man you might say of the one,
Of the other he's more of an Emerson;
C.'s the Titan, as shaggy of mind as of limb,—
E. the clear-eyed Olympian, rapid and slim;   585
The one's two thirds Norseman, the other half Greek,
Where the one's most abounding, the other's to seek;
C.'s generals require to be seen in the mass,—
E.'s specialties gain if enlarged by the glass;
C. gives nature and God his own fits of the blues,   590
And rims common-sense things with mystical hues,—
E. sits in a mystery calm and intense,
And looks coolly around him with sharp common-sense;
C. shows you how every-day matters unite
With the dim transdiurnal recesses of night,—   595
While E., in a plain, preternatural way,
Makes mysteries matters of mere every day;
C. draws all his characters quite *à la* Fuseli,—[43]
Not sketching their bundles of muscles and thews illy,
He paints with a brush so untamed and profuse,   600
They seem nothing but bundles of muscles and thews;

---

[42] An investigation after death.
[43] Henry Fuseli (1741–1825), an Anglo-Swiss painter particularly famous for his illustrations of Shakespearean characters. In his later years he served as professor of painting at the Royal Academy, London.

E. is rather like Flaxman,[44] lines strait and severe,
And a colorless outline, but full, round, and clear;—
To the men he thinks worthy he frankly accords
The design of a white marble statue in words.   605
C. labors to get at the centre, and then
Take a reckoning from there of his actions and men;
E. calmly assumes the said centre as granted,
And, given himself, has whatever is wanted.

* * * * * * * * *

"Yonder, calm as a cloud, Alcott [45] stalks in a dream,   610
And fancies himself in thy groves, Academe,
With the Parthenon nigh, and the olive-trees o'er him,
And never a fact to perplex him or bore him,
With a snug room at Plato's when night comes, to walk to,
And people from morning till midnight to talk to,   615
And from midnight till morning, nor snore in their listening;—
So he muses, his face with the joy of it glistening,
For his highest conceit of a happiest state is
Where they'd live upon acorns, and hear him talk gratis;
And indeed, I believe, no man ever talked better,—   620
Each sentence hangs perfectly poised to a letter;
He seems piling words, but there's royal dust hid
In the heart of each sky-piercing pyramid.
While he talks he is great, but goes out like a taper,
If you shut him up closely with pen, ink, and paper;   625
Yet his fingers itch for 'em from morning till night,
And he thinks he does wrong if he don't always write;
In this, as in all things, a lamb among men,
He goes to sure death when he goes to his pen.

* * * * * * * * *

"There is Willis,[46] all *natty* and jaunty and gay,   630
Who says his best things in so foppish a way,

---

[44] John Flaxman (1755–1826), an English draftsman and sculptor especially noted for his representations of figures and scenes in the *Iliad* and
Odyssey. In his later years he held the post of professor of sculpture at the
Royal Academy, London.
[45] Amos Bronson Alcott (1799–88), Transcendentalist philosopher.
[46] Nathaniel Parker Willis (1806–67), a prolific and well-known New
York writer of the period, but one whose fame proved exceedingly ephem-
eral.

With conceits and pet phrases so thickly o'erlaying 'em,
That one hardly knows whether to thank him for saying 'em;
Over-ornament ruins both poem and prose,
Just conceive of a Muse with a ring in her nose!   635
His prose had a natural grace of its own,
And enough of it, too, if he'd let it alone;
But he twitches and jerks so, one fairly gets tired,
And is forced to forgive where one might have admired;
Yet whenever it slips away free and unlaced,   640
It runs like a stream with a musical waste,
And gurgles along with the liquidest sweep;—
'Tis not deep as a river, but who'd have it deep?
In a country where scarcely a village is found
That has not its author sublime and profound,   645
For some one to be slightly shallow's a duty,
And Willis's shallowness makes half his beauty.
His prose winds along with a blithe, gurgling error,
And reflects all of Heaven it can see in its mirror:
'Tis a narrowish strip, but it is not an artifice;   650
'Tis the true out-of-doors with its genuine hearty phiz;
It is Nature herself, and there's something in that,
Since most brains reflect but the crown of a hat.
Few volumes I know to read under a tree,
More truly delightful than his A l'Abri,[47]   655
With the shadows of leaves flowing over your book,
Like ripple-shades netting the bed of a brook;
With June coming softly your shoulder to look over,
Breezes waiting to turn every leaf of your book over,
And Nature to criticise still as you read,—   660
The page that bears that is a rare one indeed.

"He's so innate a cockney,[48] that had he been born
Where plain bare-skin's the only full-dress that is worn,
He'd have given his own such an air that you'd say
'T had been made by a tailor to lounge in Broadway.   665
His nature's a glass of champagne with the foam on't,

---

[47] Willis published in 1839 a series of sketches of the Susquehanna valley
in Pennsylvania under the title of *À L'Abri, or The Tent Pitch'd*.
[48] Originally, a native of London; here, a city-dweller.

As tender as Fletcher, as witty as Beaumont; [49]
So his best things are done in the flush of the moment;
If he wait, all is spoiled; he may stir it and shake it,
But, the fixed air once gone, he can never remake it.   670
He might be a marvel of easy delightfulness,
If he would not sometimes leave the *r* out of sprightfulness;
And he ought to let Scripture alone—'tis self-slaughter,
For nobody likes inspiration-and-water.
He'd have been just the fellow to sup at the Mermaid,[50]   675
Cracking jokes at rare Ben,[51] with an eye to the barmaid,
His wit running up as Canary ran down,—
The topmost bright bubble on the wave of The Town.

/   *   *   *   *   *   *   *   *   *

"There is Bryant, as quiet, as cool, and as dignified,
As a smooth, silent iceberg, that never is ignified,   680
Save when by reflection 'tis kindled o' nights
With a semblance of flame by the chill Northern Lights.
He may rank (Griswold says so) first bard of your nation
(There's no doubt that he stands in supreme ice-olation),
Your topmost Parnassus he may set his heel on,   685
But no warm applauses come, peal following peal on,—
He's too smooth and too polished to hang any zeal on:
Unqualified merits, I'll grant, if you choose, he has 'em,
But he lacks the one merit of kindling enthusiasm;
If he stir you at all, it is just, on my soul,   690
Like being stirred up with the very North Pole.

"He is very nice reading in summer, but *inter
Nos,*[52] we don't want *extra* freezing in winter;
Take him up in the depth of July, my advice is,
When you feel an Egyptian devotion to ices.   695

---

[49] John Fletcher (1579–1625), one of Shakespeare's most notable contemporaries in playwriting.
  Francis Beaumont (1584–1616), collaborator with Fletcher in some
outstanding plays of the English stage between 1607 and 1613.
[50] Mermaid Tavern, the chief rendezvous of the playwrights in Elizabethan London.
[51] Ben Jonson (1573?–1637), founder of the English comedy of humors,
and the most learned "wit" among the London dramatists of the early
seventeenth century.
[52] Between ourselves.

But, deduct all you can, there's enough that's right good in him,
He has a true soul for field, river, and wood in him;
And his heart, in the midst of brick walls, or whe'er it is,
Glows, softens, and thrills with the tenderest charities—
To you mortals that delve in this trade-ridden planet?   700
No, to old Berkshire's hills, with their limestone and granite.
If you're one who *in loco* (add *foco* here) *desipis*,[53]
You will get of his outermost heart (as I guess) a piece;
But you'd get deeper down if you came as a precipice,
And would break the last seal of its inwardest fountain,   705
If you only could palm yourself off for a mountain.
Mr. Quivis,[54] or somebody quite as discerning,
Some scholar who's hourly expecting his learning,
Calls B. the American Wordsworth; but Wordsworth
May be rated at more than your whole tuneful herd's worth.   710
No, don't be absurd, he's an excellent Bryant;
But, my friends, you'll endanger the life of your client,
By attempting to stretch him up into a giant:
If you choose to compare him, I think there are two per-
-sons fit for a parallel—Thomson [55] and Cowper; [56]   715
I don't mean exactly,—there's something of each,
There's T.'s love of nature, C.'s penchant to preach;
Just mix up their minds so that C.'s spice of craziness
Shall balance and neutralize T.'s turn for laziness,
And it gives you a brain cool, quite frictionless, quiet,   720
Whose internal police nips the buds of all riot,—
A brain like a permanent strait-jacket put on
The heart which strives vainly to burst off a button,—

---

[53] If you're one who plays the fool on occasion (add here, 'at your own
hearth').—This line is a play on words in allusion to Bryant's political
affiliations. The Locofocos were the extreme left wing of the Democratic
Party in the 1830's and '40's. Bryant as editor of the *New York Evening
Post* supported the Locofoco principles.

[54] Mr. What-You-Please.

[55] James Thomson (1700–48), the finest nature poet of early eighteenth-
century England.

[56]   To demonstrate quickly and easily how per-
              versely absurd 'tis to sound this name *Cowper*,
              As people in general call him named *super*,
              I remark that he rhymes it himself with horse-trooper.
                                                  [Lowell's note.]
William Cowper (1731–1800), an English poet who depicted homely rural
scenes and characters in a moralistic vein.

A brain which, without being slow or mechanic,
Does more than a larger less drilled, more volcanic;   725
He's a Cowper condensed, with no craziness bitten,
And the advantage that Wordsworth before him had written.

"But, my dear little bardlings, don't prick up your ears
Nor suppose I would rank you and Bryant as peers;
If I call him an iceberg, I don't mean to say   730
There is nothing in that which is grand in its way;
He is almost the one of your poets that knows
How much grace, strength, and dignity lie in Repose;
If he sometimes fall short, he is too wise to mar
His thought's modest fulness by going too far;   735
'Twould be well if your authors should all make a trial
Of what virtue there is in severe self-denial,
And measure their writings by Hesiod's [57] staff,
Which teaches that all has less value than half.

"There is Whittier, whose swelling and vehement heart   740
Strains the strait-breasted drab of the Quaker apart,
And reveals the live Man, still supreme and erect,
Underneath the bemummying wrappers of sect;
There was ne'er a man born who had more of the swing
Of the true lyric bard and all that kind of thing;   745
And his failures arise (though he seem not to know it)
From the very same cause that has made him a poet,—
A fervor of mind which knows no separation
'Twixt simple excitement and pure inspiration,
As my Pythoness erst sometimes erred from not knowing   750
If 'twere I or mere wind through her tripod was blowing;
Let his mind once get head in its favorite direction
And the torrent of verse bursts the dams of reflection,
While, borne with the rush of the metre along,
The poet may chance to go right or go wrong,   755
Content with the whirl and delirium of song;
Then his grammar's not always correct, nor his rhymes,
And he's prone to repeat his own lyrics sometimes,
Not his best, though, for those are struck off at white-heats
When the heart in his breast like a trip-hammer beats,   760
And can ne'er be repeated again any more

---

[57] A Greek didactic poet (c. 750 B.C.), who wrote *Works and Days*.

Than they could have been carefully plotted before:
Like old what's-his-name there at the battle of Hastings
(Who, however, gave more than mere rhythmical bastings),
Our Quaker leads off metaphorical fights   765
For reform and whatever they call human rights,
Both singing and striking in front of the war,
And hitting his foes with the mallet of Thor;
Anne haec, one exclaims, on beholding his knocks,
Vestis filii tui, O leather-clad Fox? [58]   770
Can that be thy son, in the battle's mid din,
Preaching brotherly love and then driving it in
To the brain of the tough old Goliath of sin,
With the smoothest of pebbles from Castaly's spring [59]
Impressed on his hard moral sense with a sling?   775

  "All honor and praise to the right-hearted bard
Who was true to The Voice when such service was hard,   .
Who himself was so free he dared sing for the slave
When to look but a protest in silence was brave;

  *   *   *   *   *   *   *   *   *

  "There is Hawthorne, with genius so shrinking and rare   780
That you hardly at first see the strength that is there;
A frame so robust, with a nature so sweet,
So earnest, so graceful, so lithe and so fleet,
Is worth a descent from Olympus to meet;
'Tis as if a rough oak that for ages had stood,   785
With his gnarled bony branches like ribs of the wood,
Should bloom, after cycles of struggles and scathe,
With a single anemone trembly and rathe; [60]
His strength is so tender, his wildness so meek,
That a suitable parallel sets one to seek,—   790

---

[58] But is not this, one exclaims, on beholding his knocks, the coat of thy
son, O leather-clad Fox?   (Cf. the query made of Jacob concerning Joseph's
coat in Genesis xxxvii: 33.)—George Fox, the founder of the Quaker sect,
was noted for wearing a leather suit on his preaching missions. Lowell's
figure here may well have been suggested by Thomas Carlyle's vivid passage
on Fox and his suit in *Sartor Resartus,* Bk. III, Chap. i.

[59] The fountain of Castalia on Mount Parnassus in Phocis, Greece, was
sacred to Apollo and the Muses.

[60] Early in the season.

He's a John Bunyan Fouqué, a Puritan Tieck; [61]
When Nature was shaping him, clay was not granted
For making so full-sized a man as she wanted,
So, to fill out her model, a little she spared
From some finer-grained stuff for a woman prepared,   795
And she could not have hit a more excellent plan
For making him fully and perfectly man.
The success of her scheme gave her so much delight,
That she tried it again, shortly after, in Dwight; [62]
Only, while she was kneading and shaping the clay,   800
She sang to her work in her sweet childish way,
And found, when she'd put the last touch to his soul,
That the music had somehow got mixed with the whole.

"Here's Cooper, who's written six volumes to show
He's as good as a lord: well, let's grant that he's so;   805
If a person prefer that description of praise,
Why, a coronet's certainly cheaper than bays;
But he need take no pains to convince us he's not
(As his enemies say) the American Scott.
Choose any twelve men, and let C. read aloud   810
That one of his novels of which he's most proud,
And I'd lay any bet that, without ever quitting
Their box, they'd be all, to a man, for acquitting.
He has drawn you one character, though, that is new,
One wildflower he's plucked that is wet with the dew   815
Of this fresh Western world, and, the thing not to mince,
He has done naught but copy it ill ever since;
His Indians, with proper respect be it said,
Are just Natty Bumppo, [63] daubed over with red,

[61] John Bunyan (1628–88) was an English Non-Conformist preacher of the strictest morality.

    Baron Friedrich Heinrich Karl de la Motte Fouqué (1777–1843), German author of the Romantic school, who wrote many novels, epics, and plays.

    Johann Ludwig Tieck (1773–1853), German poet, playwright, novelist, and critic, who became an outstanding figure in the European Romantic Movement and whose influence was important in American literature of the earlier nineteenth century.

[62] John Sullivan Dwight (1813–93), well-known musical critic of the day.

[63] The hero of Cooper's first Leatherstocking novel, *The Pioneers* (1823), who reappeared under different names in the remaining volumes of the

And his very Long Toms [64] are the same useful Nat,   820
Rigged up in duck pants and a sou'wester hat
(Though once in a Coffin, a good chance was found
To have slipped the old fellow away underground).
All his other men-figures are clothes upon sticks,
The *dernière chemise* [65] of a man in a fix   825
(As a captain besieged, when his garrison's small,
Sets up caps upon poles to be seen o'er the wall);
And the women he draws from one model don't vary,
All sappy as maples and flat as a prairie.
When a character's wanted, he goes to the task   830
As a cooper would do in composing a cask;
He picks out the staves, of their qualities heedful,
Just hoops them together as tight as is needful,
And, if the best fortune should crown the attempt, he
Has made at the most something wooden and empty.   835

"Don't suppose I would underrate Cooper's abilities;
If I thought you'd do that, I should feel very ill at ease;
The men who have given to *one* character life
And objective existence are not very rife;
You may number them all, both prose-writers and singers,   840
Without overrunning the bounds of your fingers,
And Natty won't go to oblivion quicker
Than Adams the parson or Primrose the vicar.[66]

"There is one thing in Cooper I like, too, and that is
That on manners he lectures his countrymen gratis;   845
Not precisely so either, because, for a rarity,
He is paid for his tickets in unpopularity.
Now he may overcharge his American pictures,
But you'll grant there's a good deal of truth in his strictures;
And I honor the man who is willing to sink   850
Half his present repute for the freedom to think,
And, when he has thought, be his cause strong or weak,
Will risk t'other half for the freedom to speak,

---

series, but maintained throughout his sturdy, sincere, gallant frontiersman
character.
[64] Long Tom Coffin of Nantucket is a character in *The Pilot* (1823).
[65] Last resort (lit., last shirt).
[66] See note on p. 183.
Dr. Primrose, the vicar of Wakefield in Oliver Goldsmith's famous novel.

Caring naught for what vengeance the mob has in store,
Let that mob be the upper ten thousand or lower.   855

  "There are truths you Americans need to be told,
And it never'll refute them to swagger and scold;

*   *   *   *   *   *   *   *   *

  "You steal [67] Englishmen's books and think Englishmen's
          thought,
With their salt on her tail your wild eagle is caught;
Your literature suits its each whisper and motion   860
To what will be thought of it over the ocean;
The cast clothes of Europe your statesmanship tries
And mumbles again the old blarneys and lies;—
Forget Europe wholly, your veins throb with blood,
To which the dull current in hers is but mud: 865
Let her sneer, let her say your experiment fails,
In her voice there's a tremble e'en now while she rails,
And your shore will soon be in the nature of things
Covered thick with gilt driftwood of castaway kings,
Where alone, as it were in a Longfellow's Waif, [68]   870
Her fugitive pieces will find themselves safe.
O my friends, thank your god, if you have one, that he
'Twixt the Old World and you set the gulf of a sea;
Be strong-backed, brown-handed, upright as your pines,
By the scale of a hemisphere shape your designs,   875
Be true to yourselves and this new nineteenth age,
As a statue by Powers, [69] or a picture by Page, [70]
Plough, sail, forge, build, carve, paint, make all over new,
To your own New-World instincts contrive to be true,

[67] The absence of an international copyright law until 1891 led many
American publishers to reprint English books without payment of royalties
to the authors.
[68] Longfellow edited in 1845 an anthology entitled *The Waif: A Collection of Poems*.
[69] Hiram Powers (1805–73), an outstanding American sculptor of the
nineteenth century, created an international artistic sensation by his nude
female figure, *The Greek Slave*, in 1843. From 1837 onwards he lived in
Florence, Italy, where his residence became a center of hospitality and art
for Americans abroad, and was visited by Longfellow and Hawthorne.
[70] William Page (1811–85), a celebrated American portrait painter whose
pictures now hang in the leading art galleries of the United States. Lowell
knew him well from 1842 and later sat for him. In 1843 Lowell dedicated
his second volume of poems to Page.

Keep your ears open wide to the Future's first call,   880
Be whatever you will, but yourselves first of all. . . ."

* * * * * * * * *

Here Miranda [71] came up, and said, "Phœbus! you know
That the Infinite Soul has its infinite woe,
As I ought to know, having lived cheek by jowl,
Since the day I was born, with the Infinite Soul;   885
I myself introduced, I myself, I alone,
To my Land's better life authors solely my own,
Who the sad heart of earth on their shoulders have taken,
Whose works sound a depth by Life's quiet unshaken,
Such as Shakespeare, for instance, the Bible, and Bacon,   890
Not to mention my own works; Time's nadir is fleet,
And, as for myself, I'm quite out of conceit—"

"Quite out of conceit!   I'm enchanted to hear it,"
Cried Apollo aside.   "Who'd have thought she was near it?
To be sure, one is apt to exhaust those commodities   895
One uses too fast, yet in this case as odd it is
As if Neptune should say to his turbots and whitings,
'I'm as much out of salt as Miranda's own writings'
(Which, as she in her own happy manner has said,
Sound a depth, for 'tis one of the functions of lead).   900
She often has asked me if I could not find
A place somewhere near me that suited her mind;
I know but a single one vacant, which she,
With her rare talent that way, would fit to a T.
And it would not imply any pause or cessation   905
In the work she esteems her peculiar vocation,—
She may enter on duty to-day, if she chooses,
And remain Tiring-woman for life to the Muses."

* * * * * * * * *

"There comes Poe, with his raven, like Barnaby Rudge,[72]
Three fifths of him genius and two fifths sheer fudge,   910
Who talks like a book of iambs and pentameters,
In a way to make people of common sense damn metres,
Who has written some things quite the best of their kind,
But the heart somehow seems all squeezed out by the mind,

---

[71] Lowell's pseudonym for Margaret Fuller Ossoli.

[72] A half-witted, pathetic character, prominently depicted along with his
pet raven, Grip, in Charles Dickens' novel, *Barnaby Rudge* (1841).

Who—but hey-day! What's this? Messieurs Mathews [73] and
    Poe,   915
You mustn't fling mud-balls at Longfellow so,
Does it make a man worse that his character's such
As to make his friends love him (as you think) too much?
Why, there is not a bard at this moment alive
More willing than he that his fellows should thrive: 920
While you are abusing him thus, even now
He would help either one of you out of a slough;
You may say that he's smooth and all that till you're hoarse,
But remember that elegance also is force;
After polishing granite as much as you will,   925
The heart keeps its tough old persistency still;
Deduct all you can, *that* still keeps you at bay;
Why, he'll live till men weary of Collins and Gray.[74]
I'm not over-fond of Greek metres in English,
To me rhyme's a gain, so it be not too jinglish,   930
And your modern hexameter verses are no more
Like Greek ones than sleek Mr. Pope is like Homer;
As the roar of the sea to the coo of a pigeon is,
So, compared to your moderns, sounds old Melesigenes; [75]
I may be too partial, the reason, perhaps, o't is   935
That I've heard the old blind man recite his own rhapsodies,
And my ear with that music impregnate may be,
Like the poor exiled shell with the soul of the sea,
Or as one can't bear Strauss [76] when his nature is cloven
To its deeps within deeps by the stroke of Beethoven;   940
But, set that aside, and 'tis truth that I speak,
Had Theocritus [77] written in English, not Greek,
I believe that his exquisite sense would scarce change a line
In that rare, tender, virgin-like pastoral Evangeline.

---

[73] Cornelius Mathews (1817–89), a second-rate poet and critic in his
day, who won some prominence in the 1840's as part editor of *Arcturus*, a
monthly journal of literature.

[74] William Collins (1720–56), English poet best known for his odes.
Thomas Gray (1716–71), English poet famed for his *Elegy Written in
a Country Churchyard*.

[75] Melos-born: an epithet for Homer, who was supposed to have been
born on this island in the Aegean Sea.

[76] Johann Strauss (1804–49), the first of the famous Viennese musicians
by that name.

[77] The outstanding Greek pastoral poet, born in Sicily *c.* 270 B.C.

That's not ancient nor modern, its place is apart   945
Where time has no sway, in the realm of pure Art,
'Tis a shrine of retreat from Earth's hubbub and strife
As quiet and chaste as the author's own life.

*   *   *   *   *   *   *   *   *

"What!   Irving? thrice welcome, warm heart and fine brain,
You bring back the happiest spirit from Spain,   950
And the gravest sweet humor, that ever were there
Since Cervantes met death in his gentle despair;
Nay, don't be embarrassed, nor look so beseeching,
I sha'n't run directly against my own preaching,
And, having just laughed at their Raphaels and Dantes,   955
Go to setting you up beside matchless Cervantes;
But allow me to speak what I honestly feel,—
To a true poet-heart add the fun of Dick Steele,
Throw in all of Addison, *minus* the chill,
With the whole of that partnership's stock and good-will,   960
Mix well, and while stirring, hum o'er, as a spell,
The fine *old* English Gentleman, simmer it well,
Sweeten just to your own private liking, then strain,
That only the finest and clearest remain,
Let it stand out of doors till a soul it receives   965
From the warm lazy sun loitering down through green leaves,
And you'll find a choice nature, not wholly deserving
A name either English or Yankee,—just Irving.

*   *   *   *   *   *   *   *   *

"There's Holmes, who is matchless among you for wit;
A Leyden-jar always full-charged, from which flit   970
The electrical tingles of hit after hit;
In long poems 'tis painful sometimes, and invites
A thought of the way the new Telegraph writes,
Which pricks down its little sharp sentences spitefully
As if you got more than you'd title to rightfully,   975
And you find yourself hoping its wild father Lightning
Would flame in for a second and give you a fright'ning.
He has perfect sway of what *I* call a sham metre,
But many admire it, the English pentameter,
And Campbell,[78] I think, wrote most commonly worse,   980

---

[78] Thomas Campbell (1774–1844), a Scottish poet widely known in the nineteenth century.

With less nerve, swing, and fire in the same kind of verse,
Nor e'er achieved aught in't so worthy of praise
As the tribute of Holmes to the grand *Marseillaise*.
You went crazy last year over Bulwer's New Timon; [79]—
Why, if B., to the day of his dying, should rhyme on,   985
Heaping verses on verses and tomes upon tomes,
He could ne'er reach the best point and vigor of Holmes.
His are just the fine hands, too, to weave you a lyric
Full of fancy, fun, feeling, or spiced with satiric
In a measure so kindly, you doubt if the toes   990
That are trodden upon are your own or your foes'.

"There is Lowell, who's striving Parnassus to climb
With a whole bale of *isms* tied together with rhyme,
He might get on alone, spite of brambles and boulders,
But he can't with that bundle he has on his shoulders,   995
The top of the hill he will ne'er come nigh reaching
Till he learns the distinction 'twixt singing and preaching:
His lyre has some chords that would ring pretty well,
But he'd rather by half make a drum of the shell,
And rattle away till he's old as Methusalem,   1000
At the head of a march to the last new Jerusalem.

*   *   *   *   *   *   *   *   *

"But what's that? a mass-meeting?   No, there come in lots
The American Bulwers, Disraelis,[80] and Scotts,
And in short the American everything elses,
Each charging the others with envies and jealousies;—   1005
By the way, 't is a fact that displays what profusions
Of all kinds of greatness bless free institutions,
That while the Old World has produced barely eight
Of such poets as all men agree to call great,
And of other great characters hardly a score   1010
(One might safely say less than that rather than more),
With you every year a whole crop is begotten,

[79] *The New Timon,* a narrative poem of London life, by Edward Bulwer,
first Lord Lytton (1803–73), was in the first edition published anonymously and by parts during 1845–46. The work created an immediate
sensation on both sides of the Atlantic with its satirical sketches of contemporary giants in literature and politics. Tennyson, for example, was
referred to as "school-miss Alfred."
[80] Benjamin Disraeli (1805–81), Earl of Beaconsfield, an eminent English statesman who wrote many novels.

They're as much of a staple as corn is, or cotton;
Why, there's scarcely a huddle of log-huts and shanties
That has not brought forth its own Miltons and Dantes;   1015
I myself know ten Byrons, one Coleridge, three Shelleys,
Two Raphaels, six Titians (I think), one Apelles,[81]
Leonardos [82] and Rubenses [83] plenty as lichens,
One (but that one is plenty) American Dickens,
A whole flock of Lambs, any number of Tennysons,—   1020
In short, if a man has the luck to have any sons,
He may feel pretty certain that one out of twain
Will be some very great person over again.

      *   *   *   *   *   *   *   *

"Nature fits all her children with something to do,
He who would write and can't write can surely review,   1025
Can set up a small booth as critic and sell us his
Petty conceit and his pettier jealousies;
Thus a lawyer's apprentice, just out of his teens,
Will do for the Jeffrey [84] of six magazines;
Having read Johnson's lives of the poets half through,   1030
There's nothing on earth he's not competent to;
He reviews with as much nonchalance as he whistles,—
He goes through a book and just picks out the thistles;
It matters not whether he blame or commend,
If he's bad as a foe, he's far worse as a friend: 1035
Let an author but write what's above his poor scope,
He goes to work gravely and twists up a rope,
And, inviting the world to see punishment done,
Hangs himself up to bleach in the wind and the sun;
'Tis delightful to see, when a man comes along   1040
Who has anything in him peculiar and strong,
Every cockboat that swims clear its fierce (pop) gundeck at him,
And makes as he passes its ludicrous Peck [85] at him—"

---

81 The most famous of the Greek painters, friend of Alexander the Great.
82 Leonardo da Vinci (1452–1519), an outstanding scholar, painter, and
engineer of the Italian Renaissance.
83 Peter Paul Rubens (1577–1640), distinguished Flemish painter who
worked in France and Italy as well as in Antwerp.
84 Francis, Lord Jeffrey (1773–1850), literary critic and founder of the
Edinburgh Review, who heartily disapproved of the Lake school of poetry,
i.e., Wordsworth, Coleridge, and others.
85 A satirical play on the name of George Washington Peck (1817–59),
who wrote articles on music and drama for the Boston Post in the earlier
1840's and edited the Boston Musical Review, 1845–47.

Here Miranda came up and began, "As to that—"
Apollo at once seized his gloves, cane, and hat,   1045
And, seeing the place getting rapidly cleared,
I too snatched my notes and forthwith disappeared.

Meliboeus—Hipponax

THE

BIGLOW PAPERS [1]

EDITED,

WITH AN INTRODUCTION, NOTES,

GLOSSARY, AND COPIOUS INDEX,

By

HOMER WILBUR, A.M.,

PASTOR OF THE FIRST CHURCH IN JAALAM, AND

(PROSPECTIVE) MEMBER OF MANY LITERARY,

LEARNED, AND SCIENTIFIC SOCIETIES . . .

---

[1] This series of satirical squibs constitued for Lowell a journalistic *jeu d'esprit*, by which he could vent his scorn of the Mexican War as a conflict based on false pretenses and voice his protest at the continued toleration of slavery in America. He wrote and published at intervals over a period of somewhat more than two years (June, 1846–September, 1848) nine Biglow papers, the first four in the *Boston Courier* and the rest in the *National Anti-Slavery Standard*. When in the autumn of 1848 he set about collecting the separate newspaper compositions to form a volume, he elaborated very considerably the humorous role of the parson-editor by adding, in Wilbur's name, copious prefaces, notes, glossary, and index. He also revised to some sort of consistency the dialectical peculiarities of the verse in the separate poems. Their Yankee *patois* had sprung up in his mind with utter spontaneity. Lowell later explained his linguistic *tour de force* thus: "I was born and bred in the country, and the dialect was homely to me." (*Letters,* I, 296.) Lowell's statement is not strictly correct, for his Cambridge surroundings hardly constituted a genuinely rural environment. T. W. Higginson, a Cambridge contemporary, has remarked that the Biglow language corresponded to the speech used by the farmer youth who, in order to get on, came to towns like Cambridge and took up service in the better households as "hired men," and that therefore Lowell's early contact with and absorption of this lingo occurred right at home. (*Old Cambridge,* 28.) Higginson's comment probably presents the more accurate picture of Lowell's means for contact with the Yankee vernacular during his youth.

THE BIGLOW PAPERS

First Series

No. I

A LETTER [2]

FROM MR. EZEKIEL BIGLOW OF JAALAM TO THE HON.
JOSEPH T. BUCKINGHAM, EDITOR OF THE BOSTON
COURIER, INCLOSING A POEM OF HIS SON, MR. HOSEA
BIGLOW.

JAYLEM, june 1846.

MISTER EDDYTER:—Our Hosea wuz down to Boston last week,
and he see a cruetin Sarjunt [3] a struttin round as popler as a hen
with 1 chicking, with 2 fellers a drummin and fifin arter him like
all nater. the sarjunt he thout Hosea hed n't gut his i teeth cut
cos he looked a kindo's though he'd jest com down, so he cal'lated
to hook him in, but Hosy woodn't take none o' his sarse for all
he hed much 'as 20 Rooster's tales stuck onto his hat and eena-
most enuf brass a bobbin up and down on his shoulders and
figureed onto his coat and trousis, let alone wut nater hed sot in
his featers, to make a 6 pounder out on.

wal, Hosea he com home considerabal riled, and arter I'd gone
to bed I heern Him a thrashin round like a short-tailed Bull in
flitime. The old Woman ses she to me ses she, Zekle, ses she, our
Hosee's gut the chollery or suthin anuther ses she, don't you Bee
skeered, ses I, he's oney amakin pottery [4] ses i, he's ollers on
hand at that ere busynes like Da & martin,[5] and shure enuf, cum

The Biglow papers in book form came out about November 10, 1848
(Letters, I, 143), and sold so rapidly that the first edition of 1500 copies
was exhausted within a week or two.

[2] Published in the Boston Courier on June 17 (Bunker Hill Day), 1846.

[3] President Polk, authorized by a Congressional act of May 13, 1846,
called for 50,000 volunteers from the nation at large to carry on the Mexican War, and requested from Massachusetts as its quota 777 men. On
May 26 Governor Briggs of Massachusetts by proclamation gave official sanction to the enrollment of the volunteer regiment, the recruiting of which
was bitterly opposed by the Abolitionists and by many Whigs.

[4] *Aut insanit, aut versos facit* (Either he is out of his mind, or he is
making poetry).—H. W. [Lowell's note.]

[5] Day and Martin were well-known makers of shoe polish who advertised
their product in verse.

mornin, Hosy he cum down stares full chizzle, hare on eend
and cote tales flyin, and sot rite of to go reed his varses to Parson
Wilbur bein he haint aney grate shows o' book larnin himself,
bimeby he cum back and sed the parson wuz dreffle tickled with
'em as i hoop you will Be, and said they wuz True grit.

Hosea ses taint hardly fair to call 'em hisn now, cos the parson
kind o' slicked off sum o' the last varses, but he told Hosee he
didn't want to put his ore in to tetch to the Rest on 'em, bein
they wuz verry well As thay wuz, and then Hosy ses he sed
suthin a nuther about Simplex Mundishes [6] or sum sech feller,
but I guess Hosea kind o' didn't hear him, for I never hearn o'
nobody o' that name in this villadge, and I've lived here man
and boy 76 year cum next tater diggin, and thair aint no wheres
a kitting spryer 'n I be.

If you print 'em I wish you 'd jest let folks know who Hosy's
father is, cos my ant Keziah used to say it's nater to be curus ses
she, she aint livin though and he's a likely kind o' lad.

                                        EZEKIEL BIGLOW.

> Thrash away, you'll *hev* to rattle
>   On them kittle-drums o' yourn,—
> 'Taint a knowin' kind o' cattle
>   Thet is ketched with mouldy corn;
> Put in stiff, you fifer feller,   5
>   Let folks see how spry you be,—
> Guess you'll toot till you are yeller
>   'Fore you git ahold o' me!
>
> Thet air flag's a leetle rotten,
>   Hope it aint your Sunday's best;—   10
> Fact! it takes a sight o' cotton
>   To stuff out a soger's chest:
> Sence we farmers hev to pay fer 't,
>   Ef you must wear humps like these,
> Sposin' you should try salt hay fer 't,   15
>   It would du ez slick ez grease.
>
> 'Twould n't suit them Southun fellers,
>   They're a dreffle graspin' set,

---

[6] A humorous garbling of Horace's well-known phrase in reference to the
flirtatious Pyrrha (*Odes*, I, 5: 5). He praises her as *simplex munditiis,* i.e.,
dressed in simple neatness.

We must ollers blow the bellers
    Wen they want their irons het;   20
May be it's all right ez preachin',
    But *my* narves it kind o' grates,
Wen I see the overreachin'
    O' them nigger-drivin' States.

Them thet rule us, them slave-traders,   25
    Haint they cut a thunderin' swarth
(Helped by Yankee renegaders),
    Thru the vartu o' the North!
We begin to think it's nater
    To take sarse an' not be riled;—   30
Who'd expect to see a tater
    All on eend at bein' biled?

Ez fer war, I call it murder,—
    There you hev it plain an' flat;
I don't want to go no furder   35
    Than my Testyment fer that;
God hez sed so plump an' fairly,
    It's ez long ez it is broad,
An' you've gut to git up airly
    Ef you want to take in God.   40

'Taint your eppyletts an' feathers
    Make the thing a grain more right;
'Taint afollerin' your bell-wethers
    Will excuse ye in His sight;
Ef you take a sword an' dror it,   45
    An' go stick a feller thru,
Guv'ment aint to answer for it,
    God'll send the bill to you.

Wut's the use o' meetin'-goin'
    Every Sabbath, wet or dry,   50
Ef it's right to go amowin'
    Feller-men like oats an' rye?
I dunno but wut it's pooty
    Trainin' round in bobtail coats,—

But it's curus Christian dooty   55
   This 'ere cuttin' folks's throats.

They may talk o' Freedom's airy
   Tell they're pupple in the face,—
It's a grand gret cemetary
   Fer the barthrights of our race;   60
They jest want this Californy
   So's to lug new slave-states in
To abuse ye, an' to scorn ye,
   An' to plunder ye like sin.

Aint it cute to see a Yankee   65
   Take sech everlastin' pains,
All to git the Devil's thankee
   Helpin' on 'em weld their chains?
Wy, it's jest ez clear ez figgers,
   Clear ez one an' one makes two,   70
Chaps thet make black slaves o' niggers
   Want to make wite slaves o' you.

Tell ye jest the eend I've come to
   Arter cipherin' plaguy smart,
An' it makes a handy sum, tu,   75
   Any gump could larn by heart;
Laborin' man an' laborin' woman
   Hev one glory an' one shame.
Ev'y thin' thet's done inhuman
   Injers all on 'em the same.   80

'Taint by turnin' out to hack folks
   You're agoin' to git your right,
Nor by lookin' down on black folks
   Coz you're put upon by wite;
Slavery aint o' nary color,   85
   'Taint the hide thet makes it wus,
All it keers fer in a feller
   'S jest to make him fill its pus.

Want to tackle *me* in, du ye?
   I expect you'll hev to wait;   90

Wen cold lead puts daylight thru ye
    You'll begin to kal'late;
S'pose the crows wun't fall to pickin'
    All the carkiss from your bones,
Coz you helped to give a lickin'   95
    To them poor half-Spanish drones?

Jest go home an' ask our Nancy
    Wether I'd be sech a goose
Ez to jine ye,—guess you'd fancy
    The etarnal bung wuz loose!   100
She wants me fer home consumption,
    Let alone the hay's to mow,—
Ef you're arter folks o' gumption,
    You've a darned long row to hoe.

Take them editors thet's crowin'   105
    Like a cockerel three months old,—
Don't ketch any on 'em goin',
    Though they *be* so blasted bold;
Aint they a prime lot o' fellers?
    'Fore they think on't guess they'll sprout   110
(Like a peach thet's got the yellers),
    With the meanness bustin' out.

Wal, go 'long to help 'em stealin'
    Bigger pens to cram with slaves,
Help the men thet's ollers dealin'   115
    Insults on your fathers' graves;
Help the strong to grind the feeble,
    Help the many agin the few
Help the men thet call your people
    Witewashed slaves an' peddlin' crew!   120

Massachusetts, God forgive her,
    She's akneelin' with the rest,[7]
She, thet ough' to ha' clung ferever

---

[7] An allusion to the fact that of the seven members of the House of
Representatives from Massachusetts, all of them Whigs, two voted to accede
to President Polk's request of May 11, 1846, for $10,000,000 with which to
pursue the war against Mexico.

In her grand old eagle-nest;
She thet ough' to stand so fearless   125
   W'ile the wracks are round her hurled,
Holdin' up a beacon peerless
   To the oppressed of all the world!

Ha'n't they sold your colored seamen?
   Ha'n't they made your env'ys w'iz? [8]   130
Wut'll make ye act like freemen?
   Wut'll git your dander riz?
Come, I'll tell ye wut I'm thinkin'
   Is our dooty in this fix,
They'd ha' done 't ez quick ez winkin'   135
   In the days o' seventy-six.

Clang the bells in every steeple,
   Call all true men to disown
The tradoocers of our people,
   The enslavers o' their own;   140
Let our dear old Bay State proudly
   Put the trumpet to her mouth,
Let her ring this messidge loudly
   In the ears of all the South:—

"I'll return ye good fer evil   145
   Much ez we frail mortils can,
But I wun't go help the Devil
   Makin' man the cus o' man;
Call me coward, call me traiter,
   Jest ez suits your mean idees,—   150
Here I stand a tyrant-hater,
   An' the friend o' God an' Peace!"

Ef I'd *my* way I hed ruther
   We should go to work an' part,—
   They take one way, we take t' other,   155

---

[8] In 1844 Governor Briggs of Massachusetts, on petition of the legislature, appointed Mr. Samuel Hoar agent to Charleston, South Carolina, and Mr. George Hubbard to New Orleans, to act on behalf of colored citizens of the Bay State, who had been mistreated or sold into slavery upon entrance at these ports. Mr. Hoar, however, was expelled from South Carolina by legislative order, and Mr. Hubbard had to depart from Louisiana for fear of personal violence.

Guess it wouldn't break my heart;
Man hed ough' to put asunder
Them thet God has noways jined;
An' I shouldn't gretly wonder
Ef there's thousands o' my mind.   160

[The first recruiting sergeant on record I conceive to have been that individual who is mentioned in the Book of Job as *going to and fro in the earth, and walking up and down in it*.[9] Bishop Latimer [10] will have him to have been a bishop, but to me that other calling would appear more congenial. The sect of Cainites is not yet extinct, who esteemed the first-born of Adam to be the most worthy, not only because of that privilege of primogeniture, but inasmuch as he was able to overcome and slay his younger brother. That was a wise saying of the famous Marquis Pescara [11] to the Papal Legate, that *it was impossible for men to serve Mars and Christ at the same time*. Yet in time past the profession of arms was judged to be κατ' ἐξοχήν [12] that of a gentleman, nor does this opinion want for strenuous upholders even in our day. Must we suppose, then, that the profession of Christianity was only intended for losels,[13] or, at best, to afford an opening for plebeian ambition? Or shall we hold with that nicely metaphysical Pomeranian, Captain Vratz, who was Count Konigsmark's chief instrument in the murder of Mr. Thynne,[14] that the Scheme of Salvation has been arranged with

---

[9] Satan made this remark to the Lord (Job 1:7).

[10] Hugh Latimer (c. 1490–1555), Bishop of Worcester, one of the chief promoters of the Reformation in England.

[11] Ferdinando Francesco d'Avalos, Marquis of Pescara (?1489–1525), a Neapolitan general.

[12] Preeminently.

[13] Ne'er-do-wells.

[14] Thomas Thynne of Longleat Hall, Wilts, (1648–82), commonly known as "Tom of Ten Thousand" (a year), and the "Issachar" of Dryden's *Absalom and Achitophel* (1681), was shot in his coach on St. Alban's Street, near the Haymarket, London, on February 12, 1682, presumably at the instigation of a Swedish nobleman, Count Carl Johann Von Königsmarck (d. 1686). Königsmarck had been an unsuccessful suitor of Elizabeth Percy (1667–1722), daughter of the last Earl of Northumberland and widow of Henry Cavendish, Earl of Ogle. Lady Ogle had married Thynne in 1681, but shortly after the wedding fled from Thynne into Holland. Thynne was waylaid by three assassins, the leader of whom proved to be Colonel Christopher Vratz, a German soldier of some repute for his bravery at the siege of Mons.

an especial eye to the necessities of the upper classes, and that
"God would consider *a gentleman* and deal with him suitably to
the condition and profession he had placed him in"? [15]   It may
be said of us all, *Exemplo plus quam ratione vivimus.*[16]—H. W.]

No. III

WHAT MR. ROBINSON THINKS [17]

[A few remarks on the following verses will not be out of
place. The satire in them was not meant to have any personal,
but only a general, application. Of the gentleman upon whose
letter they were intended as a commentary Mr. Biglow had never
heard, till he saw the letter itself. The position of the satirist is
oftentimes one which he would not have chosen, had the election
been left to himself. In attacking bad principles, he is obliged to
select some individual who has made himself their exponent, and
in whom they are impersonate, to the end that what he says may
not, through ambiguity, be dissipated *tenues in auras.*[18]   For
what says Seneca [19]?   *Longum iter per præcepta, breve et effi-
cace per exempla.*[20] A bad principle is comparatively harmless
while it continues to be an abstraction, nor can the general mind
comprehend it fully till it is printed in that large type which all
men can read at sight, namely, the life and character, the sayings
and doings, of particular persons. It is one of the cunningest
fetches of Satan, that he never exposes himself directly to our
arrows, but, still dodging behind this neighbor or that acquaintance, compels us to wound him through them, if at all. He
holds our affections as hostages, the while he patches up a truce
with our conscience.

---

[15] On March 10, 1682, Colonel Vratz was executed for his part in the
murder of Thynne. As he went to the gallows, he remarked, according to
John Evelyn, that "he did not value dying of a rush, and hoped and believed God would deal with him like a gentleman." (See the *Diary of
John Evelyn* under this date.) Lowell here has set down his own more
colorful phrasing of Vratz' remark.

[16] We live more by example than by reason.

[17] Written at one sitting, according to Lowell's testimony. (*Letters,* I,
296.)

[18] Into thin air.

[19] Lucius Annaeus Seneca (*c.* 5 B.C.–65 A.D.), Roman Stoic philosopher,
moralist, and tragedian.

[20] Long is the road by way of injunctions; short and effectual is that by
way of examples.

Meanwhile, let us not forget that the aim of the true satirist is not to be severe upon persons, but only upon falsehood, and, as Truth and Falsehood start from the same point, and sometimes even go along together for a little way, his business is to follow the path of the latter after it diverges, and to show her floundering in the bog at the end of it. Truth is quite beyond the reach of satire. There is so brave a simplicity in her, that she can no more be made ridiculous than an oak or a pine. The danger of the satirist is, that continual use may deaden his sensibility to the force of language. He becomes more and more liable to strike harder than he knows or intends. He may be careful to put on his boxing-gloves, and yet forget that, the older they grow, the more plainly may the knuckles inside be felt. Moreover, in the heat of contest, the eye is insensibly drawn to the crown of victory, whose tawdry tinsel glitters through that dust of the ring which obscures Truth's wreath of simple leaves. I have sometimes thought that my young friend, Mr. Biglow, needed a monitory hand laid on his arm,—*aliquid sufflaminandus erat.*[21] I have never thought it good husbandry to water the tender plants of reform with *aqua fortis,*[22] yet, where so much is to do in the beds, he were a sorry gardener who should wage a whole day's war with an iron scuffle on those ill weeds that make the garden-walks of life unsightly, when a sprinkle of Attic salt will wither them up. *Est ars etiam maledicendi,*[23] says Scaliger,[24] and truly it is a hard thing to say where the graceful gentleness of the lamb merges in downright sheepishness. We may conclude with worthy and wise Dr. Fuller,[25] that "one may be a lamb in private wrongs, but in hearing general affronts to goodness they are asses which are not lions."—H. W.]

GUVENER B.[26] is a sensible man;
 He stays to his home an' looks arter his folks;
 He draws his furrer ez straight ez he can,

---

[21] He ought to have been checked somewhat.

[22] Nitric acid (lit., strong water).

[23] There is even an art to slandering.

[24] Julius Caesar Scaliger (1484–1558), prominent French critic and philosopher of the Renaissance.

[25] Thomas Fuller (1608–61), an Anglican clergyman, who as moralist and antiquary wrote *The History of the Worthies of England* (1661).

[26] George N. Briggs, Whig Governor of Massachusetts from 1844 to 1851. The campaign here mentioned was the gubernatorial election of 1847.

An' into nobody's tater-patch pokes;
        But John P.
        Robinson [27] he
    Sez he wunt vote fer Guvener B.

My! ain't it terrible?   Wut shall we du?
    We can't never choose him o' course,—thet 's flat;
Guess we shall hev to come round, (don't you?)
    An' go in fer thunder an' guns, an' all that;
        Fer John P.
        Robinson he
    Sez he wunt vote fer Guvener B.

Gineral C. [28] is a dreffle smart man:
    He's ben on all sides thet gives places or pelf;
But consistency still wuz a part of his plan,—
    He's ben true to *one* party,—an' thet is himself;—
        So John P.
        Robinson he
    Sez he shall vote fer Gineral C.

Gineral C. he goes in fer the war;
    He don't vally principle more 'n an old cud;
Wut did God make us raytional creeturs fer,
    But glory an' gunpowder, plunder an' blood?
        So John P.
        Robinson he
    Sez he shall vote fer Gineral C.

We were gittin' on nicely up here to our village,
    With good old idees o' wut's right an' wut aint,
We kind o' thought Christ went agin war an' pillage,
    An' thet eppyletts worn't the best mark of a saint;
        But John P.
        Robinson he
    Sez this kind o' thing's an exploded idee.

5

10

15

20

25

30

35

[27] John P. Robinson (1799–1864) of Lowell, Massachusetts, a prominent Whig politician of the Bay State, who in this 1847 contest came out in support of the Democratic candidate.
[28] Brigadier General Caleb Cushing of Newburyport, leader of the Massachusetts Regiment of Volunteers, who ran on the Democratic ticket against Briggs in 1847 and was defeated by 14,000 votes.

The side of our country must ollers be took,
  An' Presidunt Polk, you know, *he* is our country.
An' the angel thet writes all our sins in a book
  Puts the *debit* to him, an' to us the *per contry;*
          An' John P.   40
          Robinson he
      Sez this is his view o' the thing to a T.

Parson Wilbur he calls all these argimunts lies;
  Sez they're nothin' on airth but jest *fee, faw, fum;*
An' thet all this big talk of our destinies   45
  Is half on it ign'ance, an' t' other half rum;
          But John P.
          Robinson he
      Sez it aint no sech thing; an', of course, so must we.

Parson Wilbur sez *he* never heerd in his life   50
  Thet th' Apostles rigged out in their swaller-tail coats,
An' marched round in front of a drum an' a fife,
  To git some on 'em office, an' some on 'em votes;
          But John P.
          Robinson he   55
      Sez they didn't know everythin' down in Judee.

Wal, it's a mercy we've gut folks to tell us
  The rights an' the wrongs o' these matters, I vow,—
God sends country lawyers, an' other wise fellers,
  To start the world's team wen it gits in a slough;   60
          Fer John P.
          Robinson he
      Sez the world'll go right, if he hollers out Gee!

[The attentive reader will doubtless have perceived in the
foregoing poem an allusion to that pernicious sentiment,—"Our
country, right or wrong." It is an abuse of language to call a
certain portion of land, much more, certain personages, elevated
for the time being to high station, our country. I would not
sever nor loosen a single one of those ties by which we are united
to the spot of our birth, nor minish by a tittle the respect due to
the Magistrate. I love our own Bay State too well to do the one,
and as for the other, I have myself for nigh forty years exercised,

however unworthily, the function of Justice of the Peace, having been called thereto by the unsolicited kindness of that most excellent man and upright patriot, Caleb Strong. *Patriae fumus igne alieno luculentior* [29] is best qualified with this,—*Ubi libertas, ibi patria.*[30] We are inhabitants of two worlds, and owe a double, but not a divided, allegiance. In virtue of our clay, this little ball of earth exacts a certain loyalty of us, while, in our capacity as spirits, we are admitted citizens of an invisible and holier fatherland. There is a patriotism of the soul whose claim absolves us from our other and terrene fealty. Our true country is that ideal realm which we represent to ourselves under the names of religion, duty, and the like. Our terrestrial organizations are but far-off approaches to so fair a model, and all they are verily traitors who resist not any attempt to divert them from this their original intendment. When, therefore, one would have us to fling up our caps and shout with the multitude,— *"Our country, however bounded!"* [31] he demands of us that we sacrifice the larger to the less, the higher to the lower, and that we yield to the imaginary claims of a few acres of soil our duty and privilege as liegemen of Truth. Our true country is bounded on the north and the south, on the east and the west, by Justice, and when she oversteps that invisible boundary-line by so much as a hair's-breadth, she ceases to be our mother, and chooses rather to be looked upon *quasi noverca.*[32] That is a hard choice when our earthly love of country calls upon us to tread one path and our duty points us to another. We must make as noble and becoming an election as did Penelope between Icarius and Ulysses. Veiling our faces, we must take silently the hand of Duty to follow her. . . . H. W.]

---

[29] The smoke of one's native land seems more bright than the fire of a foreign country.

[30] Where there is liberty, *there* is one's native land.

[31] A quotation from a speech by Congressman Robert C. Winthrop of Boston, a "Cotton" Whig, in Faneuil Hall, July 4, 1845, in which he deprecated all secession sentiment and more or less implied support of the Mexican War project.

[32] As a stepmother.

No. VI

THE PIOUS EDITOR'S CREED [33]

I du believe in Freedom's cause,
    Ez fur away ez Payris [34] is;
I love to see her stick her claws
    In them infarnal Phayrisees;
It's wal enough agin a king   5
    To dror resolves an' triggers,—
But libbaty's a kind o' thing
    Thet don't agree with niggers.

I du believe the people want
    A tax on teas an' coffees,   10
Thet nothin' ain't extravygunt,—
    Purvidin' I'm in office;
Fer I hev loved my country sence
    My eye-teeth filled their sockets,
An' Uncle Sam I reverence,   15
    Partic'larly his pockets.

I du believe in *any* plan
    O' levyin' the texes,
Ez long ez, like a lumberman,
    I git jest wut I axes;   20
I go free-trade thru thick an' thin,
    Because it kind o' rouses
The folks to vote,—an' keeps us in
    Our quiet custom-houses.

I du believe it's wise an' good   25
    To sen' out furrin missions,

---

[33] Written the latter part of April, 1848. (*Letters,* I, 128.) At the time Lowell looked upon this bit of satiric poetry with highest approval. "It is not so humorous as some of Hosea's productions, but it is by far the wittiest." (*Ibid.*) The verse was printed in the *National Anti-Slavery Standard* on May 4.

[34] An ironic reference to the oratorical exuberance of various Democratic congressmen over the triumph of freedom and popular government by the French revolution of 1848. The same orators, however, took great pains to avoid discussion of the practical applications of these principles at home.

Thet is, on sartin understood
　　An' orthydox conditions;—
I mean nine thousan' dolls. per ann.,
　　Nine thousan' more fer outfit,   30
An' me to recommend a man
　　The place 'ould jest about fit.

I du believe in special ways
　　O' prayin' an' convartin';
The bread comes back in many days,   35
　　An' buttered, tu, fer sartin;
I mean in preyin' till one busts
　　On wut the party chooses,
An' in convartin' public trusts
　　To very privit uses.   40

I du believe hard coin the stuff
　　Fer 'lectioneers to spout on;
The people's ollers soft enough
　　To make hard money out on;
Dear Uncle Sam pervides fer his,   45
　　An' gives a good-sized junk to all,—
I don't care *how* hard money is,
　　Ez long ez mine's paid punctooal.

I du believe with al my soul
　　In the gret Press's freedom,   50
To pint the people to the goal
　　An' in the traces lead 'em;
Palsied the arm thet forges yokes
　　At my fat contracts squintin',
An' withered be the nose thet pokes   55
　　Inter the gov'ment printin'!

I du believe thet I should give
　　Wut's his'n unto Caesar,
Fer it's by him I move an' live,
　　Frum him my bread an' cheese air;   60
I du believe thet all o' me
　　Doth bear his superscription,—

Will, conscience, honor, honesty,
   An' things o' thet description.

I du believe in prayer an' praise   65
   To him thet hez the grantin'
O' jobs,—in every thin' thet pays,
   But most of all in CANTIN';
This doth my cup with marcies fill,
   This lays all thought o' sin to rest,—   70
I *don't* believe in princerple,
   But oh, I *du* in interest.

I du believe in bein' this
   Or thet, ez it may happen
One way or 't other hendiest is   75
   To ketch the people nappin';
It aint by princerples nor men
   My preudunt course is steadied,—
I scent wich pays the best, an' then
   Go into it baldheaded.   80

I du believe thet holdin' slaves
   Comes nat'ral to a Presidunt,
Let 'lone the rowdedow it saves
   To hev a wal-broke precedunt;
Fer any office, small or gret,   85
   I couldn't ax with no face,
'uthout I'd ben, thru dry an' wet,
   Th' unrizzest kind o' doughface.

I du believe wutever trash
   'll keep the people in blindness,—   90
Thet we the Mexicuns can thrash
   Right inter brotherly kindness,
Thet bombshells, grape, an' powder 'n' ball
   Air good-will's strongest magnets,
Thet peace, to make it stick at all,   95
   Must be druv in with bagnets.

In short, I firmly du believe
   In Humbug generally,

Fer it's a thing thet I perceive
　　To hev a solid vally;　　　　　　　　　100
This heth my faithful shepherd ben,
　　In pasturs sweet heth led me,
An' this'll keep the people green
　　To feed ez they hev fed me.

THE BIGLOW PAPERS

Second Series [1]

Introduction

. . . When, more than twenty years ago, I wrote the first of
the series I had no definite plan and no intention of ever writing
another. Thinking the Mexican war, as I think it still, a national crime committed in behoof of Slavery, our common sin,
and wishing to put the feeling of those who thought as I did in
a way that would tell, I imagined to myself such an upcountry
man as I had often seen at antislavery gatherings, capable of
district-school English, but always instinctively falling back into
the natural stronghold of his homely dialect when heated to the
point of self-forgetfulness. When I began to carry out my con-

---

[1] Friendly pressure as early as 1859 put into Lowell's mind the idea of
resuscitating the Biglow vein in order to treat of the momentous issues
created by the dissension between the North and the South. Lowell, however, was reluctant to undertake such a poetic resurrection, since he rightly
felt that grave artistic dangers were involved in revivals of this sort. Yet
by the end of 1860 he was thinking seriously about the composition of
fresh Biglow papers. On December 31 he wrote: "As for new 'Biglow
Papers,' God knows how I should like to write them, if they would only
make me as they did before. But I am so occupied and bothered that I
have no time to *brood,* which with me is as needful a preliminary to hatching anything as with a clucking hen. However, I am going to try my
hand, and see what will come of it." (*Letters,* I, 308.) Not until the next
December did the brooding of the poet produce any result. Then the first
paper of the second series was written and made its appearance in the
Atlantic Monthly of January, 1862. Lowell followed with five more papers
in successive monthly numbers of the *Atlantic.* This rapid endeavor more
or less exhausted the satirical vein, though sporadic Biglow efforts were
published in the *Atlantic* of February, 1863; April, 1865; May, 1866. And,
finally, two more papers, now numbered VIII and IX, were added to the
collected volume of the *Biglow Papers, Second Series,* which Lowell brought
out in the fall of 1866.

ception and to write in my assumed character, I found myself in a strait between two perils. On the one hand, I was in danger of being carried beyond the limit of my own opinions, or at least of that temper with which every man should speak his mind in print, and on the other I feared the risk of seeming to vulgarize a deep and sacred conviction. I needed on occasion to rise above the level of mere *patois,* and for this purpose conceived the Reverend Mr. Wilbur who should express the more cautious element of the New England character and its pedantry, as Mr. Biglow should serve for its homely common-sense vivified and heated by conscience. The parson was to be the complement rather than the antithesis of his parishioner, and I felt or fancied a certain humorous element in the real identity of the two under a seeming incongruity. Mr. Wilbur's fondness for scraps of Latin, though drawn from the life, I adopted deliberately to heighten the contrast. Finding soon after that I needed some one as a mouthpiece of the mere drollery, for I conceive that true humor is never divorced from moral conviction, I invented Mr. Sawin for the clown of my little puppet-show. I meant to embody in him that half-conscious *un*morality which I had noticed as the recoil in gross natures from a puritanism that still strove to keep in its creed the intense savor which had long gone out of its faith and life. In the three I thought I should find room enough to express, as it was my plan to do, the popular feeling and opinion of the time. For the names of two of my characters, since I have received some remonstrances from very worthy persons who happened to bear them, I would say that they were purely fortuitous, probably mere unconscious memories of signboards or directories. Mr. Sawin's sprang from the accident of a rhyme at the end of his first epistle, and I purposely christened him by the impossible surname of Birdofredum not more to stigmatize him as the incarnation of "Manifest Destiny," in other words, of national recklessness as to right and wrong, than to avoid the chance of wounding any private sensitiveness.

The success of my experiment soon began not only to astonish me, but to make me feel the responsibility of knowing that I held in my hand a weapon instead of the mere fencing-stick I had supposed. Very far from being a popular author under my own name, so far, indeed, as to be almost unread, I found the verses of my pseudonym copied everywhere; I saw them pinned

up in workshops; I heard them quoted and their authorship debated; I once even, when rumor had at length caught up my
name in one of its eddies, had the satisfaction of overhearing it
demonstrated, in the pauses of a concert, that *I* was utterly in-
competent to have written anything of the kind. I had read too
much not to know the utter worthlessness of contemporary reputation, especially as regards satire, but I knew also that by giving
a certain amount of influence it also had its worth, if that influence were used on the right side. I had learned, too, that
the first requisite of good writing is to have an earnest and definite purpose, whether æsthetic or moral, and that even good
writing, to please long, must have more than an average amount
either of imagination or common-sense. The first of these falls
to the lot of scarcely one in several generations; the last is within
the reach of many in every one that passes; and of this an author
may fairly hope to become in part the mouthpiece. If I put on
the cap and bells and made myself one of the court-fools of King
Demos, it was less to make his majesty laugh than to win a passage to his royal ears for certain serious things which I had
deeply at heart. I say this because there is no imputation that
could be more galling to any man's self-respect than that of being
a mere jester. I endeavored, by generalizing my satire, to give
it what value I could beyond the passing moment and the immediate application. How far I have succeeded I cannot tell,
but I have had better luck than I ever looked for in seeing my
verses survive to pass beyond their nonage.

In choosing the Yankee dialect, I did not act without forethought. It had long seemed to me that the great vice of American writing and speaking was a studied want of simplicity, that
we were in danger of coming to look on our mother-tongue as
a dead language, to be sought in the grammar and dictionary
rather than in the heart, and that our only chance of escape was
by seeking it at its living sources among those who were, as
Scottowe says of Major-General Gibbons,[2] "divinely illiterate."
President Lincoln, the only really great public man whom these

---

[2] See *Massachusetts; or, The first planters of New-England* . . . (Boston, 1696) by Joshua Scottow (1615–98), one of the earliest American
historians.—Edward Gibbons (d. 1654), Boston merchant, major-general
of the Massachusetts militia 1649–51, and one of the commissioners to
negotiate the confederation of 1643 between the colonies of Massachusetts,
Plymouth, Connecticut, and New Haven.

latter days have seen, was great also in this, that he was master—witness his speech at Gettysburg—of a truly masculine English, classic because it was of no special period, and level at once to the highest and lowest of his countrymen. But whoever should read the debates in Congress might fancy himself present at a meeting of the city council of some city of southern Gaul in the decline of the Empire, where barbarians with a Latin varnish emulated each other in being more than Ciceronian. Whether it be want of culture, for the highest outcome of that is simplicity, or for whatever reason, it is certain that very few American writers or speakers wield their native language with the directness, precision, and force that are common as the day in the mother country. We use it like Scotsmen, not as if it belonged to us, but as if we wished to prove that we belong to it, by showing our intimacy with its written rather than with its spoken dialect. And yet all the while our popular idiom is racy with life and vigor and originality, bucksome (as Milton used the word) to our new occasions, and proves itself no mere graft by sending up new suckers from the old root in spite of us. It is only from its roots in the living generations of men that a language can be reinforced with fresh vigor for its needs; what may be called a literate dialect grows ever more and more pedantic and foreign, till it becomes at last as unfitting a vehicle for living thought as monkish Latin. That we should all be made to talk like books is the danger with which we are threatened by the Universal Schoolmaster, who does his best to enslave the minds and memories of his victims to what he esteems the best models of English composition, that is to say, to the writers whose style is faultily correct and has no blood-warmth in it. No language after it has faded into *diction,* none that cannot suck up the feeding juices secreted for it in the rich mother-earth of common folk, can bring forth a sound and lusty book. True vigor and heartiness of phrase do not pass from page to page, but from man to man, where the brain is kindled and the lips suppled by downright living interests and by passion in its very throe. Language is the soil of thought, and our own especially is a rich leaf-mould, the slow deposit of ages, the shed foliage of feeling, fancy, and imagination, which has suffered an earth-change, that the vocal forest, as Howell [3] called it, may clothe itself anew

---

[3] James Howell (*c.* 1595–1666), historiographer-royal under Charles II, in 1640 published a poem entitled *Dodona's Grove, or the Vocal Forest.*

with living green.   There is death in the dictionary; and, where language is too strictly limited by convention, the ground for expression to grow in is limited also; and we get a *potted* literature, Chinese dwarfs instead of healthy trees. . . .

THE COURTIN' [4]

God makes sech nights, all white an' still
    Fur 'z you can look or listen,
Moonshine an' snow on field an' hill,
    All silence an' all glisten.

Zekle crep' up quite unbeknown   5
    An' peeked in thru' the winder,
An' there sot Huldy all alone,
    'ith no one nigh to hender.

A fireplace filled the room's one side
    With half a cord o' wood in—   10
There warn't no stoves (tell comfort died)
    To bake ye to a puddin'.

The wa'nut logs shot sparkles out
    Towards the pootiest, bless her,
An' leetle flames danced all about   15
    The chiny on the dresser.

Agin the chimbley crook-necks hung,
    An' in amongst 'em rusted
The ole queen's-arm thet gran'ther Young
    Fetched back f'om Concord busted.   20

---

[4] This brief piece of Yankee pastoral had a most fortuitous beginning. When the introduction to the *Biglow Papers, First Series,* was going through the press, it was discovered that a blank page must be filled.   Therefore Lowell dashed off another "notice to the press" which chiefly contained a brief extract from a supposed ballad by Mr. Biglow.   In a later issue of the *First Series* he patched on a conclusion in answer to numerous requests. Subsequent demand from the reading public induced him eventually to add more stanzas and to sketch in a connected story.   The final and complete version Lowell printed for the first time at the end of the introduction to the collected volume of *Biglow Papers, Second Series.*

The very room, coz she was in,
    Seemed warm f'om floor to ceilin',
An' she looked full ez rosy agin
    Ez the apples she was peelin'.

'Twas kin' o' kingdom-come to look   25
    On sech a blessed cretur,
A dogrose blushin' to a brook
    Ain't modester nor sweeter.

He was six foot o' man, A 1,
    Clean grit an' human natur',   30
None couldn't quicker pitch a ton
    Nor dror a furrer straighter.

He'd sparked it with full twenty gals,
    Hed squired 'em, danced 'em, druv 'em,
Fust this one, an' then thet, by spells—   35
    All is, he couldn't love 'em.

But long o' her his veins 'ould run
    All crinkly like curled maple,
The side she breshed felt full o' sun
    Ez a south slope in Ap'il.   40

She thought no v'ice hed sech a swing
    Ez hisn in the choir;
My! when he made Ole Hunderd ring,
    She *knowed* the Lord was nigher.

An' she'd blush scarlit, right in prayer,   45
    When her new meetin'-bunnet
Felt somehow thru' its crown a pair
    O' blue eyes sot upun it.

Thet night, I tell ye, she looked *some!*
    She seemed to've gut a new soul,   50
For she felt sartin-sure he'd come,
    Down to her very shoe-sole.

She heered a foot, an' knowed it tu,
    A-raspin' on the scraper,—

All ways to once her feelins flew   55
   Like sparks in burnt-up paper.

He kin' o' l'itered on the mat,
   Some doubtfle o' the sekle,
His heart kep' goin' pity-pat,
   But hern went pity Zekle.   60

An' yit she gin her cheer a jerk
   Ez though she wished him furder,
An' on her apples kep' to work,
   Parin' away like murder.

"You want to see my Pa, I s'pose?"   65
   "Wal . . . no . . . I come dasignin' "—
"To see my Ma?   She's sprinklin' clo'es
   Agin to-morrer's i'nin'."

To say why gals acts so or so,
   Or don't, 'ould be presumin';   70
Mebby to mean *yes* an' say *no*
   Comes nateral to women.

He stood a spell on one foot fust,
   Then stood a spell on t' other,
An' on which one he felt the wust   75
   He couldn't ha' told ye nuther.

Says he, "I'd better call agin";
   Says she, "Think likely, Mister":
Thet last word pricked him like a pin,
   An' . . . Wal, he up an' kist her.   80

When Ma bimbeby upon 'em slips,
   Huldy sot pale ez ashes,
All kin' o' smily roun' the lips
   An' teary roun' the lashes.

For she was jes' the quiet kind   85
   Whose naturs never vary,
Like streams that keep a summer mind
   Snowhid in Jenooary.

The blood clost roun' her heart felt glued
    Too tight for all expressin',   90
Tell mother see how metters stood,
    An' gin 'em both her blessin'.

Then her red come back like the tide
    Down to the Bay o' Fundy,[5]
An' all I know is they was cried   95
    In meetin' come nex' Sunday.

No. VI

SUNTHIN' IN THE PASTORAL LINE [6]

TO THE EDITORS OF THE ATLANTIC MONTHLY

JAALAM, 17th May, 1862.

GENTLEMEN,—At the special request of Mr. Biglow, I intended to inclose, together with his own contribution, (into which, at my suggestion, he has thrown a little more of pastoral sentiment than usual,) some passages from my sermon on the day of the National Fast, from the text, "Remember them that are in bonds, as bound with them" Heb. xiii. 3. But I have not leisure sufficient at present for the copying of them, even were I altogether satisfied with the production as it stands. I should prefer, I confess, to contribute the entire discourse to the pages of your respectable miscellany, if it should be found acceptable upon perusal, especially as I find the difficulty in selection of greater magnitude than I had anticipated. What passes without challenge in the fervour of oral delivery, cannot always stand the colder criticism of the closet. I am not so great an enemy of Eloquence as my friend Mr. Biglow would appear to be from some passages in his contribution for the current month. I would not, indeed, hastily suspect him of covertly glancing at myself in his somewhat caustick animadversions, albeit some of the phrases he girds at are not entire strangers to my lips. I am a more hearty admirer of the Puritans than seems now to be the fashion, and believe, that, if they Hebraized a little too much in their speech, they showed remarkable practical sagacity as states-

---

[5] An inlet of the Atlantic ocean separating Nova Scotia from New Brunswick. The tides there sometimes rise over 70 feet.

[6] Published first in the *Atlantic Monthly*, June, 1862.

men and founders.   But such phenomena as Puritanism are the
results rather of great religious than of merely social convulsions,
and do not long survive them.   So soon as an earnest conviction
has cooled into a phrase, its work is over, and the best that can be
done with it is to bury it.   *Ite, missa est.*[7]   I am inclined to agree
with Mr. Biglow that we cannot settle the great political questions which are now presenting themselves to the nation by the
opinions of Jeremiah or Ezekiel as to the wants and duties of
the Jews in their time, nor do I believe that an entire community
with their feelings and views would be practicable or even agreeable at the present day.   At the same time I could wish that
their habit of subordinating the actual to the moral, the flesh to
the spirit, and this world to the other, were more common.
They had found out, at least, the great military secret that soul
weighs more than body.—But I am suddenly called to a sick-
bed in the household of a valued parishioner.

With esteem and respect,
Your obedient servant,
HOMER WILBUR.

Once git a smell o' musk into a draw,
An' it clings hold like precerdents in law:
Your gra'ma'am put it there,—when, goodness knows,—
To jes' this-worldify her Sunday-clo'es;
But the old chist wun't sarve her gran'son's wife,   5
(For, 'thout new funnitoor, wut good in life?)
An' so ole clawfoot, from the precinks dread
O' the spare chamber, slinks into the shed,
Where, dim with dust, it fust or last subsides
To holdin' seeds an' fifty things besides;   10
But better days stick fast in heart an' husk,
An' all you keep in 't gits a scent o' musk.

Jes' so with poets: wut they've airly read
Gits kind o' worked into their heart an' head,
So 's 't they can't seem to write but jest on sheers   15
With furrin countries or played-out ideers,
Nor hev a feelin', ef it doesn't smack
O' wut some critter chose to feel 'way back:
This makes 'em talk o' daisies, larks, an' things,

---

[7] Go, it is finished.

Ez though we'd nothin' here that blows an' sings,—   20
(Why, I'd give more for one live bobolink
Than a square mile o' larks in printer's ink,)—
This makes 'em think our fust o' May is May,
Which 't ain't, for all the almanicks can say.

O little city-gals, don't never go it   25
Blind on the word o' noospaper or poet!
They're apt to puff, an' May-day seldom looks
Up in the country ez 't doos in books;
They're no more like than hornets'-nests an' hives,
Or printed sarmons be to holy lives.   30
I, with my trouses perched on cowhide boots,
Tuggin' my foundered feet out by the roots,
Hev seen ye come to fling on April's hearse
Your muslin nosegays from the milliner's,
Puzzlin' to find dry ground your queen to choose,   35
An' dance your throats sore in morocker shoes:
I've seen ye an' felt proud, thet, come wut would,
Our Pilgrim stock wuz pethed with hardihood.
Pleasure doos make us Yankees kind o' winch,
Ez though 't wuz sunthin' paid for by the inch;   40
But yit we du contrive to worry thru,
Ef Dooty tells us thet the thing's to du,
An' kerry a hollerday, ef we set out,
Ez stiddily ez though 't wuz a redoubt.

I, country-born an' bred, know where to find   45
Some blooms thet make the season suit the mind,
An' seems to metch the doubtin' bluebird's notes,—
Half-vent'rin' liverworts in furry coats,
Bloodroots, whose rolled-up leaves ef you oncurl,
Each on 'em's cradle to a baby-pearl,—   50
But these are jes' Spring's pickets; sure ez sin,
The rebble frosts 'll try to drive 'em in;
For half our May's so awfully like May n't,
't would rile a Shaker [8] or an evrige saint;
Though I own up I like our back'ard springs   55
Thet kind o' haggle with their greens an' things,

---

[8] A very strict, religious sect, who hold that Christ's second coming has already occurred.

An' when you 'most give up, 'uthout more words
Toss the fields full o' blossoms, leaves, an' birds;
Thet's Northun natur', slow an' apt to doubt,
But when it *doos* git stirred, ther' 's no gin-out!   60

Fust come the blackbirds clatt'rin' in tall trees,
An' settlin' things in windy Congresses,—
Queer politicians, though, for I'll be skinned
Ef all on 'em don't head aginst the wind.
'fore long the trees begin to show belief,—   65
The maple crimsons to a coral-reef,
Then saffern swarms swing off from all the willers
So plump they look like yaller caterpillars,
Then gray hossches'nuts leetle hands unfold
Softer 'n a baby's be at three days old: 70
Thet's robin-redbreast's almanick; he knows
Thet arter this ther' 's only blossom-snows;
So, choosin' out a handy crotch an' spouse,
He goes to plast'rin' his adobe house.

Then seems to come a hitch,—things lag behind,   75
Till some fine mornin' Spring makes up her mind,
An' sez, when snow-swelled rivers cresh their dams
Heaped-up with ice thet dovetails in an' jams,
A leak comes spirtin' thru some pin-hole cleft,
Grows stronger, fercer, tears out right an' left,   80
Then all the waters bow themselves an' come,
Suddin, in one gret slope o' shedderin' foam,
Jes' so our Spring gits everythin' in tune
An' gives one leap from Aperl into June:
Then all comes crowdin' in; afore you think,   85
Young oak-leaves mist the side-hill woods with pink;
The catbird in the laylock-bush is loud;
The orchards turn to heaps o' rosy cloud;
Red-cedars blossom tu, though few folks know it,
An' look all dipt in sunshine like a poet;   90
The lime-trees pile their solid stacks o' shade
An' drows'ly simmer with the bees' sweet trade;
In ellum-shrouds the flashin' hangbird clings
An' for the summer vy'ge his hammock slings;
All down the loose-walled lanes in archin' bowers   95

The barb'ry droops its strings o' golden flowers,
Whose shrinkin' hearts the school-gals love to try
With pins,—they'll worry yourn so, boys, bimeby!
But I don't love your cat'logue style,—do you?—
Ez ef to sell off Natur' by vendoo; [9]   100
One word with blood in 't 's twice ez good ez two:
'nuff sed, June's bridesman, poet o' the year,
Gladness on wings, the bobolink, is here;
Half-hid in tip-top apple-blooms he swings,
Or climbs aginst the breeze with quiverin' wings,   105
Or, givin' way to 't in a mock despair,
Runs down, a brook o' laughter, thru the air.

I ollus feel the sap start in my veins
In Spring, with curus heats an' prickly pains,
Thet drive me, when I git a chance, to walk   110
Off by myself to hev a privit talk
With a queer critter thet can't seem to 'gree
Along o' me like most folks,—Mister Me.
Ther' 's times when I'm unsoshle ez a stone,
An' sort o' suffercate to be alone,—   115
I'm crowded jes' to think thet folks are nigh,
An' can't bear nothin' closer than the sky;
Now the wind's full ez shifty in the mind
Ez wut it is ou'-doors, ef I ain't blind,
An' sometimes, in the fairest sou'west weather,   120
My innard vane pints east for weeks together,
My natur' gits all goose-flesh, an' my sins
Come drizzlin' on my conscience sharp ez pins:
Wal, et sech times I jes' slip out o' sight
An' take it out in a fair stan'-up fight   125
With the one cuss I can't lay on the shelf,
The crook'dest stick in all the heap,—Myself.

'T wuz so las' Sabbath arter meetin'-time:
Findin' my feelin's wouldn't noways rhyme
With nobody's, but off the hendle flew   130
An' took things from an east-wind pint o' view,
I started off to lose me in the hills
Where the pines be, up back o' 'Siah's Mills:

---

[9] I.e., by vendue, or auction.

Pines, ef you're blue, are the best friends I know,
They mope an' sigh an' sheer your feelin's so,— 135
They hesh the ground beneath so, tu, I swan,
You half-forgit you've gut a body on.
Ther' 's a small school'us' there where four roads meet,
The door-steps hollered out by little feet,
An' side-post carved with names whose owners grew 140
To gret men, some on 'em, an' deacons, tu;
't ain't used no longer, coz the town hez gut
A high-school, where they teach the Lord knows wut:
Three-story larnin' 's pop'lar now; I guess
We thriv' ez wal on jes' two stories less, 145
For it strikes me ther' 's sech a thing ez sinnin'
By overloadin' children's underpinnin':
Wal, here it wuz I larned my A B C,
An' it's a kind o' favorite spot with me.

We're curus critters: Now ain't jes' the minute 150
Thet ever fits us easy while we're in it;
Long ez 't wuz futur', 't would be perfect bliss,—
Soon ez it's past, *thet* time's wuth ten o' this;
An' yit there ain't a man thet need be told
Thet Now's the only bird lays eggs o' gold. 155
A knee-high lad, I used to plot an' plan
An' think 't wuz life's cap-sheaf to be a man;
Now, gittin' gray, there's nothin' I enjoy
Like dreamin' back along into a boy:
So the ole school'us' is a place I choose 160
Afore all others, ef I want to muse;
I set down where I used to set, an' git
My boyhood back, an' better things with it,—
Faith, Hope, an' sunthin', ef it is n't Cherry,
It's want o' guile, an' thet's ez gret a rerrity,— 165
While Fancy's cushin', free to Prince and Clown,
Makes the hard bench ez soft ez milk-weed-down.

Now, 'fore I knowed, thet Sabbath arternoon
When I sot out to tramp myself in tune,
I found me in the school'us' on my seat, 170
Drummin' the march to No-wheres with my feet.
Thinkin' o' nothin', I've heerd ole folks say,

Is a hard kind o' dooty in its way:
It's thinkin' everythin' you ever knew,
Or ever hearn, to make your feelin's blue.   175
I sot there tryin' thet on for a spell:
I thought o' the Rebellion, then o' Hell,
Which some folks tell ye now is jest a metterfor
(A the'ry, p'raps, it wun't *feel* none the better for);
I thought o' Reconstruction, wut we'd win   180
Patchin' our patent self-blow-up agin:
I thought ef this 'ere milkin' o' the wits,
So much a month, warn't givin' Natur' fits,—
Ef folks warn't druv, findin' their own milk fail,
To work the cow thet hez an iron tail,   185
An' ef idees 'thout ripenin' in the pan
Would send up cream to humor ary man:
From this to thet I let my worryin' creep,
Till finally I must ha' fell asleep.

Our lives in sleep are some like streams thet glide   190
'twixt flesh an' sperrit boundin' on each side,
Where both shores' shadders kind o' mix an' mingle
In sunthin' thet ain't jes' like either single;
An' when you cast off moorin's from To-day,
An' down towards To-morrer drift away,   195
The imiges thet tengle on the stream
Make a new upside-down'ard world o' dream:
Sometimes they seem like sunrise-streaks an' warnin's
O' wut'll be in Heaven on Sabbath-mornin's,
An', mixed right in ez ef jest out o' spite,   200
Sunthin' thet says your supper ain't gone right.
I'm gret on dreams, an' often when I wake,
I've lived so much it makes my mem'ry ache,
An' can't skurce take a cat-nap in my cheer
'thout hevin' 'em, some good, some bad, all queer.   205

Now I wuz settin' where I'd ben, it seemed,
An' ain't sure yit whether I r'ally dreamed,
Nor, ef I did, how long I might ha' slep',
When I hearn some un stompin' up the step,
An' lookin' round, ef two an' two make four,   210
I see a Pilgrim Father in the door.

He wore a steeple-hat, tall boots, an' spurs
With rowels to 'em big ez ches'nut-burrs,
An' his gret sword behind him sloped away
Long 'z a man's speech thet dunno wut to say.—   215
"Ef your name's Biglow, an' your given-name
Hosee," sez he, "it's arter you I came;
I'm your gret-gran'ther multiplied by three."—
"My *wut?*" sez I.—"Your gret-gret-gret," sez he:
"You would n't ha' never ben here but for me.   220
Two hundred an' three year ago this May
The ship I come in sailed up Boston Bay; [10]
I'd been a cunnle in our Civil War,— [11]
But wut on airth hev *you* gut up one for?
Coz we du things in England, 't ain't for you   225
To git a notion you can du 'em tu:
I'm told you write in public prints: ef true,
It's nateral you should know a thing or two."—
"Thet air's an argymunt I can't endorse,—
't would prove, coz you wear spurs, you kep' a horse: 230
For brains," sez I, "wutever you may think,
Ain't boun' to cash the drafs o' pen-an'-ink,—
Though mos' folks write ez ef they hoped jes' quickenin'
The churn would argoo skim-milk into thickenin';
But skim-milk ain't a thing to change its view   235
O' wut it's meant for more'n a smoky flue.
But du pray tell me, 'fore we furder go,
How in all Natur' did you come to know
'bout our affairs," sez I, "in Kingdom-Come?"—
"Wal, I worked round at sperrit-rappin' some,   240
An' danced the tables till their legs wuz gone,
In hopes o' larnin' wut wuz goin' on,"
Sez he, "but mejums lie so like all-split
Thet I concluded it wuz best to quit.
But, come now, ef you wun't confess to knowin',   245
You've some conjectures how the thing's a-goin'."—
"Gran'ther," sez I, "a vane warn't never known
Nor asked to hev a jedgment of its own;
An' yit, ef 't ain't gut rusty in the jints,

---

[10] I.e., 1659.
[11] I.e., the English Civil War, 1642–49, between the Royalists and the Parliamentarians.

It's safe to trust its say on certin pints: 250
It knows the wind's opinions to a T,
An' the wind settles wut the weather'll be."
"I never thought a scion of our stock
Could grow the wood to make a weather-cock;
When I wuz younger'n you, skurce more'n a shaver, 255
No airthly wind," sez he, "could make me waver!"
(Ez he said this, he clinched his jaw an' forehead,
Hitchin' his belt to bring his sword-hilt forrard.)—
"Jes so it wuz with me," sez I, "I swow,
When *I* wuz younger'n wut you see me now,— 260
Nothin' from Adam's fall to Huldy's bonnet,
Thet I warn't full-cocked with my jedgment on it;
But now I'm gittin' on in life, I find
It's a sight harder to make up my mind,—
Nor I don't often try tu, when events 265
Will du it for me free of all expense.
The moral question's ollus plain enough,—
It's jes' the human-natur' side thet's tough;
Wut's best to think may n't puzzle me nor you,—
The pinch comes in decidin' wut to *du;* 270
Ef you *read* History, all runs smooth ez grease,
Coz there the men ain't nothin' more'n idees,—
But come to *make* it, ez we must to-day,
Th' idees hev arms an' legs an' stop the way:
It's easy fixin' things in facts an' figgers,— 275
They can't resist, nor warn't brought up with niggers;
But come to try your the'ry on,—why, then
Your facts an' figgers change to ign'ant men
Actin' ez ugly—"—"Smite 'em hip an' thigh!"
Sez gran'ther, "and let every man-child die! 280
Oh for three weeks o' Cromwle [12] an' the Lord!
Up, Isr'el, to your tents an' grind the sword!"—
"Thet kind o' thing worked wal in ole Judee,
But you forgit how long it's ben A.D.;
You think thet's ellerkence,—I call it shoddy, 285
A thing," sez I, "wun't cover soul nor body;
I like the plain all-wool o' common-sense,
Thet warms ye now, an' will a twelve-month hence.

---

[12] Oliver Cromwell (1599–1658), the great Puritan leader who overthrew the Stuart monarchy in the English Civil War.

You took to follerin' where the Prophets beckoned,
An', fust you knowed on, back come Charles the Second;[13] 290
Now wut I want's to hev all *we* gain stick,
An' not to start Millennium too quick;
We hain't to punish only, but to keep,
An' the cure's gut to go a cent'ry deep."
"Wall, milk-an'-water ain't the best o' glue," 295
Sez he, "an' so you'll find afore you're thru;
Ef reshness venters sunthin', shilly-shally
Loses ez often wut's ten times the vally.
Thet exe of ourn, when Charles's neck gut split,[14]
Opened a gap thet ain't bridged over yit: 300
Slav'ry's your Charles, the Lord hez gin the exe"—
"Our Charles," sez I, "hez gut eight million necks.
The hardest question ain't the black man's right,
The trouble is to 'mancipate the white;
One's chained in body an' can be sot free, 305
But t' other's chained in soul to an idee:
It's a long job, but we shall worry thru it;
Ef bagnets fail, the spellin'-book must du it."
"Hosee," sez he, "I think you're goin' to fail:
The rettlesnake ain't dangerous in the tail; 310
This 'ere rebellion's nothing but the rettle,—
You'll stomp on thet an' think you've won the bettle;
It's Slavery thet's the fangs an' thinkin' head,
An' ef you want selvation, cresh it dead,—
An' cresh it suddin, or you'll larn by waitin' 315
Thet Chance wun't stop to listen to debatin'!"—
"God's truth!" sez I,—"an' ef *I* held the club,
An' knowed jes' where to strike,—but there's the rub!"—
"Strike soon," sez he, "or you'll be deadly ailin',—
Folks thet's afeared to fail are sure o' failin'; 320
God hates your sneakin' creturs thet believe
He'll settle things they run away an' leave!"
He brought his foot down fercely, ez he spoke,
An' give me sech a startle thet I woke.

---

[13] He ascended the English throne in 1660 after the restoration of the Stuart monarchy.

[14] Charles I was beheaded in 1649 by the Cromwellians or Parliamentarians.

FITZ ADAM'S STORY [1]

THE NEXT whose fortune 't was a tale to tell
Was one whom men, before they thought, loved well,
And after thinking wondered why they did,
For half he seemed to let them, half forbid,
And wrapped him so in humors, sheath on sheath,   5
'T was hard to guess the mellow soul beneath;
But, once divined, you took him to your heart,
While he appeared to bear with you as part
Of life's impertinence, and once a year
Betrayed his true self by a smile or tear,   10
Or rather something sweetly-shy and loath,
Withdrawn ere fully shown, and mixed of both.
A cynic? Not precisely: one who thrust
Against a heart too prone to love and trust,
Who so despised false sentiment he knew   15
Scarce in himself to part the false and true,
And strove to hide, by roughening-o'er the skin,
Those cobweb nerves he could not dull within.

---

[1] This poem was originally conceived by Lowell as early as 1850. At the time he had in mind to make it one of a connected series of tales with the general heading, "The Nooning," a title suggested by his wife Maria. Concerning the dramatic framework of the larger poem he wrote to C. F. Briggs on January 23, 1850: "My plan is this. I am going to bring together a party of half a dozen old friends at Elmwood. They go down to the river and bathe, and then one proposes that they shall go up into a great willow-tree (which stands at the end of the causey near our house, and has seats in it) to take their nooning. There they agree that each shall tell a story or recite a poem of some sort." (*Letters,* I, 171.) During the next fifteen years or so Lowell worked sporadically at various parts of his ambitious narrative project. In the early fall of 1866 he had a sudden inspiration to work upon the embryonic tale which was to be *Fitz Adam's Story,* and to complete it speedily. On October 19 he wrote to Norton: "I have taken up one of the unfinished tales of *The Nooning,* and it grew to a poem of near seven hundred lines! It is mainly descriptive. First, a sketch of the narrator, then his 'prelude,' then his 'tale.' I describe an old inn and its landlord, bar-room, etc. It is very homely, but right from nature." (*Letters,* I, 372–73.) The poem shortly appeared in the January, 1867, issue of the *Atlantic Monthly.* Its publication in book form was delayed many years, no doubt because Lowell thought he might sometime finish *The Nooning.* Finally he printed *Fitz Adam's Story* as a separate piece in *Heartsease and Rue* (1888).

Gentle by birth, but of a stem decayed,
He shunned life's rivalries and hated trade;   20
On a small patrimony and larger pride,
He lived uneaseful on the Other Side
(So he called Europe), only coming West
To give his Old-World appetite new zest;
Yet still the New World spooked it in his veins,   25
A ghost he could not lay with all his pains;
For never Pilgrims' offshoot scapes control
Of those old instincts that have shaped his soul.
A radical in thought, he puffed away
With shrewd contempt the dust of usage gray,   30
Yet loathed democracy as one who saw,
In what he longed to love, some vulgar flaw,
And, shocked through all his delicate reserves,
Remained a Tory by his taste and nerves.
His fancy's thrall, he drew all ergoes [2] thence,   35
And thought himself the type of common sense;
Misliking women, not from cross or whim,
But that his mother shared too much in him,
And he half felt that what in them was grace
Made the unlucky weakness of his race.   40
What powers he had he hardly cared to know,
But sauntered through the world as through a show;
A critic fine in his haphazard way,
A sort of mild La Bruyère [3] on half-pay.
For comic weaknesses he had an eye   45
Keen as an acid for an alkali,
Yet you could feel, through his sardonic tone,
He loved them all, unless they were his own.
You might have called him, with his humorous twist,
A kind of human entomologist: 50
As these bring home, from every walk they take,
Their hat-crowns stuck with bugs of curious make,
So he filled all the lining of his head
With characters impaled and ticketed,
And had a cabinet behind his eyes   55

---

[2] Conclusions (lit., therefores).

[3] Jean de La Bruyère (1646–96), French satirist noted for his *Characters
of Theophrastus, translated from the Greek, with the Characters or Manners
of this Age* (1688).

For all they caught of mortal oddities.
He might have been a poet—many worse—
But that he had, or feigned, contempt of verse;
Called it tattooing language, and held rhymes
The young world's lullaby of ruder times.   60
Bitter in words, too indolent for gall,
He satirized himself the first of all,
In men and their affairs could find no law,
And was the ill logic that he thought he saw.

   Scratching a match to light his pipe anew,   65
With eyes half shut some musing whiffs he drew
And thus began: "I give you all my word,
I think this mock-Decameron [4] absurd;
Boccaccio's garden! how bring that to pass
In our bleak clime save under double glass?   70
The moral east-wind of New England life
Would snip its gay luxuriance like a knife;
Mile-deep the glaciers brooded here, they say,
Through æons numb; we feel their chill to-day.
These foreign plants are but half-hardy still,   75
Die on a south, and on a north wall chill.
Had we stayed Puritans! *They* had some heat,
(Though whence derived I have my own conceit,)
But you have long ago raked up their fires;
Where they had faith, you've ten sham-Gothic spires.   80
Why more exotics?   Try your native vines,
And in some thousand years you *may* have wines;
Your present grapes are harsh, all pulps and skins,
And want traditions of ancestral bins
That saved for evenings round the polished board   85
Old lava-fires, the sun-steeped hillside's hoard.
Without a Past, you lack that southern wall
O'er which the vines of Poesy should crawl;
Still they're your only hope; no midnight oil
Makes up for virtue wanting in the soil;   90
Manure them well and prune them; 't won't be France,

---

[4] The *Decameron,* or *Ten Days' Entertainment,* by the Italian novelist,
Giovanni Boccaccio (1313–75), is a world-known collection of one hundred stories, supposed to be told by a party of ladies and gentlemen stopping
at a country house near Florence while the plague is raging in that city.

Nor Spain, nor Italy, but there's your chance.
You have one story-teller worth a score
Of dead Boccaccios,—nay, add twenty more,—
A hawthorn asking spring's most dainty breath,   95
And him you're freezing pretty well to death.
However, since you say so, I will tease
My memory to a story by degrees,
Though you will cry, 'Enough!' I'm wellnigh sure,
Ere I have dreamed through half my overture.   100
Stories were good for men who had no books,
(Fortunate race!) and built their nests like rooks
In lonely towers, to which the Jongleur [5] brought
His pedler's-box of cheap and tawdry thought,
With here and there a fancy fit to see   105
Wrought in quaint grace in golden filigree,—
Some ring that with the Muse's finger yet
Is warm, like Aucassin and Nicolette; [6]
The morning newspaper has spoilt his trade,
(For better or for worse, I leave unsaid,)   110
And stories now, to suit a public nice,
Must be half epigram, half pleasant vice.

    "All tourists know Shebagog County: there
The summer idlers take their yearly stare,
Dress to see Nature in a well-bred way,   115
As 't were Italian opera, or play,
Encore the sunrise (if they're out of bed),
And pat the Mighty Mother on the head:
These have I seen,—all things are good to see,—
And wondered much at their complacency.   120
This world's great show, that took in getting-up
Millions of years, they finish ere they sup;
Sights that God gleams through with soul-tingling force
They glance approvingly as things of course,
Say, 'That's a grand rock,' 'This a pretty fall,'   125
Not thinking, 'Are we worthy?'   What if all
The scornful landscape should turn round and say,
'This is a fool, and that a popinjay'?

---

[5] A wandering minstrel of the Middle Ages.
[6] A pair of devoted lovers in a famous medieval French romance by the
same name.

I often wonder what the Mountain thinks
Of French boots creaking o'er his breathless brinks,   130
Or how the Sun would scare the chattering crowd,
If some fine day he chanced to think aloud.
I, who love Nature much as sinners can,
Love her where she most grandeur shows,—in man:
Here find I mountain, forest, cloud, and sun,   135
River and sea, and glows when day is done;
Nay, where she makes grotesques, and moulds in jest
The clown's cheap clay, I find unfading zest.
The natural instincts year by year retire,
As deer shrink northward from the settler's fire,   140
And he who loves the wild game-flavor more
Than city-feasts, where every man's a bore
To every other man, must seek it where
The steamer's throb and railway's iron blare
Have not yet startled with their punctual stir   145
The shy, wood-wandering brood of Character.

  "There is a village, once the county town,
Through which the weekly mail rolled dustily down,
Where the courts sat, it may be, twice a year,
And the one tavern reeked with rustic cheer;   150
Cheeshogquesumscot erst, now Jethro hight,
Red-man and pale-face bore it equal spite.
The railway ruined it, the natives say,
That passed unwisely fifteen miles away,
And made a drain to which, with steady ooze,   155
Filtered away law, stage-coach, trade, and news.
The railway saved it; so at least think those
Who love old ways, old houses, old repose.
Of course the Tavern stayed: its genial host
Thought not of flitting more than did the post   160
On which high-hung the fading signboard creaks,
Inscribed, 'The Eagle Inn, by Ezra Weeks.'

  "If in life's journey you should ever find
An inn medicinal for body and mind,
'T is sure to be some drowsy-looking house   165
Whose easy landlord has a bustling spouse:
He, if he like you, will not long forego

Some bottle deep in cobwebbed dust laid low,
That, since the War we used to call the 'Last,'
Has dozed and held its lang-syne memories fast: 170
From him exhales that Indian-summer air
Of hazy, lazy welcome everywhere,
While with her toil the napery is white,
The china dustless, the keen knife-blades bright,
Salt dry as sand, and bread that seems as though   175
'T were rather sea-foam baked than vulgar dough.

"In our swift country, houses trim and white
Are pitched like tents, the lodging of a night;
Each on its bank of baked turf mounted high
Perches impatient o'er the roadside dry,   180
While the wronged landscape coldly stands aloof,
Refusing friendship with the upstart roof.
Not so the Eagle; on a grass-green swell
That toward the south with sweet concessions fell
It dwelt retired, and half had grown to be   185
As aboriginal as rock or tree.
It nestled close to earth, and seemed to brood
O'er homely thoughts in a half-conscious mood,
As by the peat that rather fades than burns
The smoldering grandam nods and knits by turns,   190
Happy, although her newest news were old
Ere the first hostile drum at Concord rolled.
If paint it e'er had known, it knew no more
Than yellow lichens spattered thickly o'er
That soft lead-gray, less dark beneath the eaves   195
Which the slow brush of wind and weather leaves.
The ample roof sloped backward to the ground,
And vassal lean-tos gathered thickly round,
Patched on, as sire or son had felt the need,
Like chance growths sprouting from the old roof's seed,   200
Just as about a yellow-pine-tree spring
Its rough-barked darlings in a filial ring.
But the great chimney was the central thought
Whose gravitation through the cluster wrought;
For 't is not styles far-fetched from Greece or Rome,   205
But just the Fireside, that can make a home;
None of your spindling things of modern style,

Like pins stuck through to stay the card-built pile,
It rose broad-shouldered, kindly, debonair,
Its warm breath whitening in the October air,   210
While on its front a heart in outline showed
The place it filled in that serene abode.

  "When first I chanced the Eagle to explore,
Ezra sat listless by the open door;
One chair careened him at an angle meet,   215
Another nursed his hugely-slippered feet;
Upon a third reposed a shirt-sleeved arm,
And the whole man diffused tobacco's charm.
'Are you the landlord?' 'Wahl, I guess I be,'
Watching the smoke, he answered leisurely.   220
He was a stoutish man, and through the breast
Of his loose shirt there showed a brambly chest;
Streaked redly as a wind-foreboding morn,
His tanned cheeks curved to temples closely shorn;
Clean-shaved he was, save where a hedge of gray   225
Upon his brawny throat leaned every way
About an Adam's-apple, that beneath
Bulged like a boulder from a brambly heath.
The Western World's true child and nursling he,
Equipt with aptitudes enough for three: 230
No eye like his to value horse or cow,
Or gauge the contents of a stack or mow;
He could foretell the weather at a word,
He knew the haunt of every beast and bird,
Or where a two-pound trout was sure to lie,   235
Waiting the flutter of his home-made fly;
Nay, once in autumns five, he had the luck
To drop at fair-play range a ten-tined buck;
Of sportsmen true he favored every whim,
But never cockney [7] found a guide in him;   240
A natural man, with all his instincts fresh,
Not buzzing helpless in Reflection's mesh,
Firm on its feet stood his broad-shouldered mind,
As bluffly honest as a northwest wind;
Hard-headed and soft-hearted, you'd scarce meet   245
A kindlier mixture of the shrewd and sweet;

[7] See note on p. 208.

Generous by birth, and ill at saying 'No,'
Yet in a bargain he was all men's foe,
Would yield no inch of vantage in a trade,
And give away ere nightfall all he made.   250

" 'Can I have lodging here?' once more I said.
He blew a whiff, and, leaning back his head,
'You come a piece through Bailey's woods, I s'pose,
Acrost a bridge where a big swamp-oak grows?
It don't grow, neither; it's ben dead ten year,   255
Nor th' ain't a livin' creetur, fur nor near,
Can tell wut killed it; but I some misdoubt
'T was borers, there's sech heaps on 'em about.
You did n' chance to run ag'inst my son,
A long, slab-sided youngster with a gun?   260
He'd oughto ben back more 'n an hour ago,
An' brought some birds to dress for supper—sho!
There he comes now. 'Say, Obed, wut ye got?
(He'll hev some upland plover like as not.)
Wal, them's real nice uns, an'll eat A 1,   265
Ef I can stop their bein' over-done;
Nothin' riles *me* (I pledge my fastin' word)
Like cookin' out the natur' of a bird;
(Obed, you pick 'em out o' sight an' sound,
Your ma'am don't love no feathers cluttrin' round;)   270
Jes' scare 'em with the coals,—thet's *my* idee.'
Then, turning suddenly about on me,
'Wal, Square, I guess so. Calliate to stay?
I'll ask Mis' Weeks; 'bout *thet* it's hern to say.'

"Well, there I lingered all October through,   275
In that sweet atmosphere of hazy blue,
So leisurely, so soothing, so forgiving,
That sometimes makes New England fit for living.
I watched the landscape, erst [8] so granite glum,
Bloom like the south side of a ripening plum,   280
And each rock-maple on the hillside make
His ten days' sunset doubled in the lake;
The very stone walls draggling up the hills
Seemed touched, and wavered in their roundhead wills.

---

[8] Formerly.

Ah! there's a deal of sugar in the sun!   285
Tap me in Indian summer, I should run
A juice to make rock-candy of,—but then
We get such weather scarce one year in ten.

"There was a parlor in the house, a room
To make you shudder with its prudish gloom.   290
The furniture stood round with such an air,
There seemed an old maid's ghost in every chair,
Which looked as it had scuttled to its place
And pulled extempore [9] a Sunday face,
Too smugly proper for a world of sin,   295
Like boys on whom the minister comes in.
The table, fronting you with icy stare,
Strove to look witless that its legs were bare,
While the black sofa with its horse-hair pall
Gloomed like a bier for Comfort's funeral.   300
Each piece appeared to do its chilly best
To seem an utter stranger to the rest,
As if acquaintanceship were deadly sin,
Like Britons meeting in a foreign inn.
Two portraits graced the wall in grimmest truth,   305
Mister and Mistress W. in their youth,—
New England youth, that seems a sort of pill,
Half wish-I-dared, half Edwards on the Will,[10]
Bitter to swallow, and which leaves a trace
Of Calvinistic colic on the face.   310
Between them, o'er the mantel, hung in state
Solomon's temple, done in copperplate;
Invention pure, but meant, we may presume,
To give some Scripture sanction to the room.
Facing this last, two samplers you might see,   315
Each, with its urn and stiffly-weeping tree,
Devoted to some memory long ago
More faded than their lines of worsted woe;
Cut paper decked their frames against the flies,

---

[9] Without preparation.
[10] Jonathan Edwards (1703–58), eminent New England theologian of the
stern Calvinist faith, who published in 1754 *A Careful and Strict Enquiry
into the Modern Prevailing Notions of that Freedom of Will which is Supposed to be Essential to Moral Agency, Vertue and Vice, Reward and Punishment, Pride and Blame.*

Though none e'er dared an entrance who were wise,   320
And bushed asparagus in fading green
Added its shiver to the franklin [11] clean.

"When first arrived, I chilled a half-hour there,
Nor dared deflower with use a single chair;
I caught no cold, yet flying pains could find   325
For weeks in me,—a rheumatism of mind.
One thing alone imprisoned there had power
To hold me in the place that long half-hour:
A scutcheon this, a helm-surmounted shield,
Three griffins argent on a sable field;   330
A relic of the shipwrecked past was here,
And Ezra held some Old-World lumber dear.
Nay, do not smile; I love this kind of thing,
These cooped traditions with a broken wing,
This freehold nook in Fancy's pipe-blown ball,   335
This less than nothing that is more than all!
Have I not seen sweet natures kept alive
Amid the humdrum of your business hive,
Undowered spinsters shielded from all harms,
By airy incomes from a coat of arms?"   340

He paused a moment, and his features took
The flitting sweetness of that inward look
I hinted at before; but, scarcely seen,
It shrank for shelter 'neath his harder mien,
And, rapping his black pipe of ashes clear,   345
He went on with a self-derisive sneer:
"No doubt we make a part of God's design,
And break the forest-path for feet divine;
To furnish foothold for this grand prevision
Is good, and yet—to be the mere transition,   350
That, you will say, is also good, though I
Scarce like to feed the ogre By-and-by.
Raw edges rasp my nerves; my taste is wooed
By things that are, not going to be, good,
Though were I what I dreamed two lustres gone,   355
I'd stay to help the Consummation on,
Whether a new Rome than the old more fair,

---

[11] I.e., Franklin stove.

Or a deadflat of rascal-ruled despair;
But *my* skull somehow never closed the suture
That seems to knit yours firmly with the future,   360
So you'll excuse me if I'm sometimes fain
To tie the Past's warm nightcap o'er my brain;
I'm quite aware 't is not in fashion here,
But then your northeast winds are *so* severe!

  "But to my story: though 't is truly naught   365
But a few hints in Memory's sketchbook caught,
And which may claim a value on the score
Of calling back some scenery now no more.
Shall I confess? The tavern's only Lar [12]
Seemed (be not shocked!) its homely-featured bar.   370
Here dozed a fire of beechen logs, that bred
Strange fancies in its embers golden-red,
And nursed the loggerhead [13] whose hissing dip,
Timed by nice instinct, creamed the mug of flip [14]
That made from mouth to mouth its genial round,   375
Nor left one nature wholly winter-bound;
Hence dropt the tinkling coal all mellow-ripe
For Uncle Reuben's talk-extinguished pipe;
Hence rayed the heat, as from an indoor sun,
That wooed forth many a shoot of rustic fun.   380
Here Ezra ruled as king by right divine;
No other face had such a wholesome shine,
No laugh like his so full of honest cheer;
Above the rest it crowed like Chanticleer.

  "In this one room his dame you never saw,   385
Where reigned by custom old a Salic law; [15]
Here coatless lolled he on his throne of oak,
And every tongue paused midway if he spoke.
Due mirth he loved, yet was his sway severe;
No blear-eyed driveller got his stagger here;   390
'Measure was happiness; who wanted more,
Must buy his ruin at the Deacon's store;'

[12] Ancient Roman household god.
[13] A long-handled iron dipper.
[14] Ale nog.
[15] Old Frankish law which excluded females from the throne of France.

None but his lodgers after ten could stay,
Nor after nine on eves of Sabbath-day.
He had his favorites and his pensioners,   395
The same that gypsy Nature owns for hers:
Loose-ended souls, whose skills bring scanty gold,
And whom the poor-house catches when they're old;
Rude country-minstrels, men who doctor kine,
Or graft, and, out of scions ten, save nine;   400
Creatures of genius they, but never meant
To keep step with the civic regiment.
These Ezra welcomed, feeling in his mind
Perhaps some motions of the vagrant kind;
These paid no money, yet for them he drew   405
Special Jamaica from a tap they knew,
And, for their feelings, chalked behind the door
With solemn face a visionary score.
This thawed to life in Uncle Reuben's throat
A torpid shoal of jest and anecdote,   410
Like those queer fish that doze the droughts away,
And wait for moisture, wrapt in sun-baked clay;
This warmed the one-eyed fiddler to his task,
Perched in the corner on an empty cask,
By whose shrill art rapt suddenly, some boor   415
Rattled a double-shuffle on the floor;
'Hull's Victory' was, indeed, the favorite air,
Though 'Yankee Doodle' claimed its proper share.

  " 'T was there I caught from Uncle Reuben's lips,
In dribbling monologue 'twixt whiffs and sips,   420
The story I so long have tried to tell;
The humor coarse, the persons common,—well,
From Nature only do I love to paint,
Whether she send a satyr [16] or a saint;
To me Sincerity's the one thing good,   425
Soiled though she be and lost to maidenhood.
Quompegan is a town some ten miles south
From Jethro, at Nagumscot river-mouth,
A seaport town, and makes its title good
With lumber and dried fish and eastern wood.   430

---

[16] A lascivious or wanton man.

Here Deacon Bitters dwelt and kept the Store,
The richest man for many a mile of shore;
In little less than everything dealt he,
From meeting-houses to a chest of tea;
So dextrous therewithal a flint to skin,   435
He could make profit on a single pin;
In business strict, to bring the balance true
He had been known to bite a fig in two,
And change a board-nail for a shingle-nail.
All that he had he ready held for sale,   440
His house, his tomb, whate'er the law allows,
And he had gladly parted with his spouse.
His one ambition still to get and get,
He would arrest your very ghost for debt.
His store looked righteous, should the Parson come,   445
But in a dark back-room he peddled rum,
And eased Ma'am Conscience, if she e'er would scold,
By christening it with water ere he sold.
A small, dry man he was, who wore a queue,
And one white neckcloth all the week-days through,—   450
On Monday white, by Saturday as dun [17]
As that worn homeward by the prodigal son.
His frosted earlocks, striped with foxy brown,
Were braided up to hide a desert crown;
His coat was brownish, black perhaps of yore;   455
In summer-time a banyan [18] loose he wore;
His trousers short, through many a season true,
Made no pretence to hide his stockings blue;
A waistcoat buff his chief adornment was,
Its porcelain buttons rimmed with dusky brass.   460
A deacon he, you saw it in each limb,
And well he knew to deacon-off a hymn,
Or lead the choir through all its wandering woes
With voice that gathered unction in his nose,
Wherein a constant snuffle you might hear,   465
As if with him 't were winter all the year.
At pew-head sat he with decorous pains,
In sermon-time could foot his weekly gains,

---

[17] Dingy.

[18] A loose woolen shirt similar to that worn in India by the banians, a
caste of Hindu merchants who abstain from all meat.

Or, with closed eyes and heaven-abstracted air,
Could plan a new investment in long-prayer.   470
A pious man, and thrifty too, he made
The psalms and prophets partners in his trade,
And in his orthodoxy straitened more
As it enlarged the business at his store;
He honored Moses, but, when gain he planned,   475
Had his own notion of the Promised Land.

  "Soon as the winter made the sledding good,
From far around the farmers hauled him wood,
For all the trade had gathered 'neath his thumb.
He paid in groceries and New England rum,   480
Making two profits with a conscience clear,—
Cheap all he bought, and all he paid with dear.
With his own mete-wand measuring every load,
Each somehow had diminished on the road;
An honest cord in Jethro still would fail   485
By a good foot upon the Deacon's scale,
And, more to abate the price, his gimlet eye
Would pierce to cat-sticks that none else could spy;
Yet none dared grumble, for no farmer yet
But New Year found him in the Deacon's debt.   490

  "While the first snow was mealy under feet,
A team drawled creaking down Quompegan street.
Two cords of oak weighed down the grinding sled,
And cornstalk fodder rustled overhead;
The oxen's muzzles, as they shouldered through,   495
Were silver-fringed; the driver's own was blue
As the coarse frock that swung below his knee.
Behind his load for shelter waded he;
His mittened hands now on his chest he beat,
Now stamped the stiffened cowhides of his feet,   500
Hushed as a ghost's; his armpit scarce could hold
The walnut whipstock slippery-bright with cold.
What wonder if, the tavern as he past,
He looked and longed, and stayed his beasts at last,
Who patient stood and veiled themselves in steam   505
While he explored the bar-room's ruddy gleam?

"Before the fire, in want of thought profound,
There sat a brother-townsman weather-bound:
A sturdy churl, crisp-headed, bristly-eared,
Red as a pepper; 'twixt coarse brows and beard   510
His eyes lay ambushed, on the watch for fools,
Clear, gray, and glittering like two bay-edged pools;
A shifty creature, with a turn for fun,
Could swap a poor horse for a better one,—
He'd a high-stepper always in his stall;   515
Liked far and near, and dreaded therewithal.
To him the in-comer, 'Perez, how d'ye do?'
'Jest as I'm mind to, Obed; how do you?'
Then, his eyes twinkling such swift gleams as run
Along the levelled barrel of a gun   520
Brought to his shoulder by a man you know
Will bring his game down, he continued, 'So,
I s'pose you're haulin' wood? But you're too late;
The Deacon's off; Old Splitfoot couldn't wait;
He made a bee-line las' night in the storm   525
To where he won't need wood to keep him warm.
'Fore this he's treasurer of a fund to train
Young imps as missionaries; hopes to gain
That way a contract that he has in view
For fireproof pitchforks of a pattern new.   530
It must have tickled him, all drawbacks weighed,
To think he stuck the Old One in a trade;
His soul, to start with, was n't worth a carrot,
And all he'd left 'ould hardly serve to swear at.'

"By this time Obed had his wits thawed out,   535
And, looking at the other half in doubt,
Took off his fox-skin cap to scratch his head,
Donned it again, and drawled forth, 'Mean he's dead?'
'Jesso; he's dead and t'other d that follers
With folks that never love a thing but dollars.   540
He pulled up stakes last evening, fair and square,
And ever since there's been a row Down There.
The minute the old chap arrived, you see,
Comes the Boss-devil to him, and says he,
"What are you good at?   Little enough, I fear;   545
We callilate to make folks useful here."

"Well," says old Bitters, "I expect I can
Scale a fair load of wood with e'er a man."
"Wood we don't deal in; but perhaps you'll suit,
Because we buy our brimstone by the foot: 550
Here, take this measurin'-rod, as smooth as sin,
And keep a reckonin' of what loads comes in.
You'll not want business, for we need a lot
To keep the Yankees that you send us hot;
At firin' up they're barely half as spry   555
As Spaniards or Italians, though they're dry;
At first we have to let the draught on stronger,
But, heat 'em through, they seem to hold it longer."

    " 'Bitters he took the rod, and pretty soon
A teamster comes, whistling an ex-psalm tune.   560
A likelier chap you wouldn't ask to see,
No different, but his limp, from you or me'—
'No different, Perez!   Don't your memory fail?
Why, where in thunder was his horns and tail?'
'They're only worn by some old-fashioned pokes;   565
They mostly aim at looking just like folks.
Sech things are scarce as queues and top-boots here;
'T would spoil their usefulness to look too queer.
Ef you could always know 'em when they come,
They'd get no purchase on you: now be mum.   570
On come the teamster, smart as Davy Crockett,[19]
Jinglin' the red-hot coppers in his pocket,
And clost behind, ('t was gold-dust, you'd ha' sworn,)
A load of sulphur yallower 'n seed-corn;
To see it wasted as it is Down There   575
Would make a Friction-Match Co. tear its hair!
"Hold on!" says Bitters, "stop right where you be;
You can't go in athout a pass from me."
"All right," says t'other, "only step round smart;
I must be home by noon-time with the cart."   580
Bitters goes round it sharp-eyed as a rat,
Then with a scrap of paper on his hat
Pretends to cipher.   "By the public staff,
That load scarce rises twelve foot and a half."

---

[19] David Crockett (1786–1836), a famed Tennessee hunter and adven-
turer who lost his life in the Texan revolt against Mexico.

"There's fourteen foot and over," says the driver,   585
"Worth twenty dollars, ef it's worth a stiver;
Good fourth-proof brimstone, that'll make 'em squirm,—
I leave it to the Headman of the Firm;
After we masure it, we always lay
Some on to allow for settlin' by the way.   590
Imp and full-grown, I've carted sulphur here,
And gi'n fair satisfaction, thirty year."
With that they fell to quarrellin' so loud
That in five minutes they had drawed a crowd,
And afore long the Boss, who heard the row,   595
Comes elbowin' in with "What's to pay here now?"
Both parties heard, the measurin'-rod he takes,
And of the load a careful survey makes.
"Sence I have bossed the business here," says he,
"No fairer load was ever seen by me."   600
Then, turnin' to the Deacon, "You mean cus,
None of your old Quompegan tricks with us!
They won't do here: we're plain old-fashioned folks,
And don't quite understand that kind o' jokes.
I know this teamster, and his pa afore him,   605
And the hard-working Mrs. D. that bore him;
He would n't soil his conscience with a lie,
Though he might get the custom-house thereby.
Here, constable, take Bitters by the queue,
And clap him into furnace ninety-two,   610
And try this brimstone on him; if he's bright,
He'll find the masure honest afore night.
He is n't worth his fuel, and I'll bet
The parish oven has to take him yet!"'

"This is my tale, heard twenty years ago   615
From Uncle Reuben, as the logs burned low,
Touching the walls and ceiling with that bloom
That makes a rose's calyx of a room.
I could not give his language, wherethrough ran
The gamy flavor of the bookless man   620
Who shapes a word before the fancy cools,
As lonely Crusoe improvised his tools.
I liked the tale,—'t was like so many told

By Rutebeuf [20] and his brother Trouvères [21] bold;
Nor were the hearers much unlike to theirs,   625
Men unsophisticate, rude-nerved as bears.
Ezra is gone and his large-hearted kind,
The landlords of the hospitable mind;
Good Warriner of Springfield was the last;
An inn is now a vision of the past;   630
One yet-surviving host my mind recalls,—
You'll find him if you go to Trenton Falls." [22]

THE NIGHTINGALE IN THE STUDY [1]

"COME forth!" my catbird calls to me,
"And hear me sing a cavatina [2]

---

[20] The pseudonym of an unknown French poet (*c.* 1230–*c.* 1285), the most vigorous versifier of his age.

[21] French epic poets of the Middle Ages.

[22] An autobiographical touch. In March, 1855, Lowell spent a week-end at Trenton Falls (twelve miles from Utica, New York), where a certain Mr. Moore, who kept a hotel, showed Lowell warm hospitality. "After tea Mr. Moore and I smoked and talked together. I found him a man with tastes for medals, pictures, engravings, music, and fruit culture. He played very well on a parlor organ, and knew many artists whom I also knew. Moreover, he was a Unitarian. So we got along nicely." (*Letters*, I, 226.)

[1] Written June 29–30, 1867. Published in the *Atlantic Monthly*, September, 1867, and then in the volume, *Under the Willows and Other Poems*, 1868. On June 30 Lowell submitted the poem to J. T. Fields, editor of the *Atlantic*, with the comment: "The possibility of doing this came to me like a flash as I was walking out of town last night after club. I happened to look up at the stars, and my mind was loosened like brooks in spring. I wrote down a few stanzas before I went to bed, so as to be sure of it, and this morning it slid like sand. Here I am, pleased with it, and in a week, goodness knows how flat it will seem!" (*Letters*, I, 388.) The poem was an outburst of long-felt admiration for the famous Spanish writer, Pedro Calderon de la Barca. On August 23, 1890, just a year before he died, he wrote to Norton of Calderon: "He always entertains and absorbs me after everybody else has given it up. . . . If his horizon be not of the widest, heat-lightnings of fancy are forever winking around the edges of it. . . . There are greater poets, but none so constantly delightful. . . . His mind is a kaleidoscope, at every turn making a new image of the same bits of colored glass. . . . These are fragments from painted windows deepened in hue with incense fumes and thrilled through and through with organ and choir." (*Letters*, II, 413.)

[2] Short simple Italian song.

That, in this old familiar tree,
   Shall hang a garden of Alcina.

"These buttercups shall brim with wine   5
   Beyond all Lesbian [3] juice or Massic; [4]
May not New England be divine?
   My ode to ripening summer classic?

"Or, if to me you will not hark,
   By Beaver Brook [5] a thrush is ringing   10
Till all the alder-coverts dark
   Seem sunshine-dappled with his singing.

"Come out beneath the unmastered sky,
   With its emancipating spaces,
And learn to sing as well as I,   15
   Without premeditated graces.

"What boot your many-volumed gains,
   Those withered leaves forever turning,
To win, at best, for all your pains,
   A nature mummy-wrapt in learning?   20

"The leaves wherein true wisdom lies
   On living trees the sun are drinking;
Those white clouds, drowsing through the skies,
   Grew not so beautiful by thinking.

" 'Come out!' with me the oriole cries,   25
   Escape the demon that pursues you!
And, hark, the cuckoo weatherwise,
   Still hiding farther onward, wooes you."

"Alas, dear friend, that, all my days,
   Hast poured from that syringa thicket   30
The quaintly discontinuous lays
   To which I hold a season-ticket,

---

   [3] The wine from the Greek island of Lesbos off the coast of Asia Minor was noted among the ancients.

   [4] Mt. Massicus in Campania, Italy, was also famed for its wine.

   [5] One of Lowell's haunts, four to five miles west of Elmwood towards Waltham.

"A season-ticket cheaply bought
  With a dessert of pilfered berries,
And who so oft my soul hast caught   35
  With morn and evening voluntaries,

"Deem me not faithless, if all day
  Among my dusty books I linger,
No pipe, like thee, for June to play
  With fancy-led, half-conscious finger.   40

"A bird is singing in my brain
  And bubbling o'er with mingled fancies,
Gay, tragic, rapt, right heart of Spain
  Fed with the sap of old romances.

"I ask no ampler skies than those   45
  His magic music rears above me,
No falser friends, no truer foes,—
  And does not Doña Clara love me?

"Cloaked shapes, a twanging of guitars,
  A rush of feet, and rapiers clashing,   50
Then silence deep with breathless stars,
  And overhead a white hand flashing.

"O music of all moods and climes,
  Vengeful, forgiving, sensuous, saintly,
Where still, between the Christian chimes,   55
  The Moorish cymbal tinkles faintly!

"O life borne lightly in the hand,
  For friend or foe with grace Castilian!
O valley safe in Fancy's land,
  Not tramped to mud yet by the million!   60

"Bird of to-day, thy songs are stale
  To his, my singer of all weathers,
My Calderon, my nightingale,
  My Arab soul in Spanish feathers.

"Ah, friend, these singers dead so long,   65
  And still, God knows, in purgatory,
Give its best sweetness to all song,
  To Nature's self her better glory."

THE CATHEDRAL [1]

FAR through the memory shines a happy day,
Cloudless of care, down-shod to every sense,
And simply perfect from its own resource,
As to a bee the new campanula's

---

[1] The original draft of this poem was composed during July and August, 1869, in a period of exultant poetic inspiration. "How happy I was while I was writing it! For weeks it and I were alone in the world, till Fanny [i.e., Mrs. Lowell] well-nigh grew jealous." (*Letters,* II, 79.) During the ensuing autumn Lowell worked over the text considerably, but apparently he ceased his labored efforts at revision about the end of November, since he put the finishing touch to the copy for book publication on the twenty-ninth of that month by a dedicatory letter addressed to James Fields. The poem first appeared in the January, 1870, number of the *Atlantic Monthly* with the title "The Cathedral," and shortly thereafter it was published as a small volume by itself. Lowell himself had originally given the work a different title, as he reported to Leslie Stephen: "The name was none of my choosing. I called it 'A Day at Chartres,' and Fields rechristened it." (*Ibid.,* II, 57.) That earlier title suggests more explicitly the autobiographical experience from which the poem slowly derived its genesis. In July, 1855, he visited Chartres for the first time and enjoyed an extremely memorable day, about which he wrote Norton with some of the descriptive imagery that later he wove into the poem: "I must only tell you of one wonderful thing I saw in France—the Cathedral of Chartres. It is very grand—with mossy saints and angels looking down upon you out of that hoary, inaccessible past. It is the home now of innumerable swallows and sparrows, who build upon the shoulders of those old great ones—as we little folks do too, I am afraid. . . . The day, also, was superb—clear and lucent, with a great white cloud here and there to make the blue companionable for the imagination, and to dapple the green landscape with shadow." (*Ibid.,* I, 237, 239.) With the experience at Chartres, however, Lowell's imagination fused the figure of the Gothic cathedral which much earlier had gripped his fancy as the symbol of religious disparity between the Middle Ages and the present. On May 12, 1848, he wrote to Briggs: "The Gothic style is just as fit for a church (meeting-house) as ever; the difficulty is that The Church has shrunk so as not to fill her ancient idea. . . . While our church-buildings are poor and jejune because our Church is dead, our ships, our railroad stations, and our shops are our best specimens of architecture because commerce, trade, and stocks are our religion. These are our temples we erect to Mammon, our God." (*Ibid.,* I, 132, 134.)

POEMS 275

Illuminate seclusion swung in air.   5
Such days are not the prey of setting suns,
Nor ever blurred with mist of afterthought;
Like words made magical by poets dead,
Wherein the music of all meaning is
The sense hath garnered or the soul divined,   10
They mingle with our life's ethereal part,
Sweetening and gathering sweetness evermore,
By beauty's franchise disenthralled of time.

I can recall, nay, they are present still,
Parts of myself, the perfume of my mind,   15
Days that seem farther off than Homer's now
Ere yet the child had loudened to the boy,
And I, recluse from playmates, found perforce
Companionship in things that not denied
Nor granted wholly; as is Nature's wont,   20
Who, safe in uncontaminate reserve,
Lets us mistake our longing for her love,
And mocks with various echo of ourselves.

These first sweet frauds upon our consciousness,
That blend the sensual with its imaged world,   25
These virginal cognitions, gifts of morn,
Ere life grow noisy, and slower-footed thought
Can overtake the rapture of the sense,
To thrust between ourselves and what we feel,
Have something in them secretly divine.   30
Vainly the eye, once schooled to serve the brain,
With pains deliberate studies to renew
The ideal vision: second-thoughts are prose;
For beauty's acme hath a term as brief
As the wave's poise before it break in pearl.   35
Our own breath dims the mirror of the sense,
Looking too long and closely: at a flash
We snatch the essential grace of meaning out,
And that first passion beggars all behind,
Heirs of a tamer transport prepossessed.   40
Who, seeing once, has truly seen again
The gray vague of unsympathizing sea
That dragged his Fancy from her moorings back

To shores inhospitable of eldest time,
Till blank foreboding of earth-gendered powers,   45
Pitiless seignories [2] in the elements,
Omnipotences blind that darkling smite,
Misgave him, and repaganized the world?
Yet, by some subtler touch of sympathy,
These primal apprehensions, dimly stirred,   50
Perplex the eye with pictures from within.
This hath made poets dream of lives foregone
In worlds fantastical, more fair than ours;
So Memory cheats us, glimpsing half-revealed.
Even as I write she tries her wonted spell   55
In that continuous redbreast boding rain:
The bird I hear sings not from yonder elm;
But the flown ecstasy my childhood heard
Is vocal in my mind, renewed by him,
Haply made sweeter by the accumulate thrill   60
That threads my undivided life and steals
A pathos from the years and graves between.

I know not how it is with other men,
Whom I but guess, deciphering myself;
For me, once felt is so felt nevermore.   65
The fleeting relish at sensation's brim
Had in it the best ferment of the wine.
One spring I knew as never any since:
All night the surges of the warm southwest
Boomed intermittent through the wallowing elms,   70
And brought a morning from the Gulf adrift,
Omnipotent with sunshine, whose quick charm
Startled with crocuses the sullen turf
And wiled the bluebird to his whiff of song:
One summer hour abides, what time I perched,   75
Dappled with noonday, under simmering leaves,
And pulled the pulpy oxhearts, while aloof
An oriole clattered and the robins shrilled,
Denouncing me an alien and a thief:
One morn of autumn lords it o'er the rest,   80
When in the lane I watched the ash-leaves fall,
Balancing softly earthward without wind,

---

[2] Domains.

Or twirling with directer impulse down
On those fallen yesterday, now barbed with frost,
While I grew pensive with the pensive year: 85
And once I learned how marvellous winter was,
When past the fence-rails, downy-gray with rime,
I creaked adventurous o'er the spangled crust
That made familiar fields seem far and strange
As those stark wastes that whiten endlessly   90
In ghastly solitude about the pole,
And gleam relentless to the unsetting sun:
Instant the candid chambers of my brain
Were painted with these sovran images;
And later visions seem but copies pale   95
From those unfading frescos of the past,
Which I, young savage, in my age of flint,
Gazed at, and dimly felt a power in me
Parted from Nature by the joy in her
That doubtfully revealed me to myself.   100
Thenceforward I must stand outside the gate;
And paradise was paradise the more,
Known once and barred against satiety.

What we call Nature, all outside ourselves,
Is but our own conceit of what we see,   105
Our own reaction upon what we feel;
The world's a woman to our shifting mood,
Feeling with us, or making due pretence;
And therefore we the more persuade ourselves
To make all things our thought's confederates,   110
Conniving with us in whate'er we dream.
So when our Fancy seeks analogies,
Though she have hidden what she after finds,
She loves to cheat herself with feigned surprise.
I find my own complexion everywhere: 115
No rose, I doubt, was ever, like the first,
A marvel to the bush it dawned upon,
The rapture of its life made visible,
The mystery of its yearning realized,
As the first babe to the first woman born;   120
No falcon ever felt delight of wings
As when, an eyas, from the stolid cliff

Loosing himself, he followed his high heart
To swim on sunshine, masterless as wind;
And I believe the brown earth takes delight   125
In the new snowdrop looking back at her,
To think that by some vernal alchemy
It could transmute her darkness into pearl;
What is the buxom peony after that,
With its coarse constancy of hoyden [3] blush?   130
What the full summer to that wonder new?

But, if in nothing else, in us there is
A sense fastidious hardly reconciled
To the poor makeshifts of life's scenery,
Where the same slide must double all its parts,   135
Shoved in for Tarsus [4] and hitched back for Tyre.[5]
I blame not in the soul this daintiness,
Rasher of surfeit than a humming-bird,
In things indifferent by sense purveyed;
It argues her an immortality   140
And dateless incomes of experience,
This unthrift housekeeping that will not brook
A dish warmed-over at the feast of life,
And finds Twice stale, served with whatever sauce.
Nor matters much how it may go with me   145
Who dwell in Grub Street [6] and am proud to drudge
Where men, my betters, wet their crust with tears:
Use can make sweet the peach's shady side,
That only by reflection tastes of sun.

But she, my Princess, who will sometimes deign   150
My garret to illumine till the walls,
Narrow and dingy, scrawled with hackneyed thought
(Poor Richard [7] slowly elbowing Plato out),
Dilate and drape themselves with tapestries

---

[3] Flamboyant and unmannerly.

[4] Ancient city of Asia Minor, famed as the birthplace of the Apostle Paul.

[5] The largest city and port of ancient Phœnicia, on the Mediterranean sea-coast of modern Syria.

[6] A London street inhabited by needy authors and literary hacks in the eighteenth century.

[7] The pseudonym used by Benjamin Franklin (1706–90) in his almanac, which was filled with homely and wise sayings.

Nausikaa [8] might have stooped o'er, while, between,   155
Mirrors, effaced in their own clearness, send
Her only image on through deepening deeps
With endless repercussion of delight,—
Bringer of life, witching each sense to soul,
That sometimes almost gives me to believe   160
I might have been a poet, gives at least
A brain desaxonized, an ear that makes
Music where none is, and a keener pang
Of exquisite surmise outleaping thought,—
Her will I pamper in her luxury: 165
No crumpled rose-leaf of too careless choice
Shall bring a northern nightmare to her dreams,
Vexing with sense of exile; hers shall be
The inviitate [9] firstlings of experience,
Vibrations felt but once and felt life long: 170
Oh, more than half-way turn that Grecian front
Upon me, while with self-rebuke I spell,
On the plain fillet that confines thy hair
In conscious bounds of seeming unconstraint,
The *Naught in overplus,* thy race's badge!   175

One feast for her I secretly designed
In that Old World so strangely beautiful
To us the disinherited of eld,[10]—
A day at Chartres, with no soul beside
To roil with pedant prate [11] my joy serene   180
And make the minster shy of confidence.
I went, and, with the Saxon's pious care,
First ordered dinner at the pea-green inn,
The flies and I its only customers.
Eluding these, I loitered through the town,   185
With hope to take my minster unawares
In its grave solitude of memory.
A pretty burgh, and such as Fancy loves

---

[8] The beautiful daughter of Alcinous, king of the Phaeacians. Bk. VII
of the *Odyssey* describes her father's banquet hall and the fine tapestries
woven by the women of the household.
[9] Uncontaminated or uncorrupted.
[10] To us the people cut off from antiquity.
[11] To disturb with learned talk.

For bygone grandeurs, faintly rumorous [12] now
Upon the mind's horizon, as of storm   190
Brooding its dreamy thunders far aloof,
That mingle with our mood, but not disturb.
Its once grim bulwarks, tamed to lovers' walks,
Look down unwatchful on the sliding Eure,
Whose listless leisure suits the quiet place,   195
Lisping among his shallows homelike sounds
At Concord and by Bankside heard before.
Chance led me to a public pleasure-ground,
Where I grew kindly with the merry groups,
And blessed the Frenchman for his simple art   200
Of being domestic in the light of day.
His language has no word, we growl, for Home;
But he can find a fireside in the sun,
Play with his child, make love, and shriek his mind,
By throngs of strangers undisprivacied.   205
He makes his life a public gallery,
Nor feels himself till what he feels comes back
In manifold reflection from without;
While we, each pore alert with consciousness,
Hide our best selves as we had stolen them,   210
And each bystander a detective were,
Keen-eyed for every chink of undisguise.

So, musing o'er the problem which was best,—
A life wide-windowed, shining all abroad,
Or curtains drawn to shield from sight profane   215
The rites we pay to the mysterious I,—
With outward senses furloughed and head bowed
I followed some fine instinct in my feet,
Till, to unbend me from the loom of thought,
Looking up suddenly, I found mine eyes   220
Confronted with the minster's vast repose.
Silent and gray as forest-leaguered cliff
Left inland by the ocean's slow retreat,
That hears afar the breeze-borne rote [13] and longs,

---

[12] Indistinct.

[13] According to Lowell (*Letters*, II, 66–7), a word of Elizabethan vintage,
perpetuated along the New England coast, and expressing "the dull and
continuous burden of the sea heard inland before and after a great storm."

Remembering shocks of surf that clomb and fell,   225
Spume-sliding down the baffled decuman,[14]
It rose before me, patiently remote
From the great tides of life it breasted once,
Hearing the noise of men as in a dream.
I stood before the triple northern port,   230
Where dedicated shapes of saints and kings,
Stern faces bleared with immemorial watch,
Looked down benignly grave and seemed to say,
Ye come and go incessant; we remain
Safe in the hallowed quiets of the past;   235
Be reverent, ye who flit and are forgot,
Of faith so nobly realized as this.
I seem to have heard it said by learnëd folk
Who drench you with æsthetics till you feel
As if all beauty were a ghastly bore,   240
The faucet to let loose a wash of words,
That Gothic is not Grecian, therefore worse;
But, being convinced by much experiment
How little inventiveness there is in man,
Grave copier of copies, I give thanks   245
For a new relish, careless to inquire
My pleasure's pedigree, if so it please,
Nobly, I mean, nor renegade to art.
The Grecian gluts me with its perfectness,
Unanswerable as Euclid, self-contained,   250
The one thing finished in this hasty world,
Forever finished, though the barbarous pit,
Fanatical on hearsay, stamp and shout
As if a miracle could be encored.
But ah! this other, this that never ends,   255
Still climbing, luring fancy still to climb,
As full of morals half-divined as life,
Graceful, grotesque, with ever new surprise
Of hazardous caprices sure to please,
Heavy as nightmare, airy-light as fern,   260
Imagination's very self in stone!
With one long sigh of infinite release
From pedantries past, present, or to come,

---

[14] The checked peak-wave (lit., tenth in a series of ten).

I looked, and owned myself a happy Goth.
Your blood is mine, ye architects of dream,   265
Builders of aspiration incomplete,
So more consummate, souls self-confident,
Who felt your own thought worthy of record
In monumental pomp! No Grecian drop
Rebukes these veins that leap with kindred thrill,   270
After long exile, to the mother-tongue.

Ovid in Pontus,[15] puling for his Rome
Of men invirile and disnatured dames
That poison sucked from the Attic bloom decayed,
Shrank with a shudder from the blue-eyed race [16]   275
Whose force rough-handed should renew the world,
And from the dregs of Romulus express [17]
Such wine [18] as Dante poured, or he who blew
Roland's [19] vain blast, or sang the Campeador [20]
In verse that clanks like armor in the charge,   280
Homeric juice, though brimmed in Odin's horn.[21]
And they could build, if not the columned fane
That from the height gleamed seaward many-hued,
Something more friendly with their ruder skies:
The gray spire, molten now in driving mist,   285
Now lulled with the incommunicable blue;
The carvings touched to meaning new with snow,
Or commented with fleeting grace of shade;
The statues, motley as man's memory,
Partial as that, so mixed of true and false,   290

---

[15] Publius Ovidius Naso (B.C. 43–A.D. 18), a well-known Roman poet, was banished at the age of fifty by the Emperor Augustus to a town in Pontus, a district of Asia Minor on the shore of the Black Sea. There Ovid wrote poems on the sorrows of his exile.

[16] I.e., the Goths.

[17] From the dregs of the Roman race squeeze out.

[18] I.e., poetry.

[19] The nephew of Charlemagne (742–814), King of the Franks. The *Song of Roland,* the great medieval French epic, tells of Roland's death after he had vainly blown his horn for more warriors to help defend the Roncesvalles pass against the Moors.

[20] "The Champion," the name given by the Moors to the famous Spanish warrior, Rodrigo Diaz (1040–99), also called the Cid. A medieval Spanish epic, *Poem of the Cid,* relates his exploits.

[21] Poured to the brim in the drinking horn of Odin or Wodin, the chief of the old Scandinavian gods.

History and legend meeting with a kiss
Across this bound-mark where their realms confine;
The painted windows, freaking [22] gloom with glow,
Dusking the sunshine which they seem to cheer,
Meet symbol of the senses and the soul,   295
And the whole pile, grim with the Northman's thought
Of life and death, and doom, life's equal fee,—
These were before me: and I gazed abashed,
Child of an age that lectures, not creates,
Plastering our swallow-nests on the awful Past,   300
And twittering round the work of larger men,
As we had builded what we but deface.
Far up the great bells wallowed in delight,
Tossing their clangors o'er the heedless town,
To call the worshippers who never came,   305
Or women mostly, in loath twos and threes.
I entered, reverent of whatever shrine
Guards piety and solace for my kind
Or gives the soul a moment's truce of God,
And shared decorous in the ancient rite   310
My sterner fathers held idolatrous.
The service over, I was tranced in thought:
Solemn the deepening vaults, and most to me,
Fresh from the fragile realm of deal and paint,
Or brick mock-pious with a marble front;   315
Solemn the lift of high-embowered roof,
The clustered stems that spread in boughs disleaved,
Through which the organ blew a dream of storm,
Though not more potent to sublime with awe
And shut the heart up in tranquillity,   320
Than aisles to me familiar that o'erarch
The conscious silences of brooding woods,
Centurial shadows, cloisters of the elk:
Yet here was sense of undefined regret,
Irreparable loss, uncertain what: 325
Was all this grandeur but anachronism,
A shell divorced of its informing life,
Where the priest housed him like a hermit-crab,
An alien to that faith of elder days
That gathered round it this fair shape of stone?   330

_____
[22] Dappling.

Is old Religion but a spectre now,
Haunting the solitude of darkened minds,
Mocked out of memory by the sceptic day?
Is there no corner safe from peeping Doubt,
Since Gutenberg [23] made thought cosmopolite   335
And stretched electric threads from mind to mind?
Nay, did Faith build this wonder? or did Fear,
That makes a fetish and misnames it God
(Blockish or metaphysic, matters not),
Contrive this coop to shut its tyrant in,   340
Appeased with playthings, that he might not harm?

I turned and saw a beldame [24] on her knees;
With eyes astray, she told mechanic beads
Before some shrine of saintly womanhood,
Bribed intercessor with the far-off Judge: 345
Such my first thought, by kindlier soon rebuked,
Pleading for whatsoever touches life
With upward impulse: be He nowhere else,
God is in all that liberates and lifts,
In all that humbles, sweetens, and consoles: 350
Blessèd the natures shored on every side
With landmarks of hereditary thought!
Thrice happy they that wander not life long
Beyond near succor of the household faith,
The guarded fold that shelters, not confines!   355
Their steps find patience in familiar paths,
Printed with hope by loved feet gone before
Of parent, child, or lover, glorified
By simple magic of dividing Time.
My lids were moistened as the woman knelt,   360
And—was it will, or some vibration faint
Of sacred Nature, deeper than the will?—
My heart occultly felt itself in hers,
Through mutual intercession gently leagued.

Or was it not mere sympathy of brain?   365
A sweetness intellectually conceived

  [23] Johann Gutenberg (c. 1400–68), the German inventor of the printing
  press.
  [24] Old woman.

In simpler creeds to me impossible?
A juggle of that pity for ourselves
In others, which puts on such pretty masks
And snares self-love with bait of charity? 370
Something of all it might be, or of none:
Yet for a moment I was snatched away
And had the evidence of things not seen;
For one rapt moment; then it all came back,
This age that blots out life with question-marks, 375
This nineteenth century with its knife and glass
That make thought physical, and thrust far off
The Heaven, so neighborly with man of old,
To voids sparse-sown with alienated stars.

'T is irrecoverable, that ancient faith, 380
Homely and wholesome, suited to the time,
With rod or candy for child-minded men:
No theologic tube, with lens on lens
Of syllogism transparent, brings it near,—
At best resolving some new nebula, 385
Or blurring some fixed-star of hope to mist.
Science was Faith once; Faith were Science now,
Would she but lay her bow and arrows by
And arm her with the weapons of the time.
Nothing that keeps thought out is safe from thought. 390
For there's no virgin-fort but self-respect,
And Truth defensive hath lost hold on God.
Shall we treat Him as if He were a child
That knew not His own purpose? nor dare trust
The Rock of Ages to their chemic tests, 395
Lest some day the all-sustaining base divine
Should fail from under us, dissolved in gas?
The armëd eye that with a glance discerns
In a dry blood-speck between ox and man
Stares helpless at this miracle called life, 400
This shaping potency behind the egg,
This circulation swift of deity,
Where suns and systems inconspicuous float
As the poor blood-disks in our mortal veins.
Each age must worship its own thought of God, 405
More or less earthy, clarifying still

With subsidence continuous of the dregs;
Nor saint nor sage could fix immutably
The fluent image of the unstable Best,
Still changing in their very hands that wrought: 410
To-day's eternal truth To-morrow proved
Frail as frost-landscapes on a window-pane.
Meanwhile Thou smiledst, inaccessible,
At Thought's own substance made a cage for Thought,
And Truth locked fast with her own master-key;   415
Nor didst Thou reck what image man might make
Of his own shadow on the flowing world;
The climbing instinct was enough for Thee.
Or wast Thou, then, an ebbing tide that left
Strewn with dead miracle those eldest shores,   420
For men to dry, and dryly lecture on,
Thyself thenceforth incapable of flood?
Idle who hopes with prophets to be snatched
By virtue in their mantles left below;
Shall the soul live on other men's report,   425
Herself a pleasing fable of herself?
Man cannot be God's outlaw if he would,
Nor so abscond him in the caves of sense
But Nature still shall search some crevice out
With messages of splendor from that Source   430
Which, dive he, soar he, baffles still and lures.
This life were brutish did we not sometimes
Have intimation clear of wider scope,
Hints of occasion infinite, to keep
The soul alert with noble discontent   435
And onward yearnings of unstilled desire;
Fruitless, except we now and then divined
A mystery of Purpose, gleaming through
The secular confusions of the world,
Whose will we darkly accomplish, doing ours.   440
No man can think nor in himself perceive,
Sometimes at waking, in the street sometimes,
Or on the hillside, always unforewarned,
A grace of being, finer than himself,
That beckons and is gone,—a larger life   445
Upon his own impinging, with swift glimpse

Of spacious circles luminous with mind,
To which the ethereal substance of his own
Seems but gross cloud to make that visible,
Touched to a sudden glory round the edge.   450
Who that hath known these visitations fleet
Would strive to make them trite and ritual?
I, that still pray at morning and at eve,
Loving those roots that feed us from the past,
And prizing more than Plato things I learned   455
At that best academe, a mother's knee,
Thrice in my life perhaps have truly prayed,
Thrice, stirred below my conscious self, have felt
That perfect disenthralment which is God;
Nor know I which to hold worst enemy,   460
Him who on speculation's windy waste
Would turn me loose, stript of the raiment warm
By Faith contrived against our nakedness,
Or him who, cruel-kind, would fain obscure,
With painted saints and paraphrase of God,   465
The soul's east-window of divine surprise.
Where others worship I but look and long;
For, though not recreant to my fathers' faith,
Its forms to me are weariness, and most
That drony vacuum of compulsory prayer,   470
Still pumping phrases for the Ineffable,
Though all the valves of memory gasp and wheeze.
Words that have drawn transcendent meanings up
From the best passion of all bygone time,
Steeped through with tears of triumph and remorse,   475
Sweet with all sainthood, cleansed in martyr-fires,
Can they, so consecrate and so inspired,
By repetition wane to vexing wind?
Alas! we cannot draw habitual breath
In the thin air of life's supremer heights,   480
We cannot make each meal a sacrament,
Nor with our tailors be disbodied souls,—
We men, too conscious of earth's comedy,
Who see two sides, with our posed selves debate,
And only for great stakes can be sublime!   485
Let us be thankful when, as I do here,

We can read Bethel [25] on a pile of stones,
And, seeing where God *has* been, trust in Him.

Brave Peter Fischer [26] there in Nuremberg,
Moulding Saint Sebald's miracles in bronze,   490
Put saint and stander-by in that quaint garb
Familiar to him in his daily walk,
Not doubting God could grant a miracle
Then and in Nuremberg, if so He would;
But never artist for three hundred years   495
Hath dared the contradiction ludicrous
Of supernatural in modern clothes.
Perhaps the deeper faith that is to come
Will see God rather in the strenuous doubt,
Than in the creed held as an infant's hand   500
Holds purposeless whatso is placed therein.

Say it is drift, not progress, none the less,
With the old sextant of the fathers' creed,
We shape our courses by new-risen stars,
And, still lip-loyal to what once was truth,   505
Smuggle new meanings under ancient names,
Unconscious perverts of the Jesuit, Time.
Change is the mask that all Continuance wears
To keep us youngsters harmlessly amused;
Meanwhile some ailing or more watchful child,   510
Sitting apart, sees the old eyes gleam out,
Stern, and yet soft with humorous pity too.
Whilere, men burnt men for a doubtful point,
As if the mind were quenchable with fire,
And Faith danced round them with her war-paint on,   515
Devoutly savage as an Iroquois;
Now Calvin [27] and Servetus [28] at one board

---

[25] I.e., the house of God. See Genesis xxviii: 16–19.

[26] Peter Vischer (1455–1529), the renowned sculptor who labored thirteen years (1506–19) in the Church of St. Sebald, Nuremberg, on the richly adorned bronze sarcophagus and canopy of St. Sebald's shrine, one of the masterpieces of German art.

[27] See note on p. 122.

[28] Michael Servetus (Miguel Serveto) (1511–53), Spanish physician and antitrinitarian theologian, who with the knowledge and approval of Calvin was burned alive at Champel, Switzerland, for religious heresy.

Snuff in grave sympathy a milder roast,
And o'er their claret settle Comte [29] unread.
Fagot and stake were desperately sincere: 520
Our cooler martyrdoms are done in types;
And flames that shine in controversial eyes
Burn out no brains but his who kindles them.
This is no age to get cathedrals built:
Did God, then, wait for one in Bethlehem?   525
Worst is not yet: lo, where his coming looms,
Of Earth's anarchic children latest born,
Democracy, a Titan who hath learned
To laugh at Jove's old-fashioned thunderbolts,—
Could he not also forge them, if he would?   530
He, better skilled, with solvents merciless,
Loosened in air and borne on every wind,
Saps unperceived: the calm Olympian height
Of ancient order feels its bases yield,
And pale gods glance for help to gods as pale.   535
What will be left of good or worshipful,
Of spiritual secrets, mysteries,
Of fair religion's guarded heritage,
Heirlooms of soul, passed downward unprofaned
From eldest Ind?   This Western giant coarse,   540
Scorning refinements which he lacks himself,
Loves not nor heeds the ancestral hierarchies,
Each rank dependent on the next above
In orderly gradation fixed as fate.
King by mere manhood, nor allowing aught   545
Of holier unction than the sweat of toil;
In his own strength sufficient; called to solve,
On the rough edges of society,
Problems long sacred to the choicer few,
And improvise what elsewhere men receive   550
As gifts of deity; tough foundling reared
Where every man's his own Melchisedek,[30]
How make him reverent of a King of kings?

---

[29] Auguste Comte (1798–1857), one of the foremost French thinkers,
whose philosophical system under the name of Positivism proved widely
influential in the nineteenth century and almost from its inception aroused
particular interest in the United States.

[30] King of Salem and "priest of God Most High," who anointed and
blessed Abraham as a leader among his people.   (Genesis xiv, 18.)

Or Judge self-made, executor of laws
By him not first discussed and voted on?   555
For him no tree of knowledge is forbid,
Or sweeter if forbid.   How save the ark,
Or holy of holies, unprofaned a day
From his unscrupulous curiosity
That handles everything as if to buy,   560
Tossing aside what fabrics delicate
Suit not the rough-and-tumble of his ways?
What hope for those fine-nerved humanities
That made earth gracious once with gentler arts,
Now the rude hands have caught the trick of thought   565
And claim an equal suffrage with the brain?

The born disciple of an elder time,
(To me sufficient, friendlier than the new,)
Who in my blood feel motions of the Past,
I thank benignant nature most for this,—   570
A force of sympathy, or call it lack
Of character firm-planted, loosing me
From the pent chamber of habitual self
To dwell enlarged in alien modes of thought,
Haply distasteful, wholesomer for that,   575
And through imagination to possess,
As they were mine, the lives of other men.
This growth original of virgin soil,
By fascination felt in opposites,
Pleases and shocks, entices and perturbs.   580
In this brown-fisted rough, this shirt-sleeved Cid,
This backwoods Charlemagne of empires new,
Whose blundering heel instinctively finds out
The goutier foot of speechless dignities,
Who, meeting Caesar's self, would slap his back,   585
Call him "Old Horse," and challenge to a drink,
My lungs draw braver air, my breast dilates
With ampler manhood, and I front both worlds,
Of sense and spirit, as my natural fiefs,
To shape and then reshape them as I will.   590
It was the first man's charter; why not mine?
How forfeit? when deposed in other hands?

Thou shudder'st, Ovid?   Dost in him forebode
A new avatar [31] of the large-limbed Goth,
To break, or seem to break, tradition's clue, ·   595
And chase to dreamland back thy gods dethroned?
I think man's soul dwells nearer to the east,
Nearer to morning's fountains than the sun;
Herself the source whence all tradition sprang,
Herself at once both labyrinth and clue.   600
The miracle fades out of history,
But faith and wonder and the primal earth
Are born into the world with every child.
Shall this self-maker with the prying eyes,
This creature disenchanted of respect   605
By the New World's new fiend, Publicity,
Whose testing thumb leaves everywhere its smutch,
Not one day feel within himself the need
Of loyalty to better than himself,
That shall ennoble him with the upward look?   610
Shall he not catch the Voice that wanders earth,
With spiritual summons, dreamed or heard,
As sometimes, just ere sleep seals up the sense,
We hear our mother call from deeps of Time,
And, waking, find it vision,—none the less   615
The benediction bides, old skies return,
And that unreal thing, preëminent,
Makes air and dream of all we see and feel?
Shall he divine no strength unmade of votes,
Inward, impregnable, found soon as sought,   620
Not cognizable of sense, o'er sense supreme?
Else were he desolate as none before.
His holy places may not be of stone,
Nor made with hands, yet fairer far than aught
By artist feigned or pious ardor reared,   625
Fit altars for who guards inviolate
God's chosen seat, the sacred form of man.
Doubtless his church will be no hospital
For superannuate forms and mumping [32] shams,
No parlor where men issue policies   630

---

[31] Incarnation.
[32] Cheating.

Of life-assurance on the Eternal Mind,
Nor his religion but an ambulance
To fetch life's wounded and malingerers in,
Scorned by the strong; yet he, unconscious heir
To the influence sweet of Athens and of Rome,   635
And old Judæa's gift of secret fire,
Spite of himself shall surely learn to know
And worship some ideal of himself,
Some divine thing, large-hearted, brotherly,
Not nice in trifles, a soft creditor,   640
Pleased with his world, and hating only cant.
And, if his Church be doubtful, it is sure
That, in a world, made for whatever else,
Not made for mere enjoyment, in a world
Of toil but half-requited, or, at best,   645
Paid in some futile currency of breath,
A world of incompleteness, sorrow swift
And consolation laggard, whatsoe'er
The form of building or the creed professed,
The Cross, bold type of shame to homage turned,   650
Of an unfinished life that sways the world,
Shall tower as sovereign emblem over all.

The kobold [33] Thought moves with us when we shift
Our dwelling to escape him; perched aloft
On the first load of household-stuff he went;   655
For, where the mind goes, goes old furniture.
I, who to Chartres came to feed my eye
And give to Fancy one clear holiday,
Scarce saw the minster for the thoughts it stirred
Buzzing o'er past and future with vain quest.   660
Here once there stood a homely wooden church,
Which slow devotion nobly changed for this
That echoes vaguely to my modern steps.
By suffrage universal it was built,
As practised then, for all the country came   665
From far as Rouen,[34] to give votes for God,
Each vote a block of stone securely laid
Obedient to the master's deep-mused plan.

---

[33] Familiar spirit.
[34] The capital of Normandy in the Middle Ages.

Will what our ballots rear, responsible
To no grave forethought, stand so long as this?   670
Delight like this the eye of after days
Brightening with pride that here, at least, were men
Who meant and did the noblest thing they knew?
Can our religion cope with deeds like this?
We, too, build Gothic contract-shams, because   675
Our deacons have discovered that it pays,
And pews sell better under vaulted roofs
Of plaster painted like an Indian squaw.
Shall not that Western Goth, of whom we spoke,
So fiercely practical, so keen of eye,   680
Find out, some day, that nothing pays but God,
Served whether on the smoke-shut battlefield,
In work obscure done honestly, or vote
For truth unpopular, or faith maintained
To ruinous convictions, or good deeds   685
Wrought for good's sake, mindless of heaven or hell?
Shall he not learn that all prosperity,
Whose bases stretch not deeper than the sense,
Is but a trick of this world's atmosphere,
A desert-born mirage of spire and dome,   690
Or find too late, the Past's long lesson missed,
That dust the prophets shake from off their feet
Grows heavy to drag down both tower and wall?
I know not; but, sustained by sure belief
That man still rises level with the height   695
Of noblest opportunities, or makes
Such, if the time supply not, I can wait.
I gaze round on the windows, pride of France,
Each the bright gift of some mechanic guild
Who loved their city and thought gold well spent   700
To make her beautiful with piety;
I pause, transfigured by some stripe of bloom,
And my mind throngs with shining auguries,
Circle on circle, bright as seraphim,
With golden trumpets, silent, that await   705
The signal to blow news of good to men.

Then the revulsion came that always comes
After these dizzy elations of the mind:

And with a passionate pang of doubt I cried,
"O mountain-born, sweet with snow-filtered air   710
From uncontaminate wells of ether drawn
And never-broken secrecies of sky,
Freedom, with anguish won, misprized till lost,
They keep thee not who from thy sacred eyes
Catch the consuming lust of sensual good   715
And the brute's licence of unfettered will.
Far from the popular shout and venal breath
Of Cleon [35] blowing the mob's baser mind
To bubbles of wind-piloted conceit,
Thou shrinkest, gathering up thy skirts, to hide   720
In fortresses of solitary thought
And private virtue strong in self-restraint.
Must we too forfeit thee misunderstood,
Content with names, nor inly wise to know
That best things perish of their own excess,   725
And quality o'er-driven becomes defect?
Nay, is it thou indeed that we have glimpsed,
Or rather such illusion as of old
Through Athens glided menadlike [36] and Rome,
A shape of vapor, mother of vain dreams   730
And mutinous traditions, specious plea
Of the glaived [37] tyrant and long-memoried priest?"

I walked forth saddened; for all thought is sad,
And leaves a bitterish savor in the brain,
Tonic, it may be, not delectable,   735
And turned, reluctant, for a parting look
At those old weather-pitted images
Of bygone struggle, now so sternly calm.
About their shoulders sparrows had built nests,
And fluttered, chirping, from gray perch to perch,   740
Now on a mitre poising, now a crown,
Irreverently happy.   While I thought
How confident they were, what careless hearts

---

[35] An Athenian demagogue (d. 422 B.C.), who out of selfish interest championed, successfully for a time, the stupid continuance of the Peloponnesian War.

[36] A maenad was a reveling priestess of Bacchus, god of wine.

[37] Sworded.

Flew on those lightsome wings and shared the sun,
A larger shadow crossed; and looking up,   745
I saw where, nesting in the hoary towers,
The sparrow-hawk slid forth on noiseless air,
With sidelong head that watched the joy below,
Grim Norman baron o'er this clan of Kelts.
Enduring Nature, force conservative,   750
Indifferent to our noisy whims!   Men prate
Of all heads to an equal grade cashiered
On level with the dullest, and expect
(Sick of no worse distemper than themselves)
A wondrous cure-all in equality;   755
They reason that To-morrow must be wise
Because To-day was not, nor Yesterday,
As if good days were shapen of themselves,
Not of the very lifeblood of men's souls;
Meanwhile, long-suffering, imperturbable,   760
Thou quietly complet'st thy syllogism,
And from the premise sparrow here below
Draw'st sure conclusion of the hawk above,
Pleased with the soft-billed songster, pleased no less
With the fierce beak of natures aquiline.   765

Thou beautiful Old Time, now hid away
In the Past's valley of Avilion,
Haply, like Arthur, till thy wound be healed,[38]
Then to reclaim the sword and crown again!
Thrice beautiful to us; perchance less fair   770
To who possessed thee, as a mountain seems
To dwellers round its bases but a heap
Of barren obstacle that lairs the storm
And the avalanche's silent bolt holds back
Leashed with a hair,—meanwhile some far-off clown,   775
Hereditary delver of the plain,
Sees it an unmoved vision of repose,

---

[38] According to the famous account by Sir Thomas Malory of King
Arthur's earthly passing, the king, mortally wounded, was placed in a barge
presided over by black-hooded ladies. As the barge moved away from the
shore, Sir Bedivere cried out in grief and Arthur spoke then to comfort
him. Among other things the king said, "I will into the vale of Avilion to
heal me of my grievous wound." See *Morte d'Arthur,* Bk. XXI, Chap. v.

Nest of the morning, and conjectures there
The dance of streams to idle shepherds' pipes,
And fairer habitations softly hung   780
On breezy slopes, or hid in valleys cool,
For happier men.   No mortal ever dreams
That the scant isthmus he encamps upon
Between two oceans, one, the Stormy, passed,
And one, the Peaceful, yet to venture on,   785
Has been that future whereto prophets yearned
For the fulfilment of Earth's cheated hope,
Shall be that past which nerveless poets moan
As the lost opportunity of song.

O Power, more near my life than life itself   790
(Or what seems life to us in sense immured),
Even as the roots, shut in the darksome earth,
Share in the tree-top's joyance, and conceive
Of sunshine and wide air and wingèd things
By sympathy of nature, so do I   795
Have evidence of Thee so far above,
Yet in and of me!   Rather Thou the root
Invisibly sustaining, hid in light,
Not darkness, or in darkness made by us.
If sometimes I must hear good men debate   800
Of other witness of Thyself than Thou,
As if there needed any help of ours
To nurse Thy flickering life, that else must cease,
Blown out, as 't were a candle, by men's breath,
My soul shall not be taken in their snare,   805
To change her inward surety for their doubt
Muffled from sight in formal robes of proof:
While she can only feel herself through Thee,
I fear not Thy withdrawal; more I fear,
Seeing, to know Thee not, hoodwinked with dreams   810
Of signs and wonders, while, unnoticed, Thou,
Walking Thy garden still,[39] commun'st with men,
Missed in the commonplace of miracle.

---

[39] God walked in the Garden of Eden "in the cool of the day," and spoke
to Adam.   See Genesis iii: 8–10.

THE PETITION [1]

OH, TELL me less or tell me more,
Soft eyes with mystery at the core,
That always seem to meet my own
Frankly as pansies fully grown,
Yet waver still 'tween no and yes!   5

So swift to cavil and deny,
Then parley with concessions shy,
Dear eyes, that make their youth be mine
And through my inmost shadows shine,
Oh, tell me more or tell me less!   10

THE SECRET [1]

I HAVE a fancy: how shall I bring it
Home to all mortals wherever they be?
Say it or sing it?   Shoe it or wing it,
So it may outrun or outfly ME,
Merest cocoon-web whence it broke free?   5

Only one secret can save from disaster,
Only one magic is that of the Master:
Set it to music; give it a tune,—
Tune the brook sings you, tune the breeze brings you,
Tune the wild columbines nod to in June!   10

This is the secret: so simple, you see!
Easy as loving, easy as kissing,
Easy as—well, let me ponder—as missing,
Known, since the world was, by scarce two or three.

---

[1] Written in 1879 and first published in *Heartsease and Rue* (1888).

[1] Written in 1882 and first published in the *Atlantic Monthly,* January, 1888.   During this latter year it also was printed in *Heartsease and Rue.*

ELEANOR MAKES MACAROONS [1]

Light of triumph in her eyes,
Eleanor her apron ties;
As she pushes back her sleeves,
High resolve her bosom heaves.
Hasten, cook! impel the fire   5
To the pace of her desire;
As you hope to save your soul,
Bring a virgin casserole,
Brightest bring of silver spoons,—
Eleanor makes macaroons!   10

Almond-blossoms, now adance
In the smile of Southern France,
Leave your sport with sun and breeze,
Think of duty, not of ease;
Fashion, 'neath their jerkins brown,   15
Kernels white as thistle-down,
Tiny cheeses made with cream
From the Galaxy's mid-stream,
Blanched in light of honeymoons,—
Eleanor makes macaroons!   20

Now for sugar,—nay, our plan
Tolerates no work of man.
Hurry, then, ye golden bees;
Fetch your clearest honey, please,
Garnered on a Yorkshire moor,   25
While the last larks sing and soar,
From the heather-blossoms sweet
Where sea-breeze and sunshine meet,
And the Augusts mask as Junes,—
Eleanor makes macaroons!   30

Next the pestle and mortar find,
Pure rock-crystal,—these to grind
Into paste more smooth than silk,

---

[1] Written on Lowell's sixty-fifth birthday, February 22, 1884, and first
published in *Heartsease and Rue* (1888).

Whiter than the milkweed's milk:
Spread it on a rose-leaf, thus,   35
Cate [2] to please Theocritus; [3]
Then the fire with spices swell,
While, for her completer spell,
Mystic canticles she croons,—
Eleanor makes macaroons!   40

Perfect! and all this to waste
On a graybeard's palsied taste!
Poets so their verses write,
Heap them full of life and light,
And then fling them to the rude   45
Mumbling of the multitude.
Not so dire her fate as theirs,
Since her friend this gift declares
Choicest of his birthday boons,—
Eleanor's dear macaroons!   50

THE RECALL [1]

COME back before the birds are flown,
Before the leaves desert the tree,
And, through the lonely alleys blown,
Whisper their vain regrets to me
Who drive before a blast more rude,   5
The plaything of my gusty mood,
In vain pursuing and pursued!

Nay, come although the boughs be bare,
Though snowflakes fledge the summer's nest,
And in some far Ausonian [2] air   10
The thrush, your minstrel, warm his breast.
Come, sunshine's treasurer, and bring
To doubting flowers their faith in spring,
To birds and me the need to sing!

[2] A choice viand or a dainty.
[3] See note on p. 217.

[1] Written in 1884 and first published in *Heartsease and Rue*.
[2] I.e., Italian.   The *Ausones* were a primitive people of lower Italy.

THE BROKEN TRYST [1]

WALKING alone where we walked together,
When June was breezy and blue,
I watch in the gray autumnal weather
The leaves fall inconstant as you.

If a dead leaf startle behind me,   5
I think 't is your garment's hem,
And, oh, where no memory could find me,
Might I whirl away with them!

THE LESSON [1]

I SAT and watched the walls of night
With cracks of sudden lightning glow,
And listened while with clumsy might
The thunder wallowed to and fro.

The rain fell softly now; the squall,   5
That to a torrent drove the trees,
Had whirled beyond us to let fall
Its tumult on the whitening seas.

But still the lightning crinkled keen,
Or fluttered fitful from behind   10
The leaden drifts, then only seen,
That rumbled eastward on the wind.

Still as gloom followed after glare,
While bated breath the pine-trees drew,
Tiny Salmoneus [2] of the air,   15
His mimic bolts the firefly threw.

---

[1] Published in *Heartsease and Rue*.

[1] Published in *Heartsease and Rue*.

[2] The son of Æolus, who tried to imitate lightning by means of blazing torches. As a punishment Jupiter with a lightning-bolt hurled him into the infernal regions.

He thought, no doubt, "Those flashes grand,
That light for leagues the shuddering sky,
Are made, a fool could understand,
By some superior kind of fly.   20

"He's of our race's elder branch,
His family-arms the same as ours,
Both born the twy-forked flame to launch,
Of kindred, if unequal, powers."

And is man wiser?   Man who takes   25
His consciousness the law to be
Of all beyond his ken, and makes
God but a bigger kind of Me?

LETTERS

ELMWOOD

(Original drawing by Julian F. Bechtold.)

LETTERS

1. To C. F. Briggs. (L., I, 104–7) [1]

Elmwood, Feb. 18, 1846.

My dear Friend,— . . . Transmitted peculiarities and family resemblances have always been a matter of interesting speculation with me, and I sometimes please myself with the fancy that the motto of our family arms—*Occasionem cognosce* [2]—may indicate a similar feeling to my own in the mind of the ancestor who first adopted it. Be that as it may, I never wrote a letter which was not a sincere portrait of my mind at the time, and therefore never one whose contents can hold a rod over me. My pen has not yet traced a line of which I am either proud or ashamed, nor do I believe that many authors have written less from *without* than I, and therefore more piously.

. . . My calling is clear to me. I am never lifted up to any peak of vision—and moments of almost fearful inward illumination I have sometimes—but that, when I look down in hope to see some valley of the Beautiful Mountains, I behold nothing but blackened ruins; and the moans of the down-trodden the world over—but chiefly here in our own land—come up to my ear, instead of the happy songs of the husbandmen reaping and binding the sheaves of light; yet these, too, I hear not seldom. Then I feel how great is the office of poet, could I but even dare to hope to fill it. Then it seems as if my heart would break in

---

[1] The following abbreviations are consistently used to indicate the works from which this selection of letters is reprinted:

L. = *Letters of James Russell Lowell,* edited by Charles Eliot Norton, 2 vols., New York, 1894.

N.L. = *New Letters of James Russell Lowell,* edited by M. A. DeWolfe Howe, New York, 1932.

Scudder = H. E. Scudder, *James Russell Lowell: A Biography,* 2 vols., Boston, 1901.

[2] Recognize your opportunity.

pouring out one glorious song that should be the gospel of Reform, full of consolation and strength to the oppressed, yet falling gently and restoringly as dew on the withered youth-flowers
of the oppressor. That way my madness lies, if any.[3]   Were I to
hang my harp (if we moderns may keep up the metaphor, at
least, of the old poets after losing their spirit) on a tree surrounded only by the very sweetest influence of summer nature,
and the wind should breathe through its strings, I believe they
would sound with a warlike clang.

I do not value much the antislavery feeling of a man who
would not have been abolitionist even if no such abomination as
American Slavery ever had existed. Such a one would come
home from an antislavery meeting to be the unhired overseer of
his wife and children and *help* (for I love our Yankee word,
teaching, as it does, the true relation, and its being equally
binding on master and servant), or he would make slaves of
them that he might go to one.   It is a very hard thing in society,
as at present constituted, for a male human being (I do not say
for a man) to avoid being a slaveholder.   I never see Maria
mending my stockings, or Ellen bringing the water for my
shower-bath in the morning, without hearing a faint tinkle of
chains.   Yet how avoid it?   Maria laughs when I propose to
learn darning, and Ellen flies into open rebellion and snatches
the pail out of my hands when I would fain assume half of the
old Israelitish drudgery, and become my own drawer of water.
After prolonged controversy and diplomatic negotiation day
after day on the cellar-stairs a treaty was concluded by which
I was always to bring up my own coal, and yet on this very
morning I surprised Ellen, in flagrant violation of the treaty,
half way upstairs on her way to my garret with a hodful.

. . . I read "Margaret"[4] when it first came out, having seen
extracted in a newspaper the account of Margaret's first visit to
the meeting-house. The book, as a whole, is clumsily con-
structed and not very well written, but there is a lovely *aura*

---

[3] Cf. Lear's "Oh, that way madness lies" (*King Lear,* III, iv, 20).
[4] A novel (1845) by the Reverend Sylvester Judd (1813–53), an American Unitarian clergyman.

about it which makes us love it, apart from its many glimpses of rare beauty and touches of genuine humor. Deacon Ramsdill is the first real Yankee I have seen in print. And this reminds me that I have always had it in my mind to write a New England novel which will astonish my friends if it ever gets delivered. Your amazement at a Puseyite Yankee [5] is unphilosophical. The cathedral-and-surplice-mania is the natural reaction from the old *slam-seat* (do you remember the racket after the "long" prayer, which the boys had established into as recognized a part of the services as the scarcely more harmonious noise of wind and catgut in the gallery, and which, being a free motion of the spirit and a genuine enjoyment, I consider as real worship?) meeting-houses and the puritanical creed. Shut Nature out at the door, and she will in at the window, says Sir Roger L'Estrange.[6] If men have not enough spirituality to find an inward beauty in Religion (a creed within the creed—recognized alike by Gentile and Christian), they will begin to bedizen her exterior. You never heard of a poet's sending a pair of earrings as a gift to his beloved (though he would find a lovely meaning in them if she chanced to wear them), yet it is a love of the same Beauty (though of a more savage and rude kind) which prompts such a gift in others. I had reserved Blanche [7] as the kernel of my letter, but I have filled it already, and she is so lovely that she will keep till my next. With much affectionate remembrance to you and yours,

We remain your loving friends,

her

Maria Lowell, Blanche X Lowell, and J.R.L.

mark

---

[5] I.e., a Yankee with a love for ritualism.—A Puseyite was a follower of the tenets of Dr. E. B. Pusey (1800–82), one of the leaders in the Tractarian movement within the Church of England. Puseyism strongly emphasized ceremonial and sacramental symbolism.

[6] Sir Roger L'Estrange (1616–1704), licenser of the press under Charles II and first professional English journalist, published in 1692 a widely read work, *The Fables of Aesop and other eminent Mythologists, with Moral Reflections*. One of his reflections (1699 edition, p. 61) reads: "How impossible it is to make Nature change her biass, and that if we shut her out of the door, she'll come in at the window."

[7] His baby daughter, born December 31, 1845.

2. To the Same. (L., I, 130–31)

Elmwood, May 12, 1848.

My dear Friend,— . . . Here I am in my garret. I slept here when I was a little curly-headed boy, and used to see visions between me and the ceiling, and dream the so often recurring dream of having the earth put into my hand like an orange. In it I used to be shut up without a lamp—my mother saying that none of her children should be afraid of the dark—to hide my head under the pillows, and then not be able to shut out the shapeless monsters that thronged around me, minted in my brain. It is a pleasant room, facing, from the position of the house, almost equally towards the morning and the afternoon. In winter I can see the sunset, in summer I can see it only as it lights up the tall trunks of the English elms in front of the house, making them sometimes, when the sky behind them is lead-colored, seem of the most brilliant yellow. When the sun, towards setting, breaks out suddenly after a thunder-shower and I see them against an almost black sky, they have seemed of a most peculiar and dazzling green tint, like the rust on copper. In winter my view is a wide one, taking in a part of Boston. I can see one long curve of the Charles, and the wide fields between me and Cambridge, and the flat marshes beyond the river, smooth and silent with glittering snow. As the spring advances and one after another of our trees puts forth, the landscape is cut off from me piece by piece, till, by the end of May, I am closeted in a cool and rustling privacy of leaves. Then I begin to bud with the season. Towards the close of winter I become thoroughly wearied of closed windows and fires. I feel dammed up, and yet there is not flow enough in me to gather any head of water. When I can sit at my open window and my friendly leaves hold their hands before my eyes to prevent their wandering to the landscape, I can sit down and write. . . .

Your dear friend,

J. R. L.

3. To the Same. (L., I, 138–41)

Elmwood, Sunday, Sept. 3, 1848.

My dear Friend,— . . . For your other gift, of "Keats's Life," [1]
I have other thanks to offer.   It is a book that I have long desired
to see.   Indeed, I once meditated the raising of such a monument to him myself (it was in 1840), and I think, had even gone
so far as to write a letter to his brother George—which I never
sent.   Keats was a rare and great genius.   He had, I think, the
finest and richest fancy that has been seen since Shakespeare.
And his imagination gave promise of an equal development.
Ought we to sorrow for his early death, or to be glad that we
have in his works an eternal dawn of poesy, as in Shakespeare
we have early morning and full day?   Forever and forever shall
we be able to bathe our temples in the cool dew which hangs
upon his verse.

I love above all other reading the early letters of men of genius.
In that struggling, hoping, confident time the world has not
slipped in with its odious consciousness, its vulgar claim of con-
fidantship, between them and their inspiration.   In reading these
letters I can recall my former self, full of an aspiration which had
not learned how hard the hills of life are to climb, but thought
rather to alight down upon them from its winged vantage-
ground. Whose fulfilment has ever come nigh the glorious greatness of his yet never-balked youth?   As we grow older, art becomes to us a definite faculty, instead of a boundless sense of
power.   Then we felt the wings burst from our shoulders; they
were a gift and a triumph, and a bare flutter from twig to twig
seemed aquiline to us; but now our vans, though broader grown
and stronger, are matters of every day.   We may reach our
Promised Land; but it is far behind us in the Wilderness, in the
early time of struggle, that we have left our Sinais and our per-

---

[1] *Life, Letters, and Literary Remains of John Keats,* edited by Richard
Monckton Milnes, Lord Houghton (1809–85), and first published at London
in 1848.

sonal talk with God in the bush.[2]   I think it fortunate to have
dear friends far away.   For not only does absence have something of the sanctifying privilege of death, but we dare speak in
the little closet of a letter what we should not have the face to at
the corner of the street, and the more of our confidence we give
to another, the more are we ourselves enlarged.   It is good also,
on another account, to pour ourselves out, for it gives room for
other thoughts to be poured in. The mind and the heart must
have this outlet or they would stagnate. . . .

Your loving friend,
J. R. L.

4. To Robert Carter [1]

Rome, Saturday, 6th March, 1852.
68 Capo le Case, 3° P^o.[2]

My dear Friend,

I was very glad indeed to get your letter, and also the file of
the "Commonwealth" which you sent by W.W.S.[3]   It was odd
to be reading your quarrels here in the solemn quiets of old
Rome.   Shall I say that I was glad to be so far away?   Your
noise and confusion there made me almost dizzy.   'Twas like
stand[ing] on firm land and seeing a torrent rush by one carrying in a confused whirl houses, churches, oxen, trees, horses,
men and pigs in one swift headlong of higgledy-piggledy.   These
political freshets, I know, are the order of nature in America,
and we scramble unconcernedly upon firm land again, dry ourselves, and run up a shanty of repose that will last till the next

---

[2] God talked to Moses on Mt. Sinai and, earlier, out of a burning bush
on Mt. Horeb.   See Exodus iii and xxiv.

[1] Carter (1819–79) was an early intimate of Lowell's in Cambridge, and
in 1843 had edited with the latter a short-lived literary monthly, *The Pioneer*.
This letter now reposes in the University of Cincinnati Library, and the
portion written at Rome is here printed for the first time.
[2] Third floor.
[3] William Wetmore Story.   See note on p. 3.

election-flood. Even my dear old Study at Elmwood used to
shiver and tremble now and then. I am glad to learn from John
Holmes's [4] letter that you have got out of it, and are now engaged
in an editorial occupation which I hope will be permanent. The
Americans seem determined to carry the *fuss* of their institutions
with them, as the French do the milliner part of theirs. Accordingly a ball was got up for the 22nd February—with a committee
of Generals, Honorables and Esquires—to which none but Americans were admitted. I confess myself opposed to this importa-
tion of 4th Julyism. I did not go, but I understand that the
Committee had the satisfaction of spending six hundred and odd
dollars in providing a bore for one hundred and fourteen of their
countrymen. Bores (as the stock reports say) must be lively
when they are "quoted" at six dollars a head.

You will wish to have some of my impressions of Rome, but
I hardly know where to begin. I was quite unprepared for two
things—the modern appearance of the city, and the great beauty
of the mountain-horizon which shuts it in on two sides. As a
Christian (in distinction from an Imperial) city, the oldest-
looking things in it are the Romanesque *campaniles* [5] of some
of the churches, the façades and interiors of nearly all having
been restored by some Pope or Cardinal in what to me is rather
an *op*pressive than an *im*pressive style of architecture. Even
buildings really old do not look so—they are built so strongly
and the climate is so *antiseptic,* so to speak. The side of the
King's Chapel on School Street,[6] seems more weatherworn and
more ancient than the back of the capitol here, which we know
was built in the time of the Republic, and even the *Cloaca
Maxima,*[7] which is of Etruscan masonry, does not show so great

---

[4] John Holmes (1812–99), the younger brother of Dr. Oliver Wendell
Holmes, was a life-long Cambridge friend.

[5] Bell-towers.

[6] A famous Boston landmark located on the corner of Tremont and
School Streets, and dating from 1745.

[7] The great conduit which was first built about the sixth century B.C. to
drain into the Tiber River the marshy ground beneath the Roman Forum.
Only the side walls are now visible by the Tiber bank near the Palatine
Bridge.

symptoms of senility as that drain which they discovered in digging the foundations of the Brattle House.[8] Even the Roman costumes have in a great measure disappeared. Some of the women go so far as to wear bonnets, and one must go into the country to see what was once universal in the streets of Rome. In the Trastevere,[9] you may see a little of it—but not much— and that chiefly among the men—who still wear the tall hat with the brim turned up on one side and a cock's or peacock's feather, or a flower (real or artificial) twisted into the band, as an Irishman carries his pipe—a short velvet jacket, velvet breeches held up by a bright sash tied round the waist, and white stockings. The dress of the women at this season is a gown made of coarse plaid in which the colors of grey and muddy purple predominate. The headcloth has almost wholly gone out of wear, but the bonnet has not yet (fortunately) taken its place, so that the head is only covered by the magnificent hair, on which a good deal of pains is bestowed, and which is the only part of their persons in which they are neat. Carnival taught me to lament the disappearance of the costumes. During carnival week, the women of the lower class dress themselves in the peculiar costume of their native place, and either ride in the Corso,[10] or sit along the sides of the street. The brilliant *bustos* [11] and skirts of satin are picturesque in themselves and especially becoming to a race of women distinguished above any I have seen for the noble proportions of the neck and bosom and for the peculiar dignity with which the head and shoulders are carried—the result in part, no doubt, of the universal habit of bearing waterjars upon the head. I think I never before saw so many beautiful women—nor does the mere word beautiful by any means express all. One must add the epithet magnificent, and then say further that they are characterized by a

---

[8] A now vanished hostelry, opened in 1850 on Brattle Square, near Harvard Square, in the heart of old Cambridge.

[9] "The District across the Tiber," i.e., the region along the west bank of the river to the south of St. Peter's and Vatican City.

[10] The long straight avenue running northward from the Capitoline Hill, the ancient center of Rome, to the People's Square, where the Flaminian Way begins.

[11] Shirtwaists.

dignity and grace of manner quite peculiar to them. At least I have not found it in the higher class here whether Italian or foreign, least of all in the English, who are noisy and pushing, not so much from ignorance as from arrogance, and the cause of whose unpopularity on the continent is plain at a glance. The more I see of the Romans the better I like them. Not much less civil than the Tuscans,[12] their bearing is more independent— more American I should say, if you could add to the American character a certain natural ease and repose of manner. They seem a very amiable people. I have only seen one quarrel since I have been in Rome. I have never even heard the boys quarreling in their play. Of course, I do not consider this as proving that such things do not take place, but it does prove that they are rare, for I have been all over Rome on foot and have watched the people pretty closely. I think I would give more for a Roman's word than for that of a Tuscan. In Florence a hackman is scarcely ever satisfied with the fare agreed upon. In Rome I have never been asked for more than the stipulated sum. Now, *a fortiori,*[13] a good quality which can be predicated of this class of society, may be safely predicated of all, for I take it that, except *Red Republicans,*[14] there is no part of the population so thoroughly execrated and feared by Europeans in general as this.

After all, except so far as Art is concerned, I doubt if one gains much by staying long in Europe. I fancy that one of our rapid American travelers, (supposing him to have real eyes in his head) who should keep an accurate journal, so that his brain did not lose images as rapidly as a kaleidoscope, would carry away more vivid impressions of places than those who spend more time. The eye so soon gets toned to a particular key and the mind adjusted to a new standard, that in a few weeks things the most strange become commonplace. It is only by a definite

---

[12] Inhabitants of the old duchy of Tuscany, the territory adjoining the old Roman kingdom on the north. The ducal seat was Florence.

[13] With stronger reason.

[14] I.e., extreme political radicals.—The term came into being at the time of the French Revolution (1789), when a red liberty cap was the badge of the extreme republicans.

exercise of the mind that I can appreciate, for instance, the height and size of buildings here. I realize it, however, when I find myself speaking of our *little* parlor which is larger than any room at Elmwood, and when I look at the *baldacchino* [15] in St. Peter's which looks in that vast solitude about as high as your house, and *is* ninety four feet in height. Perhaps the first thing that will strike an American in Rome is the immense number of priests in their peculiar costume, and the troops of boys and young men from the different public educational establishments dressed in clerical habits of different colors. The students of the German College you see alighted in a long string on some promontory of the Pincio [16] like a flock of flamingoes—their costume being scarlet with a long trailer fluttering from each shoulder. You would think that priests, soldiers and *gens d'armes* [17] formed the bulk of the population, indeed, they cannot be far from a fourth part of it. As for the church ceremonies, they are all alike, and all tedious, nor have I found them even picturesque except in St. Peter's where one can get sufficient distance to group and mass the colors a little. Yet middleaged Englishmen, who, one would say, might find enough to do in endeavoring to solve their own social problem, come hither and get converted, and fancy they have got an idea when they have only received a sensation.

April 28th.

My dear Friend, you know me well enough and have enough trust in my thorough love and esteem for you, to forgive me for being a month and a half in writing a letter. I sit down to finish this in a spare minute on the day before leaving Rome for Naples. My trunk is packed, my contract with the *vetturino* [18] signed, and I am awaiting the pleasant visit of my *padrona di casa* [19] to go over the inventory of cups and spoons and chairs and every et cetera that you can think of. Since I began this

[15] The ornamental bronze canopy over the high altar.
[16] See note on p. 6.
[17] Policemen.
[18] Cab-driver.
[19] Landlady.

letter we have had Holy Week and you may fancy how fond
I am of Catholic ceremonies when I tell you that I walked out
of town on Easter Sunday and spent the day at what they call
the Grotto of Egeria.[20] The illumination of St. Peter's in the
evening, however, is something miraculous—a thing to cross the
ocean for—and the Girandola [21] was certainly the most tasteful
as it was the most brilliant display of fireworks I ever saw. I
wish you would tell Professor Pierce with my kindest regards,
that I gave his Astronomical Journal to Padre Secchi the head
of the Observatory here—and that he will doubtless write an
acknowledgment. Tell him also that his pamphlet was the
means of making me acquainted with the Padre himself, a most
intelligent (you know I do not apply such terms at random)
and kindhearted Jesuit who has just made some discoveries (I
believe they are) in the light and heat of the sun which he will
probably communicate ere long to Professor P. Through Padre
Secchi I became acquainted with Padre Marchi, another Jesuit
of whom you have often heard our friend the Count speak as a
"most distinguished archaeologue."

April 30. Terracina.[22]

At this point of my letter came my *padrona* and after that
came friends to bid goodbye and now * here [23] I am at Terracina,
with a magnificent cliff opposite my window crowned by twelve
arches of what is called the Palace of Theodoric. I have just
come in from seeing the Cathedral, the dirtiest church I have
seen in Italy, (with a very picturesque old campanile, however)

---

[20] A grotto in which, according to legend, the nymph Egeria gave lessons
in statecraft to Numa Pompilius, successor to Romulus as king of Rome.
The grotto with its fountain in the form of a nymph is located on the side
of a wooded eminence about two miles south of Rome to the east of the
Appian Way.

[21] Lit., the Pinwheel: this fireworks festival at Rome was so called because large and elaborate pinwheels originally formed the principal element
in the display. See p. 319 for further description.

[22] A seashore resort for the fashionable society of ancient Rome, lying
about seventy-five miles southeast of the capital.

[23] The portion of this letter between the two asterisks was printed in
H. E. Scudder, *James Russell Lowell*, I, 343–44.

and the remains of the old Roman Port, which astonished me by their size even after all I had seen of Roman hugeness. The port is now filled with soil and there is a fine orange garden where vessels used to lie. Terracina is nothing like what I expected to see. The Inn (or "Grand' Albergo" as it is called) is one of the least cutthroat-looking places I ever saw. It is quite out of the town between the great cliff and the sea. Behind it, on the beach, the scene is quite Neapolitan—forty or fifty bare-legged fishermen are drawing a great seine out of the water and forty or fifty dirty, laughing, ragged, happily-wretched children gather round you and beg for *caccose* or *caccò* by which they mean *qualche cosa*.[24] The women sit round the doors nasty and contented urging on their offspring in their professional career. They are the most obstinate beggars I have seen yet. In Rome the waving of the two first fingers of the hand and a decided *non c'è* [25] is generally sufficient, but here I tried every expedient in vain.—The prickly pear grows bloatedly in all the ledges of the cliff, an olive orchard climbs halfway up the back of it where the hill is less steep, and farther to the left there are tall palms in a convent-garden—but I cannot see them.—The drive over the Pontine Marshes is for more than twenty miles a perfectly straight, smooth avenue, between double rows of elms. I had been told it was very dull—but did not find it so—for there were mountains on one side of us, cultivated, or cattle and horse-covered fields or woods on the other, and the birds sang and the sun shone all the way. It seemed like the approach to some prince's pleasure-house. . . . On the whole, the result of my experience thus far is that I am glad I came abroad—though the knowledge one acquires must rust for want of use in a great measure at home. To be sure one's political ideas are also some-what modified—I don't mean retrograded.* . . . In my next letter, I will give you some fine art news for your paper. The following is *not* for the paper but for yourself—Story has made a very successful bust of me which I am going to have put in

---

[24] Something.
[25] Nothing (lit., there is not).

marble. It is (I believe) the fifth likeness of me, either begun
or completed in Rome. The good old Chevalier Kestner (son
of Goethe's Charlotte) [26] also wished to do me. Expecting to
see you now in the course of six months, I remain, as ever, most
affectionately yours

J. R. L.

Don't mention the bust except to the Dr. and John.[27]

5. To Miss Rebecca Russell Lowell [1]
(Scudder, I, 338–41)

Rome, April 13, 1852.

. . . We are now within a fortnight of bidding farewell to
what I am now forced to call dear old Rome. In spite of its
occupation by an army of ten thousand French soldiers, in spite
of its invasion by that more terrible force, the column of English
travellers, in spite of the eternal drumming and bugling and
sentinelling in the streets, and the crowding of that insular Bull [2]
—*qui semper habet foenum in cornu* [3]—there is an insensible
charm about the place which grows upon you from hour to hour.
There must be few cities where one can command such absolute
solitude as here. One cannot expect it, to be sure, in the Colosseum by moonlight, for thither the English go by carriage loads

---

[26] Charlotte Buff (1753–1828), intimate friend of Goethe at Wetzlar in
1772–73. He provided the wedding ring on her marriage to Georg Kestner
in 1773, and then introduced her as a character, Lotte, in his novel
Werther (1774).

[27] Dr. Estes Howe, the husband of Mrs. Lowell's sister, and John Holmes.
These two, together with Lowell, Carter, and one or two other Cambridge
men formed the Whist Club, which lasted for some forty years until Lowell's
death in 1891.

[1] Lowell's older sister, b. 1809, d. unmarried 1872.
[2] I.e., the Englishman.
[3] Who always is a dangerous fellow (lit., who always has hay on the
horn). The figure is drawn from the old Roman practice of covering with
hay the horns of a bull who is apt to gore. Cf. Horace, *Satires*, I, 4: 34.

to be lonely with a footman in livery behind them, and to quote
Byron's stuff out of Murray's Guide;[4] there perch the French
in voluble flocks, under the necessity (more painful to them than
to any other people) of being poetical—chattering *Mon Dieu!
qu'un joli effet!*[5]   But an hour's walk will take one out into the
Campagna,[6] where you will look across the motionless heave of
the solitude dotted here and there with lazy cattle to the double
wall of mountain, the nearest opaline with change of light and
shadow, the farther Parian[7] with snow that only grows whiter
when the cloud shadows melt across it—the air overhead rippling
with larks too countless to be watched, and the turf around you
glowing with strange flowers, each a wonder, yet so numberless
that you would as soon think of gathering a nosegay of grass
blades.   On Easter Sunday I spent an incomparable day at the
Fountain of Egeria,[8] stared at sullenly, now and then, by one of
those great gray Campagna bulls, but totally safe from the English variety which had gone to get broken ribs at St. Peter's.
The show-box unholiness of Holy Week is at last well over.   The
best part of it was that on Holy Thursday all the Vatican was
open at once—fifteen miles of incomparable art.   For me the
Pope washed perfumed feet, and the Cardinal Penitentiary
wielded his long rod in vain.   I dislike such spectacles naturally,
and saw no reason why I should undergo every conceivable sort
of discomfort and annoyance for the sake of another discomfort
or annoyance at the end. . . .

The finest *show* I have seen in Rome is the illumination of
St. Peter's.   Just after sunset I saw from the head of the *scali-
nata*,[9] the little points of light creeping down from the cross
and lantern (trickling, as it were) over the dome.   Then I

---

[4] Byron in *Childe Harold's Pilgrimage* (Canto IV, stanzas 128–30) pictures "this vast and wondrous monument" in the moonlight.—John Murray
(1808–92), London publisher, started in 1836 the first series of travelers'
handbooks.

[5] My goodness!   What a lovely effect!

[6] The low pastoral plain to the south and east of Rome.

[7] I.e., white as the marble of Paros, one of the Greek islands in the Ægean
Sea.

[8] See note on p. 315.

[9] Flight of steps.

walked over to the Piazza di San Pietro, and the first glimpse I caught of it again was from the Ponte Sant' Angelo. I could not have believed it would have been so beautiful. There was no time or space to pause here. Foot passengers crowding hither and thither as they heard the shout of *Avanti!* [10] from the coachmen behind—dragoon-horses getting unmanageable just where there were most women to be run over—and all the while the dome drawing all eyes and thoughts the wrong way, made a hubbub to be got out of as soon as possible. Five minutes more of starting and dodging, and we were in the piazza. You have seen it and know how it seems, as if the setting sun had lodged upon the horizon and then burnt out, the fire still clinging to its golden ribs as they stand out against the evening sky. You know how, as you come nearer, you can see the soft travertine of the façade suffused with a tremulous golden gloom like the innermost shrine of a water-lily. And then the change comes as if the wind had suddenly fanned what was embers before into flame. If you could see *one* sunset in a lifetime and were obliged to travel four thousand miles to see it, it would give you a similar sensation; but an everyday sunset does not, for we take the gifts of God as a matter of course.

After wondering long enough in the piazza, I went back to the Pincio (or rather the Trinità dei Monti [11]) and watched it for an hour longer. I did not wish to see it go out. To me it seemed better to go home with the consciousness that it was still throbbing, as if I could make myself believe that there was a kind of permanence in it, and that I should see it there again some happy evening. Before leaving it, I went away and came back several times, and at every return it was a new miracle—the more miraculous for being a human piece of fairy work.

Last night there was another wonder, the Girandola,[12] which we saw excellently well from the windows of the American legation. Close behind me, by the way, stood Silvio Pellico (a

---

[10] Look out ahead!

[11] A large, picturesque square adjoining the Villa Medici Gardens near the Pincio.

[12] See p. 315 and note.

Jesuit now), a little withered old man in spectacles, looking so very dry that I could scarce believe he had ever been shut up in a *damp* dungeon in his life. This was (I mean the Girandola) the most brilliant and at the same time tasteful display of fireworks I ever saw. I had no idea that so much powder could be burned to so good purpose. For the first time in my life I saw rockets that seemed endowed with life and intelligence. They might have been thought filled with the same vivacity and enjoyment so characteristic of the people. Our rockets at home seem businesslike in comparison. They accomplish immense heights in a steady straightforward way, explode as a matter of course, and then the stick hurries back to go about its terrestrial affairs again. And yet why should I malign those beautiful slow curves of fire, that I have watched with Charlie and Jemmie [13] from Simonds's Hill,[14] and which I would rather see again than twenty Girandolas? If Michelangelo had designed our fireworks, and if it did not by some fatal coincidence always rain on the evening of 4th July, doubtless they would be better. . . .

6. To C. F. Briggs (L., I, 205–6)

Elmwood, Nov. 25, 1853.

My dear old Friend,—Your letter came while I was sadly sealing up and filing away my old letters, for I feel now for the first time old, and as if I had a past—something, I mean, quite alien to my present life, and from which I am now exiled. How beautiful that past was and how I cannot see it clearly yet for my tears I need not tell you. I can only hope and pray that the sweet influences of thirteen years spent with one like her may be seen and felt in my daily life henceforth. At present I only feel that there *is* a chamber whose name is Peace, and which

---

[13] His nephews, Charles Russell Lowell, Jr., and James Jackson Lowell.

[14] A piece of high ground formerly located to the east of Elmwood near the bank of the Charles River, but long since leveled away. Its crest was approximately on the site of the present Cambridge Hospital, Mt. Auburn Street.

opens towards the sunrising, and that I am not in it. I keep repeating to myself "by and by," "by and by," till that trivial phrase has acquired an intense meaning. I know very well that this sunset-glow, even of a life like hers, will fade by degrees; that the brisk, busy day will return with its bills and notes and beef and beer, intrusive, distracting—but in the meantime I pray. I do abhor sentimentality from the bottom of my soul, and cannot wear my grief upon my sleeves, but yet I look forward with agony to the time when she may become a memory instead of a constant presence. She promised to be with me if that were possible, but it demands all the energy of the soul to believe without sight, and all the unmetaphysical simplicity of faith to distinguish between fact and fancy. I know that the little transparent film which covers the pupil of my eye is the only wall between her world and mine, but that hair-breadth is as effectual as the space between us and the sun. I cannot see her, I cannot feel when I come home that she comes to the door to welcome me as she always did. I can only hope that when I go through the last door that opens for all of us I may hear her coming step upon the other side. That her death was so beautiful and calm and full of faith as it was gives me no consolation, for it was only that rare texture of her life continuing to the very end, and makes me feel all the more what I had and what I have not.

I began this upon a great sheet because it reminded me of the dear old times that are dead and buried now. But I cannot write much more. I keep myself employed most of the time—in something mechanical as much as possible—and in walking. . . .

So God bless you, and think of me always as your more loving friend,

J. R. L.

7. To Miss Mabel Lowell.[1] (N.L., 59–61)

Delmonico's Hotel, New York, 1st June, 1855.

Darling little pussy,—so it seems that Papa need not have said goodbye in such a hurry, after all, for the ship will not sail till Monday. However, I have plenty to do while I stay here, in dodging dinners. I have been on board the ship and looked at the little stateroom in which I am to be shut up and find it as good as I expected.

The ship is named the Saint Nicholas, and under the bowsprit is a great figure of the Saint holding up his hand in the act of blessing. I hope he will keep the waves smooth—don't you?

Yesterday afternoon I went into Barnum's Museum [2] to see if I could find something that you would like to hear about, and I found there two tall ostriches, taller than men, and big enough to carry Miss Hopkins very easily. They were in a kind of pen downstairs. Upstairs there was a giantess—the biggest one I ever saw, and a fat girl that looked as if she had been meant for a mammoth pumpkin, and had grown into a girl by mistake, and a very little dwarf girl, and an albino—ask Miss Dunlap [3] what an albino is. But the greatest curiosity of all was the woman with a beard—that is, she was the greatest except her baby, which had whiskers almost as large as papa's.

It was very droll indeed to see all these sitting upon a platform in a row to be stared at. How would you like it? But then you need not be troubled, for very few people but papa would give a quarter of a dollar to see you.

Darling, I would give a great deal—and I thought of coming home again—but would rather not have to say goodbye again. Your likeness is a great pleasure to me. I looked at it the last thing before I went to bed, and the first when I got up this morning. I have been to Newark today, and little cousin Manna

---

[1] Lowell's second daughter, b. Sept. 9, 1847.

[2] See note on p. 43.

[3] Frances Dunlap, Mabel's governess, who in 1857 became the second Mrs. Lowell.

was very sorry for Mabel because her Papa was going away.
Be a good little girl and I will try to be a good little Papa, for
it would not do at all for a little girl to be better than her Papa,
would it?   You forgot to give me a lock of your hair.

This is a monstrous kiss,
like the fat girl I saw at the
museum—a kiss that has been
growing on the kiss-tree ever since
I saw you last and just dropt off. It is
shaped a little like a pear—and those are
the sweetest, because when they are not
pairs they are good for nothing. God
bless you, sweetest little daughter! I shall
write to you again before I sail. Give
my love to Miss Dunlap and Aunt
Lois.

PAPA

8. TO MISS ANNA LORING. (L., I, 240–42)

No. 4, Kleine Schiessgasse, Dresden, Oct. 3, 1855.

. . . I am *beim* [1] Herrn Hofrath Dr. Reichenbach, who is one
of the kindest of men, and Madame is a "first-rate fullah" too,
as my nephew Willie would say. I have a large room *am
Parterre,* [2] with a glass door opening upon a pretty garden.   My
walls are hung with very nice pictures painted by the *gnädige
Frau* [3] herself; and they were so thoughtful as to send down

[1] At the house of.
[2] On the ground floor.
[3] Gracious lady.

before I came a large case with American birds very well stuffed
and mounted, so that I might have some friends. Some of them
are very familiar, and I look at the oriole sometimes till I hear
him whistling over the buttercups in the dear old times at Elmwood. Ah, how deep out of the past his song comes! But *hin
ist hin, verloren ist verloren!* [4] Then I have one of those solemn
ceremonials, a German bed—with a feather-bed under which I
engrave myself at night and dream that I am awaiting the last
trump. Then I have the prettiest writing-table, bought *exprès
pour moi* [5] by Madame, *weil ich ein Dichter bin* [6]—and at which
I am now sitting—with drawers for everything and nothing.
I rack my brains for what to put in 'em. I am fast turning into
a "regular" German, according to the definition of that Italian
innkeeper at Amalfi, who told me, speaking of a man that was
drowned, "bisognerebbe che fosse un Tedesco perchè sempre
stava a casa, e non faceva niente che fumare e studiare." [7] I get
up *um sieben Uhr,* [8] and *das Mädchen* [9] brings me my coffee and
Butterbrod [10] at 8. Then I begin to study. I am reading for
my own amusement (*du lieber Gott!*) [11] the *aesthetische For-
schungen von* [12] Adolf Zeising, pp. 568, large octavo! Then I
overset something *aus* [13] German into English. Then comes
dinner at 1 o'clock, with *ungeheuer* [14] German dishes. *Nach-
mittag* [15] I study Spanish with a nice young Spaniard who is in
the house, to whom I teach English in return. *Um sechs Uhr
ich gehe spazieren,* [16] and at 7 come home, and Dr. R. dictates
and I write. *Aber potztausend Donnerwetter!* [17] what a lan-

---

[4] Gone is gone, lost is lost!
[5] Especially for me.
[6] Because I am a poet.
[7] He must have been a German because he always stayed at home, and
did nothing but smoke and study.
[8] At seven o'clock.
[9] The maid-servant.
[10] Bread and butter.
[11] Thou dear God!
[12] Studies in aesthetics of, etc.
[13] From.
[14] Huge.
[15] In the afternoon.
[16] At six o'clock I go and take a walk.
[17] But a thousand damnations (lit., thunderstorms)!

guage it is to be sure! with nominatives sending out as many
roots as that witch-grass which is the pest of all child-gardens,
and sentences in which one sets sail like an admiral with sealed
orders, not knowing where the devil he is going to till he is in
mid-ocean! Then, after tea, we sit and talk German—or what
some of us take to be such—and which I speak already like a
native—of some other country. But Madame R. is very kind
and takes great pains to set me right. The confounded genders!
If I die I will have engraved on my tombstone that I died of *der,
die, das,* not because I caught 'em, but because I couldn't. Dr.
R. is one of the most distinguished *Naturwissenschaftsgelehr-
ten* [18] (!!) in Europe—a charming, friendly, simple-hearted man.
I attend his *Vorlesungen und etwas verstehe.*[19] . . .

9. To Mrs. Estes Howe. (N.L., 70–72)

Dresden, 4th November, 1855.

My dear Lois,—I was very glad, as I always am and shall be,
to hear from you. I am afraid I was in one of my moods when
I wrote my last letter to you. If I was, please burn it and forget it.
It is tolerably lonely over here, you may be sure—lonely as it is
for a boy the first week or two at a boardingschool—but worse,
because with a man of my age the loneliness is inside instead of
outside, and so *lasts*. But I am busy all the time and that is the
best medicine. It is not Time, as people are apt to say, but
activity that heals mental wounds. Time is no doctor at all,
on the contrary, if one has nothing to do but think, Time only
exasperates our old sores. The cut skins over, but the twinges
come back whenever it is cloudy weather. Death only practises
on Sir Kenelm Digby's theory of sympathetic cures,[1] and repairs

---

[18] Most distinguished and most learned natural scientists.
[19] Lectures and understand *somewhat*.

[1] See note on p. 4. Digby first described his "sympathetic" principle
for curing wounds and disease in "A late Discourse. . . . Touching the
Cure of wounds by the Powder of Sympathy" (1658). A bandage was
laid upon the wound, then taken from it, immersed in the "powder of sympathy" (really powdered vitriol), and kept there until the wound healed.

the evil he has done with a touch of the same arrow that caused it. Do you know what today is? It is the fifteenth anniversary of the happiest day of my life—the day of my betrothal with the noblest woman I have ever known. Dear Lois, it is little to say that such a loss is irreparable—it becomes every day a greater loss—and a real sorrow is forever at compound interest. I look sadly at my weddingring and it is empty as a magic circle after the Prospero [2] is dead who traced it—the obedient spirits come no more. My greatest comfort over here is that I know I am doing what she would have liked, and I thank God that I can say with a clear front that thus far I have been faithful in deed and thought to so pure a memory. I have a great deal of love to spare now, dear Lois, and you must consent to take a large part of it.

But I meant to write you a purely domestic letter, and instead of being in Dresden, I have been sitting on the hill in Watertown on a hazy November afternoon, and putting asters into the hole in the rock, (do you remember it?) that was always full of water and which we used to call the Fairy Well. [3] The village basks below me in the tremulous Indian Summer air. The roofs seem to ripple in the streaming sunwarmth—the fields lie broad and still, and a sweet voice recites the ballad of Binnorie [4] —but the whole vision splits and splinters in the prism of tears. My God, what an enchantress is Memory that she can make it seem better to *have* lived than to live! If I could only command *her* as she commands her good and evil spirits, I should be perfectly happy. I would live forever in the two or three brightest days of my life, and only look forward when the gates of the next world opened, when the inner side of the veil which drops be-

Digby's method of cure has been copied widely by quack doctors and is still in existence.

[2] The magician in Shakespeare's *The Tempest*.

[3] Howe (*N.L.*, 71) prints "Fairy Wall," an obvious misreading.

[4] An English border ballad, the burden of which is "Bínnorie, O Bínnorie." It is usually entitled "The Cruel Sister" and relates a sad tale of love and violence. The elder of two sisters who were in love with the same man pushed the younger into the water one day and caused her death by drowning. After the body had been recovered by a miller, a passing harper took the breast-bone and the yellow hair of the dead sister and made a harp therefrom. This instrument, on being taken to the hall of the girl's father, began to play a tune all alone and to chant a revealing lament.

tween us and life began to glow with faint reflections of the splendor beyond. Dear Lois, forgive me but I *must* run over now and then or I should go stark staring mad some fine afternoon as I was laughing and joking with my evil spirit ever at my elbow. I have nobody to say a word to here, and I cannot pour myself out in verses, for I have to work all the time. And work enough I have before me. I have just bought Goethe in forty volumes and I must read him and a great deal more in the course of the winter. I am at it from the time I get up till I go to bed except my hours for dinner and walking. . . .

The Cholera is here in Dresden, but you need fear nothing about my health. I have nothing but the old pain in my side which I have almost got used to now as one does to the striking of a clock so that one does not hear it. Did I ever laugh at your chillblains? If I did, a judgment is come upon me, for I have had them scandalously as if an army of fleas had encamped on each foot and were digging trenches. I do nothing but rub one foot atop of tother and say *Creuz Donner Wetter! Empfehle mich dem gnädigen Fräulein Fay. Ich möchte gern einen Brief von ihr bekommen.*[5]—Goodbye, dear Lois, I have got to the end of my sheet just in time, for here comes Madame R. to go and visit a painter—whose pictures I wish were—hung! God bless you!

J. R. L.

10. To William W. Story [1]
(N.L., 72-4; H.C.L. Ms. Am. 183.30)

Dresden, den 10 Nov. 1855.

Hochwohlgeborner Edelmann! [2]—do you think, because you don't write to me, that I shall know nothing about you? Don't

---

[5] Say thunder and damnation [lit., cross-thunder-weather]! Commend me to the gracious Miss Fay [Mrs. Howe's maiden name]. I should like to receive a letter from her.

[1] This letter, now in the possession of the Harvard College Library, is here printed in its entirety for the first time. Howe omitted a considerable number of highly interesting remarks and also made slight revisions.

[2] Honorable Sir (lit., high and noble gentleman)!

you know enough of human nature yet, (*you,* in the neighborhood of Forty—is that written plainly enough?) to conceive that
I shall hear no good of you unless you write it yourself? Don't
I know that you want to buy a great estate in Cambridge, and
that you also want to buy it for nothing? Now let me reason
with you a little. *What* do you want fifteen acres for? Do you
expect to supply Europe with wheat? Do you mean to raise
your own potatoes and pay three and ninepence apiece for 'em?
Go rather and dig those of one of your neighbors and have the
good of the exercise! Do you want to raise fruittrees? Farewell, then, your peace of mind forever! There are (ask Dr.
Harris) if I remember, ninety-six varieties of insects with a
penchant [3] for pears, forty-three with an appetite for apples,
thirty-one that poison peaches, and twenty-seven and three
quarters that puncture plums. Your imagination will be as full
of bugs as a drop of water under the solar mikroscope. You
will go through every form of disease to which your pets are
incident—(and all the beds in your garden will be beds in a
hospital)—Edelmann Storg.[4] You will have the blackwart with
the plums, the yellow with the peaches, the cracks (or whatever
they call it) with the pears, and worst of all, be bored with the
apples—*Crede Experto!* [5] Or do you want fifteen acres to walk
over perhaps? Again I say walk over your neighbor's land and
wear that out—there is some sense in that. Is it a sense of
proprietorship you wish to buy? Then buy a dog with nomadic
propensities, and you won't forget for five minutes at a time
that you own something. Archimedes [6] was the only man who
ever had right notions about landed property—enough to stand

---

[3] Liking.

[4] According to F. H. Underwood (as quoted by Howe in *New Letters,*
72n) Lowell's humorous appellation "Storg" grew out of a Swiss innkeeper's
misreading of the name "Story" on one occasion when Lowell and his friend
were traveling together. Frank P. Stearns (*Cambridge Sketches,* 107)
claims that Story really was an "edelmann," or "nobleman," by virtue of a
patent given him by King "Bomba," or Ferdinand II, of the Two Sicilies
(1810–59). The King issued the patent to reward Story for selling to
American friends in Rome some oil paintings belonging to the Sicilian king.

[5] Believe an experienced person.

[6] Noted Greek mathematician and engineer (*c*. 287–212 B.C.), who discovered the law of specific gravity.

on for the time being was all he asked for,—and that a man can always borrow. Two feet square will hold a man with all his joys and sorrows, farreaching hopes, and highpoising imaginations. *Cujus est solum, ejus est usque ad coelum,*[7] you know, and even to two feet square that is a very handsome piece of property, and one that takes most of us a good while to walk *to the other end of*. Perhaps you have eaten of the insane root Speculation? You mean to buy property that will rise? Invest in a basin of soapsuds and a tobacco pipe, then; it is inexpensive, and will amuse the children. If you *buy* land, it won't go up any more than a balloon with carbonic acid gas in it. *Nothing* will start it. Everything and everybody conspires against you. They build railways in other directions on purpose—they put up offensive manufactures on the next lot—they swindle you with taxes—they run highways through you and make you pay for 'em—they carry off your rails for fuel and your stone walls for the fun of it—and your land stays on your hands as a plain girl sits beside her mother in a ballroom—*eternumig: sedebit*[8]— and no one enquires after it.

The only gleam of reason in your plan is the desire to buy in Cambridge. *That* is sensible. There stick. 'Tis as good a climate to raise statues in as any in the world, not to speak of the resident gentry—some of the most agreeable of whom are now unhappily in Europe. But they will come back if they live. So, be a good boy and buy a house in Cambridge, but suppress all ambition. You can't expect to rival the *great hereditary proprietors*—that would be madness—but buy a modest house and you will not find even the Duke of Thompsonlot[9] too proud to come and eat *maccaroni in tamburro*[10] with you.

Maccaroni—that reminds me of what an Italian feast I have

---

[7] Whosesoever is the soil, it is his up to the sky.

[8] Eternally: it will sit.

[9] A humorous title which Lowell conceived and bestowed upon himself as a Cambridge landowner.

[10] Lit., macaroni in a drum.—This phrase is not a recognised Italian idiom, but was evidently coined by Lowell's humorous fancy to denote macaroni which is cooked and served in a casserole or a round receptacle of some kind.

been having. La Ristori [11] has been playing here—a head and shoulders greater than she was in Rome. The Germans call her *eine der am grössten tragischen Erscheinungen,*[12] or something of the sort, but they don't go to see her because the prices are raised, and because—she is an Italienerina. They would choose sourkrout rather than ambrosia because it is Dutch. They think no country beautiful, fertile, no people wise, brave, beautiful—out of this confounded Dutchland. However, there is one accomplished foreigner in Dresden and *he* goes every night and shouts *brava!* in the hope of giving a grammatical flavor to the *bravoes* of the audience, which of course the modest *schauspieler* [13] who leads in the heroine takes all to himself and blushes with pleasure through his paint. But she [*i.e.,* Ristori] is splendid and I don't know whether it's association, for I saw her in happier times—but she makes me quite drunk with the sweetness of her Italian. I can't go to sleep after it.

But I am stealing the time to write this and I mustn't go on about Ristori or I shall need another sheet. Would you know my condition—fancy yourself a savage without a squaw, who has to get all his food by the chase, to make his own moccasins, and to darn his own stockings—only they don't wear any—I forgot that. Well, who *would* have to if he did wear 'em. I read nothing but German and as I have considerable appetite for learning, you may fancy the excursions I had to make at first into the forest of the dictionary. *Now* I have a tolerable winter's store of this vocabulary venison salted and dried, so that I live more at my ease. But nothing have I got without my own hard work—for I found I knew intolerably little Dutch when I came here. I am in a state of nature, æsthetically considered, and shall continue more or less so for some time to come. And how is Emmeline? [14] as I used to call her in the old, old times—times

---

[11] Adelaide Ristori (1822–1906), famous Italian tragic actress, during the winter of 1855–56 was touring Europe in presumable rivalry with France's premier tragedienne, Rachel, who was that season visiting the United States.

[12] One of the very grandest appearances in tragic drama.

[13] Actor.

[14] Mrs. W. W. Story, whose Christian name was Emelyn.

before the flood—God forgive me! Dear old times when the daughters of God loved the sons of men—the reverse of what it was before Noah—and horribly the reverse of what it is now, only in another sense. Goodbye. Be good and make a *Big* Beethoven.[15] I heard from Cranch [16] the other day. He is well—and poor as St. Francis. Give my love to Emelyn. And has the boy a name yet? The splendid great placidity! Tell him that Unku Dames has not forgotten him. Dinner! *zu Tisch!* [17]—Ever yours

J. R. L.

Write me a good long circumstantial letter. You don't have to study Dutch!

P.S. [on inside page] I never enjoyed any piece of property so much as a stack of hay which I saw carried off bodily by an inundation of the Charles. I was proud of the undecayed forces of my native stream and sacrificed the hay [with] exultation. I suppose he and his nereids stuffed their *beds* with it.

Tell Emelyn that I use those things she gave me for my bills and that there is not one on the "unpaid" side!

Tell me about Rachel.[18] I have not seen an American paper, not even *Galignani* [19] for five weeks.

I tried to write this straight but my hands are too cold. I know it's offensive to a well-regulated mind to see such scrimble-scramble—but I can't help it. Fancy it talked and it will all be straight enough.

---

[15] A humorous injunction to his sculptor friend to make a *large* bust or statue of the great German composer.

[16] Christopher Pearse Cranch (1813–92), a lifelong acquaintance of Lowell's, was an American painter, poet, and critic of inferior attainments.

[17] To dinner (lit., to table)!

[18] Elisabeth Rachel-Felix (1821–58), celebrated French tragic actress, born in Switzerland of Jewish parents. Her American tour of 1855 was not an unqualified success, and brought about a physical breakdown in 1856, from which she never recovered.

[19] *Galignani's Messenger,* a news gazette of great popularity with the English-speaking residents on the Continent during the nineteenth century. It was founded at Paris in 1814 by Giovanni Galignani (1752–1821), a well-known Italian publisher.

11. To Miss Jane Norton. (L., I, 269–72)

Cambridge, Sept. 9, 1856.
Mabel's Birthday.

. . . You see that I no longer date my letters "Elmwood," but simple "Cambridge." After thirty-seven years spent in the ship-house, only hearing afar the tumults of the sea, I am launched at last, and have come to anchor in *Professors' Row.*[1] Or am I rather a tree with my taproot cut? Or a moss-gathering bowlder gripped up by that cold iceberg Necessity, and dropped here at the corner of Oxford Street? We never find out on how many insignificant points we have fastened the subtile threads of asso-ciation—which is almost love with sanguine temperaments—till we are forced to break them; and perhaps, as we grow older, Fancy is more frugal of her web: spins it more for catching flies than from an overplus that justifies whim and wastefulness. . . .

. . . I will envy you a little your delightful two months in England—and a picture rises before me of long slopes washed with a cool lustre of watery sunshine—a swan-silenced reach of sallow-fringed river—great humps of foliage contrasting taper spires—cathedral closes, gray Gothic fronts elbowed by red-brick deaneries—broad downs clouded with cumulous sheep—nay, even a misty, moisty morning in London, and the boy with the pots of porter, and the hansom cab just losing itself in the uni-versal gray—even these sights I envy you. . . .

I suppose you think you are having all the green to yourselves over there—but there never was a greater mistake. The fates have given us an exceptional August—so unlike the common ones that I don't believe even the oysters found out what *r*-less month it was—rain every other day, so that trees and grass are like June, while at the same time we have the ripeness of the

---

[1] On his return from Europe in July, Lowell went to reside at the house of Dr. and Mrs. Estes Howe, located near the corner of Kirkland and Oxford Streets in the line of faculty mansions which faced the Harvard campus and was then called "Professors' Row."

middle-aged year instead of the girlishness of a season in its
teens. . . . The hills that you see beyond Charles as you go
towards Boston are superb, and then we have all the while those
glorious skies of ours, with the clouds heaped up like white foam-
bursts to set them off in full perfection. And the sunsets!
Europe has lost the art of shining skies as of staining glass—or
is it that our unthrift New World squanders like a young heir
just come into his estate, while grandam Europe is growing
close-fisted? Is our Nature Venetian with her gorgeous color,
or only Indian, painting herself savagely with the fiercest pigments? I am delighted with your *ma*triotism. "Rome, Venice,
Cambridge!" I take it for an ascending scale, Rome being the
first step and Cambridge the glowing apex. But you wouldn't
know Cambridge—with its railroad and its water-works and its
new houses. You remember our bit of Constantinopolitanism—
the burnt-out shell of the school-house on the Common? It is
gone, and a double house stares like an opera-glass in its place.
Think of a car passing our corner at Elmwood every fifteen minutes! Think of the most extraordinary little "Accommodation"
—an omnibus that holds four, with an Irish driver whose pride
in it is in the inverse ratio of its size—to carry one to the cars!
Think of a reservoir behind Mr. Wells's![2] And then think of
Royal Morse and John Holmes [3] and me in the midst of these phenomena! I seem to see our dear old village wriggling itself out
of its chrysalis and balancing its green wings till the sun gives
them color and firmness. Soon it will go fluttering with the
rest over the painted garden of this fool's paradise, trying to suck
honey from flowers of French crape.[4] For my part, I stick where
I was, and don't believe in anything new except butter.

To-morrow (for there is a gap of a week in this letter) we are

[2] Mr. William Wells (d. 1860), an Englishman of some learning, who
after an unsuccessful attempt to launch a publishing business in Boston,
set up a classical preparatory school for boys at the Fayerweather house in
Tory Row, now Brattle Street, not far from Elmwood. Lowell attended
this school during his teens.

[3] For Holmes see note on p. 311. Morse, a kinsman of Holmes, was a
schoolmate and playfellow of Lowell's.

[4] Flowers made of crinkled silk, or perhaps cotton, cloth; in other words,
artificial flowers.

to inaugurate Greenough's Franklin [5] with a tremendous procession—which I look at solely from a Mabelian point of view.[6] Did I say solely? Well, let it stand. But I may just mention that the American Academy [7] comes in before the governor, and Charles [8] perhaps can tell you who *some* of the fellows are. *It is thought* that they will find carriages provided for them. That under these circumstances I should find composure to write to you is a curious biological (I believe that's the word now) fact. There are to be two addresses and an oration. Only think how interesting! and we shall find out that Franklin was born in Boston, and invented being struck with lightning and printing and the Franklin medal, and that he had to move to Philadelphia because great men were so plenty in Boston that he had no chance, and that he revenged himself on his native town by saddling it with the Franklin stove, and that he discovered the almanac, and that a penny saved is a penny lost, or something of the kind. So we put him up a statue. *I* mean to invent something—in order to encourage sculptors. How to make butter from cocoanut milk, for example—or, by grafting the cocoanut with the breadfruit-tree, to make this last bear buttered muffins. Or, still better, if I could show folks how to find the penny they are to save. That has always been my difficulty. Or would it be enough to do as the modern poets, who invent the new by exaggerating the old, and be original by saying a *dollar* saved is a *dollar* lost—or we shall never feather our nests from the eagles we have let fly? . . .

---

[5] Richard Saltonstall Greenough (1819–1904), a leading American sculptor of the nineteenth century, made a bronze statue of Franklin, heroic in size, which stands in front of the Boston City Hall on a four-square pedestal of green marble adorned with bronze bas-reliefs. This splendid monument was unveiled with ceremonies of unprecedented extravagance for Boston.

[6] I.e., the point of view of a child who loves spectacle and pageantry. Lowell's daughter Mabel was just nine years old at the time.

[7] American Academy of Arts and Sciences was founded at Boston in 1780 under the chief sponsorship of John Adams as an elective body of notable men in the learned and creative fields.

[8] Charles Eliot Norton, her brother.

12. To C. E. Norton. (L., I, 272–73)

Cambridge, Sept. 16, 1856.

. . . I have just come in from a walk up the little lane that runs down behind the hill to Fresh Pond.[1] It is one of the few spots left *something* like what it was when I was a boy, and I can pick hazelnuts from the same bushes which brought me and the chipmunks together thirty years ago. I really think it is bad for our moral nature here in America that so many of the links that bind us to our past are severed in one way or another, and am grateful for anything that renews in me that capacity for mere delight which made my childhood the richest part of my life. It seems to me as if I had never seen nature again since those old days when the balancing of a yellow butterfly over a thistlebroom was spiritual food and lodging for a whole fore-noon. This morning I have had it all over again. There were the same high-heaped shagbark-trees—the same rosebushes with their autumn corals on—the same curving golden-rods and wide-eyed asters—the same heavy-headed goatsbeard—the same frank blue sky—the same cloud-shadows I used to race with—the same purple on the western hills—and, as I walked along, the great-grandchildren of the same metallic devil's-darning-needles slid sideways from the path and were back again as soon as I had passed. Nature has not budged an inch in all these years, and meanwhile over how many thistles have I hovered and thought I was—no matter what; it is splendid, as girls say, to dream backward so. One feels as if he were a poet, and one's own Odyssey sings itself in one's blood as he walks. I do not know why I write this to you so far away, except that as this world goes it is something to be able to say, "I have been happy for two hours." I wanted to tell you, too, what glorious fall weather we are having, clear and champagney, the northwest wind crisping Fresh Pond to steel-blue, and curling the wet lily-pads over till they bloom in a sudden flash of golden sunshine. How I do

---

[1] Located about a mile northwest of Elmwood, and now the city reservoir.

love the earth! I feel it thrill under my feet. I feel somehow as if it were conscious of my love, as if something passed into my dancing blood from it, and I get rid of that dreadful duty-feeling —"what right have I to be?"—and not a golden-rod of them all soaks in the sunshine or feels the blue currents of the air eddy about him more thoughtlessly than I.

I wish I could reach you a cup of this wine over those briny leagues. I drink your health in it, and then the glass shatters as usual. . . .

13. To O. W. Holmes. (L., I, 288–89)

Cambridge, Dec. 19, 1858.

My dear Wendell,—Thank you ever so much for the "Autocrat," [1] who comes at last drest like a gentleman. The color of the paper is just that which knowers love to see in old lace.

"Run out" indeed!—who has been suggesting the danger of that to you? I hope you will continue to run out in the style of the first "Professor." [2] The comparison of the bung and the straw is excellent and touched a very tender spot in me, who was born between two cider-mills, and drew in much childish belly-ache from both, turned now by memory into something like the result that might follow nectar.

You have been holding-in all this while—*possumus omnes,*[3] we all play the 'possum—and are now getting your second wind. I like the new Professor better than the old Autocrat. You have filled no ten pages so wholly to my liking as in the January number. I have just read it and am delighted with it. The "Old Boston" is an inspiration.[4] You have never been so wise

---

[1] *The Autocrat of the Breakfast Table* was the title of the first series of essays (in the form of dramatic monologues), which Holmes contributed to the *Atlantic Monthly* after its inception in 1857. They brought him immediate fame and were published in a collected volume during 1858.

[2] The second series of his essays, beginning in the *Atlantic* for January, 1859, Holmes entitled *The Professor at the Breakfast Table*.

[3] We all can.

[4] Lowell mistakenly refers to "Old Boston" instead of "Little Boston":

and witty as in this last number. I hold up my left foot in token of my unanimity.

The religious press (a true sour-cider press with belly-ache privileges attached) will be at you, but after smashing one of them you will be able to furnish yourself with a Samson's weapon for the rest of the Philisterei.[5] Good-by.

Always affectionately yours,

J. R. Lowell.

14. To C. E. NORTON. (L., I, 289–90)

Cambridge, 2d day of Holy Week, May, 1859.

. . . I miss you *like thunder—ça va sans dire* [1]—especially in this George-Herbert's-Sunday kind of weather, which is cool and calm and bright as can be thought.[2] I fancy you listening to the bobolinks among the lush grass on the lawn. I heard them yesterday on my way to the printing-office for the first time this spring. That liquid tinkle of theirs is the true fountain of youth if one can only drink it with the right ears, and I always date the New Year from the day of my first draught. Messer Roberto di Lincoln, with his summer alb over his shoulders, is the true chorister for the bridals of earth and sky. There is no bird that seems to me so thoroughly happy as he, so void of all *arrière pensée* [3] about getting a livelihood. The robin sings matins and vespers somewhat conscientiously, it seems to me—makes a business of it and pipes as it were by the yard—but Bob

---

the nickname given to a life-long Bostonian at the Professor's Table, "a little deformed body, mounted on a high stool."

[5] Samson, the celebrated strong man among the Israelites, when taken by his fellow countrymen to the Philistines as a bound hostage, burst his bonds asunder in rage, seized the jawbone of a newly killed ass, and slew a thousand Philistines therewith. (See Judges xv: 14–17.) For Philisterei see note on p. 96.

[1] That goes without saying.

[2] An allusion to the following lines in *Virtue*, a poem by George Herbert (1593–1632):

Sweet day, so cool, so calm, so bright,
The bridal of the earth and sky.

[3] Mental reservation.

squanders song like a poet, has no rain-song (as the robin has, who prophesies the coming wet that will tempt the worms out— with an eye to grub), and seems to have no other tune than, *mihi est propositum in taberna mori,*[4] with a long unpaid score chalked up against him behind the door. He never forebodes or remembers anything, won't sing in wet weather, but takes a thoughtless delight in present sunshine. I am sure he leaves debts behind him when he comes up from Carolina in May. Well, you see I was happy yesterday on my way to Riverside. I indulged in my favorite pastime of sitting on a fence in the sunshine and basking. The landscape was perfect. . . . Sweet Auburn [5] pink with new-leaved oaks, Corey's Hill [6] green in the hay-fields and brown with squares of freshly turned furrows (*versus,* the farmer's poem), the orchards rosy with apple-blooms, the flowering grasses just darkening the meadows to set off the gold of the buttercups, here and there pale splashes of Houstonia dropt from the Galaxy,[7] and the river all blue and gold. This is Cambridge, sir! What is Newport to this? But I am bobolink-ing instead of attending to business. . . .

15. To John Ruskin. (N.L., 98–99)

Cambridge, Massachusetts, 22nd Novr., 1859.

My dear Mr. Ruskin,—to have made one man happy in a life-time is worth living for, and you have made me happy and proud too in writing to Norton that you counted me "among your friends." *That* you may take for granted, but I must go farther and say "among your debtors as well." My proportion of a debt which I share with all who speak or read the English tongue may be small as far as it concerns you, but to me it is great and

---

[4] I am resolved to die in a tavern.

[5] The early nineteenth-century name of what was originally called "Stone's Woods" on the western boundary of Cambridge between the Charles River and the Watertown road. These woods in Lowell's boyhood were owned by the Massachusetts Horticultural Society, but in 1831 were sold and dedicated as Mount Auburn Cemetery

[6] A height located in Brighton across the Charles River from Elmwood.

[7] Splashes of bluets (or quaker-ladies) dropt from the Milky Way.

lifelong. We all quarrel with you sometimes, but what good could we get from a man who prophesied smooth things? and I am sure that I am not assuming too much when I say that in giving you my hearty thanks for what you have done, I am only doing what all the men whose opinion you would care for in America would gladly do if they had the same pretext for it that I have. I offer you my hand with all my heart, and I pay you my fealty also as to the man who has done for Art what Wordsworth wished to do for Poetry.

Now what is the use of a friend unless he can ask us now and then to do him a kindness, and like us all the better if we say him nay? So I am going to ask a favor of you. I am editor of a Magazine which Norton may tell you about if he likes. As the old poet of Kalevala [1] says, "it is not of the best, nor is it of the worst." I should be as happy as an Editor can be if you would write something for it upon any topic that interests you. I can promise you (reckoning à la Buckle) [2] at least a hundred thousand readers—for its subscribers are nearly forty thousand— readers who will be glad to be taught. Not a bad congregation, and moreover we pay our preacher at the rate of ten dollars (2 guineas) a page of the size of *Blackwood*. [3]

I do not ask this because I want your *name*, but because I want what you would write.

You need not answer this. A *yes* or *no* when you are writing to Norton will be enough,

and whether or no,

I remain most faithfully

Your friend

J. R. Lowell [4]

i go in for the A buv
like all git eout
    Hosea Biglow [5]

---

[1] The Finnish national epic (Kaleva = Finland), a mythological account of Finland's rise and development.

[2] See note on p. 112.

[3] *Blackwood's Magazine*, an important literary monthly founded at Edinburgh in 1817 by the Scottish publisher, William Blackwood (1776–1834).

[4] Lowell's appeal was altogether without avail, for Ruskin never contributed an article to the *Atlantic*.

[5] This bit of Biglow dialect is interesting evidence that a second series

16. To Nathaniel Hawthorne. (L., I, 305–6)

Cambridge, Aug. 5, 1860.

My dear Hawthorne,—I have no masonic claim upon you except community of tobacco, and the young man who brings this does not smoke.

But he wants to look at you, which will do you no harm, and him a great deal of good. His name is Howells,[1] and he is a fine young fellow, and has written several *poems* in the *Atlantic,* which of course you have never read, because you don't do such things yourself, and are old enough to know better.

When I think how much you might have profited by the perusal of certain verses of somebody who shall be nameless— but, no matter! If my judgment is good for anything, this youth has more in him than any of our younger fellows in the way of rhyme.

Of course he can't hope to rival the *Consule Planco* men.[2] Therefore let him look at you, and charge it

To yours always,
J. R. Lowell.

17. To Judge E. R. Hoar. (N.L., 107–11)

Elmwood, 18ᵗʰ Novʳ, 1862.

My dear Judge,—to turn boldly on a caviler and ask him, "Well, then, how would *you* go to work?" has before now spiked many a canon of criticism with its charge rammed home for a new attack. My dear friend, what shall I say? . . .

. . . It seems to me that one great element of the picturesque is Age. I think the greatest loss we ever had, and an irreparable

of Biglow Papers was beginning to run in Lowell's head some two years before a new poem of the sort came off to satisfy him.

[1] William Dean Howells (1837–1920), well-known American novelist and editor.
[2] The men in the good old days of our youth (lit., the men in the consulship of Plancus). See Horace, *Odes,* I, 14: 28.

one, was the old Harvard Hall. Well, is it absolutely irreparable? Can you not build something old-fashioned, which will
seem old? If a reproduction of Old Harvard Hall would not
be suitable to your purpose—why not something in that style?
It seems to me that the theory should be something (adapted to
present wants) in a style coëval with the founding of the College. Anything older would be bad, but such a building would
soon acquire the prestige of antiquity. It should be of brick,
and brick is capable of great effects both of dignity and picturesqueness. Remember Bologna, Bruges, and Nürnberg.[1]
Now there are some very simple shifts by which the *factory*-look
of our present style may be avoided. First by gables. The
gambrel-roof [2] (Dr. Holmes is mistaken in his derivation of the
name, by the way) seems to me much prettier—no, that is not
the word—but more agreeable to the eye, and more *sedate, a*
thing to be considered in a College-building, than the Mansard [3]
which is so fashionable now, but which has a Chinese look. The
gambrel gives quite as good chambers under the roof, and has
a New England air—a great merit in my eyes. Massachusetts
Hall, for example, is on the whole our best-looking building,
though the College Carpenter has done all he could to spoil it
by taking away the balustrade on the roof. Well, then, my first
suggestion is *gables*—and let the chimneys be solid and with
panels or breaks of some sort in them. Our modern chimneys
are so slender they look like pins thrust through the cardhouses
to keep them from blowing away. Large chimneys are safer,
too, as well as handsomer. But the great thing is the windows.
The front of a dormitory is mainly made up of windows and they
may just as well be made an ornament as a deformity. Let them
have hoods to give a little shadow; let them be wide and low
rather than high and narrow. Look at a photograph of Trinity
College, Cambridge. That is of brick and both venerable and

---

[1] Old cities in Italy, Belgium, and Germany respectively—each of them
noted for centuries-old brick architecture.

[2] "A curb roof of the same section in all parts, with a lower steeper slope
and an upper flatter one, so that each gable is pentagonal." (Webster's *New
International Dictionary*.)

[3] A roof on which each face has two slopes, the lower one steeper than
the upper.

picturesque though not very old. Don't be afraid of having
bay-windows here and there. Be willing to give something for
beauty as well as use. A building outlasts many generations of
Professors, and gives its silent lecture on æsthetics to class after
class of students. Consider what you spend in ornament as
the endowment of a perpetual lecturer on the principles of good
taste. 'Twill be money well laid out!

. . . Even ugly buildings may gain a kind of dignity from
Mass. Our buildings . . . have no relation so far as mass is
concerned, but are tailed on one behind another like caterpillars
on a twig. . . . I think there is some sense in what I have suggested. Namely—a touch of archaism—not *too* old; a New
England sentiment in the style . . . Simplicity is the first element of dignity . . . At least, my dear Friend, for God's sake
try to give us something that an association can love to cling
round. Fancy an "Ode on a distant (the farther the better)
prospect of *Harvard* College"![4] And yet why might it not have
been so built that a poet might love it? It would have cost no
more, and what a perpetual income of delight to the eye and to
the memory!

. . . So my dear Judge, I have jotted down what came into
my head—without any order (unless composite) and maybe with
a savor of impracticability. But look at engravings and photographs of buildings similar in character in England before you
make up your minds. At least spare us any more abominations,
and remember that the College builds forever, or should.

Hoping to see you at the next Club,[5]

I remain affectionately yours

J. R. Lowell.

18. To the Rev. W. L. Gage. (N.L., 115–16)

Elmwood, 7th Dec^r, 1863.

My dear Sir,—When I was editing the "Atlantic Monthly," I
was in the habit of sending all the new books which came to me

---

[4] Cf. Thomas Gray's *Ode on a Distant Prospect of Eton College* (1747).
[5] I.e., the next Saturday Club meeting.

as editor, to the College Library. I suppose "Leaves of Grass" [1] must have been one of them. It is a book I never looked into farther than to satisfy myself that it was a solemn humbug. Still, I think the business of a library is to have *every* book in it, and I should be sorry to have it supposed that I thought well of every volume I have sent to Gore Hall [2]—nay, that I did not think ill of many of them.

As for the evil influence of this particular book, I doubt if so much harm is done by downright *animality* as by a more refined sensuousness. There is worse in Schleiermacher.[3] Wordsworth would have tabooed "Wilhelm Meister." [4] Where shall the line be drawn? Would you have a library without Byron? or a Byron with his most characteristic work left out? For my part I should like to see a bonfire made of a good deal of ancient and modern Literature—but 'tis out of the question.

I am obliged to you, however, for calling my attention to a part of this book of which I knew nothing, and I will take care to keep it out of the way of the students.

Very truly yours
J. R. Lowell

19. To Miss Jane Norton. (L., I, 345-47)

Elmwood, July 25, 1865.

My dear Jane,—However statures and wits may degenerate, and we become, as Donne says, "our fathers' shadows cast at noon," [1]

---

[1] Walt Whitman's epoch-making volume of poems, published in 1855.

[2] At this time the home of the Harvard College Library.

[3] Friedrich Ernst Daniel Schleiermacher (1768–1834), a German philosopher and theologian.

[4] *Wilhelm Meister's Apprenticeship* (1795–96) and *Wilhelm Meister's Travels* (1821), Goethe's fictional studies of the mental and moral development of a reflective young man.

[1]   . . . mankind decays so soon,
         We're scarce our fathers' shadows cast at noon;
         Only death add t'our length: . . .
             John Donne, *An Anatomie of the World. The first Anniversary*, ll. 143–45.

July keeps his old force and is pleasing himself today with a noble display of it. It is so hot that the very locusts are dumb and cannot endure to carry on their own trade of spinning out "their longdrawn, red-hot wires of shrilly song," as they are called in a lost poem of Pindar's,[2] from which I translate by direct inspiration of a scholiast turned table-tipper. Each under his cool leaf is taking his siesta. There is an unpleasing moisture even in the slender palms of the flies that fondle the restiff tip of my nose. The thin gray lives of mosquitoes are burnt up and evaporate. My anxious shirt-collar still stiffly holds its undiminished state, but with a damp foreboding of its doom. In short, dear Jane, it is just such a day as the Clerk of the Weather, abusing his opportunities, invariably appoints for public festivities—just such a day as were the Wednesday, Thursday, and Friday of last week. Nevertheless, I am here among my books and I am in a literal sense alive. I eat and smoke and sleep and go through all the nobler functions of a man mechanically still, and wonder at myself as at something outside of and alien to Me. For have I not worked myself lean on an "Ode for Commemoration"? Was I not so rapt with the fervor of conception as I have not been these ten years, losing my sleep, my appetite, and my flesh, those attributes to which I before alluded as nobly uniting us in a common nature with our kind? Did I not for two days exasperate everybody that came near me by reciting passages in order to try them on? Did I not even fall backward and downward to the old folly of hopeful youth, and think I had written something *really* good at last? And am I not now enduring those retributive dumps which ever follow such sinful exultation, the Erynnyes[3] of Vanity? Did not I make John Holmes[4] and William Story[5] shed tears by my recitation of it (my ode) in the morning, both of 'em fervently declaring it was "noble"? Did not even the silent Rowse[6] declare 'twas in a higher mood

[2] A Greek poet (*c.* 520–440 B.C.) especially renowned for his odes.
[3] The Eumenides or Furies. See note on p. 7.
[4] See note on p. 311.
[5] See note on p. 3.
[6] Samuel Worcester Rowse (1822–91), an American illustrator and a painter noted especially for his portraits.

than much or most of later verse? Did not I think, in my
nervous exhilaration, that 'twould be *the* feature (as reporters
call it) of the day? And, after all, have I not a line in the *Daily
Advertiser* calling it a "graceful poem" (or "some graceful
verses," I forget which), which "was received with applause"?
Why, Jane, my legs are those of grasshoppers, and my head is
an autumn threshing-floor, still beating with the alternate flails
of strophe and antistrophe,[7] and an infinite virtue is gone out of
me somehow—but it seems *not* into my verse as I dreamed.
Well, well, Charles will like it—but then he always does, so
what's the use? I am Icarus [8] now with the cold salt sea over
him instead of the warm exulting blue of ether. I am gone
under, and I will never be a fool again. You read between the
lines, don't you, my dear old friend, if I may dare to call a woman
so? You know my foibles—women always know our foibles,
confound them!—though they always wink at the right moment
and seem not to see—bless them! Like a boy, I mistook my
excitement for inspiration, and here I am in the mud. You see
also I am a little disappointed and a little few (*un petit peu*)
vexed. I did *not* make the hit I expected, and am ashamed at
having been again tempted into thinking I could write *poetry,*
a delusion from which I have been tolerably free these dozen
years. . . .

26th.

The Storys have got home and look as young as ever. I first
saw William on Commencement day, and glad enough I was.
A friendship counting nearly forty years is the finest kind of
shade-tree I know of. One is safe from thunder beneath it, as
under laurel—nay, more safe, for the critical bolts do not respect
the sacred tree any more than if it were so much theatrical green
baize. To be sure, itself is of the harmless theatrical kind often

---

[7] Two divisions in Greek choral odes, representing a passage and a
counterpassage of recitation.
[8] The son of Dædalus, an Athenian artificer. He took to the air from
Crete with wings of his father's manufacture, but he flew higher than he
ought. The sun melted the wax by which his wings were attached, and
he fell into the Ægean Sea.

enough. Well, he and two more came up hither after dinner, and we talked and laughed and smoked and drank Domdechanei [9] till there wasn't a bald head nor a gray hair among us. Per Bacco [10] and tobacco, how wisely silly we were! I forgot for a few blessed hours that I was a professor, and felt as if I were something real. But Phi Beta came next day, and *wasn't* I tired! Presiding from 9 A.M. till 6½ P.M. is no joke, and then up next morning at ½ past 4 to copy out and finish my ode.[11] I have not got cool yet (I mean as to nerves), and lie awake at night thinking how much better my verses might have been, only I can't make 'em so. Well, I am printing fifty copies in 4to, and Charles will like it, as I said before, and I sha'n't, because I thought too well of it at first. . . .

Yours always,
J. R. L.

20. To Leslie Stephen. (L., I, 358–64)

Elmwood, April 10, 1866.

My dear Stephen,—I am not very good at writing letters at any rate, and this is the first one I have sent across the Atlantic since our war began. That is now five years ago, but so crowded with events that it seems hardly yesterday that Sumter was fired on. Montaigne, and Byron after him (and both of 'em after Plutarch, if I remember), are all wrong in saying that life is long in proportion to its eventfulness or the movement of thought it has forced upon us. On the contrary, I am persuaded that periods of revolution and excitement cheat us of half our days; and that a pioneer backwoodsman, who knows no changes of ministry but those of the seasons, and whose greatest events are the coming into office and falling of the leaves, is the only mortal who knows what length of years is. It seems to me as if it were

---

[9] Wine from the Dodecanese, Italian islands in the Aegean Sea.

[10] Through Bacchus (the Greek god of wine).

[11] Ode recited at the Harvard Commemoration held on July 21, 1865, in honor of the Harvard men who had died in the Civil War.

only a day or two since I parted with you at the corner of the lane, since we walked together to Beaver Brook, since I told you, as we came down the hill on our way home, that I had no gift of prophecy, but that I had an *instinct* that the American people would come out of the war stronger than ever. I confess I have had an almost invincible repugnance to writing again to England. I share with the great body of my countrymen in a bitterness (half resentment and half regret) which I cannot yet get over. I do not mean that, if my heart could be taken out after death, *Delenda est Anglia* [1] would be found written on it—for I know what the land we sprung from, and which we have not disgraced, is worth to freedom and civilization; but I cannot forget the insult so readily as I might the injury of the last five years. But I love my English friends none the less—nay, perhaps the more, because they have been *her* friends, too, who is dearer to me for her trials and for the victory which I am sure she will be great enough to use gently. There! Like a true New-Englander I have cleared my conscience, and I can allow a little play to my nature. . . .

I was interested in what you told me of the professorship.[2] I have heard very little about it, having abstained from English newspapers for these five years as strictly as a Pythagorean from beans.[3] They need not be frightened, so far as we are concerned. We do not want to make Socinians [4] of 'em, poor fellows! Their sow shall farrow in spite of the Black Douglas.[5]

---

[1] England must be destroyed.

[2] Yates Thompson proposed to establish at Cambridge University an annual series of lectures by outstanding American scholars, but the proposal was not accepted by the university.

[3] The followers of Pythagoras (see note on p. 99) placed taboos on many foods and practiced an ascetic diet.

[4] I.e., heretics or unbelievers. The Socinians were the followers of Faustus Socinus (Sozzoni), celebrated Italian theologian (1539–1604) whose anti-trinitarian tenets shocked alike the orthodox Catholics and Protestants of the sixteenth and seventeenth centuries. The term "Socinian" was also used to denote the adherents of English Unitarianism in the eighteenth century, for this latter movement succeeded to the rationalism and anti-trinitarianism of the older Socinian sect.

[5] The Black Douglas was the name applied to Sir James Douglas (1286?–1330), a Scottish chieftain who invaded the north of England in 1319 and struck terror to the hearts of the inhabitants there by his savage plundering.

What amused me most was the suggestion that we should have
sent Mr. Bancroft,[6] of all men in the world! Wouldn't you
smile if I were to write you seriously that I hoped the English
Government would not send out Roebuck [7] as minister at Washington? Country parsons know as little about the other world
as about this—and one really sees no means they have of knowing even so much. I should pity their parishes if they were not
made up of "Britishers," as you persist in thinking that we call
you. But, seriously, I doubt if the lectureship would have done
much good. England *can't* like America, do what she or we
will, and I doubt if I could, were I an Englishman. But I think
the usages of society should hold between nations, and see no particular use in her taking every opportunity to *tell* us how disagreeable and vulgar we are. What *riled* me was the quiet
assumption that we hadn't, couldn't, and had no right to have,
a country over here. They seem to forget that more than half
the people of the North have roots, as I have, that run down
more than two hundred years deep into this new-world soil—
that we have not a thought nor a hope that is not American—
and they may make up their minds that it is not what Mr. Disraeli [8] calls a "territorial democracy," but democracy itself, that
makes us strong. If they could only understand that we feel
like an *old* country over here, and not a sutler's camp, they would
be less afraid of any active propagandism of ours. We would
not rob you of a single one of your valuable institutions—state-
church, peerage, pauperage—so long as you like 'em and like to
pay for 'em. We really have no use for such things, and you
can leave your doors unlocked, so far as we are concerned. *I*
don't understand your English taste for what you call "respect-

Hence his name became so formidable a symbol of terrible force that in
after time the English women used to threaten refractory children with
the "Black Douglas," and thus coined a long-standing household phrase.

[6] George Bancroft (1800–91), well-known American diplomat and historian, who served as American minister to Great Britain, 1846–49, and
again as minister to Germany, 1867–74.

[7] John A. Roebuck (1802–79), an English lawyer and member of Parliament, who was an active pamphleteer of liberal persuasions.

[8] Benjamin Disraeli (1804–81), first Earl of Beaconsfield, English author
and statesman, prime minister 1868, 1874–80.

ability" (I should call it "whitechokerism" [9]), thinking, as I do, that the one thing worth striving for in this world is a state founded on pure manhood, where everybody has a chance given him to better himself, and where the less costume and the more reality there is, the better. As for "Socinianism," heavens! we've got several centuries ahead of *that,* some of us, or behind it, if you please. Why couldn't they have said "Semi-Pelagianism"? [10] There is a plesiosaurian [11] word long enough to scare one a little! If you should infect 'em with that, 'twould be worse than the rinderpest.[12] But, alas, there doesn't seem to be such a thing as an *esel*pest! [13] *That* kind of animal seems to have a prodigious constitution. How they do survive everything, wagging their sacred ears in the pulpit, sticking their pens behind 'em in the Foreign Office (they're very convenient for that—I mean the ears), and never hearing anything through 'em on the Bench or in Parliament! Sacred animal, as safe from ideas as the laurel from lightning!

We have one of the breed, I fear, just now for President, with all the obstinacy of a weak mind and a strong constitution. But I think the people will hold out longer than he, and show how much stronger an united purpose is than a selfish one. Johnson is really foolish enough to think that he can make himself President for a second term by uniting in his favor the loyalty of both ends of the country. As if the Southern people, whose notion of the chase is to hunt loyalists the moment our troops are withdrawn (you know their passion for field-sports was one of the grounds of sympathy which was discovered between you and them), would ever forgive *him*. But I have the same confidence as ever (impudent Yankee that I am) in the sense and nerve of the people; and as they put down the same combination in the field, so they will at the polls, so soon as they understand what

---

[9] "White tie-ism," i.e., belief in the dominance of the aristocracy.

[10] Pelagianism, the formerly heretical doctrine of a British monk, Pelagius (d. *circa* 418 A.D.), emphasizes that humanity is not tainted by original sin, that man is the author of his own salvation, without need of God's grace, and that man has perfect freedom of the will.

[11] I.e., extinct. See note on p. 44.

[12] Cattle disease.

[13] Ass disease.

it means. Meanwhile we are gaining time—a great thing; the Southerners are learning again to be interested in *national* politics—a still greater thing; and matters are settling in a natural way, as they should and must at last by the necessities of trade and agriculture. Mr. Hosea Biglow addresses his constituents on this matter in the *May* number of the *Atlantic Monthly,* and I should like you to read his speech (especially as it is to be his last), if the magazine is to be come at in any London reading-room. I would not have you spend a shilling for it, nor will I send it, for fear it should cost you its weight in gold, after I had paid the postage; for the wonders of our international postal system are past my finding out.

We are having an April whimsical beyond the womanly privilege of April. Last Thursday my thermometer marked 76° of Fahrenheit in the shade, and on Sunday morning there were three inches of snow on the ground. But the grass is beginning to green, the lilac buds are swelling, and I can hear the chirping of a brood of chickens in the cellar as I write. What a blessing is the quiet indifference of nature amid all our hurry and worry and turmoil! But for that it seems to me as if I could never have endured the last five years. However, we are all tougher than we think, and have also our kind of dogged persistency in living. Our constitutions adapt themselves to the slow poison of the world till we become mithridatized [14] at last.

Now remember that your first dinner in America is to be eaten with me, and I only hope you won't arrive on one of those days of household dyspepsia—washing or ironing day. But, after all, the real flavor of a dinner is the welcome, and yours will be hearty. You shall have a new brier-wood pipe—though I am sorry to say that the war has somehow got into the tobacco—and I have some excellent materials for the making of nightcaps, in which there shall be acres of pleasant dreams without a single toadstool of headache (and how full-grown they do get sometimes in a night!) in their whole expansion.

I am desired by the American Eagle (who is a familiar of mine

---

[14] Immunized from poison.—Mithridates VI, king of Pontus (d. 63 B.C.), is said to have produced in himself immunity from poison by the administration of gradually increased doses of it.

caught on the coins of my country) to request you to present
her compliments to the British Lion, and say to him that she
does *not* (as he seems to think) spend *all* her time in trying to
find a chance to pick out his eyes, having vastly more important
things to occupy her mind about. She really can't conceive
how they can quarrel when *his* place is on the ground and *hers*
in the air—a moral on which she begs him to meditate. *She*
doesn't wish to change, having a natural fondness for large
views. "As for Fenians," [15] she adds, "tell him to spell it
Fainéants,[16] as we do over here, and he will enjoy his dinner
again."

Isn't it lucky that I don't write often? Like a woman, I put
the main thing in my P.S., which is, that I am, with the kindli-
est recollections,

Very truly your friend,
J. R. Lowell.

21. To C. E. Norton.[1] (L., I, 366–67; Scudder, II, 98–100)

Elmwood, July 10, 1866.

. . . The hot weather we have been having for some time—
95° for nearly a week together—has pretty nearly used me up.
It has made me bilious and blue, my moral thermometer sinking
as the atmospheric rose. But Sunday afternoon we had one of
the finest thunderstorms I ever saw, beginning in the true way
with a sudden whirl of wind that filled the air with leaves and
dust and twigs (*dinanzi va superbo* [2]), followed in due time by
a burst of rain. One flash struck close by us somewhere, and

---

[15] The Fenian Association or Brotherhood was founded in Ireland about
1858 with the avowed object of making England's rule in Ireland impossible
and of achieving this end by force and rebellion.

[16] I.e., idlers; the French term here is an intended pun on Fenian. The
implication is that the Fenians through their policy of negation and their
acts of sporadic violence behave like rowdy good-for-nothings and do not
deserve to be taken seriously.

[1] Norton and Scudder each print different passages from this letter. The
separate extracts are here pieced together to form a more connected and
interesting epistle.

[2] The beginning is superb.

I heard distinctly the crack of a bough at the moment of its most intense redness. Just at sunset the cloud lifted in the west, and the effect was one that I always wish all my friends could be at Elmwood to see. The tops of the English elms were turned to sudden gold, which seen against a leaden background of thundercloud had a supernatural look. Presently that faded, and after the sun had set came a rainbow more extravagant than any I ever saw. There were seven lines of the glory looking like the breaking of quiet surf on the beach of a bay. First came one perfect bow—the more brilliant that the landscape was dark everywhere by the absence of the sunlight. Gradually another outlined itself at some distance above, and then the first grew double, triple, till at last six arches of red could be counted. The other colors I could only see in the two main bows. I thought it a trick of vision, but Fanny and her sister counted as I did. A triple arch was the most I had ever seen before. Here is a diagram. . . . *d* is the spectator for whom this wonderful show was exhibited. I should have made *d* a capital, thus, D, to indicate his importance in the scene. For have I not read in some old moralist that God would not have created so much beauty without also creating an eye to see and a soul to feel it? As if God could not be a poet! The author of the book of Genesis knew better. However, it is something to have had an eye see what we are seeing; it seems to double the effect by some occult sympathy, and my rainbows are always composed of one part rain, one part sunshine, and one part blessed Henry Vaughan with his 'Still young and fine,' and his 'World's gray fathers in one knot'! [3] The older I grow the more I am convinced that

---

[3] The phrases quoted here by Lowell come from *The Rainbow* by Henry Vaughan (*c.* 1622–95). The opening stanzas are as follows:

> Still young and fine! but what is still in view
> We slight as old and soil'd, though fresh and new.
> How bright wert thou, when Shem's admiring eye
> Thy burnish'd, flaming arch did first descry!

> When Terah, Nahor, Haran, Abram, Lot,
> The youthful world's grey fathers in one knot,
> Did with intensive looks watch every hour
> For thy new light, and trembled at each shower!

[there] are no satisfactions so deep and so permanent as our sympathies with outward nature. I have not said just what I meant, for we are thrilled even more by any spectacle of human heroism. But the others seem to bind our lives together by a more visible and unbroken chain of purifying and softening emotion. In this way the flowering of the buttercups is always a great and I may truly say religious event in my year. But I am talking too unguardedly. You know what a deep distrust I have of the poetical temperament, with its self-deceptions, its real unrealities, and its power of sometimes unblest magic, building its New Jerusalems in a sunset cloud rather than in the world of actuality and man.

In some moods I heartily despise and hate myself, there is so much woman in me (. . . I mean no harm. I was designed, sketched rather, for a man). Why, I found myself the other day standing in a muse with something like tears in my eyes, before a little *pirus* that had rooted itself on the steep edge of the runnel that drains the meadow above Craigie's pond, and thinking—what do you suppose? Why, how happy and careless the life of such a poor shrub was compared with ours! But I was in a melancholy and desponding mist of mind, and I snatched myself back out of it to manlier thoughts. But the reality and sincerity of the emotion struck me as I mused over it, and I set it down on the debtor side of my account. Still, *can* one get away from his nature? That always puzzles me. Your close-grained, strong fellows tell you that you can, but they forget that they are only acting out their complexion, not escaping it. I did not expect to chase my rainbow into such a miserable drizzle, but for that very reason I will let it go as I have written it, though I am rather ashamed of having uncovered my nakedness so plumply. In spite of the heat we have had rain enough to keep the country beautiful, and my salt marshes have been in their glory. The salt grass is to other grass like fur compared with hair, and the color of the 'black grass,' and even its texture at the right distance remind one of sable. I have been making night studies of late, having enjoyed, as folks say, a season of sleeplessness, and I saw the dawn begin the other night at two

o'clock. The first bird to sing was a sparrow. The cocks followed close upon him, and the phoebe upon them. The crows
were the latest to shake the night out of them.

. . . I am called away to the hayfield, so good-by. I work
more or less every day out of doors and like it. I am getting
back as well as I can to my pristine ways of life. . . .

22. To Judge E. R. Hoar. (N.L., 132–34)

Elmwood, 14ᵗʰ April, 1869.

My dear Judge,—Cowper in one of his letters says that the tallest
and loudest fellow among his thoughts is one crying continually
actum est de te, periisti! [1] I heard the same voice this morning
at breakfast as I opened my paper and read the nominations.
'Tis plain I was not born under the sign of Pisces.[2] At the same
time, as I always try to eliminate self from my judgment of men
and things, I must say that I think Mʳ. Sandford [3] [*sic*] a much
fitter nomination for Spain than I should have been. Mr. Jay's [4]
is also an eminently proper one. I knew all along that I had no
claims. And yet I could not help having a kind of hope. I am
only a poor poet, though I am not so modest as to think my name
would have done any *dis*credit to the administration. What a
spider hope is! Mine still contrives to hitch a filament strong
enough to hang by on Rome. I should not have cared for a
mission except that I thought it would give me a few years for
poetry pure and simple, and bridge over the gap till I could sell

---

[1] It is all over with thee, thou hast perished!—William Cowper (1731–
1800), English poet who also showed extraordinary talent as a letter-writer,
wrote on August 21, 1781, to the Reverend John Newton, his former rector:
"My thoughts are clad in sober livery, for the most part as grave as that
of a bishop's servants. They turn too upon spiritual subjects; but the tallest
fellow and the loudest among them all is he who is continually crying with
a loud voice, *Actum est de te; periisti!*"

[2] The sign of the Fishes, the twelfth sign of the zodiac; in astrology, to
be born under this sign is assurance of good fortune.

[3] Henry S. Sanford (1823–91), appointed Minister to Spain by President
Grant.

[4] John Jay (1817–94), named minister to Austria-Hungary by President
Grant.

my land and be able to command that leisure which is half the battle in literature. However, I have had my little experience of place-hunting which is worth something to me. It unsettled me, though I never allowed myself to count upon anything, and made me realize the pathetic force of Spenser's anathema upon it because it makes us

> To lose good days that might be better spent.[5]

Now that it is all over, I begin to feel "like the Monument," as Johnson said when *Irene* failed.[6] And as for Rome, I look upon it as a plentiful disqualification that I have lived there eight months and understand Italian. A diplomatist who can make himself understood is unfit for his business and might do mischief.

However, all I write for now is to say that I value in my new experience mainly that fresh proof it has given me of your friendship and esteem. Life with all its cheats gives us something substantial *there*. I shall always be proud of having had you for my advocate.[7] And I have the satisfaction of thinking that, as what service I may have done for good principles, was done without any hope of reward, so my convictions have not been vulgarized by receiving any. Which being interpreted means merely Swift's extra beatitude, "Blessed are they which expect nothing, for they shall surely not be disappointed." [8]

Meanwhile the birds sing (more shame to them!) as if nothing

---

[5] *Mother Hubberds Tale,* l. 897.

[6] Dr. Samuel Johnson finished in 1737 a tragedy in blank verse, entitled *Irene,* but was not able to get the play produced until 1749, when his friend, David Garrick, actor-manager of the Drury Lane Theater, had *Irene* acted there February 6–20.—"The Monument," a fluted Doric column 200 feet high, was erected by Christopher Wren in Fish Street near London Bridge to commemorate the great fire of 1666, and constituted a notable landmark in eighteenth-century London. Johnson's remark (quoted by Boswell in his *Life of Johnson,* Chap. vii) simply meant that the good Doctor continued, despite *Irene's* failure, as firm and unmoved as the famous column.

[7] Hoar was Attorney-General in the new Grant Cabinet.

[8] Lowell mistakes Swift for Alexander Pope, who wrote on Oct. 16, 1727, to John Gay: "I have many years ago . . . repeated to you a ninth beatitude, added to the eighth in the Scripture: 'Blessed is he who expects nothing, for he shall never be disappointed.'" On Sept. 23, 1725, Pope quoted almost the same beatitude in a letter to Wm. Fortescue.

had happened, and we had yesterday our true New England snowdrops in a fall of snow. I have begun my spring plough-ing, the lettuces and other vegetables make my hotbeds green and I have three broods of chickens. If *I* don't start for Europe, Mabel does in the "Russia" on the 29th, where she will have the pleasure of M[r]. Jay's company. I have discovered a new fact in proverbial philosophy and that is that one *may* count chalk eggs, and a great many times too, before they are hatched. There are none on which the old hen Fancy sits so sedulously or with such assurance of thumping broods. I shan't worry Sibley by getting my name into Capitals in the College Catalogue[9] but I shall always be most heartily yours

J. R. Lowell.

late Minister Resident at the (I mean near the) Court of Bara-taria.[10]

23. To Miss Mabel Lowell. (N.L., 140–42)

Elmwood, 12th July, 1869.

My dearest Hopkins,—your nice long letter from Winandermere came on Saturday while we were at tea, and was read with great satisfaction. I am sorry that you should have gone through the cathedral of St. Andrews without knowing that it was mainly built by a collateral ancestor of yours, Robert Traill, who was Archbishop in 14—. Also that I had not thought to ask Mr. Fields to get you an introduction to the Laings in Edinboro, able men all of them and Scotch cousins of yours. I was shocked by the picture you draw of Scotch civilization as contrasted with English. I could hardly believe it till you mentioned the fact

---

[9] The triennial catalogue of the graduates of Harvard College at this period printed in capitals the names of the alumni who had attained public distinction in official positions. The custom has long since been abandoned.

[10] A humorous comparison by Lowell of his own state of mind to the disappointment of Sancho Panza in *Don Quixote,* when the latter was made governor of Barataria, the island city, and was invited to an inauguration feast. At the banquet every dish was taken away before Sancho could taste it, and he was forced to go away hungry. (Part II, Chap. xlvii.)

of their ignorance of the authorship of the *Biglow Papers*. That indeed opens to Imagination an abyss of darkness at which she covers her eyes in horror. That they should know Burns and not Biglow is heartrending. However, I have met with such people before, and shuddered to think of their doom in another and more *enlightened* world. Pity them, my dear child, and hope for better things. Dumfries, by your account of it, seems to have been in a condition such as you would probably have found its most famous Citizen in if you had been there in his day.[1] (By the way, let me suggest to you that one of the *idiotisms* of our mother-tongue is that there are two forms of the participle *drunk*. We say "the waiter was drunk"—but a "drunk*en* waiter.") . . .

There is no home news except that I have bought a cow and of all places in the world at No. 69 Broad street in Boston. That cows should be pastured in that once busy avenue of commerce is a sad result of our Civil War, which your English friends will readily understand. But in truth I bought her without seeing her on the strength of her owner's face which had a kind of bovine honesty that pleased me. She is coming today and is said to be a beauty—half Durham and half Ayrshire. I hope she won't try her horns on William.[2] She is described as having one horn of each breed and this may naturally tempt her to test the respective qualities of each. William is wanting in some of the qualities that go to the making of a hero—and especially in this that his flesh has not that impenetrable character which detracts somewhat, I think, from our admiration of Achilles and Siegfried. We are having the best early potatoes we ever raised, our peas and beans are excellent and in a day or two we shall be having *tomatuses* as Wm. calls 'em. Our hay is all in the barn, twelve tons of it—as bright as ever was seen. W. is at this moment watering the peartrees from the cesspool, and as all my windows are open, I—well, the peartrees like it. I should have written you yesterday, but it was so hot that, though there was a strong breeze, I sat and literally dribbled. If I had written,

---

[1] Robert Burns moved to Dumfries in 1791 and died there in 1796. His fondness for drinking is generally known.

[2] The veteran hired-man at Elmwood.

I should have illustrated the other and metaphorical form of the same verb. At dinner whirled up a magnificent thunderstorm, during which the lightning knocked down one of the chimneys on the "Fresh Pond Hotel, Fourth House." If this was not a mistake, or a bad shot, it would seem to squint toward a judgment—for a Unitarian Sunday School picnicked there last week. It was probably at a fireplace in this unhallowed pile of brick that the viands were cooked for their profane orgies. The stroke made a fine sharp report which rolled off southward with a fitful redoubling and ended in one of those great thumps the thunder likes to give just as you think it over. After the storm came Rowse and spent the night. The evening was superb with a new moon and a gardenful of fireflies. Yes, real fireflies, Miss, flashing their dark-lanterns among the leaves as if they were the watchmen of our coleopterous [3] fellowcitizens. What do you think of my style? That last periphrasis [4] strikes me as rather good for plain bugs, and it is well to get ready betimes, for we shall be giving them the suffrage before long. . . .

> your loving and dutiful *Cobus*.[5]

24. To R. W. Emerson. (N.L., 150–51)

Elmwood, 18ᵗʰ Novʳ, 1869.

My dear Mʳ Emerson,—I take this time of thanksgiving to acknowledge your volumes—for they would make a festival of a dinner of herbs. Gratitude is always a pleasant feeling, but for moral and mental service it is incomparably sweet. Let them say what they will of America, there is some new and rare element in the soil that bears such fruit as these books, and Columbus need not be so sorry after all for his stumble. How much

---

3 Sheath-winged.—The Coleoptera are the insect order of beetles and weevils.

4 Roundabout way of speaking.

5 A humorous abbreviation for Jacobus, the Latin form of James. Lowell had used this abbreviation as a kind of pseudonym in a story for children which appeared in *Our Young Folks,* July, 1866, under the title "Uncle Cobus's Story."

good you have done me personally I have always been glad to say, but it is as a public benefaction that I am most thankful for you. Your sayings thrust above our deadlevel like snow-peaks, and we are not wholly left to ourselves while we have them on our horizon. The older I grow and the more I read, I find myself only the more confirmed in the singular value I set upon you. After all these thirty years I still remember passages from "Nature" as if I had read them yesterday. I am truly glad to get your prose writings all together. In this common channel they reinforce each other and seem to run with a deeper current. And to think that people should say, "Mr Emerson *used to be* a preacher"! "The Teachers shall shine with the glory of the firmament, and they that turn many to righteousness as the stars forever and ever." [1] I am so much younger than you, that I may claim to speak for posterity when I say

> how gratefully and affectionately
> I am always yours
> J. R. Lowell.

25. To C. E. Norton. (L., II, 74–76)

Elmwood, Sept. 5, 1871.

. . . Yesterday, as I was walking down the Beacon Street mall, the yellowing leaves were dozily drifting from the trees, and the sentiment of autumn was in all the air; though the day, despite an easterly breeze, was sultry. I enjoyed the laziness of everything to the core, and sauntered as idly as a thistledown, thinking with a pleasurable twinge of sympathy that the fall was beginning for me also, and that the buds of next season were pushing our stems from their hold on the ever-renewing tree of Life. I am getting to be an old fellow, and my sheaves are not so many as I hoped; but I am outwardly more prosperous than ever before—indeed, than ever I dreamed of being. If none of my stays give way, I shall have a clear income of over four thou-

---

[1] Slightly misquoted from Daniel xii: 3, the first part of which reads: "And the teachers shall shine as the firmament; . . ."

sand a year, with a house over my head, and a great heap of what I have always found the best fertilizer of the mind—leisure. I cannot tell you how this sense of my regained paradise of Independence enlivens me. It is something I have not felt for years—hardly since I have been a professor. . . . Meanwhile I am getting a kind of fame—though I never valued *that*, as you know—and what is better, a certain respect as a man of some solid qualities, which I *do* value highly. I have always believed that a man's fate is born with him, and that he cannot escape from it nor greatly modify it—and that consequently every one gets in the long run exactly what he deserves, neither more nor less. At any rate, this is a cheerful creed, and enables one to sleep soundly in the very shadow of Miltiades' trophy.[1] What I said long ago is literally true, that it is only for the sake of those who believed in us early that we desire the verdict of the world in our favor. It is the natural point of honor to hold our endorsers harmless. . . . It is always my happiest thought that with all the drawbacks of temperament (of which no one is more keenly conscious than myself) I have never lost a friend. For I would rather be loved than anything else in the world. I always thirst after affection, and depend more on the expression of it than is altogether wise. And yet I leave the letters of those I love unanswered so long! It is because the habits of authorship are fatal to the careless unconsciousness that is the life of a letter, and still more, in my case, that I have always something on my mind—an uneasy sense of disagreeable duties to come, which I cannot shake myself free from. But worse than all is that lack of interest in one's self that comes of drudgery—for I hold that a letter which is not mainly about the writer of it lacks the prime flavor. The wine must smack a little of the cask. You will recognize the taste of my old wood in this! . . .

---

[1] Miltiades (died *c.* 488 B.C.), the chief figure in the famous victory of the Greeks over the Persians at Marathon (490 B.C.), was peculiarly rewarded for his services. A subsequent attack with a Greek fleet on the island of Paros proved unsuccessful and brought about his impeachment at Athens and the imposition of a heavy fine. Soon after, he died of a leg wound contracted at Paros. Later, ironically enough, a monument was erected at Marathon.

RNETT.[1] (N.L., 185–89)

Hotel de Lorraine,
7 Rue de Beaune,
Paris, 8th April, 1873.

…s happened since I last
…mersons and the depar-
… latter to the station,
… all. I had got his
… rest of it, and had
…patiently sounded)
… a *depêchez-vous,*
… *faut monter en*
… I rushed back
…ble explication
… scales and who
… understand. How-
…John had only lingered
… expected and ten times as
…ellow, he will be missed by all
… his lame knee. I wonder how he
… without a word of the language that even
…omprehend—for I endeavored to give him a few
…eedful phrases. But his kindly face makes friends
…, and a lamb so closely shorn as he will have the wind
…for him somehow.

… a little scene in the street the other day which I saved
…n my memory for you. It was in the Rue de Seine down
…which Wendell Holmes saw the grisette Clemence trip forty
years ago.[5] A pony-carriage was drawn up opposite a pastry-

---

[1] Mabel Lowell married Edward Burnett of Southborough, Massachusetts, on April 2, 1872.

[2] John Holmes. See note on p. 311.

[3] Hurry up, sir, the train is going to depart immediately; you must get into the car.

[4] Dialect.

[5] Oliver Wendell Holmes (1809–94), while a medical student at Paris

cook's, and its mistress l
each corner of the back seat
tocratic indifference to the aff
foot, two snowwhite curled
about his neck a blue ribbo
order of the Garter. On
bull-terrier of the most d
dirty and defiant, his h
merable fights in back
canine *émeute*[7] aga
contemplating the
look of envious dis
expression of fac
Calédonèe[8] at th
St. Germain[9]
print, "If it we
livery of servitu
of a tail. *Cependa*
le beau régime de la C
que veut dire la fraternit
that in a back lane after dark

I went the other day to Duc d

---

from 1833 to 1835, wrote a sweetly sad lyric entitle
lished it in the first volume of his poems, 1836. The ly

> Ah, Clemence! when I saw thee last
> Trip down the Rue de Seine, . . .

[6] Street-urchin.

[7] Insurrection.

[8] New Caledonia, a large French possession in the west Pacifi
maintained from 1868 to 1898 a penal settlement on Nou Island close
capital city of Noumea.

[9] Formerly a fashionable section of Paris.

[10] "However, let us wait. The day will come. If ever the glorious rule
of the Common People should come back again, I would teach you what
brotherhood means, I would!"

[11] Henri Eugène Philippe Louis d'Orléans, duc d'Aumale (1822–97), the
fifth son of Louis Philippe. The Duc d'Aumale on this occasion was succeeding to the seat of the Comte de Montalembert in the French Academy.
He gained the honor because of his distinguished services as statesman and
soldier.

(through the two doors one on each side of the official chairs) presented arms. There was a more emphatic stir, a more unrepressed murmur, and then entered the Duc d'Aumale preceded by M. Guizot,[20] and followed by M. Thiers, who acted as his *parrains*[21] in the ceremony. They all three wore the Academic costume—a dark coat embroidered with green silk, and all three the broad red ribbon of the Legion of Honour and a star on the left breast. Guizot I have told you of before. Thiers is a punchy[22] little fellow who looks like his photographs except that they fail to give the expression of intense selfsatisfaction which stereotypes his countenance. It is a firm round head, looking hard enough to go through a wall and with a look that says "this is the likeness of a man who cannot by any possibility be mistaken." The upper lip is very short and the under is brought up against and over it with a firmness that had also its *soupçon*[23] of selfconceit. Take it for all in all, however, it was one of those heads that you don't get out of the way without cutting them off. Compared with that of Guizot it was emphatically *bourgeois*[24] —it was the real opposed to the ideal. On the whole I was repaid for my tribulations. The discourse of the Duc d'Aumale was admirable for its perfect good taste and its highbred delivery, and the faces of the Academy consoled me by suggesting that there is as much of the illustrious secondrate on this side of the ocean as on the other—only on a higher plane of culture. . . .

Your loving Father
J. R. L.

---

[20] Francois Pièrre Guillaume Guizot (1787–1874), one of the most famous of French historians and statesmen, was professor of modern history at the Sorbonne, minister of foreign affairs from 1840 to 1848, member of the French Academy from 1836, and author of the *History of French Civilization* (1830) and numerous other historical works.

[21] His godfathers.

[22] Short and stout.

[23] Trace.

[24] Commonplace.

27. To the Same. (N.L., 189-92)

Paris, 22nd May, 1873.

My dearest little Hopkins,—since I last wrote I have had some adventures. I have been across the channel to bid goodbye to the Nortons and spent four days in London. There I had the good luck to meet Carlyle and Ruskin and Morris [1] ("Earthly Paradise") [2] and G. H. Lewes [3] who pressed me to breakfast with him, which I had to refuse, though I wished very much to see George Eliot. Carlyle was very sweet and gentle—softened, I suppose, by the parting with the Nortons. He said nothing very memorable, and yet one thing that was characteristic. I said, "You never saw Goethe, I think?" "Naw, I naiver was in Garmany tull I went thar to gahther mahterriels for my Friedrich, and whan I got up in the mornin' at Frankfort am Main— ye'll hae been at Frankfort am Main?—thar I saw his dead marble face alookin' aht me through the winder that I had longed so to look on livin'. It was varra sahd!" Mrs. Cameron's photograph which you brought me is very like, but gives an impression of pallor which belies his complexion. The upper part of the cheeks where the beard lets it be seen is darkly ruddy, of that very deep and veiny red which the blackberry leaf takes on sometimes in autumn. It had a look of having been sharply peppered with sleet. He was very friendly and so was Ruskin, whose face and head are much smaller even than one would gather from his portraits. All that I remember of his conversation was his telling me that he couldn't endure Paris since the Commune and the barbarous destruction of historical monu-

---

[1] For Carlyle see note on p. 16 and for Ruskin note on p. 112. William Morris (1834-96), English poet, social critic, and partner with Dante Gabriel Rossetti (1828-82) in a firm which revived medieval handicrafts of all sorts.

[2] Morris' most famous poem (1870), a retelling of old myths by a group of Greek and Viking characters.

[3] George Henry Lewes (1817-78), English writer on philosophy and science, and the first husband of the noted novelist, George Eliot (1820-80).

ments. This was in answer to something I had said about the sparrows, rooks, and pigeons having taken up their lodging in the Tuileries,[4] an occupation which was more grateful to me than that of the unclean birds that housed there when I had seen it last. However, I remained unconverted, and one of my great pleasures is to watch the little creatures flying in and out and making themselves at home. Ruskin gave me the impression of a man of sentiment who seeks refuge from a sense of his own weakness in strong opinions (or at any rate the vehement assertion of them) as men reassure themselves by talking aloud in the dark. I conceived Rousseau the better for having seen him. I dined with Hughes [5] and spent a night with Stephen [6] while I was in London. One of my greatest pleasures was seeing Burne-Jones's [7] pictures and drawings in the house where Richardson [8] wrote *Clarissa*. He is something too Preraphaelite,[9] to be sure, but he has real grace and invention and that felicity of choice in his subjects which is so large a part of genius. Above all he has imagination, which always in some obscure way mixes itself with all past associations of happiness and gives us back our youth. It was easy to see that two men above all—Michel Angelo and Blake [10]—had deeply influenced him, but without fatally overlaying his originality. . . .

Your loving father
J. R. L.

---

[4] Palace of the French kings in Paris; built in 1564, burnt to the ground in 1871 by *The Commune,* the insurrectionary government of the time.

[5] Thomas Hughes (1823–96), English author known particularly for his novel *Tom Brown's School Days at Rugby* (1857).

[6] Sir Leslie Stephen (1832–1904), well-known English man of letters.

[7] Sir Edward Burne-Jones (1833–98), noted English painter, closely associated with Rossetti and Morris in the Pre-Raphaelite movement.

[8] Samuel Richardson (1689–1761), English novelist especially popular in his time for the moral sentiment of such works as *The History of Clarissa Harlowe* (1748).

[9] See note on p. 22.

[10] William Blake (1757–1828), a singular but gifted English artist and poet.

28. To T. B. Aldrich. (L., II, 98–102)

Paris, May 28, 1873.

My dear Aldrich,—I have been so busy lately with doing nothing (which on the whole demands more time, patience, and attention than any other business) that I have failed to answer your very pleasant letter of I don't know how long ago.

What you say about William amused me much.[1] You know there is a proverb that "service is no inheritance," but it was invented by the radical opposition—by some servant, that is, who was asking for higher wages. My relation with William realized the saying in an inverse sense, for I received him from my father, already partly formed by an easy master, and have, I think, pretty well finished his education. I believe I fled to Europe partly to escape his tyranny, and I am sure he is awaiting the return of his vassal to re-enter on all the feudal privileges which belong of right to his class in a country so admirably free as ours. He had all the more purchase upon me that his wife had been in our service before he was, so that he knew all my weak points beforehand. Nevertheless, he has been an excellent servant, diligent, sober, and systematic, and I have no doubt I shall end my days as his milch cow if the udders of my purse continue to have a drop in them. You would see his worst side. He has eyes all round his head for the main chance; but anybody would take advantage of *me,* and I prefer the shearer to whom I am wonted, who clips close, to be sure, but has skill enough to spare the skin. He saves me trouble, and that is a saving I would rather buy dear than any other. Beyond meat and drink, it is the only use I have ever discovered for money—unless you give it away, which is apt to breed enemies. You will forgive my saying that I feel a certain grain of pleasure (with the safe moat of ocean between) in thinking of you in your unequal struggle with Wilhelmus Conquestor.

It gives me a very odd feeling to receive a letter dated at

---

[1] Aldrich occupied Elmwood for almost two years, while Lowell was sojourning in Europe. "William" was the hired man.

Elmwood from anybody whose name isn't Lowell. I used to have a strange fancy when I came home late at night that I might find my double seated in my chair, and how should I prove my identity? Your letter revived it. I can see my study so plainly as I sit here—but I find it hard to fill my chair with anybody but myself. By the way, the study table was made of some old mahogany ones that came from Portsmouth—only I gave it to be done by a man in want of work, and of course the cheap-looking affair which affronts your eyes. 'Twas too bad, for the wood was priceless. You may have dined at it in some former generation. It is a pleasant old house, isn't it? Doesn't elbow one, as it were. It will make a frightful conservative of you before you know it. It was born a Tory and will die so. Don't get too used to it. I often wish I had not grown into it so. I am not happy anywhere else.

I am glad to hear you are writing a novel. Get it all done before you begin to print. Serials have been the bane of litera-ture. There is no more good ship-building. But I draw a good augury from your letter. You had the strength of mind to leave off at the end of your third page—though I would readily have forgiven you the fourth. This is a rare virtue, and if you will but write your book on the same principle of leaving off when you have done, I am sure I shall be glad to read it.

I shall stay out my two years, though personally I would rather be at home. In certain ways this side is more agreeable to my tastes than the other—but even the buttercups stare at me as a stranger and the birds have a foreign accent. I'll be hanged but the very clouds put on strange looks to thwart me, and turn the cold shoulder on me. However, I have learned to know and like the French during my nine months' stay among them.

I am sorry to hear they stole your fruit. It gave me a sensible pang, for the trees I have planted are part of myself, and I feel the furtive evulsion of every pear even at this distance. Get a dog. He will eat up all your chickens, keep you awake all moonlight nights, and root up all your flowers, but he will make you feel safe about your pears till they have been made booty of. Study the book of Job. It supplies one with admirable formulas of impatience, and in that way serves to reconcile one to his lot. To learn patience read the works of A.H.K.B.[2]

Give my love to Howells when you see him, and tell him that as he is pretty busy he will easily find time to write to me. I suppose he is in his new house by this time. And Bartlett's [3] house? I sha'n't know my Cambridge when I come back to it. Are you annexed yet? Before this reaches you I shall have been over to Oxford to get a D.C.L.[4] So by the time you get it this will be the letter of a Doctor and entitled to the more respect. Perhaps, in order to get the full flavor, you had better read this passage first if you happen to think of it. Do you not detect a certain flavor of parchment and Civil Law?

Mrs. Lowell joins me in kind regards to Mrs. Aldrich and yourself—and I am always

Yours cordially,

J. R. L.

P.S. I have kept this back for the Brest steamer, which saves me fourteen cents postage. We leave Paris in a day or two. I have learned to like it and the French, which is a great gain. We have had a very pleasant winter here in the most French of hotels. But Cambridge is better, as the rivers of Damascus were better than Jordan.[5] There is no place like it, no, not even for taxes! I am getting gray and fat—about ½ as large as Howells.

29. To HENRY ADAMS. (N.L., 198–201)

Bruges, 27th June, 1873.

Dear Adams,—I had meant to write my thanks to you and Madam, who twice have made a day and night good as the best

---

  [2] Lowell has mixed the initials slightly. They should read "A.K.H.B.," the initials of Andrew Kennedy Hutchinson Boyd (1825–99), minister of St. Andrews, Edinburgh, 1865–90, who began writing about 1854 in *Fraser's Magazine* under these initials and made a wide reputation for his essays of moral reflection, such as *Recreations of a Country Parson* (1860).

  [3] John Bartlett (1820–1905), the author of the famous *Familiar Quotations*.

  [4] Doctor of Civil Law.

  [5] See note on p. 97.

since Adam. Good company, good talk, good bed—a very pearl
of havens! nor was the prophet better fed by flocks of bill-less
ravens. The ills that dog a traveller's life are not what one can
call grave, who dines with Adams and his wife, with Woolner,[1]
Brooke,[2] and Palgrave.[3] I mused thereon till well across upon
my way to Flanders, foreboding not my breakfast's loss,—with
others 'twas *ganz anders*.[4] Our passengers were half High
Dutch, half sallow Portugueses, who did not seem to relish much
the least of little breezes. They gazed upon the frolic wave that
tilts the British Channel, and gradually grew as grave as, 'mong
the lions, Daniel. Byron the wild sea Muse heard shriek; for
me the steamer's whistle, (like a wire-edged neuralgic streak),
keeps time to my epistle. It blows, just when you least expect,
because the day is foggy and gives morn's eyelids that effect
called by the Fancy *groggy*. (Here I am forced to change my
views, as must historians *täglich;*[5] my Germans prove themselves rank Jews, pronouncing *schän* and *mäglich*.[6]) Soon sky
and sea come brightly out with no mist-veils to cross 'em, as
widows, overcoming doubt, from crapes to colors blossom.
Gray in the sun, in shadow blue, the smoke, with woolly motion,
to leeward trails a purplish hue across the blue-green ocean.
Oranges, crimsons, violets, grays, together wildly jumbled,—such
Turner in his latter days upon his canvas tumbled, with one
huge blur amid the rest like a transfigured bun set, and chal-
lenged Nature with her West to match him for a sunset.

The white cliffs sink; of quads I muse, of gardens, courts, and
cloisters where Fellows wait each others' shoes as tranquilly as
oysters. There, over mediaeval gates, the clustered ivy thickens,
and every sleepy stone awaits its wallflowers or its lichens.

---

[1] Thomas Woolner (1825–92), English sculptor of the Pre-Raphaelite
school.

[2] Stopford Augustus Brooke (1832–1916), English divine and man of
letters, author of a famous primer of English literature (1876).

[3] Francis Turner Palgrave (1824–97), English poet and critic, noted for
his *Golden Treasury of English Songs and Lyrics* (1861).

[4] Far otherwise.

[5] Daily.

[6] Lowell's humorous nasalization of the German words, *schön* (beautiful), and *möglich* (possible).

There, from the Present's bondage torn, the senses turn recluses; the flags by pacing feet seem worn of meditative Muses. Again I hear the Christ Church bells; a new-ennobled varlet, I flaunt among the other swells and dons my borrowed scarlet. On audit ale [7] I ride sublime, the best of mortal brewing; behind the horseman, for a time, Death seems to cease pursuing. Sure, in the gown and quadrate cap lurks such prevailing virtue, much meat and drink bring no mishap, nor Doctoring doesn't hurt you!—Like one cast down from being queen along the street to bawl soles, I feel when I compare the scene around me now with All Souls. A pupa, shorn of mealy wings, I find it to return hard from Courts where Fancy spinning sings, from Oxford and from Bernard.[8] As grim as I appear engraved, I took my place for London, but Norfolk Street her exile saved ere he was wholly undone. (From Eton, crowds the railway lined, held there by *vis inertiae,*[9] hoping to see rush by like wind the invisible Shaw of Pershy.) [10] Grave John, the stillest man alive, did, when I pulled the bell, come to say they'd all gone out to drive, and bid me pensive welcome. Then, like the pack of Christian's [11] cares, he shouldered my portmanteau, inviting me to mount the stairs, which straightway I began to. Then dinner came, and after that, digestion's purring leisure; then enter Fashion who cries, "Scat! begone, and take some pleasure!" Pleasure means coaxing dead champagne to some pretence of foam on't; so dutifully forth we train to Lady Margaret Beaumont.[12] A

---

[7] Ale of especially fine quality, brewed at the old English universities originally for use on the day of audit, that is, the day when the tenants of any college property used to come up to the college and settle their accounts, either quarterly or annual.

[8] Mountague Bernard (1820–82), fellow of All Souls College and professor of international law and diplomacy at Oxford University, acted as Lowell's host while the latter was there taking his honorary degree in June, 1873.

[9] The force of inertia.

[10] The Shah, or King, of Persia.

[11] See note on p. 25.

[12] Lady Margaret Anne De Burgh Canning (d. 1888), fourth daughter of the first Marquis of Clanricarde, county Galway, Ireland, and wife of Wentworth Blackett Beaumont, first Baron Allendale, had her town house in Piccadilly and was a fashionable London hostess. It was she who once, when Henry Adams sat at her breakfast table, made the startling remark,

multitudinous din of talk with here and there a quaver (snapt short upon its slender stalk) to give a musical flavor; a crowd all boring and all bored, all edging doorward slily, all tedious as a song encored, as solitary as Philae.[13] Such was the scene my fancy drew, dull as a psalm of Brady's;[14] but things improved on nearer view; 'twas pleasant at my lady's. Once more at home, we light our pipes and smoke till day is graying, like boors of Teniers's[15] or Cuyp's,[16] the natural man betraying. Next morn we sit us down in peace to the matutinal muffin contented as, in Southern seas, an unregenerate puffin.[17] Gravely we chat of trifling things, lightly give grave opinions; mix mutton chops with fates of kings, from High Art pass to chignons.[18] Old silver pale, a painted tile, the pattern of a trowser, no matter what, keeps Time the while as moveless as a mouser:—a mouser waiting for his spring, as I shall find tomorrow, when John my early bath shall bring and wake me to my sorrow. I had no chance to say goodbye to people in their slumbers, content to do it bye and bye in these haphazard numbers. Part rhymed I on the steamer's deck where the distraction huge is, part in this softly bedded wreck whose English name is Bruges. The meaning is, you filled my soul with peace if e'er there was peace, by changing my short London rôle from ξένος into *hospes*.[19] On your

"I don't think I care for foreigners!" (*The Education of Henry Adams,* Chap. xiii.)

[13] A small island of steep and wall-encircled shores above the cataract of Syene on the Nile. Since it was hallowed as the burying place of Osiris, and therefore only priests could live there, it came to be called in ancient times "the unapproachable place," near which neither birds nor fish were supposed to come.

[14] Nicholas Brady (1659–1726), an Anglican divine who with Nahum Tate, the then Poet Laureate, composed a metrical version of the Psalms which was used widely in the English churches from 1696.

[15] The Teniers family were celebrated Flemish painters in seventeenth-century Antwerp. Both David the Elder (1582–1649) and David the Younger (1610–90) painted pictures of carousing peasants.

[16] Albert Cuyp (1620–91), the most famous of a notable family of Dutch painters in Dordrecht, excelled in scenes of rural life.

[17] A sea-bird which, on account of dark plumage, white cheeks, and a large light plume over the eye, possesses a pompous and comical appearance.

[18] Knobs of natural or artificial hair, worn at the back or on the top of the head.

[19] From a stranger entertained in the home to a guest-friend of the family.

way home may Boreas [20] wheeze and Auster [21] only blow well enough to rock sleek Panopes! [22]   So prays yours J. R. Lowell.

30. To Miss Jane Norton. (L., II, 112–13)

Florence, Jan. 7, 1874.

. . . You find our beloved country dull, it seems.   With a library like that at Shady Hill [1] all lands are next door and all nations within visiting distance—better still, all ages are contemporary with us.   But I understand your feeling, I think. Women need social stimulus more than we.   They contribute to it more, and their magnetism, unless drawn off by the natural conductors, turns inward and irritates.   Well, when I come back I shall be a good knob on which to vent some of your superfluous electricity; though on second thoughts I am not so sure of that, for the Leyden jar [2] after a while becomes clever enough to give off sparks in return.   But, dear Jane, the world in general is loutish and dull.   I am more and more struck with it, and a certain sprightliness of brain, with which I came into life, is driven in on myself by continual rebuffs of misapprehension. I have grown wary and don't dare to let myself go, and what are we good for if our natural temperament doesn't now and then take the bit between its teeth and scamper till our hair whistles in the wind?   But indeed America is too busy, too troubled about many things, and Martha [3] is only good to make puddings. There is no *leisure,* and that is the only climate in which society is indigenous, the only one in which good-humor and wit and all the growths of art are more than half-hardy exotics.   It is not that one needs to be idle—but only to have this southern atmos-

---

[20] North wind.
[21] South wind.
[22] A sea-nymph.   (See Virgil's *Aeneid,* Bk. V, l. 246.)

[1] The Norton estate in Cambridge.
[2] A type of electrical condenser, invented in 1745 at Leyden, Holland.
[3] Sister of Mary and Lazarus, Jesus' friends in Bethany.   Once on a visit to their home Jesus reproved Martha, saying: "Martha, Martha, thou art careful and troubled about many things."   (See Luke xi: 38–42.)

phere about him. Democracies lie, perhaps, too far north. You were made—with your breadth of sympathy, the contagion of your temperament, and the social *go* of your mind—to drive the four-in-hand of a *salon,* and American life boxes us all up in a one-horse *sulky* [4] of absorbing occupation. We are isolated in our own despite, the people who have a common ground of sympathy in pursuits (or the want of them) are rare, and without partnership the highest forms of culture are impossible. . . .

31. To the Same. (L., II, 117–21)

Albergo Crocolle, Napoli,
Marzo 12, 1874.

My dear Jane,—If I should offer to explain any eccentricities of chirography by telling you my fingers were numb, you would think me joking, and be much rather inclined to account for it by the intoxication of this heavenliest of climates as you remember it. But I speak forth the words of truth and soberness when I assure you that Vesuvius is hoary with snow to his very roots, that Sorrento has just been hidden by a cloud which I doubt not is bursting in hail, for we were greeted on our arrival last night by a hailstone chorus of the most emphatic kind, so that the streets were white with it as we drove shiveringly along, and the top of the 'bus rattled to the old tune of "Pease on a Trencher." All the way from Rome I saw Virgil's too-fortunate husbandmen (he was right in his parenthetic *sua si bona norint* [1]) working with their great blue cloaks on, or crouching under hedges from the wire-edged wind. The very teeth in their harrows must have been chattering for cold. And this is the climate you so rapturously wish us joy of! *Vedi Napoli, e poi mori* [2] of a catarrh. I envy you with your foot of honest snow on the

---

[4] Light two-wheeled vehicle for a single person.

[1] If they only knew their blessings.—Virgil in his *Georgics,* Bk. II, ll. 458–59, writes: "*O fortunatos nimium, sua si bona norint, agricolas.* . . . (O too fortunate husbandmen, if they only knew their blessings)."

[2] I see Naples and then die.

ground where it ought to be, and not indigested in the atmosphere, giving it a chill beyond that of condensed Unitarianism.

We left Rome after a fortnight's visit to the Storys, which was very pleasant *quoad* [3] the old friends, but rather wild and whirling *quoad* the new. Two receptions a week, one in the afternoon and one in the evening, were rather confusing for wits so eremetical as mine. I am not equal to the *grand monde*.[4] 'Tis very well of its kind, I dare say, but it is not *my* kind, and I still think the company I kept at home better than any I have seen—especially better in its simplicity. The Old World carries too much top-hamper for an old salt like me to be easy in his hammock. There are good things west of the ocean in spite of ——'s [5] pessimism, and better things to come, let us hope. . . .

It is now (as regards my date) to-morrow the 13th. We have been twice to the incomparable Museum, which to me is the most interesting in the world. There is the keyhole through which we barbarians can peep into a Greek interior—provincial Greek, Roman Greek, if you will, but still Greek. Vesuvius should be sainted for this miracle of his—hiding Pompeii and Herculaneum [6] under his gray mantle so long, and saving them from those dreadful melters and smashers, the Dark Ages. Now we come in on them with the smell of wine still in their cups—we catch them boiling their eggs, selling their figs, and scribbling naughty things on the walls. I do not find that they were much our betters in parietal wit, but in sense of form how they dwarf us! They contrived to make commonplace graceful—or rather they could not help it. Well, we are alive (after a fashion) and they dead. That is one advantage we have over 'em. And they could not look forward to going home to Cambridge and to pleasant visits at Shady Hill. On the whole, I pity 'em. They are welcome to their poor little bronzes and things. Haven't we our newspapers, marry come up! What did they know about the Duke of Edinburgh's wedding and all the other edifying

---

[3] With respect to.

[4] High society.

[5] Probably Miss Norton's brother, Charles, who first edited this letter.

[6] Roman cities near Naples, which for centuries remained buried beneath volcanic ash and lava from Mt. Vesuvius.

things that make us wise and great, I should like to know? They were poor devils, after all, and I trample on 'em and snub 'em to my heart's content. Where were their Common Schools? They are dumb and cast down their eyes, every mother's son of 'em. Not a school-desk among all their relics! No wonder they came to grief.

It is now after dinner. I write this by installments, as the amiable bandits of this neighborhood send a man they have caught home to his friends till they pay a ransom—first one ear, then the other, and so on. I am a little cross with the table-d'hôte, because I always know so well what is coming—it is like the signs of the zodiac. I think we should be bored to death with the regular courses of the seasons were it not for the whimsicality of the weather. That saves us from suicide. On the other hand, though depressed by the inevitable *rosbif* [7] and *pollo arrostito*,[8] I am enlivened by a fiddle and guitar, and a voice singing the Naples of twenty years ago under my window. For Naples has changed for the worse (shade of Stuart Mill! [9] I mean for the better) more than any other Italian city. Fancy, there are no more *lazzaroni*,[10] there is no more *corricolo*.[11] The mountains are here, and Capri, but where is Naples? *Italia unita* [12] will be all very well one of these days, I doubt not. At present it is paper money, and the practical instead of the picturesque. Is the day of railways worse than that of Judgment? Why could not one country be taken and the other left? Let them try all their new acids of universal suffrage and what not

---

[7] Roast beef.

[8] Roast chicken.

[9] John Stuart Mill (1816–73), English philosopher and economist, strongly urged the possibility of improvement in living conditions through social planning. His chief works are *Principles of Political Economy* (1848) and *Utilitarianism* (1863).

[10] Beggars.

[11] A Neapolitan gig, formerly seen along the quays, having a single seat which accommodated one or two passengers, and drawn originally by one horse. Later, when more passengers were crowded on, a second horse was added in a crude tandem arrangement. See Alexandre Dumas' *Impressions de Voyage: Le Corricolo,* Introduction, for an amusing description of this obsolete vehicle.

[12] United Italy:—a patriotic campaign cry of that period.

on the tough body of the New World. The skin will heal again. But this lovely, disburied figure of Ausonia [13]—they corrode her marble surface beyond all cure. *Panem et circenses* [14] wasn't so bad after all. A bellyful and amusement—isn't that more than the average mortal is apt to get? more than perhaps he is capable of getting? America gives the *panem,* but do you find it particularly amusing just now? My dear Jane, you see I have had a birthday since I wrote last, and these are the sentiments of a gentleman of fifty-five—and after dinner. Change in itself becomes hateful to us as we grow older, and naturally enough, because every change in ourselves is for the worse. I am writing to you, for example, by lamp-light, and I feel what used to be a pleasure almost a sin. To-morrow morning I shall see that the crows have been drinking at my eyes. Fanny is wiser (as women always are), and is sound asleep in her armchair on the other side of the fire. The wood here, by the way, is poplar—good for the inn-keeper, but only cheering for the guest, as it reminds him of the Horatian *large super foco ligna reponens,*[15] and the old fellow in Smollett,[16] whom you never read. . . .

32. To Mrs. Francis J. Lippitt. (N.L., 206–7)

Elmwood, 21ˢᵗ August, 1874.

Dear Mrs. Lippitt,—I do not well enough remember the poem you ask about to give any intelligent opinion about it. If I recollect, it is one of those monologues of self-analysis that Browning brought into fashion and which must depend for their interest on poignancy of phrase and ingenuity of treatment rather than on any value they may possess whether metaphysical or (in the highest sense) poetical. Generally, I mean, for I think

---

[13] Poetical name for Italy.

[14] Bread and games in the arena:—the fare given to the populace by Roman politicians from ulterior motives.

[15] Piling high the wood upon the hearth. (Horace, *Odes,* I, 9: 5.)

[16] Presumably Matthew Bramble, the Welsh squire, in *Humphrey Clinker* (1771).

Browning's Caliban [1] a very wonderful psychological study. But the *form* is always a bother to me. People *don't* cross-examine their motives and dissect the nerves of their character in this fashion. If they did, to know oneself would not be the tough job it generally turns out to be. A man's ignorance in this useful department of learning holds out wonderfully against the schooling of experience, the good offices of friends and enemies, nay, even against the sharper lesson of the suffering which sooner or later is sure to be its own result. If it didn't, suicide would be much more common than it is. The ingenuity of self-love thrusts numberless buffers between our conceit of ourselves and the thrusts of conscience.

As for the aphrodisiac or cantharides style of verses, I do not believe that the sexual impulses need any spurring, nor, if they did, that the rowel would be forged of that most precious metal of poesy whereof the Shield of Achilles or the Grecian Urn could be hammered. The line between the sensuous and the sensual is that between sentiment and sentimentalism, between passion and brutish impulse, between love and appetite, between Vittoria-Colonna [2] and Madame Bovary.[3] Cleopatra, one may suspect, was much rather a harlot of the brain (that is, from political motives) than of the senses, though Shakespeare (and even Dryden) have idealized her in the only possible way by throwing around her the lurid light of a sublime passion, and even then there is the inevitable aspic at the end of the rose-strewn path of dalliance. To show her disidealized into a mere lustful animal, is to degrade her to a Catherine II,[4] and thrust her beyond the pale of poesy. Shelley almost alone (take his "Stanzas to an Indian air," for example) has trodden with an unfaltering foot

---

[1] In his dramatic monologue *Caliban upon Setebos; or, Natural Theology in the Island* (1864).

[2] See note on p. 131.

[3] Madame Bovary, the heroine of the French novel of the same name by Gustave Flaubert (1821–80). A young woman romantically inclined but married to a humdrum provincial doctor, she has an affair and then poisons herself out of fear that her unfaithfulness will be discovered.

[4] Catherine the Great (1729–96), German wife of Peter III and Empress of Russia from 1762 to 1796, usurped her husband's throne, had him assassinated thereafter, and then ruled with a violent ambition for power and domain.

the scimetar-edged bridge which leads from physical sensation to the heaven of song. No, I certainly do *not* believe in the value of any literature that renders the relation between the sexes more ticklish than nature has already made it, or which paints self-indulgence as nobler than self-restraint. That is to unsettle the only moral center of gravity we have. With love to Mrs. Bowen and Mrs. Lowell's kindest remembrances to both of you,

Your affectionate Cousin

J. R. Lowell.

33. To C. E. Norton. (L., II, 131–33)

Elmwood, Oct. 7, 1874.

My dear Charles,—The nameless author of that delightful poem, "The Squyr of Lowe Degree" [1] (may God him save and see!) gives a list of every bird he can think of that sang to comfort his hero. Here they are:

1. Lavrock,
2. Nightingale,
3. Pie,
4. Popinjay,
5. Throstil,
6. Marlyn,
7. Wren,
8. Jay,
9. Sparrow,
10. Nuthatch,
11. Starling,
12. Goldfinch,
13. Ousel.

On Monday the 5th I walked up to the Oaks [2] with Stillman,[3] and

---

[1] A fifteenth-century English narrative of chivalric love.

[2] Waverley Oaks, now a small state park about three miles west of Elmwood.

[3] William James Stillman (1828–1901), well-known painter, journalist, diplomat, and intimate friend of Lowell.

in a quarter of an hour had noted on a paper the following birds
(most of which counted by dozens):

1. Robin,
2. Wilson's thrush (singing),
3. Chewink,
4. Bluebird (warbling as in spring),
5. Phoebe (doing his best),
6. Ground sparrow (singing),
7. Tree   "   ("   ),
8. Nuthatch,
9. Flicker (laughing and crying like Andromache),
10. Chickadee (doing all he could),
11. Goldfinch,
12. Linnet,
13. Jay,
14. Crow (to balance his popinjay),
15. Catbird.

Thus I take down the gauntlet which you left hanging for
all comers in your English hedge. I don't believe that hedge
birds are a whit more respectable than hedge priests or hedge
schoolmasters. All the while we were there the air was tinkling
with one or other of them. Remember—this was in October.
Three cheers for the rivers of Damascus! [4]

Affectionately always,

Hosea Biglow.

Et ego in Arcadia,[5] says Mr. Wilbur.

34. To Mrs. S. B. Herrick. (L., II, 162–64)

Elmwood, April 19, 1876.

. . . But I did not tell you the worst. Horace confesses that
he was stout, or at any rate implies it. Thomson says plumply

---

[4] See note on p. 97.
[5] And I am in Arcadia; i.e., I am living an ideally rustic life. Arcadia
was a lovely mountain district in the Greek Peloponnesus.

that he was *fat* [1]—an odious word. I suppose Coleridge would
have admitted a certain amiable rotundity of presence. Byron
wrestled with increasing flesh, as it had been well for him to do
against growing fleshliness. But such is the weakness of our
poor human nature that never one of them could bring himself
to the shameful confession that he had lost his *waist*. There is
the tender spot, and I claim a certain amount of admiration when
I admit that *mine* has been growing more and more obscure (like
many a passage in Browning) for several years. Now, a waist
is as important in a poet's economy as in a woman's. But this
is too sad a topic. You see I disenchant you by installments—
and, how shall I say it? I am writing at this moment with
spectacles (not *nippers,* mind you, but the steel-bowed deformity
which pale young parsons love) across my prosaic nose. It is
horrible, but it is true. I have, to be sure, the saving grace of
being still a little touchy about them, and have never yet allowed
any of the servants to see me in my debasement. *Nippers* have
still a pretension of foppishness about them, and he who is foppish has not yet abandoned the last stronghold of youth, or, if he
has, he at least marches out with the honors of war. I have laid
down my arms. That steel bow is Romance's Caudine Forks.[2]
I used to have the eye of a hawk, and a few days ago I mistook
a flight of snow-birds for English sparrows! Have you still the
courage to come? If you have, we shall be all the gladder to
see you, and I will make you welcome to whatever I have contrived to save from the wreck of myself. Age makes Robinson
Crusoes of the best of us, and makes us ingenious in contrivances
and substitutes, but what cunning expedient will ever replace
youth? In one respect only I have lost nothing. I think I am
as great a fool as ever, and that is no small comfort. I believe,
too, that I still feel the blind motions of spring in my veins with
the same sense of *prickle* as trees do, for I suppose their sense of

---

[1] James Thomson (1700–48) describes himself in *The Castle of Indolence*
(1748), Canto I, l. 604, as "more fat than bard beseems."

[2] I.e., Romance's complete surrender. The Caudine Forks, or *Furculae
Caudinae,* were a pair of narrow passes in Samnium, one at each end of a
mountain-surrounded valley. There in 321 B.C. the Samnites bottled up a
Roman army and captured it entire.

April must be very much like ours when a limb that has been asleep, as we call it, is fumbling after its suspended sensation again.

Are you a stout walker? If you are, I will show you my oaks while you are here. If you are not, I will still contrive to make you acquainted with them in some more ignominious way. They will forgive you, I dare say, for the sake of so old a friend as I. Besides, they are no great pedestrians themselves unless, like Shelley's Appenine,[3] they walk abroad in the storm. We haven't much to show here. We are a flat country, you know, but not without our charm, and I love Nature, I confess, not to be always on her high horse and with her tragic mask on. Bostonians generally (I am not a Bostonian) seem to have two notions of hospitality—a dinner with people you never saw before nor ever wish to see again, and a drive in Mount Auburn cemetery, where you will see the worst man can do in the way of disfiguring nature. Your memory of the dinner is expected to reconcile you to the prospect of the graveyard. But I am getting treasonable.

Now to business. You must let me know in good season when you are coming, because I wish to make sure of some pleasant people for you to meet. Don't come till May, if you can help it, for our spring is backward and we don't do ourselves justice yet. But come at any rate. . . .

35. To Miss Grace Norton. (L., II, 198)

*Grosvenor Hotel, Park Street,
London, July 29, 1877.*

. . . I have just come in from Hyde Park, whither I go to smoke my cigar after breakfast. The day is as fine as they can make 'em in London: the sun shines and the air is meadowy. I sat and watched the sheep crawl through the filmy distance,

---

[3] The last line of Shelley's *Passage of the Apennines* (1818) reads:

And the Apennine walks abroad with the storm.

The Apennine chain of mountains extend through Italy from north to south.

unreal as in a pastoral of the last century, as if they might have
walked out of a London eclogue of Gay.[1] Fancy saw them
watched by beribboned shepherdesses and swains. Now and
then a scarlet coat would cross my eye like a stain of blood on
the innocent green. The trees lifted their cumulous outlines
like clouds, and all around was the ceaseless hum of wheels that
never sleep. . . . This scene in the Park is one of which I never
tire. I like it better than anything in London. If I look westward I am in the country. If I turn about, there is the never-
ebbing stream of coaches and walkers, the latter with more
violent contrasts of costume and condition than are to be seen
anywhere else, and with oddities of face and figure that make
Dickens seem no caricaturist. The landscape has the quiet far-
offness of Chaucer. The town is still the town of Johnson's
London. . . .

36. To William M. Evarts, Secretary of State. (N.L., 233–34)

Legation of the United States,
Madrid, 6th Feb'y, 1878.

Sir,— . . . One of the devices of Fourcarde,[1] which came within
Mr. Silvela's own knowledge when in another Department of
the Government is so ingenious and amusing as to be worth
recounting. The Frenchman's object was to smuggle petroleum
into Madrid without paying the *octroi*.[2] To this end he established his storehouses in the suburbs, and then hiring all the
leanest and least mammalian women that could be found, he
made good all their physical defects with tin cases filled with
petroleum, thus giving them what Dr. Johnson would have called
the pectorial proportions of Juno. Doubtless he blasphemed the
unwise parsimony of Nature in denying to women in general

---

[1] See note on p. 5. Gay wrote some eclogues or pastoral poems.

[1] The opening portion of this letter refers to Spanish complaints that a
New York firm, through the agency of a Frenchman, Fourcarde, was im-
porting refined oil into Spain as crude oil.

[2] Import tax.

the multitudinous breasts displayed by certain Hindu idols.
For some time these seeming milky mothers passed without
question into the unsuspecting city and supplied thousands of
households with that cheap enlightenment which cynics say is
worse than none. Meanwhile Mr. Fourcarde's pockets swelled
in exact proportion to the quaker breastworks of the improvised
wetnurses. Could he only have been moderate! Could he only
have bethought him in time of the *ne quid nimis*.[3] But one
fatal day he sent in a damsel whose contours aroused in one of
the guardians at the gates the same emotions as those of Mari-
tornes [4] in the bosom of the carrier. With the playful gallantry
of a superior he tapped the object of his admiration and—it
tinkled. He had "struck oil" unawares. Love shook his wings
and fled; Duty entered frowning; and M. Fourcarde's perambulating wells suddenly went dry.

With a gentleman so ingenious the Spanish Government is
perhaps justified in being on its guard. Even charity has eyes
and ears.

> I have the honor to be,
> Very respectfully,
> Your obedient servant,
> J. R. Lowell.

37. To Miss Grace Norton. (L., II, 224–28)

7 Cuesta de Sto. Domingo, Aug. 11, 1878.

. . . Madrid is the noisiest city I ever dwelt in. The street-
cries are endless, and given with a will and with such distortions
of face as must be seen to be believed. None are musical. One
always stirs my fancy by its association with Aladdin—the
lamparero.[1] Shall I try my luck? I think not, for in his cry I
have the material for rows of palaces, whereas if I bought a lamp
I might rub in vain. The first sound in the morning is the tinkle

---

[3] Avoidance of excess (lit., nothing too much).
[4] The Asturian wench at the inn in *Don Quixote*, Pt. I, Bk. III, Chap. 2.

[1] Lamplighter.

of bells on the necks of the she-asses that come in to be milked
at the customer's door for surety. I know not who the customers are, but there must be many if there be any truth in the
vulgar belief that children take after their nurses. Then there is
a succession of blind players on the guitar, on the pipe and
tabor, and on what I suppose to be the *gaita*.[2] They sometimes
also sing, but commonly have with them a boy or girl who shrieks
a *romance*.[3] All the tunes are the same so far as I can make out
—just as in a school of poetry. Then the town is full of parrots
and caged quails. I don't suppose we are exceptional, but there
are five parrots in this house and the next together, all birds of
remarkable talents. One hangs in the court-yard of our house
and sings, shouts, calls names, and swears all day long. In this
same *patio*,[4] by the way, I have heard songs issuing from the
servants' quarters in every floor and from the grooms in the
court-yard at the same time. The voices are seldom agreeable
and the tunes always monotonous. Indeed they seem to have
but one. I can't catch much of the words, but the other day I
heard, *"Yo soy el capitan de la tropa,"*[5] and presently, *"Yo soy
el duque de Osuna,"*[6] from which I surmised a Lord of Burleigh[7] who was gradually revealing himself. I was wrong in
saying that all the street-cries are harsh. There is a girl who
passes every day crying radishes who really makes a bit of melody
with her *Rábanos!*[8] It is seldom that one does not hear (night
or day) a thrumming or a snatch of nasal song, and I am pretty
well persuaded that it was the Spanish dominion which planted
the seeds of the Neapolitan street-music.

At this season they sleep in the day a good deal, and at night
are as lively as certain skipping insects, with which many of
them are only too familiar. Far from being a grave people, they
seem to me a particularly cheerful one, and yet I am struck with

[2] Bagpipe.
[3] Ballad.
[4] Courtyard.
[5] "I am the captain of the troop."
[6] "I am the duke of Osuna."
[7] William Cecil, Baron Burghley or Burleigh (1520–98), distinguished
English statesman and principal adviser of Queen Elizabeth.
[8] Radishes.

the number of deeply-furrowed faces one meets, the mark of hereditary toil. I turn half communist when I see them. The porters especially stir an angry sympathy in me, sometimes old men (nay, often) tottering under incredible burthens, which they carry on their backs steadied by a cord passed round the forehead. Every day I recall that passage in Dante where he stoops from sympathy, like an ox in the yoke. The traditional figures of the *genre* painters one sees rarely now, and yet there is no lack of costume. One meets constantly men in the very costume of Velasquez's "Lanzas," [9] which sometimes has a very odd effect on my fancy. The reality makes a very different impression from the attempted illusion of the stage, and has made me understand better why I don't care for such pictures as many of Meissonier's [10] and the like—clever as they are. But here is theme for a dissertation. I suppose that in some remote way the notion of *sincerity* has something to do with it, and here, I suspect, is to be found the distinction between the *reality* of Dante and modern realism. A great deal of what is called pre-Raphaelite on canvas and in verse gives me the same uncomfortable feeling of *costume*. You will guess what I mean if I am not very clear. To come back to statistics.

I never saw anything like the fruit in Madrid for abundance and variety. The oranges, plums, melons, apricots, and nectarines are the best I ever saw. I have sometimes eaten finer melons of my own growing—but my average was never so high. Then we have grapes, pomegranates, pears (not nearly so fine as ours), apples (ordinary), prickly pears, peaches (tolerable), medlars. What surprises me is how long the season is. We are never without something. Grapes begin in June and last till December.

The city of Madrid at first disappointed me greatly by its modern look. I had expected to find the "mise en scène" of

---

[9] "Surrender of Breda," also called "Las Lanzas" ("The Lances") on account of the serried rank of lances which break the sky background, is a masterpiece of historical scene by the celebrated Spanish painter, Don Diego Rodriguez de Silva y Velasquez (1599–1660).

[10] Jean Louis Ernest Meissonier (1815–91), a well known French painter, whose chief *genre* was miniatures in oils, done with amazing detail.

Calderon.[11] But I gradually became reconciled, and now like it. Moreover, I begin to suspect that I hadn't understood Calderon, and that his scenery is applicable to the present city—at least in a measure. The Prado with its continuations is fine, and the Buen Retiro as agreeable a drive as I know—more agreeable, I add on reflection, than anything of the kind I know of in any other city. But then I am bewitched with the Campiña. To me it is grander than the Campagna; of course I do not count the associations. I mean as a thing to look at and fall in love with. The Guadarramas are quite as good as or better than the Alban mountains, and their color is sometimes so ethereal that they seem visionary rather than real. The Campiña, I admit, is sombre—but its variety and shift of color, its vague undulations! At night, especially, it is like the sea, and even in the day sometimes. We are, you know, twenty-five hundred feet above the sea, but beside that, Madrid stands on hills more considerable than those of Rome and commanding wider horizons. The climate thus far has been incomparable. In our year here we have had, I believe, only three days when it rained. All blue, night and day, and such a blue! Nothing so limpid have I ever conceived. I should hate such a climate were I living in the country. I should sympathize too keenly with my trees, should be always feeling the drouth of their roots, and being wretched. But here it makes no odds. The trees are watered daily, and there are really beautiful gardens.

This is the course of my day: get up at 8, from 9 sometimes till 11 my Spanish professor, at 11 breakfast, at 12 to the Legation, at 3 home again and a cup of chocolate, then read the paper and write Spanish till a quarter to 7, at 7 dinner, and at 8 drive in an open carriage in the Prado till 10, to bed at 12 to 1. In cooler weather we drive in the afternoon. I am very well— cheerful and no gout. . . .

Your affectionate
J. R. L.

---

[11] See note on p. 38.

38. To W. D. Howells. (L., II, 239-41)

Madrid, May 2, 1879.

Dear Howells,—When Aldrich passed through here he brought
me some excuse or other from you for not having answered a
letter of mine. Was it an abominable sarcasm sent all the way
over the ocean with its subtile barb dipt in sweetened poison—
the worst kind of all? If not, the sensation is so novel that I
ought not to endanger it by any clumsy interferences of mine.
I am as sure as I well can be of anything that no man ever before
accomplished the feat of owing me a letter. Believe me, my
dear boy, it is your most exquisite literary achievement. My
own debts of this kind commonly gather and gather till bank-
ruptcy is the only possible outlet—and without a dividend.
Never a court in Christendom would whitewash me. Now I
am going to astonish you by paying you a penny in the pound.

And yet I can't say that you had wholly neglected me. I
always fancy that an author's works are more intimately addressed to his friends, have passages in them written in sympathetic ink invisible to the vulgar, but revealing themselves to
the penetrating warmth of friendship. And your "Lady of the
Aroostook" was to me a delightful instance of this cryptography.
I read it as it came out in the *Atlantic,* and was always as impatient for more as the French ladies used to be for more Arabian
Nights. It is delightful, and there was never a slyer bit of satire
than your Englishman who loves the real American flavor,
while his wife is abolishing herself as hard as she can in a second-
hand Anglicism. . . .

I am painfully struck, by the way, with the amount of discussion going on just now, which somehow implies a certain consciousness of inferiority on our part as compared with our English cousins. (I confess, let me say in passing, that I am tired
to death of [White']s [1] laborious demonstration that we have a

---

[1] Richard Grant White (1821–85), well known American critic and

right to our mother-tongue! If he would devote himself to hunting down American vulgarisms and corruptions—I observe that even the *Atlantic,* in some sort the child of my entrails, confuses *will* and *shall*—more power to his elbow!) I think we were less conscious when I was a youngster. Nowadays Europe, and especially England, seems a glass of which everybody is uncomfortably aware, an horizon which, instead of suggesting something beyond itself, cuts us all off with reflections of (perhaps I should say on) our unhappy selves. We are all the time wondering what is thought of us over there, instead of going quietly about our business.

However, my opinion is of no earthly consequence, for I feel every day more sensibly that I belong to a former age. A new generation has grown up that knows not Joseph, and I have nothing left to do but to rake together what embers are left of my fire and get what warmth out of them I may. I still take an interest, however, in what some of the young ones are doing, as a gambler who has emptied his pockets still watches the game, and especially in you who always do conscientious work. So I venture to tell you that I think your new book especially *wholesome* and admirable.

You can't imagine how far I am away from the world here—I mean the modern world. Spain is as primitive in some ways as the books of Moses and as oriental. Spaniards have, I believe, every possible fault—and yet I love the jades for a' that! They find themselves in the midst of a commercial age, poor devils! with as little knowledge of book-keeping as the Grand Turk. But there is something fine in this impenetrability of theirs, and the grand way they wrap themselves in their ragged *capa* [2] of a past and find warmth in their pride. Their indiffer-

---

editor, had undertaken an extended comparison of American and English usage of selected words and idioms. His discussion under the title, *Americanisms,* began in the *Atlantic Monthly* of which Howells was at this time editor, in April, 1878, and continued to appear at irregular intervals until May, 1880. His thesis was that *all* deviations from the best *English* usage are barbarisms.

[2] Cloak.

ence to legitimate profit is a continual comfort, and they have no
more enterprise than an Old Cambridge man.

Good-by. Write another story at once, and don't forget

Your affectionate old friend,

J. R. L.

39. To WILLIAM H. FURNESS. (N.L., 247–49)

[*Madrid*]
13 July, 1879.

Dear Dr. Furness,—It was a very kind thought in you to give
me an account of your visit to Emerson and of his actual condition, for I feared from what I had heard that his mind as well
as memory had begun to fail him. The tone of your letter,
even more than what you say, convinces that he is at least happy,
and happy from his own resources. This is as it should be, for
he of all men deserves

> An old age serene and bright,
> And lovely as a Lapland night,[1]

and so I fancy him since your letter with one daylight bending
over to kiss the other above his head. However, I cannot conceive him as an old man. I associate him always with things
vernal and in their prime, with the everlasting forces that know
not decay, and though by the common doom his bodily presence
must be taken from us ere long, there are few men of whom so
much will be left living and giving life. I have never known
a character on the whole so beautiful, so high above *self,* and so
kindly a mixture of strength and gentleness. How firmly he
always held his own and that without ever withstanding others

---

[1] The last three lines of Wordsworth's poem *To a Young Lady who had
been reproached for taking long walks in the country* read:

> But an old age serene and bright,
> And lovely as a Lapland night,
> Shall lead thee to thy grave.

but only the thing they represented. I have known a bit of scenery and now and then a Cathedral to stamp itself on my memory as he did, but no other man and no other thing. I remember as if it were of yesterday the first time I ever walked with him and the exquisite suavity of his demeanor towards me—a boy of nineteen and very young of my age. It was to the "South-Cliff" (I think they called it) in Concord, a lovely summer day forty one years ago. What another New England it was then to that we have now!

I sometimes think that it is not our own growing-old that is painful—if indeed we are altogether conscious of it—but that of those older than ourselves and associated with the better memories of our prime. With every one of them we lose a bit of our youth which survived for us still in them, and at last find ourselves alone in an unfamiliar or even alienated landscape which they tell us is the same but from which all the old landmarks that made it dear to us are gone. Even the cutting-down of a long-known tree leaves a scar in the heart that aches in bad weather, but when the *cara e buona imagine paterna* [2] of such a man as Emerson is seen no more a gap is left between us and our past that nothing can ever fill. . . .

With great respect
faithfully and cordially yours
J. R. Lowell

40. To Mrs. Hill [1]

*Hotel Danieli, Venice,
23rd Oct. 1881.*

Dear Mrs. Hill,

Your very friendly and welcome letter has found me here whither I am fled on leave of absence. Venice would give an agreeable flavour to almost anything that lacked it as your letter

---

[2] Dear and good fatherly likeness.

[1] This letter, now in the possession of the University of Cincinnati Library, is here printed for the first time.

certainly didn't. I am very glad you were pleased with my little Mark Antony speech,[2] for it was a difficult thing to do—"and therefore worth doing" you will object. True, but I was so harassed and had so little time to think it over! However, I think I managed *not to put my foot in it,* one of the main secrets of successful oratory though not mentioned in any treatise that I ever happened to read. It is so easy on such occasions to say too much, or, in evading that, to say too little. I believe my countrymen were pleased with it from what I hear.

I am grieved that Mr. Hill should have needed the operation you mention, though at his age, it is likely to be permanently successful. His eyes are too precious to be lost. Give him my kindest regards and accept them also yourself.

Faithfully yours
J. R. Lowell.

It is raining, but even that can't make Venice gray, immortal beauty as she is! Congratulate me I am off in a gondola presently.

41. To Mrs. George W. Smalley [1]

Venice, 2nd Nov. 1881.

Dear Mrs. Smalley,

I think one should be in the mood for writing a letter just as for writing a poem. But I am not. If anything could put me into it, surely such charming notes as yours might, for one of which I had to thank you yesterday. But there is no help for it. I *am* heavy this morning though the sun is shining on

---

[2] His address on President James A. Garfield, which he delivered on September 24, 1881, at the memorial meeting in Exeter Hall, London, before an audience composed largely of American citizens. Garfield had been wounded on July 2, but did not die till September 19. Lowell likens his role on this occasion to that of Mark Anthony who addressed his fellow Romans after the assassination of Julius Caesar.

[1] This letter, now in the possession of the University of Cincinnati Library, is here printed for the first time.

my paper as I write and Venice (like the true woman she is) is giving me a smile just as she is going to lose me. For a wonder we have had two clear days running and I stood on my balcony last night looking over at San Giorgio and then up the Canal towards Santa Maria della Salute and thinking how the moon flattered everything and that I liked her all the better for it. I am a pretty faithful lover and Venice never looked more beautiful in my eyes than now. It is I who need to be seen by moonlight and not she, for she has the privilege of beauty and never grows older.

Yesterday I wandered into St. Mark's and saw the high altar uncovered and then into the Doge's Palace to see the Tintoreto and find the Bacchus and Ariadne more lovely than ever. Then I took the little steamer and went to the Lido (which is grown a favourite of mine) where I walked an hour or more and thought of the dear footprints that have been washed out on its sands but which my fancy could still trace there.[2] It will soon be thirty years since I first walked there! I walked to the left this time and in the whole distance found but a single one of your roseleaves. So I was lucky the other day—if I can but get my trophies safe to London. Did I tell you that I found the Brownings [3] here? They too have been often at the Lido and I am afraid (as they started for London Tuesday) that he will forestall me. If so, I shall keep my roseleaves to myself as a kind of testimonial to character showing that I do not always forget commissions—when they are agreeable. I took good care not to remind him of *his* commission, so that I might at least have a chance of doing you a service.

There are no more gondolas to be had because the gondoliers are on a strike which began yesterday morning. They are as rare as horses and this gives Venice a strange look and a strange silence. (I have just found a hair on my paper, which seems to be from my beard, and am highly pleased to find it brown. If

---

[2] Lowell's maiden visit to Venice was made in May, 1852, with his first wife, Maria White Lowell, who died on October 27, 1853.

[3] The famous poet, Robert Browning (1812–89), and his sister Sarianna (1814–1903).

beauty draw us with a single hair, as Mr. Pope says it does,[4] you see I am willing to hold on to (what is left of) my youth by as frail a leash.)

I leave Venice tomorrow morning for Florence in company with my dear old friend Field [5] whom I found here. I shall hope for news of you there, if you have leisure and inclination. Did you get the second dove's feather I sent you?

I send you a bit of confidential news which I hope will please you. Mr. Blaine [6] has telegraphed bidding me take my house for another year. Having occasion to write to Lord Granville [7] I mentioned this in confidence and this morning received a telegram from him saying "Delighted to hear the good news. It has given me real pleasure." Will you say as much as Earl Granville, K. G.[8]?

I must end my fruitless apology for a letter, for I must go to meet Field to make some farewell calls. Half my holiday (almost) is over and I shall soon be turning northwards again. I wish I thought I were coming back a better and wiser man, but that at my age is hopeless. You have been always kind enough to tolerate me as I am and I hope therefore will like me no worse for continuing so. Give my kindest regards to Mr. Smalley and the children.

Faithfully yours always

J. R. L.

P.S. I was glad to hear you were to dine with Fanny [9] Sunday. *Addio!* [10]

---

[4] Alexander Pope (1688–1744), noted English poet and satirist, in *The Rape of the Lock*, Canto II, l. 28.

[5] John W. Field, one of Lowell's American companions during his first visit to Italy thirty years previous.

[6] James G. Blaine (1830–93), Secretary of State, simply passed on the official request of President Chester A. Arthur, who succeeded to the presidency upon Garfield's death, that Lowell continue as American minister to England.

[7] Granville George Leveson-Gower, second Earl of Granville (1815–91), English statesman, secretary for foreign affairs, 1870–74, 1880–85.

[8] Knight of the Garter.—The Order of the Garter is the highest honorary order in Great Britain.

[9] Frances Dunlap Lowell, his second wife.

[10] Good-bye!

42. To Oliver Wendell Holmes. (N.L., 262)

10 Lowndes Square,
S.W. 21st. Dec[r]*., 1881.*

Dear Doctor Holmes,—a clever and accomplished man should no more need an introduction than a fine day, but since a stranger can no longer establish a claim on us by coming in and seating himself as a suppliant at our fireside, let me ask you to be serviceable to the bearer of this, Mr. Oscar Wilde,[1] the report of whom has doubtless reached you and who is better than his report.

Faithfully yours,
J. R. Lowell

43. To T. B. Aldrich. (L., II, 267–68)

Legation of the United States,
London, May 8, 1882.

Dear Aldrich,—If I could, how gladly I would![1] But I am piecemealed here with so many things to do that I cannot get a moment to brood over anything as it must be brooded over if it is to have wings. It is as if a sitting hen should have to mind the door-bell. I speak as of the days of Æsop, which I mention lest some critic should charge me with not knowing what a mixed metaphor was—or rather an incongruous conception.

Now, you who are young and clever will at once divine what I mean you to divine from that last sentence—namely, that a man with his mind in so self-conscious a state as that can't write *any*thing to advantage, and I should wish to do my best for a

---

[1] At this date Wilde, twenty-five years of age, had not yet published any notable literary work, but had achieved notoriety for his wit and affectations.

---

[1] Mr. Aldrich, then editor of the *Atlantic Monthly,* had asked Lowell to contribute an article on his Cambridge friend of half a century, Richard Henry Dana (1815–82), who had died in January.

man so intimately associated with what is dearest to me. No, you must wait till I come home to be boycotted in my birthplace by my Irish fellow-citizens (who are kind enough to teach me how to be American), who fought all our battles and got up all our draft riots. Then, in the intervals of firing through my loopholes of retreat, I may be able to do something for the *Atlantic*.

I am now in the midst of the highly important and engrossing business of arranging for the presentation at Court of some of our fair *citoyennes*.[2] Whatever else you are, never be a Minister! With kind regards to Mrs. Aldrich,

Faithfully yours,
J. R. Lowell.

44. To C. E. Norton. (L., II, 272–73)

10 Lowndes Sq., S.W., April 22, 1883.

. . . I like London, and have learned to see as I never saw before the advantage of a great capital. It establishes one set of weights and measures, moral and intellectual, for the whole country. It is, I think, a great drawback for us that we have as many as we have States. The flow of life in the streets, too—sublimer, it seems to me often, than the tides of the sea—gives me a kind of stimulus that I find agreeable even if it prompt to nothing. For I am growing old, dear Charles, and haven't the go in me I once had. Then I have only to walk a hundred yards from my door to be in Hyde Park, where, and in Kensington Gardens, I can tread on green turf and hear the thrushes sing all winter. I often think of what you said to me about the birds here. There *are* a great many more and they sing more perennially than ours. As for the climate, it suits me better than any I ever lived in, and for the inward weather, I have never seen civilization at so high a level in some respects as here. In plain living and high thinking I fancy we have, or used to have, the advantage, and I have

---

[2] Female citizens.

never seen society, on the whole, so good as I used to meet at our Saturday Club.[1]

Always affectionately yours,

J. R. Lowell.

45. To Mrs. W. K. Clifford. (L., II, 284–85)

Hurstbourne, Nov. 16, 1884.

. . . Everybody has gone to church, and I have just come in from walking up and down the avenues of meditation, by which orientalism I mean an avenue of autumnal trees, in one of which (an elm that has changed all its leaves into fairy gold) a thrush has been singing to me, like Overbury's fair and happy milk-maid,[1] as if he never could be old. I have been thinking that the decay of nature is far more beautiful than that of man, that autumn is rather pensive than melancholy, that the fall of the leaf does not work such dilapidation on the forest as on us the fall of the hair, but gives its victims a new beauty. I have been thinking—to about as much purpose as the deer who were browsing or dozing all about me, and now I have come in to answer your letter.

I am quite willing you should prefer disagreeable men (there are enough of them!), provided you will tolerate me. For my part, I prefer agreeable women. I must keep copies of my letters if I would understand the answers to them. Could I have

---

[1] A Boston dining club which sprang chiefly out of the establishment of the *Atlantic Monthly* in 1857, and held its dinners on the last Saturday of the month at Parker's Hotel (later the Parker House) on Tremont Street. In its earlier years it was made up chiefly of literary men,—such figures as Emerson, Thoreau, Hawthorne, Holmes, Lowell, Longfellow, Howells, Aldrich, and the historians John Motley and William Prescott.

[1] Sir Thomas Overbury (1581–1613), the leading pioneer of "character writing" in seventeenth-century England, composed a score of prose portraits which were published posthumously in 1614. Among this collection was one entitled "A faire and happy Milk-mayd," wherein occurs the following passage:

. . . and when winter evenings fall early (sitting at her merry wheele) she sings a defiance to the giddy *wheele of fortune.*

been such an ass as to ask if I was charming? It is out of the
question. Even if I thought I was, I should be too clever to inquire too nicely about it, for I hold with my favorite Donne that

Who knows his virtue's name and place hath none.[2]

And yet I should infer from your letter that I had been stupid
enough to ask something of the kind. Nothing in my life has
ever puzzled me so much as my popularity here in England—
which I have done nothing and been nothing to deserve. I was
telling my wife a day or two ago that I couldn't understand it.
It must be my luck, and ought to terrify me like the ring of
Polycrates.[3]

No, the Lord Mayor's Show was pure circus and poor circus
at that. It was cheap, and the other adjective that begins with
n. 'Twas an attempt to make poetry out of commonplace by
contract. 'Twas antiquity as conceived by Mr. Sanger.[4] Why,
I saw the bottoms of a Norman knight's trousers where they had
been hitched up into a tell-tale welt round the ankle by his chain
armor! There was no pretence at illusion; nay, every elephant,
every camel, every chariot was laden with disillusion. It was
worth seeing for once, to learn how dreary prose can contrive to
be when it has full swing.

It is cold here. Twelve degrees of frost this morning. My
fingers are numb and my thoughts crawl slowly as winter flies.
Are you making notes as I bade you? I have no news about

---

[2] *A Letter to the Lady Carey and Mrs. Essex Riche, from Amyens,* l. 33.
The original reads slightly differently:
    Who knowes his Vertues name or place, hath none.
[3] Polycrates of Samos (d. 522 B.C.), one of the most ambitious, treacherous, and fortunate of the Greek tyrants, had as his ally Amasis, king of
Egypt. The latter finally came to fear that Polycrates' continual good
fortune would incur the envy of the gods, and therefore he advised that
Polycrates throw away a valuable possession and thus inflict injury on himself. Polycrates then tossed into the sea a seal ring of extraordinary beauty,
but in a few days he found the ring again in the belly of a fish which had
been presented to him by a fisherman. So terrified was Amasis by this
amazing stroke of fortune that he broke off his alliance with Polycrates.
[4] John Sanger (1816–89), one of the earliest English circus proprietors.
His equestrian pantomimes every winter at Astley's amphitheater, London,
were particularly famous during the 1870's and 1880's.

myself yet, though I have heard the name of somebody who expects to be my successor. A very agreeable man, by the way,
so you won't like him. That's some comfort.

Faithfully yours,

J. R. Lowell.

46. To O. W. Holmes. (L., II, 291–94)

31 Lowndes Square, S.W., Dec. 28, 1884.

Dear Wendell,—I was about to write thanking you for your
"Emerson," [1] when your letter was brought to me. I found the
Emerson very interesting. You, more than anybody else, have
the literary traditions of New England in your blood and brain.
It was this special flavor that pleased my palate as I read. I felt
as when I walk along one of our country lanes in early autumn—
stone walls on either hand, a somewhat thrifty landscape, and
yet fringed all along with hardhack and golden-rod. I recognize our surly limitations, but feel also the edging of poetry—
northern, not tropical, but sincere and good of its kind. Nay,
with you I may trust a homelier image. You know that odor
of sweet herbs in the New England garret and its pungency of
association, and will know what I mean when I say that I found
much of it in your book. You have never written better than
in some of the genially critical parts. There are admirable
things in the chapter about Emerson's poetry, many that made
me slap my thigh with emphatic enjoyment. You say the book
tired you, but I see no sign of it, and your wind is firm to the
end. I thank you for helping me to a conclusion (or a distinction) I was fumbling for. If Emerson show no sensuous passion in his verse, at least there is spiritual and intellectual passion enough and to spare—a paler flame, but quite as intense in
its way. I go back, you see, to my hardhack and golden-rod
again. I talked with him once about his versification, by the
way, and he humorously confessed that he couldn't see the dif-

---

[1] *Ralph Waldo Emerson* (1884) in the American Men of Letters series.

ference between a good verse and a bad one—so in that line you
cite from his "Adirondacks." [2] . . .

Affectionately yours,

J. R. Lowell.

47. To Edward J. Phelps [1]

Deerfoot Farm,
Southborough, Mass.,
U.S.A.
1st Oct: 1885.

Dear Mr. Phelps,

Many thanks for finding time to write, for I know by experience how little an American Minister [2] has to spare. Your letter
gave me a keener feeling than ever of the advantages of my
Lucretian position on the shore.[3] True I was in a sense castaway upon it and am almost as solitary as Robinson Crusoe, but
I find it wholesome and enjoy my walks over the solitary hills
where I can make as many speeches as I like to the goldenrods
and asters with no reporter to dishearten me. I think from the
way they listen that if I were a candidate for the office of Select-
man or any other within the scope of a reasonable ambition they
would all vote for me to the last seedpod. The goldenrods
especially are charmed with views on the silver question. My
fellow citizens the musquashes and woodchucks are very civil
to me (for I have taken care to hint that I am in favour of an
extension of the suffrage in their direction) and not one of them
has asked for a letter of introduction to you "with a view to be

---

[2] Holmes (*op. cit.,* Chap. xiv, p. 327) quoted ll. 73–74 of *The Adirondacs,*
In Adirondac lakes
At morn or noon the guide rows bare-headed.
and then suggested the emendation of the second line thus:
At morn or noon bare-headed rows the guide.

---

[1] This letter, now in the possession of the University of Cincinnati Library,
is here printed for the first time.
[2] Phelps (1822–1900) in June, 1885, had been appointed by President
Grover Cleveland to succeed Lowell as American minister to England.
[3] See note on p. 36.

presented at Court." You see there are some advantages in a fugitive and cloistered life, but I will not dwell upon them longer, for I do not wish to make you miserable.

My chief adventure since my return was my visit to Washington where I was charmed with Mr. Bayard,[4] who was good enough to insist on being my host and who was as amiable as possible. I saw Mr. Cleveland and thought him just the man for his place which will not be an easy one, though, if I understand the drift of Public Opinion, not so *un*easy as is generally expected. He seemed to me expressly framed by nature for the kind of rough and tumble fight that is before him—very firm on his legs, with Atlantean shoulders, and a backbone with no more *give* in it than that (or the pocket) of John Adams. But I forget that I am saying all this to one who knows him better than I.

I was in New Haven the other day—I wonder you could ever bring yourself to leave it, it is so charming—where I saw two special friends of yours Mr. Wayland and Mr. Fisher. Both were well (though Mr. Fisher has aged much since I saw him last) and both spoke most affectionately of you. At Philadelphia, by the way, somebody, I forget who, told me (what will please you more) how charmingly Mrs. Phelps received, and I told *him* that it was just what I expected.

I see that they are taxing you as they did me in the way of speeches. I read with great pleasure what you said to the Workingmen. It was excellent—full of good sense and good feeling—which is perhaps a pleonasm, since the one is the complement of the other. Perhaps I am wrong in my spelling of *complement,* for the copyists of the State Department spell it with an *i* which they have saved out of mar*i*time, where they replace it with an *a*. However, our ancestors got on very well though they left orthography altogether to Divine Providence. Were you looking up *your* ancestors, by the bye, in Somerset? There used to be men of your name there, one of whom, I think, was member of one of Oliver's Parliaments.

Don't make your speeches too good or the poison of jealousy

---

[4] Thomas Francis Bayard, secretary of state, 1885–89.

will begin to work in my veins. This by the way, as our ancients used to say when they couldn't resist a caper of digression.

I am glad you like No. 31.[5] I was sure you would, or I
shouldn't have recommended it. As for the remittance you
speak of—don't fash your—or rather my—beard about it. When
you are ready pay it in to my credit at the Barings. Meanwhile
I had rather you should have it than they. This is a very bad
pen and a manifest judgment—for I stole it from the Legation!

With kindest regards to Mrs. Phelps and to Mr. Hoppin and
Mr. White,[6]

Faithfully yours
J. R. Lowell.

48. To the Misses Lawrence. (L., II, 303–4)

Deerfoot Farm, Southborough, Mass.,
Jan. 4, 1886.

. . . I am living quietly here with my son-in-law, my daughter, and five very creditable grandchildren, in a pretty country
village, all hill and dale, and every hill a heap of boulders piled
up by glaciers Heaven knows how long ago. I like my grandchildren, and this is in their favor, for I have none of that natural
fondness for children which some people have, who also, I have
observed, like puppies in the same indiscriminate way. I like
my solitude, too, when I am allowed to have it all to myself, for
a solitude *à deux* [1] is possible only with a woman.

You must have had a pleasant continental trip, but I can't
understand your not liking Weimar.[2] I liked it immensely—a
kind of puppet-theatre of the world, with its little Schloss [3] and

---

[5] 31 Lowndes Square, Lowell's last London residence.
[6] William J. Hoppin and Henry White, secretaries of the American Legation.

---

[1] For two persons.
[2] A small German city near Leipzig, once the residence of Goethe and
Schiller who in the early nineteenth century made it a center of learning
and art.
[3] Castle.

little Park and little Army and little Play-house and little Court and little men and women. And as for the little stream that runs through the Park or along its edge, I fell in love with it, and so would you had you seen the horse-chestnuts lying in its bed, and more brilliant than balas rubies. And then there was the grand duke—a man of genius (on perpetual furlough), and one can get on very well where one has a man of genius to friend. And Frau v. Stein—one can get on very well where there is one charming woman. But I am glad you said what you did, because it confirms me in something I was going to say about Hawthorne—that men of genius can manage anywhere, because they make the best part of their own material. . . .

What you say of Weimar convinces me of how London has thrown its dust in your eyes. But I like it too, and am glad even of a bit of gossip thence now and then. . . .

You will divine, by what I say about gossip, that I am growing old. I used to be as stern about it as Wordsworth. You remember his "I am not one," [4] etc.? 'Tis senescence or London, I know not which—perhaps a mixture of both. . . .

49. To C. E. Norton. (L., II, 315-17)

40 Clarges Street, Piccadilly, W.,
July 25, 1886.

. . . What you say of Carlyle is sympathetic (as it should be) and not dyspathetic. Of course every man that has any dimensions at all must have more than one side to him, and if he have dyspepsia one of those sides will have corners, and sharp ones, that find a sort of ease in the ribs of other folks. But, after all, Carlyle was a man of genius, and it is sheer waste of time to be looking one's gift-horse in the mouth and examining his hoofs, if he have wings and can lift us away from this lower region of

---

[4] Wordsworth's sonnet *Personal Talk*, which begins:
I am not one who much or oft delight
To season my fireside with personal talk. . . .

turmoil at will. The rest is rubbish. Biographies (except Plutarch's) seldom do a man any good, and the less in proportion to the cleverness of the biographer, for your very clever one is sure to mix a good deal of auto- with his bio-graphy. The beauty and truth of impressions depend on the substance in which they are made. The main ingredient a biographer should contribute is sympathy (which includes insight). Truth is not enough, for in biography, as in law, the greater the truth sometimes the greater the libel. Happy those authors who are nothing more than airy tongues that syllable our names when they have a message for us! Most Lives are more properly Deaths, or at least might have for their title, like Chapman's D'Ambois, "The Life *and* Death of So-and-so." [1]

I am living a futile life here, but am as fond of London as Charles Lamb. The rattle of a hansom shakes new life into my old bones, and I ruin myself in them. I love such evanescent and unimportunate glimpses of the world as I catch from my flying perch. I envy the birds no longer, and learn better to converse with them. Our views of life are the same.

As for politics—I saw Gladstone [2] the other day, and he was as buoyant (*boy*ant) as when I stayed with him at Holmbury, just before he started for Scotland. I think the Fates are with him, and that the Tories will have to take up Home Rule where he left it. The great difficulty is in making up an able Cabinet. I suppose that ineptitudes will be neutralized with coronets (or signalized by them, as we mark shoals with buoys), and room made for younger and abler men. Lord Randolph Churchill [3] is taken seriously now, and will have a front seat. He ought to build a temple to the goddess Push.

[1] For Chapman see note on p. 40. Lowell has confused the full title of this long-popular Elizabethan drama, *Bussy D'Ambois: A Tragedie* (1607), with that of some other contemporary play, perhaps Shakespeare's *True Chronicle Historie of the Life and Death of King Lear* (1608).

[2] William Ewart Gladstone (1809–98), noted English statesman of the Liberal party and several times prime minister of Great Britain.

[3] Randolph Henry Spencer Churchill (1849–95), well known English politician of the Conservative party and father of Winston Leonard Spencer Churchill, prime minister 1940–45.

I spent two days in the country lately (at the George Lewises) with Burne-Jones,[4] and found him delightful. As Mrs. Lewis says, "If he were not a great artist, there would be enough left of him to make a great man of." His series of Perseus (did you see any of them?) is to my thinking the greatest achievement in art of our time or of any time. It has mannerisms which I don't like, but it is noble in conception and execution. Above all, it has the crowning gift of making an old story as new as if nobody had ever told it before. I feel as if I had heard the waves rustle under the bows of the *Argo*.[5]

I suppose you are at Ashfield,[6] and that the hills are as dear as ever, and Monadnock[7] as like a purpose unfulfilled. Is the June grass golden on the upper slopes? Do the cloud-shadows still linger and hate to leave their soft beds in the woods and grass? Above all, are you and yours well and remember me? And G.W.C.?[8] Sometimes I hear faintly the notes of S——'s violin singing *"Scheiden, ach, scheiden!"*[9] and think of many things. . . .

50. To Mrs. Owen J. Wister. (N.L., 300-3)

> *Deerfoot Farm,*
> *Southborough, Mass.*
> *Xmas, 1886.*

Dear Mrs. Wister,—I began a letter to you on Thanksgiving Day, but left it in the bud because I had not your new address. 'Twas very natural I should think of you on that day (or any other, for that matter) as one of the nice things I should be thankful for. I shan't have much corn to show for the field allotted me by the Giver, but won't I bring to harvest home my

---

[4] See note on p. 367.

[5] The ship in which Jason sailed from Greece to Colchis in search of the Golden Fleece.

[6] A summer resort in the Berkshire hills of western Massachusetts.

[7] The highest mountain of southwestern New Hampshire.

[8] George William Curtis (1824–92), American critic, editor, and essayist, most popularly known for his collection of essays entitled *Prue and I* (1856).

[9] To part, alas, to part.

hands full of the cornflowers and poppies that friendship has sown wherever the wheat-stems were thinnest and fewest! 'Tis the best of my crop, though it feeds none but myself—and me in a super-sensual way. I think very often of those pleasant days in Paris (so beyond the grave now) when I first had the happiness of really knowing you. It has been my greatest luck in life to be honoured with the partiality (to a certain extent) of many superior and delightful women. If it have done nothing else for me, it has at least kept me young. . . .

All the grandchildren are in bed after an evening of games and a day of comparing, trying, and retrying presents. The youngest boy was sent up stairs in disgrace and, as I can't help being partial to him for his dear name's sake (Frank), and he had gone away in a passion of tears, bitter seemingly as Eve's when evicted from Eden, I thought I would cheer him up a bit when I went up myself presently after. I was guided to him as Dante's eyes to the giants by the clamor of Nimrod's horn.[1] But the sounds I heard came from a penny trumpet through which the dear little fellow had puffed his tragedy away from him into infinite space and uttermost oblivion. There he sat blowing as contentedly as a rose. I couldn't help laughing and thought to myself how often I had seen men consoled by blowing their own trumpets as if their griefs had a certain merit in virtue of being *theirs*. So has the Supreme ordered it and wisely. But doesn't he, too, smile over it sometimes?

We are having a decayed-gentleman kind of winter (which I don't like) threadbare and even tattered, the naked earth showing indecently through its raiment of snow. However, it isn't so bad as in town where the snow gets used to its degradation and is grimy without minding it any more as one sees poor girls in the streets of cities do. Last night we had rain *à outrance*,[2] the real thing that drums on the roof, and to-day my ordinarily humble friend the mill-stream is inclined to be bumptious. I am very fond of the mill—'tis the only human industry that takes nature into partnership—and I stand listening some-

---

[1] See Dante's *Divine Comedy: Inferno*, Canto XXXI.
[2] Beyond measure.

times to its far-off buzz till I fancy myself under a limetree simmering with bees in mid June. The colour of the water of our
brook where it slips over the dam with the light striking through
it is more beautiful than any I ever saw—pale green shot with
gold and shifting from one to tother. This must have been the
hue of those green eyes of women which the poets used to praise.
Is it fair to find morals in Nature? I am often struck with the
fact that the colours of the after-sunset sky are far more vivid on
the surface of the frozen millpond than in the heavens above.
Must a mind freeze first in order to reflect Nature with advantage? Didn't Wordsworth?

What are you doing and reading? As for me, I find myself
more and more drawn by my old favorites and cronies, as I grow
older, and read them with ever new refreshment and delight.
I can always lose myself (isn't that what we read for? or is it to
find ourselves?) in the thickets of Montaigne. Pray tell me that
you are well and haven't forgotten me, when you have nothing
better to do. I fear I have undertaken more work than I can
do this winter—lectures and things. Must one go on lecturing
forever? Alas, there is the *pot-au-feu* [3] to be kept boiling, a
Medea's [4] cauldron that works us only woe! Never mind,
vogue la galère [5]—if one but knew the port one was bound to!
Goodbye

faithfully yours
J. R. Lowell.

51. To Miss Dora Sedgwick. (L., II, 341-43)

2 Radnor Place, Hyde Park, W.,
Aug. 18, 1887.

Dear Dora,—Many thanks for so kindly remembering me. But
how clever women are in flattering us with their pretended jeal-

[3] The kettle on the fire.
[4] A sorceress, daughter of King Æetes of Colchis on the south shore of
the Black Sea, and of Hecate, goddess of the underworld and of witchcraft.
[5] Let come what may.

ousies! No, there may be another Dora, but the first will always have that pre-eminence of priority that belongs to the first snow-drop and the first bluebird. You are Dora I, D.G.[1]

In spite of the epigraph of my paper I am really at Whitby, whither I have been every summer but '85 for the last six years. This will tell you how much I like it. A very primitive place it is, and the manners and ways of its people much like those of New England. "Sir" and "ma'am" are only half-hardy exotics here. The great difference is that everybody here will take a shilling, failing that, a six-pence, and, in desperate circumstances, even a penny, as a kind of *tabula in naufragio*,[2] God save the mark! The people with whom I lodge, but for accent, might be of Ashfield.[3] 'Tis a wonderfully picturesque place, with the bleaching bones of its Abbey standing aloof on the bluff and dominating the country for leagues. Once, they say, the monks were lords as far as they could see. The skeleton of the Abbey still lords it over the landscape, which was certainly one of the richest possessions they had, for there never was finer. Sea and moor, hill and dale; sea dotted with purple sails and white (fancy mixes a little in the purple, perhaps), moors flushed with heather in blossom, and fields yellow with corn, and the dark heaps of trees in every valley blabbing the secret of the stream that fain would hide to escape being the drudge of man. I know not why, wind has replaced water for grinding, and the huge water-wheels, green with moss and motionless, give one a sense of re-pose after toil that, to a lazy man like me, is full of comfort. Not that I am so lazy neither, for I think a good deal—only my thoughts never seem worth writing down till I meet with them afterwards written down by somebody more judiciously frugal than I. Do you know I was thinking this morning that Mon-taigne [4] was the only original man of modern times, or at any rate the only man with wit enough to see things over again in his own way, and to think it as good a way as any other, never mind how old?

[1] D.G. = *Deo gratias,* i.e., thanks be to God.
[2] Solace. (Cf. Cicero, *Epp. ad Atticum,* IV, 18: 3.)
[3] See note on p. 406.
[4] See note on p. 42.

I wish you could see the "yards"—steep flights of stone steps hurrying down from the West Cliff and the East, between which the river (whose name I can never remember) crawls into the sea, and where I meet little girls with trays bearing the family pies to the baker, and groups of rosy children making all manner of playthings of a bone or a rag. And I wish you could see the pier, with its throng of long-booted fishermen, looking the worthy descendants of the Northmen who first rowed their ships into the shelter of the cliffs and named the place. And I wish you could breathe the ample air of the moors—I mean with me.

Your little gift, dear Dora, has been very useful. I carry it in my pocket, not without fear of wearing away the birds and flowers, and so changing its summer to autumn, as my own has changed. I use it almost every day. I dare say you are in Ashfield now. Greet the hills for me, especially Peter's, and the June grass that I still see making them so beautiful in velvet. Give my love to all wherever you are, and tell Sally that I shall write to her soon. I take my letters in order, and yours came before hers; and oh, if I am tardy, remember how many I have to write and that my life is eventless.

Affectionately yours,
J. R. Lowell.

52. To C. E. Norton. (L., II, 360–62)

2 Radnor Place, Hyde Park, W.,
Nov. 11, 1888.

. . . It is noon, and I am writing by candle-light. If I look over the way I can just see the houses vague as the architecture of Piranesi.[1] But I like fogs; they leave the imagination so wholly to herself, or just giving her a jog now and then. I shall go out into the Park by and by, to lose myself in this natural

---

[1] Giovanni Battista Piranesi (1720–78), renowned Italian artist and engraver, whose etchings were generally on a grand scale with shadowy architectural backgrounds and foregrounds sharply lined in contrast. The bulk of his etchings present ancient Roman monuments, but one of his outstanding collections, Carceri (1750), is composed of fanciful themes.

poesy of London which makes the familiar strange. It is as good as travelling in the interior of Africa, without the odious duty of discovery, which makes the strange familiar. There is an ominous feel about it to which I never get wonted, as of the last day, and I listen with a shudder sometimes for the *tuba mirum spargens sonum*.[2] I am still so much of a Puritan that the English words would shock me a little, as they did the other day at —'s table, when I blurted them out to a parson's wife in my impulsive way, and made her jump as if she had heard the authentic instrument with her accounts but half made up.

There is nothing new here—there seldom is, and this is what makes it so comfortable. The Parnell Commission,[3] like a wounded snake, drags its slow length along [4] with an effect of bore silently and sootily pervasive as the fog of which I was just speaking. Unless some sudden Chinese cracker of *révélation intime* [5] should go off, the world in general will have forgotten it ere it be over. I think Gladstone has at least effected so much—that he has brought Irish and English together on a common ground. Surely this is good so far as it goes, but how long the Irish will allow any ground on which they get a footing to remain common is to me at least problematical. I for one am getting tired of seeing *our* politics playing bob to *their* kite.

The Sackville squall [6] has amused me a good deal, bringing

---

[2] The trumpet spreading abroad the wonderful sound.—Lowell, of course, has in mind here the trumpet which is supposed to herald the Last Judgment.

[3] On April 18, 1887, the *Times* published the facsimile of a purported letter of Charles S. Parnell (1846–91), leader of the Irish Home Rule party in the English Parliament. This letter extenuated the murders of the Chief and Under Secretaries for Ireland in Phoenix Park, Dublin, during May, 1882. Action for libel was instituted by Parnell and led to the appointment by Parliament of a special commission of three judges to investigate the whole affair. The commission began its formal proceedings on October 22, 1888, and finally on February 13, 1890, made its report acquitting Parnell of all connection with the Phoenix Park murders.

[4] This figure comes from Pope's *Essay on Criticism* (1711), Pt. II, l. 157.

[5] Secret revelation.

[6] On October 22, 1888, Lionel Sackville-West, Baron Sackville (1822–1908), British minister to the United States since 1881, published in the *New York Tribune* a letter in response to an open letter from an alleged naturalized citizen of British birth, Charles F. Murchison. Murchison's letter requested that the British minister advise him and citizens of like

out so strangely as it did the English genius for thinking all the
rest of mankind unreasonable.   One is reminded of the old story
of the madman who thought himself alone in his sanity.   I seldom care to discuss anything—most things seem so obvious—
least of all with the average Briton, who never is willing to take
anything for granted and whose eyes are blind to all side-lights.
Yes, there is one thing they always take for granted, namely, that
an American *must* see the superiority of England.   They have
as little tact as their *totem* [7] the bull.   I have come to the edge
of my temper several times over the Sackville business—always
introduced by them.   "All Europe is laughing at you, you
know," said Sir —— —— to me genially the other day.   "That
is a matter of supreme indifference to us," I replied blandly,
though with a keen temptation to pull a pair of ears so obtru-
sively long.   But with all that there is a manliness about them
I heartily like.   Tact, after all, is only a sensitiveness of nerve,
and there is but a hair's-breadth between this and irrita-
bility. . . .

   P.S.   Fancy!   I shall have reached David's limit in three
months.[8]

53. To Mrs. S. Weir Mitchell. (L., II, 367–69)

68 Beacon Street, Boston, March 9,
1889.

Dear Mrs. Mitchell,—I am not so clever as you show yourself to
be in the size of your sheets of paper, which reminds me of that
prudence one learns in Italy of ordering one ration (*una por-
zione*) for two persons.   Nor, though I have so many letters to

descent how favorable the attitude of the Cleveland administration was
toward England.   Sackville, apparently unaware of the political dynamite
in such a request made near the close of a bitter presidential campaign such
as Benjamin Harrison and Cleveland had been waging, gave a strictly serious reply which implied that the re-election of Cleveland would be advan-
tageous to British interests.   For obvious political reasons the administration
asked at once that Sackville be recalled, and, when this request was not
heeded, gave the British minister his passports on October 30.
   [7] Idol.
   [8] I.e., three score years and ten.   See Psalm xv: 10.

write, and using as I do a more generous sheet, can I divest myself of the feeling that there is a kind of inhospitality in leaving my fourth page blank. Am I flattering myself, as we generally do when there is a choice of motives, by assuming that we act from the better? and is this feeling but a superstition derived from those heathen times (before yours) when a single postage was 18¾ cents (written in red ink, as if in the very life-blood of the correspondent), and one felt that one didn't get an honest pennyworth unless one filled every scribable corner of his foolscap? Now, you think I mean by this that I should have answered your note sooner had I as tiny quarto as your own to write upon. But nothing of the kind. It was because I remembered that I had promised you something. . . .

I have been doing my best to be seventy, and have had a dinner, and all kinds of nice things were said about me, and it was very pleasant to think that people were so kind. But I feel that they were trying to make it up to me for having been guilty of some sort of gaucherie, as when one knocks over a stand with some frail thing on it that can't be replaced, and is condoled with, "It's not of the least consequence." Well, I have made up my mind never to do it again. But really I am quite ashamed to find how well people think of me, and yet I can't help liking it too. I feel as if it somehow justified my friends.

I often think of my pleasant week with you in Walnut Street. I have now two memories of Philadelphia, antithetic one to the other—the Quaker one of forty-five years ago, and that of yesterday so very unlike it, and both so good. How far away seems and is the first, for it is extinct as the dodo. It was very sweet in its provincial valley of self-sufficientness and contentment. It had a flavor beyond terrapin. But the telegraph has cosmopolitanized us in spite of ourselves; the whole world has but one set of nerves, and we all have the headache together. And, after all, Europe has the advantage of us still, for it has been endowed with the gift of prescience and hears what happens here before it has happened. Do what we will, they get the elder brother's portion. But I am droning. . . .

Affectionately yours,

J. R. Lowell.

54. To Mrs. Leslie Stephen. (L., II, 375–77)

Whitby, Aug. 11, 1889.

. . . The Abbey looks across over the red roofs into my window and seems to say, "Why are you not at church to-day?" and I answer fallaciously, "Because like yourself I have gone out of the business, and, moreover, I am writing to a certain saint of my own canonization who looks amazingly as your St. Hilda [1] must have looked (as I fancy her), and the thought of whom has both prayers and praise in it." The Abbey doesn't look satisfied, but I am—so the Abbey may go hang! Besides, am I not honoring the day with a white shirt and well-blackened boots? and when I presently go out shall I not crown my head with a chimney-pot hat? [2] which, rather than the cross, is the symbol of the Englishman's faith—being stiff, hollow, pervious to the rain, and divided in service between Babylon and Sion.[3]

This is my ninth year at Whitby,[4] and the place loses none of its charm for me. It is better than Cornwall, except inasmuch as Cornwall has St. Erth's in it, where sometimes one has beatific visions. I find a strange pleasure in that name too, so homely and motherly, as if some pope had suddenly bethought himself to canonize this dear old Earth of ours so good to us all, and give the body as well as the soul a share in those blessed things. My happiness is so much at the mercy of obscure sympathies and antipathies that perhaps I am less at ease among a Celtic population (though I fancy them more refined) than among these men of Danish stock with whom I own kinship of blood. But you are enough to leaven the biggest batch of Celts that ever was baked, so I am coming to you as soon as I leave Whitby, or shall it be later? . . .

---

[1] A nun of strong character (614–80), who in 657 founded at Whitby the famous double monastery for men and women.

[2] Tall, silk hat.

[3] I.e., between Man and God, or between the Flesh and the Spirit.— Babylon, the wealthy magnificent city; Sion (Zion), the Heavenly City.

[4] A coast resort in the north riding of Yorkshire.

Whitby is coming more and more into the great currents of civilization. We have a spasmodic theatre and an American circus that seems a fixture. Last year there was a delightful clown who really looked as if he couldn't help it, and was a wonderful tumbler too. How the children would have liked it! One other amusement is the Spa, where there is a band of music bad enough to please the Shah.[5] It is brilliantly lighted, and at night it is entertaining to sit above and watch the fashionable world laboriously diverting themselves by promenading to and fro in groups, like a village festival at the opera. The sea, of course, is as fine and as irreconcilable as ever. Thank God, they can't landscape-garden *him*. I think I have confessed to you before that our colors are not so southern as yours. On the land they are as good as they can be in range, variety, and fickleness. . . .

55. To the Same. (L., II, 381–83)

Whitby, Sept. 11, 1889.

. . . For the last few days we have been having American weather, except for the haze which softens and civilizes (perhaps I should say, artistically generalizes) all it touches, like the slower hand of time. It does in a moment what the other is too long about for the brevity of our lives. How I do love this unemphatic landscape, which suggests but never defines, in which so much license is left to conjecture and divination, as when one looks into the mysterious beyond. And how the robins and some other little minstrels whose names I don't know keep on pretending it is the very fresh of the year. I think few people are made as happy by the singing of birds as I, and this autumnal music (unknown at home), every bush a song, is one of the things that especially endear England to me. Even without song, birds are a perpetual delight, and the rooks alone are enough to make this country worth living in. I wish you could

---

[5] See note on p. 372.

see a rook who every morning busies himself among the chimney-pots opposite my chamber window. For a good while I used to hear his chuckle, but thought he was only flying over. But one day I got out of bed and looked out. There he was on the top of a chimney opposite, perambulating gravely, and now and then cocking his head and looking down a flue. Then he would chuckle and go to another. Then to the next chimney and *da capo*.[1] He found out what they were going to have for breakfast in every house, and whether he enjoyed an imaginary feast or reckoned on a chance at some of the leavings I know not, but he was evidently enjoying himself, and that is always a consoling thing to see. Even in the stingy back-yards of these houses too, wherever there is a disconsolate shrub a robin comes every morning to cheer it up a bit and help it along through the day.

Since I wrote what I did about the weather (one should always let the Eumenides [2] alone) it has begun to rain, but gently, like a rain that was trying to discriminate between the just and the unjust, and sympathized with those confiding enough to leave their umbrellas behind them (I hate to expose *mine* any more than I can help, for reasons of my own). So the rain let me get back dry from the beach, whither I had gone for a whiff of salt air and a few earfuls of that muffled crash of the surf which is so soothing—perpetual ruin with perpetual renewal. . . .

56. To the Same. (L., II, 389–90)

Elmwood, Nov. 9, 1889.

. . . It is a very strange feeling this of renewing my life here. I feel somehow as if Charon [1] had ferried me the wrong way, and yet it is into a world of ghosts that he has brought me, and I am slowly making myself at home among them. It is raining

---

[1] And begin over again (lit., from the beginning).
[2] See note on p. 7.

[1] The ferryman who took the souls of the dead across the river into Hades.

faintly today, with a soft southerly wind which will prevail with the few leaves left on my trees to let go their hold and join their fellows on the ground. I have forbidden them to be raked away, for the rustle of them stirs my earliest memories, and when the wind blows they pirouette so gayly as to give me cheerful thoughts of death. But oh, the changes! I hardly know the old road (a street now) that I have paced so many years, for the new houses. My old homestead seems to have a puzzled look in its eyes as it looks down (a trifle superciliously methinks) on these upstarts. "He who lives longest has the most old clothes," says the Zulu proverb, and I shall wear mine till I die.

It is odd to think that the little feet which make the old staircases and passages querulous at their broken slumbers are the second generation since my own. I try to believe it, but find it hard. I feel so anomalously young I can't persuade myself that *I* ever made such a rumpus, though perhaps the boots are thicker now.

The two old English elms in front of the house haven't changed. The sturdy islanders! A trifle thicker in the waist, perhaps, as is the wont of prosperous elders, but looking just as I first saw them seventy years ago, and it is a balm to my eyes. I am by no means sure that it is wise to love the accustomed and familiar so much as I do, but it is pleasant and gives a unity to life which trying can't accomplish.

I began this yesterday and now it is Sunday. You will have *not* gone to church five hours ago. I have just performed the chief function of a householder by winding up all the clocks and adjusting them to a *striking* unanimity. I doubt if this be judicious, for when I am lying awake at night their little differences of opinion amuse me. They persuade me how artificial a contrivance Time is. We have Eternity given us in the lump, can't believe in such luck, and cut it up into mouthfuls as if it wouldn't go round among so many. Are we to be seduced by the superstitious observances of the earth and sun into a belief in days and years? . . .

57. To the Misses Lawrence. (L., II, 392–94)

Elmwood, Cambridge, Mass.,
Jan. 2, 1890.

. . . Here I am again in the house where I was born longer ago than you can remember, though I wish you more New Year's days than I have had. 'Tis a pleasant old house just about twice as old as I am, four miles from Boston, in what was once the country and is now a populous suburb. But it still has some ten acres of open about it, and some fine old trees. When the worst comes to the worst (if I live so long) I shall still have four and a half acres left with the house, the rest belonging to my brothers and sisters or their heirs. It is a square house with four rooms on a floor, like some houses of the Georgian era I have seen in English provincial towns, only they are of brick and this is of wood. But it is solid with its heavy oaken beams, the spaces between which in the four outer walls are filled in with brick, though you mustn't fancy a brick-and-timber house, for outwardly it is sheathed with wood. Inside there is much wainscot (of deal) painted white in the fashion of the time when it was built. It is very sunny, the sun rising so as to shine (at an acute angle, to be sure) through the northern windows, and going round the other three sides in the course of the day. There is a pretty staircase with the quaint old twisted banisters —which they call balusters now, but mine are banisters. My library occupies two rooms opening into each other by arches at the sides of the ample chimneys. The trees I look out on are the earliest things I remember. There you have me in my new-old quarters. But you must not fancy a large house—rooms sixteen feet square and, on the ground floor, nine high. It was large, as things went here, when it was built, and has a certain air of amplitude about it as from some inward sense of dignity. . . . There are plenty of mice in the walls, and, now that I can't go to the play with you, I assist at their little tragedies and comedies behind the wainscot in the night-hours and build up plots in my fancy. 'Tis a French company, for I hear them distinctly say *wee, wee,*[1] sometimes. My life, you see, is not without its excitements, and what are your London mice doing that is more important? I see you are to have a Parnell scandal [2] at last, but I overheard an elopement the other night behind the wainscot, and the solicitors talking it over with the desolated husband afterwards. It was very exciting. Ten thousand grains of corn damages!

Good-by, and take care of yourselves till I come with the daffodils. I wish you both many a happy New Year and a share for me in some of them. Poets seem to live long nowadays, and I, too, live in Arcadia [3] after my own fashion.

Affectionately yours,

J. R. L.

58. To Thomas Hughes. (L., II, 397–400)

Elmwood, Cambridge, Mass., April 20, 1890.

Dear Friend,—What a good old-fashioned Scripture-measure letter was that of yours! It annihilated penny-posts and telegraphs, and grew to a quarto sheet as I read with all the complicated creases of its folding. Pleasant indeed was it to hear such good news from your Deeside hive, which through the boys bids fair to be a true *officina gentium,*[1] peopling our Western emptinesses with the right kind of stock.

And so our bright and busy-minded —— is married, and happily too. After mature deliberation with the help of a pipe, I don't think her husband's not smoking is a fatal objection. A— would tell you that Napoleon didn't, and Goethe and several other more or less successful men. I consent, therefore, on condition that he stuff his pockets with baccy for his poor parish-

---

[1] A pun on the French *oui, oui* (yes, yes).
[2] See note on p. 411.
[3] See note on p. 381.

---

[1] See note on p. 150.

ioners when he goes his rounds; they know how good it is and
how they "puff the prostitute (Fortune) away," [2] or snuff up
oblivion with its powdered particles. I remember an old crone
whom I used to meet every Sunday in Kensington Gardens when
she had her outings from the almshouse and whom I kept supplied with Maccaboy.[3] I think I made her perfectly happy for
a week and on such cheap terms as make me blush. She was a
dear old thing, and used to make me prettier curtsies than I saw
at court. Good heavens, of what uncostly material is our earthly
happiness composed—if we only knew it! What incomes have
we not had from a flower, and how unfailing are the dividends
of the seasons!

. . . Philosophy and liberty are excellent things, but I made
the discovery early in life that they had one fault—you can't eat
'em, and I found it necessary to eat something, however little.
For the celibate (if his father have a balance at his banker's)
they will serve, but on no other condition and at best not for
long. —— [4] tried it, and do you know what Mrs. —— once
said when somebody asked "if her husband didn't live with his
head always in the clouds?" "Yes, and I'm sometimes tempted
to wish he'd draw his feet up after it!" But his were the dreams
of middle-age and senescence. Those of youth are sometimes
the best possession of our old age. . . . Association with so
generous a nature as Auberon Herbert's [5] would do any man
good—unless, to be sure, they give up for the moment making
themselves good to quarrel about the best way of making other
people so. I have known that to happen. But never mind; the

---

[2] Quoted from John Dryden's *Imitation of Horace*, Book III, Ode 29, l. 84.
Lowell, however, has inserted "(Fortune)."

[3] A kind of snuff made in the Macouba district of Martinique, a French
island in the West Indies.

[4] Lowell is perhaps referring here to the celebrated Transcendentalist
philosopher, Amos Bronson Alcott (1799–1888), whose otherworldliness
became proverbial.

[5] Auberon Edward William Molyneux Herbert (1838–1906), third son
of the third Earl of Carnarvon, was an English author and political philosopher who gained widespread attention for his particular form of volun-
tarism, which held that the law of equal freedom is the supreme moral law.
Although a faddist, he at the same time displayed a broad and mellow
tolerance.

desire to sit in the *siege perilleus* [6] is a good thing in itself, if it do not end in sitting there to watch the procession of life go by, papa meanwhile paying a smart fee for young Hopeful's excellent seat.

Speaking of these things reminds me of Howells's last story, "A Hazard of New Fortunes"; [7] have you read it? If not, do, for I am sure you would like it. A noble sentiment pervades it, and it made my inherited comforts here at Elmwood discomforting to me in a very salutary way. I felt in reading some parts of it as I used when the slave would not let me sleep. I don't see my way out of the labyrinth except with the clue of co-operation, and I am not sure even of that with over-population looming in the near distance. I wouldn't live in any of the Socialist or Communist worlds into the plans of which I have looked, for I should be bored to death by the everlasting Dutch landscape. Nothing but the guillotine will ever make men equal on compulsion, and even then they will leap up again in some other world to begin again on the old terms.

You will be glad to hear that Carl Schurz [8] (a good judge), who had several talks with the new emperor [9] both as crown prince and after, thinks that he is intelligent, means business, and knows what he is about. As emperor he has done away with some of the old fusses and feathers. Once he sent for Schurz, who was ushered at once into the cabinet of the emperor, with whom he was left alone, and who pushed an easy-

---

[6] The Siege Perilous, the seat of danger at King Arthur's Round Table, was reserved for the knight who should win the quest of the Holy Grail, and would prove fatal to any other knight trying to occupy it.

[7] For Howells see note on p. 340. He published in 1889 *A Hazard of New Fortunes,* a novel which presents a middle-aged Boston couple moving to New York and there encountering unfamiliar fashions along with social evils. A mild vein of Tolstoyan humanitarianism colors the treatment of such dramatic social incidents as a street-car strike.

[8] Carl Schurz (1828–1906), distinguished German-American statesman and reformer, came to the United States in 1852, served as minister to Spain 1861–62, as United States senator from Missouri 1877–81, and as Secretary of the Interior under President Hayes 1881–83. He was editor and proprietor of the *New York Evening Post* 1892–1901.

[9] Schurz during his stay in Germany from April to November, 1888, had an audience with William II, the third German emperor, who had ascended the throne on June 15, 1888.

chair towards the fire for him, seating himself on a hard stool.
Bismarck,[10] by the way, said a good thing to Schurz with which
I am growing into sympathy—"I am beginning to think that
the best half of life is before seventy."

I am glad to be remembered by your fair neighbors, and wish
my image in their minds could, in the nature of things, be as
charming as theirs in mine.   Tell them that my power of seeing
faces with my eyes shut is a great blessing to me, since it enables
me to see two such (let their glasses fill up the blank) ones whenever I like.   I have just taken a look at them.   Love to Mrs.
Hughes.   Thanks for her kind note.

Affectionately yours,

J. R. L.

I am still doing well, but have to be very careful.   The doctor
won't hear of my going abroad this year.   Alas!

59. To the Misses Lawrence. (L., II, 410–12)

Elmwood, Cambridge, Mass., July 6, 1890.

Dear Dual-mood,—It is Sunday morning and as fair as George
Herbert's, a happy bridal of Earth and Sky [1] presaging a long
felicity of married days—all honeymoon that isn't sunshine.
Yet I can't help hoping that some spiteful fairy has hidden a
seed of storm somewhere in the *trousseau,* for we have had no
rain these three weeks, and our turf is beginning to show symptoms of jaundice.   The partiality of the solar system (due, no
doubt, to the insular prejudices of Sir Isaac Newton) gives you
a five hours' start of us; so I suppose you have both been to
church by this time, and have put away your prayer-books with
a comfortable feeling that you have played your parts in main-
taining the equilibrium of the British Constitution and have
done with religion for a week.   With us there has been a divorce

---

[10] Prince Otto Edward Leopold Bismarck-Schönhausen (1815–98), imperial chancellor of Germany, 1871–90, and an outstanding European statesman.

[1] See note on p. 337.

of Church and State, and the children are given over to their own guidance.

Why must you be so cruel as to flout me with the nightingale when you knew (or was it *because* you knew?) we hadn't him? I am not sure we would have him if we could, for, in spite of the poets, who naturally try to make the best of him, he has a bad character among you as a *somnifuge*,[2] and I have heard no music so ill-spoken of as his save only that of the barrel-organ. Even his flatterers seem savagely happy in thinking that he sings with his breast against a thorn and suffers some proportion, inadequate though it be, of the misery he inflicts.[3] In any case you need not give yourself airs, for our nights will never want for music while we have the mosquito. What is your nightingale to him, whether for assiduous song or as a prophylactic against inordinate and untimely slumber? He would have prevented the catastrophe of the Foolish Virgins [4]—not that I liken you to those—God forbid! On second thoughts I am not sure that I don't, after all, for I have been sometimes tempted to think that I liked them better than the wise. 'Tis a question of gold spectacles.

I have no news except that my smoke-trees have vapored into rosy clouds that carry on the tradition of sunrise all through the day to the sunset. Sweet-peas, too, are in blossom, and honeysuckle, but, alas, I haven't seen a humming-bird this summer. I never before knew a summer without them.

Your London world seems a great way off, for I am gone back to my old books, and live chiefly two or three centuries ago, sometimes much farther back. I find no nicer creatures than you there.

---

[2] A dispeller of sleep.

[3] See, for example, Sir Philip Sidney's *The Nightingale* (pr. 1598), which "sings out her woes, a thorn her song-book making" (l. 4).

[4] In the biblical parable of the ten virgins, who took their lamps and went forth to meet the bridegroom, there were five who were foolish, because they carried with them no oil for their lamps. When the bridegroom came at midnight for the marriage, the foolish virgins had to go and buy oil to fill their lamps. On their return they found the door already shut for the wedding, and they were not allowed to enter. See Matthew xxv 1–13.

My grandchildren grow apace and my eldest grandson goes to college this year. My contemporaries drop faster and faster about me, but one gets used to it as the leaves to the falling of their fellows and playmates in autumn. I am not conscious yet of any loosening of my stem. But who ever is?

Affectionately yours,

J. R. Lowell.